KANSAS CITY, MO. PUBLIC LIBRARY

0 0001 525034

MAIN

DATE DUE

SEP 1 3 1995			
APR 2 2 1996 DO			
JAN 1 1 1997			

155.84 J52t

Jenkins, Adelbert H.

Turning corners : the
psychology of African
c1995.

TURNING CORNERS

Turning Corners
The Psychology of African Americans

Adelbert H. Jenkins
New York University

Allyn and Bacon
Boston • London • Toronto • Sydney • Tokyo • Singapore

Copyright © 1995 by Allyn & Bacon
A Simon & Schuster Company
Needham Heights, Massachusetts 02194

All rights reserved. No part of the material protected by this copyright notice may be reproduced or utilized in any form or by any means, electronic or mechanical, including photocopying, recording, or by any information storage and retrieval system, without written permission from the copyright owner.

Also published under the title *Psychology and African Americans: A Humanistic Approach*, Second Edition

Library of Congress Cataloging-in-Publication Data

Jenkins, Adelbert H.
   Turning corners : the psychology of African Americans / Adelbert H. Jenkins.—2nd ed.
     p.   cm.
   School ed. of : Psychology and African Americans. 2nd ed. 1994.
   Includes bibliographical references and index.
   ISBN 0-205-17083-8
   1. Afro-Americans—Psychology. I. Jenkins, Adelbert H. Psychology and African Americans. II. Title.
E185.615.J474   1994
155.8'496073—dc20   94-28951
                                                                                                                                   CIP

Printed in the United States of America
10 9 8 7 6 5 4 3 2   98 97 96 95

Contents

Preface ix

Acknowledgments xiii

About the Author xv

Introduction xvii

1 African Americans: Shaping Their Destinies 1
  A Humanistic Psychological Approach to Agency 4
    Assumptions about the Causes of Behavior 4
    Conceptions of Meaning 9
    Models of the Human Mind 12
  Competence as a Humanistic Theme 16
  Conclusion 19
  Notes 21

2 African-American Self-Concept: Sustaining Self-Esteem 25
  Research: Low Self-Esteem in Black Children 27
  Research: High Self-Esteem in Black Children 30
  Self-Concept: A Many-Faceted Entity 31
    Aspects of Self: Racial and Personal 33
  Self as Active Agent 34
  Self-Concept: A Product of Dialectical Activity 39

The Black Family and Self-Concept   41
    The Black Family and Self-Awareness   44
Other Aspects of Racial Self-Concept Development   47
    Ruby: "My Skin or Me?"   48
    Attempts to Change Racial Self-Concept   51
Notes   53

3 The Active Intellect: Developing Competence   67
Assessing Intellectual Competence   72
The Anatomy of Intellectual Performance   75
    Cognitive Components of Intelligence   76
    Learning and Achievement in Intellectual
        Performance   101
    Affective/Motivational Factors and Intellectual
        Performance   105
Conclusion   119
Notes   121

4 The Black Speaker: Cherishing Pluralism   137
Black English: What Kind of Dialect?   138
    Varieties of Black English   140
    Sociolinguistic Issues   141
    Black English: Difference or Deficit?   143
Black English in the Classroom   146
    Black English Vernacular and Learning to Read   147
    The Sociolinguistic Hypothesis   148
Cherishing Pluralism   159
Notes   163

5 The Assertive Self: Emerging of a New Identity   171
Assertion and Aggression   171
    Aggression in Blacks: Selected Studies   172
Evolution of Identity   177
    Nigrescence   177
    Expression of a Collective Voice   186
Blacks in College: An Update   192
    Supporting Academic Identity   193
    Reversing "Stigma Vulnerability"   194
Life After College: Adulthood   197
Conclusion   199
Notes   200

6   **The Wayward Self: Distortion and Repair**   213
   Anxiety and Defense   215
   Mental Disorder as Disturbed Self Activity   217
       Racial Differences in Mental Disorder   218
       Diagnostic Understanding   221
   Self Disturbances and Race   224
       Depression   225
       Emotionality in African Americans   230
       Special Disorders in the Black Community   231
   Issues in Psychotherapy   232
       Psychotherapy with the Minority Poor   235
       The Therapeutic Relationship   236
       Psychotherapy and the Varieties of the Black Experience   244
   Conclusion   247
   Notes   247

Epilogue   271

References   281

Author Index   307

Subject Index   317

Preface

Viewing the African American from a psychological perspective requires that one choose some theoretical position from among the various different psychological approaches to the human individual. My background is that of a clinical psychologist trained in a psychodynamic tradition—a tradition stressing the interplay between the conscious and unconscious mind. In recent years I have been influenced by developments in psychodynamic theory that emphasize the coping aspects of personality rather than the inevitable instinctual dramas that presumably befall personality. Like most other psychologists, I am convinced that the coping characteristics are what must be developed if the human race is to survive and fully develop its potential. More specifically, however, the theoretical trends that emphasize coping and mastery seem to me to be sorely needed when choosing a psychological approach to the study of the African American. Giving more prominence to the positive and creative aspects of personality is especially needed because much of the psychological literature (in consonance with American society) paints a view of the Black American as being deficient in the mental and emotional qualities that lead to productive and creative living.

There is no question that Blacks as a group are still disproportionately numbered among the poor—especially during the decade of the 1980s—and that they suffer and have suffered personally and collectively in the United States. As an old mother says in Langston Hughes's poem:

> Well son, I'll tell you:
> Life for me ain't been no crystal stair.
> It's had tacks in it,
> And splinters,
> And boards torn up,

And places with no carpet on the floor—
Bare. [1926, p. 187]

Yet, to adopt the typical American view that Blacks as a group are unready for equal opportunity does a tragic injustice to the struggles of individual Black Americans and their collective efforts. One does not have to turn to a Benjamin Banneker, a W. E. B. DuBois, or a Marian Anderson; or to a Kareem Jabbar or a Michael Jordan—names the White community would recognize more readily—to look for competent Blacks. The evidence for nobility of the human spirit is seen in the everyday life of common Black folk, as with Hughes's old woman:

But all the time
I'se been a-climbin' on,
And reachin' landin's
and turnin' corners,
And sometimes goin' in the dark
Where there ain't been no light.
So, boy, don't you turn back. [p. 187]

In a similar vein, Alice Walker indicated in a radio interview that one of the main themes of her Pulitzer Prize-winning novel *The Color Purple* is that of *transformation*. That is, she intended the story to be an affirmation of the capacity of the characters, whose lives had been filled with violence and despair—especially the Black women in the novel—to transform themselves in positive and creative ways. Thus, Black heroes are special cases of the rule, not exceptions to it, notwithstanding the considerable social problems to which Blacks as a group have been heir.

Ralph Ellison noted some years ago that he set himself the goal as a writer: "To commemorate in fiction... that which I believe to be enduring and abiding in our situation, especially those human qualities which the American Negro has developed despite and in rejection of the obstacles and meannesses imposed upon us" (1964, p. 39). If psychology is to deal accurately with the African American, it must have a similar mission. But psychology has not been up to this task for at least two reasons. First, western psychology has been hampered by racist cultural biases; psychologists as men and women of their culture have not escaped these preconceptions. Second—and the point to which our attention will be directed in this book—in the main the reigning model in American psychology has been one proposing that drives and external events are the exclusive shapers of behavior. When this theoretical view is applied to Blacks it encourages focusing on the deleterious forces that act on them. For when the human individual is not seen as a being who takes an active, coping stance in life, then the tendency not to see active and creative features in the behavior of Blacks follows naturally.

Of course, the kind of psychological model one develops to understand Black people depends very much on what one considers appropriate for the study of any human being. I maintain that the "commemoration of the human qualities" in African Americans calls for a model that characterizes the human individual as one who can exercise some freedom of choice in life about self-conception even in the face of punishing circumstances.

After introducing a humanistic psychological view I proceed to discussions of self-concept, cognition and school performance, and speech and language processes in children. I then go on to deal with assertion and identity development in young adults and to issues related to mental health among Black persons.

Some further words on the scope of this volume. In the last decade immigration to the United States by people of color has increased dramatically. This includes Black people from Africa and the Caribbean. These people bring cultural issues that differ somewhat from those of Black Americans who are descendants of families that were brought directly to the United States from Africa generations ago. To some extent, of course, the problems of all African-derived people in America have important similarities. But to keep the discussion more focused culturally this book continues to have African Americans who are generationally native to the United States in mind.

Second, except at certain explicit points I do not distinguish between psychological issues affecting Black women as distinct from those affecting Black men. There is considerable emphasis these days on young Black men being an "endangered species." This is a problem for society at large and for the Black community in particular. On the other hand, I realize that Black women have their own sets of problems that cannot be dismissed or simply subsumed under those of men. However, in the space allotted it would take us too far afield to deal with gender differences at length, and so I focus primarily on those issues affecting the Black community as a whole.

Acknowledgments

For this second edition I wish first to acknowledge the financial support of the Harburg Foundation and particularly the interest shown in my work by my longtime friend, Dr. Ernest Harburg. I am again very appreciative of the time taken from their own work by Dr. Joseph Rychlak and Dr. Ferdinand Jones to give a careful review of the manuscript. I am also grateful for the words of counsel given me by Dr. Laura Hines regarding sections of Chapter 3.

For this edition I also had the help of two able graduate students who served as my assistants. I was fortunate, first, to have Ramani Durvasula work with me at a point when her own interests in the psychological literature on minorities was beginning to crystallize. Then Nina Sayer brought some special insights from her Peace Corps experiences in Africa. Over a two-year period her careful bibliographic reviews and her thoughtful suggestions about the manuscript were invaluable to me.

Grateful acknowledgment is made for permission to reprint the following materials: from *Selected Poems of Langston Hughes* by Langston Hughes (copyright 1926 by Alfred A. Knopf, Inc., renewed 1954 by Langston Hughes, reprinted by permission of Alfred A. Knopf, Inc.); from *Children of Crisis* by Robert Coles with permission of Little, Brown and Co.; from *Language in the Inner City* by William Labov with permission of the author and University of Pennsylvania Press; from *Discrimination, Personality and Achievement* by Robert L. Crain and Carol S. Weisman with permission of the authors and Academic Press; from *The Dynamic Assessment of Retarded Performers* by Reuven Feuerstein with permission of the author; material reprinted by permission of New York University Press, from Joseph F. Rychlak, *The Psychology of Rigorous Humanism* (2d ed., rev.), Copyright 1988 by New York University; and from Paule Marshall, "The Making of a Writer: From the Poets in the Kitchen," *New York Times Book Review,* Jan. 9, 1983, with permission of the author.

Again I thank my editorial consultant, Mary Symons Strong, for her conscientious scrutiny of this revised manuscript and for her supportive friendship, which has always gone beyond mere professional duty. I wish also to thank the staff at Allyn and Bacon, especially my editor Mylan Jaixen and his assistant, Sue Hutchinson, for their careful work in moving the manuscript through the publishing process.

And, finally, the loving interest in my work shown by my wife and son remains a source of much comfort to me.

About the Author

Adelbert H. Jenkins (Ph.D., University of Michigan) is Associate Professor of Psychology in the Faculty of Arts and Science at New York University. He has been Director of Undergraduate Studies in Psychology there and has received the College of Arts and Science *Golden Dozen* award for teaching excellence. A member of the National Association of Black Psychologists, he received its *Scholar of the Year* award in 1983. He is a Fellow of the American Psychological Association and the Society for Personality Assessment. His publications explore philosophical issues in clinical psychology and relate these themes to ethnic minorities.

Introduction

Black intellectuals have long been discontented with the inadequacy of the concepts used by American behavioral and social scientists in their research on the Black experience in the United States. Their dissatisfactions gained renewed vigor as a part of the social protests of the 1960s. The concerns and criticisms have centered on two main points. First, the accumulating literature on the individual Black person, the family, and the community reflects the common practice of looking within the Black community and Black people themselves for the sources of social disadvantage affecting their personal and collective destinies. As a result, the victims of individual and institutional racism in the White society are made responsible for their own plight. Where the role of the White society in creating problems for the Black minority is analyzed, the onus is eventually placed on Blacks for responding inadequately to the situations they face.

The second distortion—one that I am going to make an attempt to correct and refocus in this book—is the tendency to describe the psychological functioning of the Black American in negative terms. This stems in part from the almost complete lack of interest in studying the effective and constructive aspects of the psychological functioning of Black Americans. The psychological literature has neglected almost totally a serious consideration of the competent and positive aspects of their personalities, almost as if these components of their make-ups did not exist. Instead, the emphasis is almost always on their personal deficiencies—their seemingly endless failings and inabilities to cope with life. Even where the data suggest strengths and capabilities, these traits are often interpreted as defenses to cover up the deficits and insecurities that are "really there underneath." Blacks seem to be in a no-win position. Whatever their behavior, assessments of it in the literature usually turn out to be negative.

It is understandable that at the present time many Black scholars want to reject the modern myths about Blacks, circulated under the guise of being scientific findings, for their incomplete, false, and dehumanizing characterizations of Black people. Indeed, there are now some Black psychologists who advocate scrapping the entire body of theory and research on Blacks and developing entirely new approaches and new sources of data to replace it.

New approaches to the psychology of the Black American have been put forward. It has been suggested, for example, that perspectives derived from African philosophy and culture might prove fruitful. Whether or not this turns out to be a productive route to take, it is my opinion that there are existing viewpoints in contemporary Western psychology that can also be used to make a fuller and fairer assessment of the African American. In other words, there are ideas in the social and behavioral sciences that should not be overlooked as promising alternatives to the main theories and body of findings about Black Americans. At least, I think this is true in the discipline of psychology.

What are these approaches and perspectives in contemporary psychology that might lead to broadening our understanding of the psychological functioning of Black Americans? They are the same ones that hold promise for gaining through the research process a fuller grasp of the personalities of all human beings. These more promising approaches look at the human individual from a "humanistic" perspective. They posit a distinctly different image of the human being from that being defined by "mechanistic" conceptions. In the mechanistic image—still the reigning one in American psychology—the human individual is portrayed as a passive being whose responses are primarily determined either by environmental factors or by internal physiological and constitutional states. Historically the behaviorist position can be most clearly identified with the mechanistic tradition. In this appoach, behavior is seen as a function of innate or learned drives or as a function of controlling environmental "contingencies." (*Contingencies* refer to circumstances in the environment that reward or punish an event and thereby determine its likelihood of occurrence.)

Even though psychoanalytic theory is quite different from behaviorist theory in important ways, Freud's voluminous writing shows clear evidence of both mechanistic and humanistic trends (Holt, 1972). The mechanistic components reflect Freud's efforts, which were heavily influenced by the natural science of his day, to develop a "metapsychology" that would describe the basic forces governing human functioning. One aspect of Freud's mechanistic side was the positing of instinctual drives such as sexuality and aggression as the primary motivating forces in behavior. In this sense he was part of the psychological tradition of the first half of the twentieth century, which considered drive reduction as a primary aim of behavior. Much of Freud's thinking and observations about actual clinical situations led him to theorize in ways that were opposite to the prevailing mechanistic trends in science

(Cameron & Rychlak, 1985). Thus, he left important theoretical landmarks for humanistic conceptions of the person, as well. Still, in terms of his basic philosophical groundings it can be argued that he was something of a "mixed-model" theorist (Rychlak, 1981). Both mechanistic and humanistic trends are prominent in Freud's work, and the former perspectives have had a considerable influence on conceptualizations of the human being.

Counterposed against this portrayal of humankind in the passive mechanistic voice is a trend of thinking that is articulated, for example, by psychologists who could be called humanists. One such person, Isidore Chein, has described the humanistic view as one portraying the human individual as

> an active, responsible agent, not simply a helpless, powerless reagent. . . . Man, in the active image, is a being who actively does something with regard to some of the things that happen to him, a being who, for instance, tries . . . to generate circumstances that are compatible with the execution of his intentions . . . a being who seeks to shape his environment rather than passively permit himself to be shaped by the latter, a being, in short, who insists on injecting himself into the causal process of the world around him. [1972, p. 6]

A number of other psychologists have developed outlooks with similar implications for the human image. Abraham Maslow, for example, took an early and prominent part in expressing the growing dissatisfaction with the reigning emphasis on drive-reduction theories of motivation. Maslow (1968) stressed the need for a "third force" in psychology to counter the position of the other two "forces" that were influential in American psychological thought, namely, psychoanalysis and behaviorism. He acknowledged that there were important "basic" physiological and psychological "drives" within human beings that directed their behavior. However, he felt that when these drives were satisfied, other sets of motivations emerged, such as strivings for personal growth and self-realization.

Robert White also leveled criticism at both experimental and psychoanalytic psychologies. He wrote, "Something important is left out when we make drives the operating forces in animal and human behavior (1959, p. 297)." To bring back what is "left out," White developed his view that organisms, particularly the higher mammals, possess the capacity to interact "effectively" with their environments. This, to White, implied the presence in human beings of a lifelong motivation to strive for "competent" living as a universal characteristic of human development and functioning.

More recently other psychologists have begun articulating views with humanistic implications for the human image. The psychoanalyst Roy Schafer has in effect countered the mechanistic themes in psychoanalysis by developing what he calls an "action language" for psychoanalysis (1976). His work essentially develops the humanistic themes in Freud's work. (For a discussion of this point see Jenkins [1992].) Schafer sees individuals not so much as victims of instinctual forces and neurotic afflictions but as people who actively, albeit often unconsciously, construct the meanings, including the pathological ones, by which they interpret the world. "Action refers to all behavior performed in a personally meaningful, purposive or goal-directed fashion and includes all the forms of thinking and . . . feeling as well (1977, p. 61)." Schafer's emphasis on the human being as actor is basic to the humanistic conception of the individual.

Another psychologist, Joseph Rychlak (1988), reminds us that the opposing views undergirding the mechanistic and humanistic images of the human being predate by far the twentieth century in the history of philosophy. Rychlak argues, much as does Chein, that it is time to be explicit about the implications of including a humanistic perspective in accounts of human behavior. "The tie binding all humanists," he notes "is [the] assumption that the individual 'makes a difference' or contributes to the flow of events" (1976, p. 128).

The humanistic model I use here continues to develop (Rychlak, 1991) and it is one aspect of a growing antimechanistic trend in psychological theory and research (see, for example, Faulconer & Williams, 1985; Howard & Conway, 1986; Messer, Sass, & Woolfolk, 1988; Polkinghorne, 1990; Robinson, 1991; Sarbin, 1990; Secord, 1990). For that reason I think it can continue to make a contribution to understanding African-American people. It is intereting to note, too, that the "competence" notion that is a central construct in this book has also recently stimulated the work of a number of researchers (Deci & Ryan, 1985; Sternberg & Kolligian, 1990).

Chapter 1 of this volume is devoted to laying out the theoretical stance and concepts used in the following chapters to evaluate critically the literature on the psychology of Black Americans. In my earlier thinking about psycholological concepts as they related to Black Americans, Robert White's concept of competence seemed to me to be a good one in which to ground a more positive approach to the psychology of the African American. White's concept of competence implies that there is a lifelong process of self-development, one that he describes in rather straightforward psychological terms. While embodying criticisms of psychology, White's approach attempts at the same time to extend but not necessarily overturn all previous psychological work. In Joseph Rychlak's thinking I found a perspective that provided a framework for viewing most of the major personality theorists (see, for example, Rychlak, 1981) and that seemed also to subsume White's scheme. Rychlak's point of view seems to get directly to the heart of the question I wanted to address, namely, how can psychology make a contribution to a changed conception of the African American? Since space allows only a brief orientation to his thoughts, it is hoped that the reader will pursue his works more thoroughly.

At several points I illustrate how his humanistic approach can help orient our thinking about Blacks.

In Chapter 1 I introduce the key ideas of the humanistic psychological approach that I have used to examine the African-American situation. In the chapters that follow I use the humanistic perspective to review some of the psychological literature on African-Americans. I have selected studies from five areas of psychology and organized them around the topics indicated in the following chapter titles: Chapter 2, "African-American Self-Concept: Sustaining Self-Esteem"; Chapter 3, "The Active Intellect: Developing Competence"; Chapter 4, "The Black Speaker: Cherishing Pluralism"; Chapter 5, "The Assertive Self: Emerging of a New Identity"; Chapter 6, "The Wayward Self: Distortion and Repair." As mentioned, I close with an epilogue. Although the findings examined in these chapters are not exhaustive of the pertinent areas of psychology, they are important ones to address in relation to the psychological functioning of Black Americans. The extensive notes at the end of each chapter amplify issues raised in the text and provide further references and ideas that the reader can pursue.

Two final points before beginning. First, even though my attention is directed at what I affirm as universal principles in human psychology, I do not maintain that there are no differences in the psychological make-up of African Americans and Whites in the United States. For example, some of the difference in cognitive performance between African Americans and European Americans may reflect different psychological styles of approaching intellectual problems. These differences in turn may stem from the fact that different cultural heritages place different emphasis during development on one or another aspect of cognitive functioning. I discuss this issue briefly in Chapter 3.

Second, it is necessary to distinguish the term *humanistic* from the term *humanitarian.* The latter term refers to an attitude of benevolence toward humankind in general and a wish to see the best possible social condition and the highest level of personal development for all human beings. The term *humanism* as used here refers to a philosophical position that puts human individuals and their choices as central, determining factors in their fate. Such factors determine the human being's freedom and responsibility (Rychlak, 1979). Individual humanists may or may not be concerned with the broad welfare of humankind; in fact, some could be more concerned with their own welfare. By the same token, some mechanists who see the human being only as shaped by external forces might not take a back seat to anyone in their concern for bettering the human condition. Mechanists can be and often are humanitarian in outlook. My values are humanitarian (similarly to most psychologists) and humanistic. It is my belief, however, that the humanistic position articulates the potential for human development more effectively.

TURNING CORNERS

1

African Americans: Shaping Their Destinies

The focus of this book is on African Americans as actors or agents who share with all of humankind the capacity to play a part in shaping the contours of their lives. Characterizing individual Blacks in America from such an "activist" approach—as people who "make a difference" in the flow of events in their lives—involves raising questions about the usual portrayal of Blacks in the social and behavioral science literature. Blacks are commonly described as "reactors" rather than "pro-actors" to the circumstances they face. They are often said to respond either as victims who accommodate passively to discrimination and economic marginality or as aggressors who deal with their individual and group subordination by striking back violently. The options that Blacks choose are described as submissive or defensive—as reflecting powerlessness on the one hand or unthinking rage on the other. Such a picture is one of human beings who only react to their environments rather than take charge of their destinies.

In explaining this situation it has been typical to point out the limiting and debilitating psychological effects that centuries of American racism have had on Black Americans. One example of such a view in psychology was the judgment of the psychiatrists Kardiner and Ovesey ([1951] 1962) that the power of racial oppression had been such that the "Negro has no possible basis for a healthy self-esteem" (p. 297). Another example comes from the large-scale study of personality features in Black Americans by Crain & Weisman (1972) in which those authors suggest that "segregation *robs the black of some vital aspect of his personality* which in turn prevents him from realizing his ambitions" (p. 26, emphasis added). Or we could note Pettigrew's (1964) description of three reaction styles that he felt typified the responses of Black

Americans to racism: "moving toward the oppressor" (integrationist), "moving against the oppressor" (hostile), "moving away from the oppressor" (avoidant). While some of the behaviors within these types may have been positive, the categories tend to emphasize the *reaction* of Black people in response to the (often racist) initiatives of Whites.

The portrait drawn by the Black clinical psychologist Roderick Pugh in the book *Psychology and the Black Experience* (1972) is somewhat more complex. The major intent of his book is to call attention to the positive changes in the psychology of African Americans during the "Black Revolution" of the 1960s. However, in his characterization of the prerevolutionary psychology of Blacks he seems to echo some of the above mentioned trends in the literature. Pugh described the psychological attitudes of African Americans before the struggle of the 1960s as reflecting "adaptive inferiority." He proposed that African Americans had adopted this stance in order to manage the anxiety provoked by the punishing and controlling behavior of Whites toward them. This quality of the personality of Black Americans presumably came about from being made to associate negative feelings with their dark skin color. Historically the African American's dark skin was the occasion for painful abuse and limited social opportunity. To reduce the likelihood of such punishing encounters with the majority White population and to avoid the tension of the associated anxiety, Blacks learned to inhibit their aggression and assertiveness, and they came to assume a relatively deferential demeanor in interracial situations. This stance of "adaptive inferiority" was taught to their children by African-American parents, and it came to be internalized in their beliefs about themselves. Pugh acknowledged that African Americans may have experienced a sense of worth and demonstrated genuine skill in some roles, such as teacher, cook, athlete, musician, parent, for example—but this was not as a Black person. With the social upheavals of the sixties in the United States, however, Pugh believed that African Americans reclaimed a proud sense of self as persons (individual self-esteem) who are *Black* (pride in group identity).

Compared to other psychologists who have expressed somewhat similar views, Pugh's discussion is particularly poignant because it is highlighted by first-person accounts of events from his own life. Such a style is consistent with his "personological" orientation as a clinical psychologist in which he helps us to see situations through the eyes of another person. We shall have reason to refer to this descriptive mode again later in this volume. On the other hand, as sympathetic as it may be to the situation of the African American, in my view his psychological description does not go far enough in considering the way Black Americans have confronted the circumstances they historically faced.

There can be no doubt that the experiences Blacks have lived through have taken a heavy toll on their psychological adjustment, and it is necessary to recognize this cost in considering the psychology of the Black experience.

However, in discussing the nature of that experience prior to 1963, Pugh and other psychologists have tended to draw heavily upon time-honored traditions of psychological explanation—traditions that, it seems to me, are heavily laden with the more mechanistic trends in psychology. In his emphasis on how Blacks responded to social oppression by assuming an inferior stance he excludes other aspects of Black psychological adjustment. (It is important to note that, unlike most other psychological discussions of African Americans, Pugh's did introduce humanistic terms into the discussion of the post-1963 psychology of Blacks. This partly reflects his drawing on his own experience— "from the laboratory of myself," as he puts it [p. 16]—to enrich his theorizing. But I shall argue here that even the pre-1963 depiction of African Americans needs to be supplemented with more explicit humanistic considerations.)

The traditional emphasis in psychology that focuses primarily on the reduction of drive tensions or the response to environmental pressures may be a good one for understanding such notions as adaptive inferiority. Such concepts, however, present only a part of the picture of African-American psychological adjustment, even the adjustment prior to the 1960s "revolution." Something is missing when one relies solely on such constructs to account for human behavior. What is lacking is a fully developed psychological conception of human agency. Such a notion would be one that recognizes that all human beings are capable in principle of arriving at an independent construction of a given circumstance and are able to take action in that situation in accordance with *their* view of it. This conception would spell out the terms under which the human being "actively does something with regard to some of the things that happen to him," as Chein (1972) says.

I think that this missing portion of theory can be presented and applied to the circumstances of the African American. I realize that when he wrote his comments, Pugh was less concerned with the underlying issues of theory construction and philosophy than he was with making a direct statement about the refreshing changes that seemed to be developing in the situation of the African American. But, in fact, points of view about behavior do stem from (often unwitting) philosophical assumptions. I think attention to the kind of assumptions we are using to discuss such issues will pay dividends in our understanding of the Black experience.

Now the task is to determine how a carefully delineated humanistic conception of agency in psychology can be turned to advantage in examining the situation of African Americans. This will be done, first, by looking at some ways in which the humanistic and mechanistic perspectives differ on fundamental assumptions about behavior, which will clarify the humanistic position on agency. Approaches to psychological agency have been receiving more attention in recent years (e.g., Howard, 1985; Howard & Conway, 1986; Robinson, 1985, 1991). One of the most systematically developed perspectives on agency is that of Joseph Rychlak (1988), and we shall use the Rychlak perspective to illuminate the relevant issues here. We will also use the ideas of Robert White in our consideration of this notion of agency. His ideas regarding psychological "competence" will provide a specific view of the functioning of the agent as s/he "comes at" the world.

A Humanistic Psychological Approach to Agency

Rychlak defines an agent as a being who can behave so as to go along with, add to, oppose, or disregard sociocultural and/or biological stimulations (1988). Thus, such a being, and of course we are talking about a human being here, can exercise a certain freedom in the way s/he understands things and takes action. This suggests that while people are likely to be greatly influenced by their surroundings, they are not puppets of their environments.

In order to clarify this perspective on agency we must address ourselves to several key issues on which humanistic and mechanistic psychologists have basic disagreements. Put in the form of questions, these issues are:

What are our assumptions about the causes of behavior?
What are our definitions of meaning?
What is our model for how the human mind and
    human behavior work?

Assumptions about the Causes of Behavior

The question of what causes a particular behavior or event seems to be pretty straightforward at first glance. What people usually look for when confronted with a question of causation is what the forces or actions were that brought a particular event into being. It may not be easy to find the particular forces that would provide a satisfactory answer to what caused something to happen, but it doesn't occur to most people that the notion of cause itself has more than one meaning. Actually, what antecedent forces bring a thing into being is only one of the meanings of the word *cause*. There are at least three others. When trying to gain a complete understanding of the nature of an event, one can not only look at it from the point of view of the antecedent forces but can also consider, for example, the things it is made up of and even why it was made to happen or come into being. All of these contribute to what "caused" a thing to be the way it is. The reason for introducing such philosophical complications is that the adoption of some particular set of assumptions about the cause of an event such as a human behavior makes a great difference in how we understand that behavior.

In trying to get a handle on such issues, Rychlak suggests that the four perspectives that can do this descriptive job for us are those developed by Aristotle many centuries ago in his theory of knowledge. It is worth going into these points in some detail, not only because it will clarify the philosophical underpinning of our approach to the African American but also because humanists differ quite sharply from nonhumanists on the relative importance of these four issues in scientific accounts of human behavior. Specifically, humanists are inclined to use all four of the causal principles to account for the investigation of human behavior; mechanists are inclined to use only two. The four causal principles codified by Aristotle are those of "material," "efficient," "formal," and "final" cause. Mechanists emphasize the first two—the material and efficient cause. Sometimes they employ formal-cause constructs (see Rychlak, 1988), but they never wittingly employ the final-cause mode of explanation. It will be useful to take the time to illustrate these four principles of causation with some examples from everyday life so that we can see their relevance to the African American.

Substance as a Determinant

As one example, let's look at the pencil I am using to draft these paragraphs. From the perspective of the first causal principle (material cause) I can see that it is a slender tube made from a hard plastic with some graphite material inside it. What I can do with it and what I understand about it depend partly on what it is made of. To describe the pencil in this way is to use a material-cause explanation. Now, Rychlak, in trying to capture the fact that Aristotelian causal principles get at the basic meaning that a thing has for us as we encounter it, introduced another set of terms to parallel those of Aristotle. A synonym for the material of which a thing is made is its substance; hence, for Rychlak a material-cause principle can be described as a "substance construct." (In the 1981 revision of his text, *Introduction to Personality and Psychotherapy*, Rychlak has dropped these additional "basic meaning constructs." I will continue to use them here because they are useful in clarifying the discussion of these issues.) In applying a substance-construct explanation to the realm of human behavior, we can note that people's limits and potentials are determined (that is, caused) partly by their material composition, that is, their bodies. What their bodies consist of partly explains what they can and cannot do. Since human beings do not have the wings of birds, they cannot fly. However, starting with feet on the ground, a person can become, for example, a good dancer if, from a substance-construct point of view, he has sturdy limbs and is free of inner ear problems that would disturb the sense of balance. But of course such a perspective, while necessary in understanding what determines a person's choice of behaviors, is far from sufficient to fully account for behavior. Just having legs doesn't mean he will be a dancer.

Impetus as a Determinant

In turning to another use of the term *causation*, we come to the idea of efficient cause. I can further characterize my pencil by noting that a certain force was applied to the materials that make it up in order to bring the pencil into being. In other words, it is a manufactured item. Aristotle's efficient-cause idea is translated as an "impetus construct" by Rychlak. The efficient-cause or impetus-construct notion is the more familiar use of the term *cause*. An impetus construct expresses the "push, thrust, flow, bringing-about-in-motion aspect of experience" (Rychlak, 1988, p. 5). Again, by way of elaboration, an individual exercises his muscles over time to become a dancer, and of course he has to get himself to his dance classes regularly by using specific physical means (walking, driving, taking the bus). So we recognize that applying force to material form, as in manufacturing or moving the body in a disciplined way, is one of the causes of things. Note again that psychologists who are mechanists emphasize these two causal principles—the material and efficient, especially the latter—when trying to understand and control behavior.

Form and Pattern as Determinants

Looking at the third sense of the causation term, we can note that objects and events have a recognizable shape, form, or organization that makes them suitable to certain contexts or uses and that differentiates them from other objects. This is Aristotle's formal-cause principle, which is expressed in Rychlak's notion of a "pattern construct." The term *pattern* captures the idea that constituent pieces of a thing or event fit into an organizational whole that has a distinct character. It is possible, for example, to take the same ten matchsticks and arrange them into the simple form of a house or alternately to arrange them into the form of a chair. We say that this is a house or a chair not because the design is made of hard, solid objects (material cause), not because I exerted effort through time to move them from a random pile into a specific arrangement (efficient cause). We call the design a chair or a house because it has the shape or form of one or another of those things. Similarly, the shape of my pencil is quite distinguishable from that of my bicycle, and the form of the pencil is such that suits it to certain uses and not to others. Coming back to the dancer, when we watch his professional performances, we know he is a dancer. The patterning of his individual movements distinguishes him quite clearly from, for example, the quarterback on a football field, although the activities of both these athletes depend on a high degree of muscular skill. To zero in on the dance further: His practice sessions may be geared to learning the steps of a particular classical ballet. These steps will fit together as a pattern that is clearly distinguishable from another classic dance number and will be even more distinguishable from a modern dance performance.

Ends as Causes

The fourth principle, Aristotle's final cause, takes note of the fact that the dancer's practice sessions are geared *toward* something. Implied here is the notion that some events, particularly those having to do with people, can only be adequately accounted for by delineating the reason or purpose "for the sake of which" a substance was formed into a recognizable shape or "for the sake of which" something was made to happen. Rychlak describes this causal principle as an "intention construct." We can readily see the idea of an intention as being synonymous with a purpose or imagined goal. Looking at my pencil from the perspective of an intention construct, we could say that my pencil was fashioned for the manufacturer's purpose of serving the writing needs of a potential user. (It was, of course, also fashioned for the purpose of turning a profit for the manufacturer.) Returning to the dancer: He goes to class with the intention of perfecting his skill and perhaps with the further conscious intention of becoming the best dancer in the country. A psychoanalytic therapist might have occasion to point to the dancer's unconscious intention of winning his mother's not easily gained favor by the dazzling exhibitions he performs for her (and secondarily, in his conscious mind, for the rest of the audience). This last construct, which emphasizes goals or intentions as causal factors in events, has been identified as a "telic" or teleological description.

Teleological concepts have earned a bad name in the history of philosophy and science because a circularity seems involved. Rychlak notes that it is a major misconception of teleology in psychology to assert that telic descriptions must deal with goals that actually exist or that eventually come to pass. It is, therefore, as if an event came about because it exerted a "pull" on the events that preceded it. In fact, it is the *positing* of intentions (goals, reasons) in the present "for the sake of which" behavior ensues that is the crucial issue in final-cause considerations. The *accuracy* of these intentions or a goal's literal existence is not the most important factor in a teleological conception. Intentions are not seen to reside in objects or events (thereby exerting a force on the present in a kind of reversed efficient-cause way). Intentions are actions of human beings. People make premises in the present that then govern the behavior that follows. For example, the goal or intention in the mind of a Black youth to become a physician has powerful consequences *now* in determining her ensuing behavior. Whether or not she *does* become a doctor is a function of a variety of ensuing factors (some of which may be beyond her control), but this does not negate the fact that she is an active, intending being at this point with respect to this goal.

Another criticism of telic accounts flows from the fact that they involve an "introspective" perspective; that is, they involve a first-person accounting for events because of the emphasis on intentions and reasons. Criticism is perhaps rightly leveled at this tendency when telic descriptions are used to attribute purpose and intention to nature and inanimate objects leading to anthropomorphism of such phenomena. But humanistic theorists (see Chein, 1972, p. 229) are quite content to anthropomorphize human beings by describing them as intending, purposive creatures, thus bringing final-cause motivations into legitimate consideration in human behavior. Guiding behavior by the use of one's intentions is a major aspect of human agency.[1]

Now, one of the major implications of these considerations for human behavior generally is this: In its historical development, science came to rule out final-cause principles as legitimate ways of explaining human behavior (see chap. 2 in Rychlak, 1979). But personality theorists and psychotherapists often find the need (sometimes unwittingly) to introduce "pattern" and "intention" constructs in accounting for human behavior. In subsuming White's perspective under this humanistic position, I am suggesting that, when he asserts that "something is left out" when drive constructs are made the sole explanatory principles of behavior, he in effect takes issue with the position that substance and impetus constructs (material and efficient causes) are the only appropriate mode for understanding human behavior. Instead, he finds that in order to be more faithful to the complexity of human behavior it is necessary to use what amounts to a formal-final cause construct. Thus, as we shall see when we go into White's material in more detail, there are specific qualities of behavior from very early in life that seem to serve the organism's intention to relate ever more effectively to the environment in the course of one's life. Similarly, when Roy Schafer defines "action" in terms of "purposive or goal-directed" behaviors, he too is using a final-cause or intention construct.

I maintain that such a broadening of explanatory mechanisms can be useful in considering African Americans. A mechanistic persuasion would attempt to account for the behavior of Blacks primarily in what amounts to efficient-cause terms. A recent essay by Hayes (1991) provides a good example. He uses a "radical behaviorist" psychological position to portray the forces acting on Blacks. He argues that such forces (or contingencies) have been brought to bear by Whites' efforts to exert "behavioral control" over Blacks. "Behavioral control refers to the systematic manipulation of certain environmental events in such a way that the observed effect occurs in a predictable manner" (p. 76). Thus, he points out that "During slavery, whites maintained virtually complete control over the behavior of blacks through the use of aversive control [i.e., punishment]. . . . With the abolition of slavery . . . mechanisms of economic control were instituted [in addition]." (p. 76) These mechanisms served to maintain this control. Such a position sees the environmental forces constructed by Whites as sufficient, essentially, to account for the behavior of Blacks.

A humanist in psychology, however, would see the value of introducing intentions (final-cause principles) to understand the experience as well as the observable behavior of Blacks. For example, Powdermaker (1943) notes that, although Blacks showed humble and meek behavior in interracial situations historically, the intent of such behavior was often quite at variance with such a demeanor. Thus, at times Blacks intended to mock Whites by overobsequiousness; in other instances they intended in their meekness to act out of a conception of personal (Christian) dignity ("turn the other cheek") and/or moral superiority.

As an example from a different source, consider a selection from the opening passages of Ellison's *Invisible Man* (1952) in which an old Black man on his deathbed says to his son, "'I want you to overcome 'em with yeses, undermine 'em with grins, agree 'em to death and destruction.'" The writer continues, "They thought the old man had gone out of his mind. *He had been the meekest of men*" (pp. 19–20, emphasis added). The humanistic psychological position recognizes that one cannot understand the behavior without understanding the *intent* that contributes to the behavior. To recognize the intentional, purposive quality in behavior is to recognize the *active* role of mind we have been stressing here. Note that it is not that the effect of environmental events on Blacks is unimportant; it is rather that such effects are *not sufficient* to understand psychological experience in the humanistic view.

Conceptions of Meaning

A second point that differentiates the humanistic and mechanistic approaches has to do with conceptions of meaning. The dictionary definition of the word *meaning* refers to that which one intends to convey, purport, or signify. In signifying something, meanings point to or reach for "something else"—which can be called a "polar" reference. Two kinds of meaning, demonstrative and dialectical, can be identified for our purposes here. Specific, deductively ironclad meanings are called *demonstrative* or "unipolar" meanings. When we say "unipolar," we mean that a particular meaning "points" in just one direction, so to speak. Let's take a specific item such as a tree to illustrate this issue. From a unipolar point of view the aim is to describe the characteristics that pertain to the word *tree* so as to link it in a one-to-one fashion with a clear item in the real world and keep it from being confused with other items. Being specific and unipolar in our meaning aids in communicating about and controlling things in reality. Unipolar, or demonstrative, definitions are designed to increase the specificity of knowledge granted a basic set of assumptions. The syllogism, with which we are familiar from elementary logic, is another example of demonstrative reasoning: Granted that "all cats are animals"; given a cat, it *necessarily* follows that it is an animal. If one accepts the (ultimately arbitrary) basic assumption, then certain things necessarily follow. The form of this argument truly points in just one direction.

The mechanistically inclined theorist is oriented toward identifying the factors, almost always the material- and efficient-cause ones, that will help us be certain about what a thing is. The aim is to show that, with the conditions of observation carefully controlled, the object standing before us is indeed a tree, for example, and not anything else. This mode of thinking has been particularly important in the development of Western science and technology and has given us considerable control of the material environment. This mode of thinking is important for Black people, too, as they assess their social situation. While I disagreed earlier with what I saw as the narrowness of Hayes's (1991) conception, I nevertheless do agree with him that there are and have historically been formidable environmental forces of a very specific nature acting on African-American people that need to be identified in their struggle to develop. However, as with our foregoing discussion of causal forces, an additional way of addressing the issue of meaning is also necessary for a full appreciation of the human situation in general and the African-American situation in particular. I am referring here to the idea of dialectical or "bipolar" meaning.

Rychlak uses the term *dialectical* (which has been used in a number of ways in the history of Western and Eastern philosophical thought: see, for example, Rychlak, 1988, pp. 74–81) to refer to that quality in which every specific meaning is seen to suggest either its opposite or any number of other alternatives. From a dialectical view, meaning is often framed by "bipolar referents," that is, a term is defined in terms of opposing possibilities. This is particularly true of those concepts that, although fundamental to human concern, are less tangible or empirically demonstrable, such as those ancient philosophical classics of truth, beauty, and justice. Thus, for example, one cannot have a concept of "justice" without some concomitant idea of "injustice." In a more mundane dimension, the term *up* for the dialectician necessarily implies a concept of *down;* these oppositional poles are indissolubly linked in our definition of a thing's position. Even as specific a material item as a tree in the real world can be considered from a dialectical or bipolar view: assuming the existence of the tree implies other possibilities—for example, "nontree" or "no tree." Thus, one could say, "Is that really a tree out there or is it a figment of my imagination?"

This tendency of human thought to consider alternative possibilities, even in a clear stimulus situation, is a defining characteristic of this use of the term *dialectical*. It is also basic to human symbolizing capabilities (see Edelson, 1971, chap. 1) and is central to a humanistic view of agency. It is this natural capacity to propose the opposite or alternative positions that allows the person "to go along with, add to, or oppose" external stimulation, in the words of our opening definition of agency. (Note that dialectical thinking does not guarantee more *accurate* thinking. Considering alternative possibilities about the existence of the tree does not make them more correct objectively. It does allow for creativity and keeps an individual from being *only* stimulus-bound.) For our purposes I think it captures particularly well one aspect of human potential that Blacks have drawn on to survive. The mechanistic theorist is impressed by the unipolar characteristics of situations that push or pull behavior in this direction or that. A humanistic perspective supplements with a view that notes that even in the presence of unpleasant givens, Blacks have been able (dialectically) to conceptualize alternative views of themselves and other possibilities open to them. In many instances they have struggled to actualize these alternatives, and they have had varying degrees of success historically.

For example, one can understand the ceaseless though often subtle efforts at resistance to slavery partly by recognizing the alternative (dialectical) conception of self that Blacks had. Julius Lester (1968) describes this trend towards resistance anecdotally: "Ol' Aunt Jemima was always spitting in massa's soup, while ol' John out in the field couldn't pick up a hoe without it just seeming to break in his hands. And, Lord have mercy, somebody was always running away" (p. 36). Thus, we see that physical combat is only one way to resist. "In the context of America, it is an act of resistance for a poor black man to buy a Cadillac. To resist is to do whatever is necessary to maintain self-dignity." (p. 36). In this latter passage in particular, Lester points to the dialectical mode that must be taken into account in viewing Blacks' behavior. That is to say, a particular Black man's spending his meager funds on a luxury is not necessarily just an arbitrary and irrational mimicking of (overidealized) wealthy people. It may also be an act that helps this man define and express a sense of dignity that is different from the external conditions forced on him. In the terms we have been using, such an act can at times stem from the bipolar recognition of what is (poverty) and what could be (material comfort), were his opportunities not unfairly blocked and manipulated by the system. Of course, a major goal of social change would be to enable the poor to gain sufficient resources so as not to have to strain so much in order to sustain a sense of dignity. However, we should recognize the continuing striving to "make a difference" that Blacks have brought to their world.

(I recall a White working-class Michigan high school youth some years ago asking me, after I had delivered a lecture to his class on race relations, why poor Negroes spend money on fancy cars and TV sets when they don't have money for the necessities of life. From his perspective this was irrational behavior. His point of view was, of course, external to Black people and hence an "extraspective" one. The humanist would advocate taking the Black person's introspective view. Such a view will indeed be necessary on the part of Whites if they are to overcome racist attitudes.)

The dialectical mode is not seen as supplanting the demonstrative one. Many scholars sympathetic to dialectical thought recognize that an empirical science is necessary for the advancement of knowledge and it has to be based to an important degree on demonstrative and impetus-type meaning constructs. (So, for example, in the search for a cure for cancer, medical scientists look for definite physical processes. They rule out alternatives in search of *specific* causes so that they can find effective treatments.) A potential for dialectical thought in the human being, however, was seen to develop along with the demonstrative style. The importance of the dialectical mode is that it allows and predisposes a person to consider the alternative possibilities. As one contemplates an actual bird "up" in a tree, for instance, one can conjure up many other images in the so-called reality being perceived. In fact, there is a good deal of arbitrariness in what appears to be "true" or "possible" because all ideas have implicit opposites to which they point. (Presumably the greater the salience of certain aspects of a given stimulus event, the greater the possibility for a unipolar and demonstrative definition of a situation. So, for example, being *near* the tree in which the *singing* bird is sitting on a clear, sunny day would tend to enhance the singular "reality" of the idea "There is a bird up there in the tree." But, while granting this, the dialectician also insists that it is the individual who *affirms* this meaning by conforming to these probabilities derived from his or her assessment of the situation. We shall have more to say about "affirmation" later.) The capacity to contemplate polar referents is fundamental to the creative and symbolizing activities of humankind. It is interesting to note that this attitude of "but—what if . . . ?" that is so common to children and sometimes exasperating to parents is an important aspect of hypothesis generation in scientific activity. It is the dialectical capacity to take the opposite position about a given circumstance. Such hypotheses, when framed clearly, can be tested demonstratively in experimental manipulations.

Models of the Human Mind

Now let us turn to the task of distinguishing between two ways of explaining mind and behavior. These can be seen in the philosophical positions represented by John Locke and Immanuel Kant. Locke stresses the notion of mind as a blank slate, the familiar *tabula rasa*. In Locke's view, mind begins to emerge by the awakening touch, as it were, of sense impressions from the environment. The development of mind and complex abilities is held to be solely a function of the association and combination of simpler elements "put" there by experience. This is clearly consistent with a passive conception of the development and functioning of mind.

In the Kantian view, on the other hand, the infant is not simply waiting for the kiss of experience. The human individual brings certain "categories of understanding" to life situations from the moment of birth. These categories give form to (i.e., determine in a formal-cause sense) what can be known. This means, for example, that a child is innately able to make distinctions in his/her experience between the notions of "unity" and "plurality." These are not learned as separate concepts and then later associated in experience, although, of course, the words for these concepts are learned only when language develops. The child is born bringing such rudimentary (and dialectical) "meaning-framing premises" to experience. These operate like a pair of eyeglasses to give form to experience. As the individual matures and interacts with the world, such premises, of course, become more sophisticated.

Thus, mental activity or "mind" involves the *a priori* ability to organize or pattern experience in some meaningful way from birth. (This presentation of Kant's point of view is not concerned with the details of his theory of knowledge, but rather with his broad approach to mind. This perspective can provide us with a model of mental functioning.) This mental activity involves the ability to "conceptualize." "To *conceptualize* is to put a frame (order, organization, etc.) onto experience, and as such, the frame *fixes* that which can be known" (Rychlak, 1988, p. 294). To the newborn, in William James's words, the world is a "blooming, buzzing confusion." In other words, the world does not come in neat sensory packages waiting to be discovered in the form that we come to recognize. We must organize it. What the developing child comes to "know" reflects what arises from both the child's ways of categorizing and the qualities inherent in reality.

It is the child's innate capacity to order things into "one" versus "many," to return to our example, that leads to an understanding that there is a difference between "one ball" and "three balls." This contrasts with the notion that a child learns concepts only by separate experiences, that is, by seeing one ball, one truck, one horse, and then learning *separately* the concept of several balls, trucks, horses. In the latter (Lockean) view, concepts are formed additively and the person's experience with groupings of items finally leads to understanding the unity-plurality dimension. In effect, the Lockean approach takes a demonstrative stance to experience such that events come to be conceptualized as unitary phenomena that are assimilated mentally by the person. The Kantian notion is that the only reason that the child can "make sense" of an arrangement of balls is because of an innate tendency to organize along several dimensions such as unity-plurality, shape, color, for which the child at first, of course, has no words. Indeed, the child's culture will come along to show which dimensions are more important than others, and cultures will vary in their hierarchies of what is important. "What is held to be innate is the capacity to recognize or create patterns (meanings), and when in due time the conceptualizations . . . achieve a certain organization, we can speak of them as ideas" (Rychlak, 1988, p. 294). Thus, another aspect of the individual's agency is this one of bringing an independently active mentality to encounters with experience. (Recent research supports the idea that the newborn brings active mental processing into the world [Cameron & Rychlak, 1985, pp. 33–41].)

As part of their consideration of American psychology some Black writers have been particularly critical of the Lockean emphasis in American psychology (see, for example, Boykin, 1977). (Locke, of course, was only one of a number of philosophers—Hume and Hobbes were others—who adhered to a point of view identified as the British Empiricist school of philosophy.) This critique can be made clearer by noting the distinctions between Lockean and Kantian positions on the process of developing knowledge.

The Lockean perspective can be associated with a thoroughgoing "realist" position in philosophy. It assumes that there is a specific order to be known in physical reality and that it is the task of human beings to discover this reality through careful scientific observation. In this view our senses in principle transmit the real impression of the world; the observer registers things as they "really" are. Kant, by contrast, thought of himself as a "critical realist" because he, too, firmly believed that a reality is "out there." But more important for him was his insistence that what we know as reality is what we have organized through our sensory and especially our conceptual apparatus. (This latter position associates him with philosophical "idealism" in the minds of some critics.)

The conceptual "spectacles," to use Rychlak's term, that we bring from birth necessarily provide the order that characterizes our knowledge. We are always on "this side" of the spectacles as we observe nature; reality is always on the "other side." In this view, reality does not come packaged in neat units of time and space, for example; these are ideas that we impose on it. What we know is subject to the initial conceptual biases we use to frame it. While two people looking into a small furnished room may be able to communicate about the room, they see and come to know (and thus remember, incidentally) the room differently because they bring slightly (or greatly) different perspectives to it as they observe it. And who is to say which of them sees it as it *really* is—particularly if one includes aesthetic features of the room as aspects of what the room is like? Note also that in speaking of looking through the framing assumptions—the conceptual spectacles—that a person brings to a situation, we are again touching on the *introspective* view that is characteristic of a Kantian perspective toward mentality. (This point of view is consistent with modern "constructionist" approaches in psychology [Feffer, 1988; Scarr, 1985].)

With this in mind let us turn to some of the particular objections that Black psychologists have raised. The argument against the Lockean position is that in its extraspective orientation it leads observers to believe that they are standing outside of nature, as it were, registering it dispassionately, presumably free of their own biasing value systems. In assuming that scientific observation involves observation of things as they are, the Lockean runs the danger of forgetting that things are as they have been observed, *given certain basic assumptions;* these assumptions are in the minds of the observers. (It is not being maintained here that either Blacks or psychologists were the first to recognize that science is not free of cultural values. But the implications for African Americans are important enough—and it is often enough forgotten—

that it is worth raising again.) Too often, the critics argue, Western psychology can be shown to have forgotten some of its limiting assumptions. It has fallen into the general Western pattern of assuming its own cultural and behavioral framework as the standard, defining all patterns that are different from Western cultural norms as being somehow deficient.

The Lockean position epitomizes for some critics the "European" ethnocentric bias that has tended to be pejorative in its judgment of the behavior of people of African heritage (Akbar, 1991a). Thus, there is the call for discarding European philosophical perspectives in describing the African American. In fact, it is not necessary for a Lockean to be culturally biased. Such observers could recognize the limits of their measurements and assume that they had simply not observed enough to know what the real situation is in other cultures. Because the Kantian philosophical perspective recognizes *in principle* the degree to which people bring their conceptual biases (their values) even to scientific observations, it should be better prepared to meet other cultures on their own terms. This is one advantage of the Kantian perspective in viewing the African American (Boykin, 1977). Thus, as I suggested earlier in this chapter, one does not have to throw out all of psychology's Western heritage in order to retain a useful framework for viewing the African American. The Kantian view is European also.[2]

It is an interesting development that even the so-called "hard sciences" have modified their stance on what scientific observation entails. "Modern science has become more open to Kantian-like terminology because of its recognition that what one observes in the 'hard reality' is due at least in part to what one presumes from the outset. This is clearly a recognition of the telic factors in the work of science or the scientist-human who does the work" (Rychlak, 1988, p. 193).

The implication of the Kantian perspective for the African American is that Blacks, like all human beings, come to the world with mental equipment oriented toward conceptually organizing experience, not just accepting what is given. While behavior is partly shaped by environmental and constitutional factors (sometimes to a great degree), people also bring a readiness to impose their own point of view on a given situation as well. Continuation and development of this readiness through the elaboration of the intentional and dialectical potentials of the human mind throughout life are what has helped Blacks to survive in America.[3]

To sum up the discussion so far, I have been saying that a full understanding of the history—and the potential—of African Americans calls for supplementing the modes of explanation that are typical in American psychology. Humanistic psychological approaches to agency can be useful in providing the needed corrective. Thus, the humanist posits that behavior is at least partly governed by subjectively derived intentions, factors that can be just as impelling as "instinctual" drives and environmental contingencies. A person's intention to reach an imagined goal can determine behavior "come hell or high water," as the saying goes. Furthermore, the human individual brings an actively structuring mind to the world, one capable of seeing alternative meanings in any given object or event. This enables the individual in principle to rise above the environment and to create or at least imagine something new and different. Since any one event can be interpreted in different ways, one must know how the individual conceives that event. Looked at this way, the survival of Black Americans can be understood as depending to a significant degree on their capacities to imagine a dignified sense of their humanity in spite of external circumstances.[4]

Competence as a Humanistic Theme

We shall now turn to a consideration of Robert White's concept of competence as a further way of viewing the psychological literature on Black Americans in a humanistic light. His development of the competence concept amounts to a humanistic critique of extant psychological theory. In his examination of conceptions derived from both laboratory experimentation and clinical psychoanalysis, White found that there was a failure to account for important aspects of behavior. White developed a perspective to supplement the themes emphasized by these two most popular traditions in American psychology. It seems to me that his perspective has clear humanistic implications. This is the concept of competence. In choosing the term *competence* to embody this orientation to behavior, White was referring to its familiar connotation of skilled performance of a task. However, he used the concept to talk about broad aspects of behavior and development.

White does not assume that the baby springs fully competent from the mother's womb. Rather, he argues that the basis for competence is present in some of the human infant's modes of interacting with the environment from the beginning of its life. Traditionally comments about the waking behavior of the young infant concentrated on the activity that occurs as a function of (usually irritating) internal drive states that prompt responses from the caretaking environment—some adult, usually a mother, checks on the infant when it cries. In this way the child comes to learn which of its responses are associated with reduction in drive tensions. While the learning that occurs through drive reduction is an important part of the scenario of early development, White calls our attention to other ways the child learns—and here we can see the relevance of competence strivings. The very young child gradually spends more and more of its time awake and in a state in which its drive tensions are met. White argues that such states are also conducive to important learning. He notes that it is particularly in such states, when the child is comfortable in its crib with its biological needs taken care of, that it is amenable to turning its attention to the dangling objects left there for amusement.

If, on the other hand, the child were very hungry, it might indeed grab its rattle and try to suck it, but, finding the rattle unsuitable for gratifying hunger, the child would be likely to discard it quickly and move on to see what else could be sucked and swallowed. In so doing, that is, in interpreting reality objects only in terms of pressing drive tensions, the infant would be very unlikely to learn the many interesting and important non–drive-related aspects of reality that there are. However, in a mood free of basic drive tensions the child is able to evaluate these objects in their own right. Within certain limits of stimulation those objects that it can *do* the most with (in terms of movement, sound, and visual change) are those it gives the most attention.

The more the baby's interactions have pleasing *effects*, the more it is likely to repeat and expand its activities. As the child does so, it becomes more skilled in achieving such effects: that is, it becomes effective with its interactions with the environment. White calls this kind of activity "effectance" behavior; the emotion that accompanies the opportunities for effectance behavior is a "feeling of efficacy." "Effectance thus refers to the active tendency to put forth effort to influence the environment, while feeling of efficacy refers to the satisfaction that comes with producing effects" (1963, p. 185). An important consequence of this behavior is that it leads to the formation of psychological structures, so to speak; "it leads to an accumulating knowledge of what can and cannot be done with the environment" (p. 186).[5] The "meaning" (the infant's understanding) of this interaction is not waiting there to be discovered by the infant but arises from the action sequences (effectance interactions) that he or she imposes on it. "The child has a kind of beginning capacity to organize experience, to contribute something to it *from birth*, and then he builds on this organizational capacity to bring more and more knowledge to bear in an ever-expanding intellectually active sense" (Rychlak, 1988, p. 92). Obviously the child's activity does not create the rattle, but its "capacity to organize experience" does determine what the meaning of its interaction with the rattle will be (Feffer, 1988).

The neonate is confronted with a myriad of possibilities and uncertainties ("a blooming, buzzing confusion") and has to develop gradually the categories for stabilizing its experience. As Rychlak (1988) notes, "This quality of open alternatives in experience demands that the human being *affirm* [emphasis added] some . . . meaning at the outset for the sake of which behavior might then take place" (p. 295).

The connotations of an act of affirmation are important for both Rychlak and White. *Affirmation* can be used to describe a person's choosing, presuming, or deciding that a thing is so or that it has a certain character (among the possibilities conceivable in the given situation). Affirmation is "one of those *active* [emphasis added] roles assigned to mind by humanists, because which pole of a bipolarity is affirmed or which item of unipolar experience is singled out for identification is up to the individual and *not* to the environment" (Rychlak, 1988, p. 295). It is in this sense that affirmations are arbitrary.

In introducing the concept of effectance behavior, White describes one of the processes by which the infant actively comes to terms with its environment. Effectance motivation is a way of describing one kind of premise that the newborn child brings to its experience, and in White's view it is a premise that the human individual continues to bring to his or her experience throughout life. When the baby reaches out to make contact with its rattle—an (unconscious) act of "affirmation"—the contact is accompanied by an implicit "affective assessment" of the situation as being pleasing, that is, as one it "likes."[6] With repeated experience the child gradually becomes more effective in achieving this experience as it evolves toward competence. Effectance motivation has clear final-cause or intention-construct implications in that behavior is pursued for the sake of the feeling of efficacy. Eventually, as the mature person develops a sense of "self," s/he begins to order life in terms of enhancement of effectance and competence.

Through repeated and expanded contacts with the world the child develops wider ranges of effectiveness appropriate to its emerging developmental stages. In other words, the child acquires an actual competence and a "sense of competence" about his or her dealings with the environment. A person's competence represents the existing ability to interact effectively with the environment.

> Competence is the cumulative result of the history of interactions with the environment. *Sense of competence* is suggested as a suitable term for the subjective side of this, signifying one's consciously or unconsciously felt competence—one's confidence—in dealing with the various aspects of the environment. [White, 1963, p. 186]

> We can reserve the term *feeling of efficacy* for what is experienced in each individual transaction, using *sense of competence* for the accumulated and organized consequences in later stages of ego development. [1963, p. 39]

Striving to enhance competence in one's dealings with the physical and social world is ideally a lifelong process and is characteristic of human functioning in all cultural contexts.

Because the crux of the effectance concept is action on the environment, White's developing human being is, as Chein (1972) would put it, no "passive reagent" but clearly one who, even from the crib, seeks to "generate circumstances" and inject him- or herself "into the causal process of the world around him [or her]" (p. 6). While White seems particularly concerned with motor behavior, it should be emphasized that, in the humanistic sense being developed here, *action* refers to intellectual activity as well. It may or may not involve action in the sense of bodily movement, but it does involve the individual as premising "causal agent." In fact, for Schafer (1976), *mind* refers to all the things that a person does in the way of purposive and directed efforts to come to terms with the world. "Mind" represents one's continuing efforts to structure situations conceptually and affectively in the process of living. Schafer (personal communication, March 1, 1980) has suggested that White's emphasis on motor transactions with the environment is too limited to do justice to other kinds of changes in human behavior such as shifts in understanding, that is, the active restructuring of the way in which one looks at the world. This is the sort of thing that presumably happens in psychodynamic psychotherapy. While White's perspective may be limited in this sense, the scope of his concerns does seem to fit into the framework we are considering here.

The fact that behaviorally induced effects and their consequences are important in White's framework could be seen as making this position close to a (mechanistic) Skinnerian model with its emphasis on how the environment "shapes" emitted behavior.[7] However, the difference is that for White considerable weight is placed on evaluating, experiencing individuals purposefully orienting themselves toward certain features of the environment and gradually developing a "self-conscious" sense of what kinds of activities do and do not enhance a (subjective) sense of efficacy and sense of competence. The introspective and "telic" terms are important to White also, as they are to humanists generally.

Conclusion

Thus, the humanistic theory we have been describing is a "psycho-logical" theory. That is to say, it is a theory that proposes mind (psyche) as an entity imposing an order, a logic (logos), on events (thus, a formal-cause determinative principle). This patterning or conceptualization gives events their meaning and is "that for the sake of which" behavior and further understanding follow. Thus, human individuals create the "reality" to which they respond (Edelson, 1971). A student may approach college with the intention of becoming a doctor. This intention, spelled out in a set of steps held in mind—a plan of action—existing now in the present, becomes "that" which makes an essential and determining contribution to ("for the sake of which") the behavior carried out. Such behavior would involve choice of courses, choice of study habits, perhaps choice of summer jobs. Such an intention is not sufficient, of course. Native ability (a substance construct) and sufficient finances are necessary. Also the person must have freedom from competing, contradictory plans. For example, becoming extremely active in sports while leading an unusually vigorous social life might very well not be in keeping with the intention to negotiate a premed sequence with academic honors.

I have suggested that one of the universal patterns that emerges in child development is the effectance-competence striving. I have argued that seeing Blacks as imposing an order of their own making on events, one that has premises of competence striving in it, helps to make clearer their psychological survival through history. Furthermore, I would propose that one of the major contributions that a stable African background gave to the slaves and their descendants was a basis for a sense of competence as human beings. This is what stable cultural forms give to persons by the very nature of their stability and structuredness. In other words, all people look to a norm to provide the grounds ("that") that can be the initial premise for which later behavior follows. Specific cultural contents with their associated ideological components (such as specific religious and political practices, family organization patterns) that vary from culture to culture may also be supportive.

Thus, specific beliefs that all persons are equal in the sight of Allah or social practices that distribute tribal authority among women as well as men (Carey, 1979) can be supportive to individual tribal members. Kunta Kinte, as described by Haley (1976), maintained a consistent sense of self not just because he was raised an African but because his stable African background gave him the grounds for premising himself as a competent person worth more than the treatment he was getting in the United States.

What I have been trying to demonstrate is that a humanistic focus can contribute a great deal to our understanding of the African American. The humanist in contemporary psychology emphasizes the active role of the individual coming to terms with the environment. According to this view, the individual makes choices in situations that are seen as presenting more than one possibility for understanding an action. In making choices, individuals are not simply responding to environmentally determined factors but are attempting to carry out intentions and purposes of their own. As we look at the history of Blacks, we find that they have responded to the situations they confronted with underlying premises of self-worth and competence even though external circumstances did not seem to warrant positive self-appraisals. When Pugh (1972) states of Blacks in history that "the form of resistance—when present—was largely passive," he seems to dismiss such forms of Black resistance. But even passive resistance is an *act*, an intentional strategy born of a conception of self that was different from that which Whites had of Blacks. Blacks took the kind of action they were able to take under the circumstances.

Again, the focus on a drive-reduction or environmental-contingency psychology tends to see African Americans only as passive victims. It is very true that Blacks have been and continue to be victimized by this society. The more mechanistic psychological views may be able to speak to this fact rather well.

However, this focus overlooks other important aspects of human psychology and, therefore, other psychological explanations necessary to understanding Blacks' survival. Humankind's tendency not to simply react to stimuli—its tendency to be an "active agent"—stems from almost irrepressible urges to create an effective relationship with the environment. From birth on, people take actions that eventually grow into actual competencies to deal with the world. Such a conception does not preclude recognizing the individual's relationship to the environment based on drives and their primary satisfaction, including anxiety and its reduction. Rather, the humanistic theme that places emphasis on the independent striving to affirm and to make contact with the world is a necessary supplement. A psychological conception of all human individuals as potentially active shapers of their worlds makes it easier to understand how Blacks survive. It is this that is missing from much of the theorizing about the psychology of the Black experience.

Whether in the form of violent revolt or passive resistance; whether engaged in the effort to make themselves competent artisans, farmers, or professionals—throughout history, Blacks have struggled to realize a sense of themselves that was meaningful to them. A conceptualization of the person that can encompass the fact of survival of African Americans must include this quality of striving or "motivation." Chein (1972) asserts: "The essential psychological human quality is . . . one of commitment to a developing and continuing set of unending, interacting, interdependent, and mutually modifying long-range enterprises." (p. 289)

Slavery, poverty, and racism have been and are dehumanizing to the extent that they lead one to give in to being continually preoccupied with the miseries of the present. Such conditions are dehumanizing to the extent that they lead "to the abandonment of one's claims on, and one's program with regard to the relatively distant future" (Chein, 1972, pp. 289–290). At times this has happened to some Black people under the bombardment of the efforts of American society to achieve just this. But many African Americans have managed to use their creative human capacities in modest or striking and socially contributive ways to resist being dehumanized.

Notes

1. The humanist's emphasis on the introspective or subjective view—one that considers events through the perspective of the actor's intentions—contrasts with the mechanistic orientation. The latter relies on "extraspective" or third-person descriptions in attempting to account for human events primarily in terms of material and efficient causes. This effort to account for human experience and behavior in terms of *solely* material and efficient causes defines

a *reductionistic* approach (see Cameron & Rychlak, 1985, pp. 6, 13-14; Peele, 1983, chap. 2). Interestingly, though Pugh's concept of "adaptive inferiority" rests on a more mechanistic psychological base, his discussion obtains some of its appeal through his use of first-person or introspective accounts of his experiences.

2. There is some indication in literature on African culture that the Kantian perspective is compatible with the African view of a human being's relationship with nature. In the African world view there is much more recognition of the harmony between humankind and nature. People are not seen as being able to step outside of the natural world (Mbiti, 1970). This sounds much like the idea that we are identifying with Kant here, that knowledge is partly a function of what the observer brings to the observing situation. (While we will pursue some of the implications of a Kantian model in this book, it is appropriate to note that others use a different tradition in Western philosophy to oppose mechanistic views in psychology. See, for example, Messer, Sass, & Woolfolk, 1988; Rorty, 1979).

3. One current approach to constructionism argues that what we "know" about the world and even about ourselves is largely dependent on how our beliefs, organized by our socio-cultural context in a given historical time, determine our experience. This puts an emphasis on formal-cause (structured by society) influences on individual experience (Gergen, 1985; Harre, 1986). While there is some merit in such notions, this is too much on the side of a Lockean analysis in my view. There seems to me to be an overemphasis on the input of meaning *into* the individual person. As I have argued elsewhere (Jenkins, 1989), such "social constructionist" points of view leave little theoretical room for the individual to construct an alternative conceptualization from that of society through the use of independent dialectical mental processes. I maintain in this book that this latter process has been essential to the survival of African Americans. Indeed, some have argued that extreme forms of the social constructionist view that take away the possibility of individual choice among conceptions and actions—through completely *socially* determined options—undermine the possibility for moral responsibility in individual action (Cameron & Rychlak, 1985, chap. 21; Robinson, 1991).

4. Some would argue that such intentions have been sustained by the African cultural traditions that Blacks have maintained in as many spheres of life in America as possible. To what degree distinctive African cultural features are a part of African-American life is for research and scholarship to determine. More writing on this topic has emerged in the past decade (see, for example, Myers, 1988 and the Fall 1990 issue of *The Journal of Black Psychology*: "Introducing an African World View into Psychology"). The African Americans' capacity to imagine the opposite of what is presented to them makes it quite possible in principle for Blacks to have sustained African cultural perspectives of themselves in spite of the "obstacles and meannesses" imposed on them.

Such a dialectical situation is partly implied in DuBois's famous statement that the African American "ever feels his two-ness—an American, a Negro" (1961, p. 17).

However, from another dialectical perspective the African American can be seen to be a new cultural being, a blend of the African and the European in which elements of the African influence are quite recognizable but melded into something different from either simply African or European forms. A unique cultural product of the blending of these heritages is the development of jazz, a music form that has African roots yet has evolved beyond those origins in the American setting. (See the work of Ferdinand Jones [1989; 1992] on this point.) Ellison has argued in various places (e.g., Ellison & McPherson, 1970) that Blacks have made so many contributions to American popular culture that in many ways it is not possible to call this culture ethnically "White." Similarly, second-generation American citizens of other ethnic extractions are not simply transplanted Italians, Japanese, Swedes, and so forth, either. They are different culturally—and perhaps in some ways psychologically—from the persons of the "Old Country," though they are culturally distinct as groups to some degree among themselves here in this country.

5. Put another way, important consequences of effectance behavior are the building of the child's conceptions of reality and the steady exercise and development of what Freudian psychoanalysts would call the "reality testing" function of the "ego" system. This function has to do with the ability to perceive and make judgments about the world accurately, distinguish between what is a part of oneself and what is not, and use thought and action with repeated reliability in dealing with the world.

6. Affective assessment is an important concept in Rychlak's learning theory and is an example of dialectical functioning in human activity. As we shall see in Chapter 3, a considerable amount of research has been done using this theoretical notion. Affective assessments are judgments with a distinct feeling (hence, "affective") tone that human beings are able to make from birth. Such judgments give one's affirmations about experience a positive or negative value. There may be differences in degree of positive or negative assessment (e.g., "very positive" or "rather positive"), there may be mixed feelings (ambivalence), but the dialectical view holds that there is no indifference point on the dimension of affective assessment. Rychlak maintains that any time an individual conceptualizes a situation, that is, organizes it meaningfully, s/he concomitantly applies an affective assessment or affection to the situation. An affective assessment is a part of every conceptualization. Thus, a person's commitment to a belief always involves affective as well as intellectual components.

In this theory, affections are different from emotions. The latter have more of a physiological, and therefore material-cause, quality. Affections, as judgments about experience, "are purely mental phenomena, ultimately *arbitrary* and up to the person who levels such idiographic judgments from his or her (introspective) perspectives on life" (Rychlak, 1988, p. 317). Rychlak derives this notion from the Kantian idea of "transcendence," which refers to the capacity of the mind to "double back on itself," as it were, and evaluate its own evaluations. We experience emotions (e.g., anger, sadness, elation) as a function of the physiological responses that are tied to certain events in our world. Affective assessment or affection, on the other hand, refers to our capacity to reflect on our emotions in a meaningful way. The bashful, lovesick teenager gazing raptly at a picture of the high school Homecoming Queen feels crushed ("blue") that she hardly notices him, much less returns his affection. Yet for a complex of reasons he feels good (he has a positive assessment) about being in such a bad way over someone like her. He assesses his doleful emotional state as largely positive and proceeds with the activities that allow it to continue (keeping her picture pinned up in his locker, following her home from a safe distance, etc.) until he develops a different conception of what is important in his life. To return to the neonatal situation, the baby in the crib experiences not only the tactile, visual, and auditory sensations that are the direct occasion for pleasure but brings the at-first rudimentary capacity to evaluate this joyful situation as something to be repeated. White's "feeling of efficacy," the pleasure at recognizing that one is effective (and that for the sake of which behavior continues), is an affective assessment.

7. In the Skinnerian framework, when an organism makes a random response, an experimenter can increase the probability that that response will be repeated by rewarding the response. By selectively rewarding what were at first random ("emitted") responses (or, at least, responses that didn't fit the experimenter's design), the experimenter can elicit a set of responses that fit the pattern of the experimenter's intentions. This is called *operant conditioning* because it is learning that occurs by affecting the organism's operations on the environment.

For Skinner, the meaning of an act is determined by the consequences—the externally observable result—it produces, after the fact. Thus, a pigeon's peck of the red not the blue dot is "food-worthy" in meaning only in connection with the reward that follows. But to the humanist, things are more complicated for people. A person can anticipate the consequences of an action in advance and choose to proceed or not. Thus, a person might say, "Of my two favorite foods I expect the taste of pizza rather than Chinese food will satisfy me most tonight." Previous experience is necessary for the decision but not sufficient to explain this night's choice. For a more extensive critique of Skinner from his humanistic perspective, see Rychlak, 1988, pp. 255–270; 1979, pp. 85–98.

2

African-American Self-Concept: Sustaining Self-Esteem

> When I draw a white girl, I know she'll be okay, but with the colored it's not so okay. So I try to give the colored as even a chance as I can, even if that's not the way it will end up being. [Coles, 1967, p. 50]

This was the way Ruby explained to the psychiatrist Robert Coles why she rarely used the black and brown crayons when drawing herself and other Black people. Ruby was a 6-year-old Black girl—the eldest of six children of lower-class parents—and one of the first children to desegregate a New Orleans school in the late 1950s. Coles was in New Orleans attempting to evaluate the impact of school desegregation on Black and White southerners who were participants in that profound institutional change. In gathering his data he used some of the clinical methods familiar to him as a psychiatrist— primarily one-to-one interviews with people, conducted over a period of time in informal settings where rapport could be developed. With young children his interviews were put into the context of play and included asking the children to draw pictures of the life situations they were in or whatever else they chose to draw. Drawings are a natural mode of expression for children. In the case of their pictures of people it is assumed that the kinds of figures they draw represent aspects of their self-perceptions. For example, the drawing of relatively larger figures with intact bodies is thought to indicate that a person has a relatively secure sense of self—presumably a positive self-image. As to what Ruby's crayon drawings looked like when she and the researcher first started their regular meetings, Coles wrote:

She drew white people larger and more lifelike. Negroes were smaller, their bodies less intact. A white girl we both knew to be her own size appeared several times taller. While Ruby's own face . . . lacked an eye in one drawing, an ear in another, the white girl never lacked any features. [p. 47]

Ruby was the center of great controversy when she entered first grade in her New Orleans school. Almost all of the White parents chose to withdraw their children from the few desegregated schools that first year. Some joined the crowds of shrieking adults who picketed school property and lined the walk to the front door of Ruby's and other schools. Consequently, Ruby's first few years of school, which should have been joyous ones, were instead full of traumatic experiences affecting both Ruby and her family.

Ruby undoubtedly realized that she was the focus of so much attention because she was Black. The desegregation drama had brought her face to face with racial slurs and violent threats expressed openly and unequivocally. One might easily have attributed her diminished representation of Black figures and her cautious use of certain colors to the disturbing effects of being the target of racial hatred during the school desegregation crisis. That would have been too facile an explanation, because other evidence showed up in some earlier drawings made by Ruby when she attended her all-Black Sunday school class. When Coles examined some of these earlier pictures, which had been made before he or the desegregation conflict had come into her life, he found that she had been drawing Black people in a similarly incomplete way and had been careful about using the dark-colored crayons when she was a preschooler. It could only be concluded that these characteristics of her drawings reflected something relatively longstanding in her feelings about race that were not simply referable to the immediate crisis.

Ruby's preschool desegregation drawings placed the onset of her lowered self-image at a time before she entered first grade at 6 years old. Racial group membership, Coles concluded after his extended observations of Ruby and other children, had a distinct and deleterious impact on these Black children's conceptions of themselves from early preschool years. But other things were going on in their lives. In Ruby's case, she was of course frightened and saddened by the events surrounding her, but she maintained an amazing degree of poise during those trying times, much more than could have been expected of a 6-year-old child under so much pressure. In fact, her sleep, school work, and play with her friends were not disturbed. (We shall talk later of a psychiatric symptom that did develop for a time.) Like any other child she was going through the various stages of social-emotional and intellectual growth in a particular family, making good progress in many areas, and hitting some snags in others.

The example of Ruby illustrates rather well one of the dilemmas posed by the seemingly contradictory findings in the literature on the self-concept of African Americans. On the one hand, Ruby's self-esteem connected with racial membership appeared to be quite shaky from her drawings, while at the same time she seemed to be getting along well and doing a good job at growing up. By the same token, a good deal of the research literature has reported that the self-concept of Blacks has been heavily damaged by racism, while at the same time other findings have indicated that Black self-esteem has been relatively high. These contradictions in the research literature have been frequently noted and have become more and more the focus of inquiry of Black behavioral and social scientists. The direction that the reconsideration of the data has taken has stemmed from conceptual and methodological critiques. In this chapter an attempt has been made to apply a humanistic perspective in psychology as a way of supplementing and clarifying some of the current reappraisal of the data on Black self-concept.

Research: Low Self-Esteem in Black Children

Many observers have concluded that there is a considerable amount of "self-hatred" in the Black community, even among Black children. This rather widely held assumption about the low self-esteem of African Americans is based partly on research done from the late thirties through the mid-sixties. According to these studies, evidence of negative self-esteem can be elicited from Black children of nursery school age. Of the various methods that have been used to measure racial awareness and self-evaluation of Black youngsters (Brand, Ruiz, & Padilla, 1974), one of the most frequently employed has been the doll-preference technique used by Kenneth and Mamie Clark in their famous series of studies. The method consisted of presenting a pair of dolls, one brown and one white, to Black children, age 3 to 7 years, while asking them questions about the dolls to get at their knowledge of racial terms, their understanding of what racial group they belong to, and other aspects of their attitudes toward the dolls (Clark & Clark, 1952). Assuming that the answers to these questions would have implications for the children's racial feelings, the Clarks found that preschool Black children had considerable knowledge of racial labels ("colored," "Negro," "White"), and preferred the white doll as the "pretty" doll and the more desirable object of play. In general the Clarks concluded that there was evidence here of a negative attitude toward racial identity on the part of a large number of these children.

Several decades of research using variations of the doll study design produced evidence that seemed to corroborate the Clark findings about the poor self-image of Black children. In recent years, however, there has been criticism both of the methodology used in making the doll studies and the rather bleak conclusions drawn from them about the negative self-concept of Black Americans. Although this criticism was well justified when applied to some of the studies, it was not so appropriately aimed at the work of other investigators who had already recognized the methodological deficiencies of the first wave of doll studies. What had emerged from the newly designed research, however, were findings about Black self-esteem that were quite similar to conclusions of the earlier studies, although the interpretation of the findings was more cautious and qualified.

For example, Judith Porter (1971) had already taken into account the methodological weaknesses of the Clark design in her study of a large sample of northern urban Black and White nursery school children in the late sixties. To make the play situation more natural she had a small manipulable doll scene built and engaged the children in making up a "story for TV" (this was adapted from the Movie-Story Game of Evans, Chein, and Hogrefe [Evans & Chein, 1948], developed to measure racial attitudes in elementary school children). In the course of this "game" in which the children could use a set of dolls for their TV dramas—there were grown-up dolls and child dolls, both brown- and white-skinned—the children were asked questions meant to reveal racial attitudes. Employing more sophisticated statistical analyses than most previous researchers, Porter also introduced controls for social class and amount of interracial contact in the classroom. In addition, she controlled for other potentially extraneous variables about the dolls such as their sex, hair color, and color of their clothes. This enabled her to say with some degree of confidence that preferential doll choice had racial implications, particularly for the Black children she studied.

From among her several sets of findings, of particular interest to us here was that Black children showed a preference for the white doll. It was not clear, however, whether preference for a white doll always meant *rejection* of the brown doll. In a situation where the children *had* to make preferential choices between brown and white figures, white choice, Porter hypothesized, might have reflected neutral or even moderately favorable attitudes toward both dolls with a somewhat greater preference for the white one. But there was no doubt that rejection of the brown dolls was involved for some children since it could be heard in their spontaneous comments while at play.[1]

On the matter of social-class influence on doll preference, Porter reported the interesting finding that attitudes toward the dolls varied by social class. Working-class Black children showed greater preference for the brown dolls than did the middle-class Black children. Porter interpreted this as reflecting the fact that working-class Black families living in predominantly Black environments were themselves stable and had access to the supportive features of stable institutions in the Black community. In contrast, middle-class Black families were more likely to have more contact with middle-class White families than the working-class group. In comparing themselves with such families, middle-class Blacks would be under the strong pressure of American racial mores to see themselves as being of a lower status than Whites even though both Black and White families were middle class.

In a series of studies using a different kind of methodology, Williams and Morland (1976) also found that young children—both Black and White—in various regions of the country expressed a preference for light-colored objects, animals, and people over dark ones. Using pictures of black and white animals rather than human figures in one research design, they asked the children to give semantic evaluations of a pair of different-colored animals after listening to a story fragment about each pair (The Color Meaning Test). (Semantic evaluations here refer to asking subjects to rate a given stimulus item using different evaluative adjectives such as *good, clean,* and *nice* versus *bad, dirty,* and *naughty*.) Children of both races expressed a white-preference, black-avoidance tendency. A similar white-color preference was indicated by older children. Black children at the sixth-grade levels rated white more positively when they were given other tests of semantic evaluation. White-color preference has been found generally to be less strong in Blacks than in Whites in these studies.

Further studies related semantic evaluations to photographs of persons with White European ("Euro") and African-American ("Afro") characteristics using the Preschool Racial Attitude Measure (PRAM). Williams and his colleagues found that Black and White nursery and early elementary school children expressed a more positive attitude toward "Euro" characters, although again the Euro-American children clearly showed more "Euro" bias than did the African-American children. More Black children had scores in the "no-bias" range. (Porter had also noted that, on the whole, preference for the white doll was not as strong among the Black as among the White subjects in her study.)

Using a variety of measures in her study of self-concept and racial attitude in African-American children, McAdoo (1977) also found a moderate white preference among various groups of children. Her samples consisted of groups of 4- to 6-year-old children from an all-Black, rural Mississippi town; a residentially segregated suburb outside of Detroit; and children from the Washington, D.C., area. Her study was an extensive one that included retest data on her sample. We shall have more to say about her research later.

Overall, carefully designed studies have consistently indicated some out-group orientation in the attitudes of young African-American children. In other words, when children were required to express a preference for dolls or pictures of lighter as opposed to darker people or animals, they tended to choose the lighter ones. As was indicated, what seemed to be preference for the lighter did not necessarily mean a broad rejection of themselves by these children. However, since some of the preference questions had to do with physical attractiveness and preference as play objects or play partners, the data have been taken as reflecting some ambivalence about the self. (The debate about the methodology of these studies and the meaning of the "white preference" phenomenon continues [Banks, 1976; Banks, McQuater & Ross, 1979; MacMillan, 1988; Milner, 1983; Porter & Washington, 1979; Williams & Morland, 1979]. As we shall see later, it becomes further complicated by considerations regarding the stages of development in children's thinking capacities.)

Research: High Self-Esteem in Black Children

Meanwhile, other kinds of evidence had been accumulating that indicated that Black children felt neither ambivalence about nor rejection of their own group and that their self-esteem was in fact high. Hraba and Grant (1970) and Ward and Braun (1972) found that northern Black children tended overwhelmingly to prefer the dolls of their own race when they were presented with the Clark paradigm. Fish and Larr (1972) and McAdoo (1977) also discovered that the figure drawings done in the 1970s by Black children showed an increase in indicators that would identify the figures as being Black. All of these researchers interpreted their data as evidence of the positive effects of the Black Revolution on children's self-image. What seemed to show up was a new pride in themselves and their racial identity. Thus, it appeared that their self-esteem was changing for the better. (Banks [1976] has raised the question of whether greater own-race doll preference represents greater [and healthier] racial pride or greater [and not necessarily healthier] ethnocentrism.)

In addition, a number of reports (Bachman, 1970; Baughman, 1971; Powell, 1973; Taylor, 1976) indicated that, in large-scale studies, self-esteem was at least as high among Black children of varying social backgrounds as it was among White children. In one of the better known of these studies, Rosenberg and Simmons (1971) administered a six-item Gutman-type self-esteem scale to a large urban sample of third- to twelfth-grade Black and White school children in Baltimore and related the results to other social and personal characteristics gleaned in the course of extensive interviews, including questions eliciting direct statements of feelings about themselves. Not only was the self-esteem of Black children high, but more Black children reported feelings of high self-esteem than did White children of the same age.

Contrary to the studies reviewed in the previous section, this recent research indicated that a sense of competence as reflected in high self-esteem was characteristic of Black children. These findings appeared to be in clear contradiction to those studies that had shown that some Black children expressed either negative feelings or at least a degree of ambivalence about some aspects of themselves. While only a sample of the more often cited or the better-designed studies have been presented here, they are sufficient to illustrate the conflicting trends in the literature on self-concept and self-esteem in African-American children. (For a more exhaustive review of most of the studies done on self-concept and self-esteem among African Americans, see Cross, 1991; Gordon, 1977).

Self-Concept: A Many-Faceted Entity

Let us turn our attention to a reconciliation of what seem to be contradictions in the findings about self-esteem in African-American children. To some extent, trying to compare studies has been difficult because they have used different methodologies for examining self-concept (Gordon, 1977; Wylie, 1974). But equally important to how we understand the results of these studies is our understanding of what the terms *self* and *self-concept* refer to—that is, we have to clarify some underlying conceptual issues about the self before we look at the research.

In our rush to have something definitive and useful to say about self-concept and self-esteem, we often forget that people are complex. The concepts we use to account for behavior sometimes oversimplify, rather than take account of the complexity needed to do justice to the human person. It is one of the tenets of this book, for example, that trying to conceive of the human being as only an object that can be manipulated like a machine—even a complicated one—is an oversimplification and has disadvantages for the way we think about Black people. While we cannot devote a lengthy discussion to this topic of the self, we can set out some basic ideas here that will help us reorient our conception of the self in African Americans.

Traditionally the term *self* refers to those aspects of experience that the individual considers to be "I" and "me." Gradually, through experience with the world, what is self comes to be distinguished by the person from everything that is experienced as "not me." Again, from the theoretical view of this book, the concern is with the development of an important aspect of the actor's stable, introspective view of events. There is a kind of (dialectic) paradox in the idea of self. On one hand, self implies that in every person there is the feeling of being a functioning unit organized to achieve certain goals in life (White & Watt, 1981). On the other hand, this organization or patterning is made up of a variety of different personal tendencies and characteristics. Self and self-concept, while standing for the cohesiveness of the individual, are also multifaceted. Thus, a person's self-concept is an interconnected collection of the various ideas, images, and feelings that s/he holds about the self.[2] This collection is organized; that is, the different parts are meaningfully interrelated as far as the person is concerned—they are not just present in a haphazard fashion. (What is illustrated here is the "one-in-many" quality of events that dialectic focuses on. This particular unity-in-plurality notion dates back at least to the ancient Greek philosophers. The idea is that there is a oneness [identity] in the manifoldness of events. Self is a unity but patterned of many personal tendencies. See Rychlak [1988] for further discussion of this one-in-many aspect of dialectics.)

One very important aspect of the self-concept is self-esteem. *Self-esteem* refers to self-evaluations; that is, it refers to judgments that we make about our worth. Self-esteem consists of affective assessments about the self. These assessments are judgments that give our conceptions a positive or negative feeling tone or valence. So the affirmations about oneself that are a part of self-concept—for example, "I am a girl," "I am a 6-year-old," "I am a Black child"—derive important meaning from the positive or negative valence (or the ambivalence) attached to them. Just as people have feelings about all the aspects of their lives that are meaningful to them, so they have feelings about all aspects of their self-conceptualization. Some aspects of self-concept are not conscious and so some aspects of self-esteem are not conscious either. As a result, people may hold different feelings about themselves at different levels of consciousness. People strive to keep self-esteem at a positive level generally in order to support their daily encounters with the world (Epps, 1975; Epstein, 1973). We do this partly by trying to be effective in the world through activities and social relationships that we can find rewarding. One's *sense of competence* is another way of talking about self-esteem. (People whose personal development and social circumstances are or have been difficult may attempt to maintain self-esteem through various types of psychological distortions of their experience called "defenses." All of us use such maneuvers to some extent.)

Granted that maintenance of positive self-evaluation is a basic striving, there are different things that people can do to sustain this feeling:

> The individual may choose from among a number of characteristics in his efforts to maintain self-esteem. . . . One's self-esteem may be based upon such varied characteristics as athletic prowess, dress and physical appearance, attractiveness to the opposite sex, skill at verbal repartee, and skill at fighting, as well as academic achievement. [Epps, 1975, p. 305]

These multiple bases for establishing self-esteem reflect the idea that self is many-sided. People value components of themselves differently according to their personal history, the opportunity structure (the realistic chances for making use of educational achievement, for example), and ethnic and social class group membership. Black and White persons probably value some components of self-concept differently (Baldwin, 1979).

But, even more important, the individual can develop varied and even conflicting components of self. For one thing, this has implications for the measurement of self-esteem. Since self-concept is varied and components are differentially valued, tests of self-concept that measure a person's general level of self-esteem are not necessarily good at describing a more specific aspect of self-esteem. For example, if you use global measures of self-esteem, you are less likely to be able to predict academic achievement than if you use specific measures of academic self-esteem (Epps, 1975).

Related to that measurement issue is the fact that self-esteem is affected by the situation a person is confronting (Gordon, 1977). For example, students may justifiably be able to think of themselves as academically competent in one context, say in a small high school in the rural South. But upon entering a different setting, let's say a large prestigious Black college, they may find this aspect of self-esteem considerably challenged by the more rigorous classroom demands and the better student body. This would call for a different conceptualization about themselves. Both the lack of specificity of a test and the situational quality of self-esteem may be reflected in the contradictory literature on self-esteem in Black children.

Aspects of Self: Racial and Personal

Even when measurement issues are taken into account, the fact that self-esteem is multifaceted and situational does not mean that the self and its attributes are simply a random collection of characteristics. Rather, the implication is that people define themselves from a number of different perspectives while still maintaining a sense of continuity as a person. Speaking to this point, Cross (1987, 1991) suggests that a "multiple reference point" perspective may account for many of the contradictions in the literature on self-concept in Black children. By this he means that Black children have available and make use of different reference groups and their associated values in assessing themselves.[3] Based on his review of the literature, he argues that on the one hand much of the research done before the late 1960s reflected Black children's racial reference group attitudes, that is, their attitudes toward their own group and toward Whites. It is primarily from these studies that conclusions about low self-esteem in Black children have been drawn. On the other hand, studies in which test items tend not to raise issues of racial group membership have consistently yielded positive self-evaluation among Black children. These studies tap *personal* self-esteem (or "Personal Identity," as Cross puts it) rather than racial self-concept.

What happens when racial and personal self-esteem measures are included in the same study? The results are mixed, but the larger studies (McAdoo, 1977; Porter, 1971; Rosenberg & Simmons, 1971; Spencer, 1985) tend to indicate that when Black children have some degree of low self-esteem about race, they do not necessarily have a correspondingly poor concept about other aspects of themselves. In other words, racial and personal self-esteem can be different. Based on such data, Cross suggests that, while sense of personal self-esteem among African-American children is and always has been high—at least as high as among Whites—regarding racial self-evaluation prior to the late sixties, many young Black children seem to have used Whites as the reference point for what was positive. It appeared by the late 1970s as if this racial outgroup orientation among Blacks was changing as a result of events of the previous decade. (It is this aspect of self-esteem that would be consistent with Pugh's analysis [1972]. Such a trend is suggested by the Hraba and Grant [1970] and Ward and Braun [1972] studies and by the literature review conducted by Cross [1991]. It should be noted that the rather blunt presentation of questions used in such Clark doll-design studies may be less useful as a technique these days than it was in the years prior to the 1960s. Investigation in this area still awaits the updating of a design like Judith Porter's [1971], which puts experimental controls on so many important variables. Such a study should be done in different regions of the country, also, as were McAdoo's ([1977] and Spencer's [1985] studies.)[4]

In sum, what we have been saying is that self-concept is a multifaceted sense that one has about who and what one is. It is a theory about oneself. Self-esteem is a set of affective evalutions about oneself; people try by their actions to keep self-esteem at a relatively positive level. Apart from the problems of measurement of self-esteem in general and among minority persons in particular, the contradictions in the literature on the self-esteem of Black children partly reflect the fact that self-concept is multifaceted. Persons have available to themselves a variety of vantage points (or "anchor points," as Cross says) that they use to conceptualize themselves and their place in the world at any given moment. The data reflect the complexity of self-esteem and the fact that Black children have used more than one set of reference points to evaluate themselves depending partly on what they were being asked to do. If the reference point was self-esteem from the vantage point of racial group membership, it might contain some negative feelings, while at the very same moment they might feel quite positive about other parts of themselves.[5]

Self as Active Agent

The next thing we need to do is to see how some of the humanistic concepts that we have developed in Chapter 1 can help us understand the complexity of self-concept and self-esteem still further. What is required here is a clear picture of the active quality of the self. The self-concept, the (relatively static) view that we develop of ourselves as we turn our gaze toward ourselves—as an object, so to speak—is not the only sense we have of self (Keen, 1970). We are also aware of ourselves as agents. By *agents* I mean we recognize ourselves as persons who take action, take initiative, make decisions, and make choices from among possibilities. Thus, self is also a way of talking about our capacity to come to a situation that is full of possibilities (as most situations are) and make a choice in that situation. As we do this, we shape the course of our lives.

This can be seen even in young children. Let's take as an example of this choosing and affirmation activity a hypothetical 7-year-old boy, physically well coordinated, whose acknowledged enjoyment of vigorous muscular activity and his vivid imagination are fulfilled by his active interest in baseball. He avidly follows the exploits of his local major league team, which, let's say, is clearly on its way to the World Series. Every chance he gets he plays baseball, draws pictures of his favorite team, uses his still rudimentary reading skills to follow the scores in the paper and to devour simple books on the game, and watches (as much as his parents will let him) the televised games of any major league team instead of the Tom and Jerry cartoons or *Sesame Street*, which he used to enjoy. He plays ball with his friends as much as he can and plays catch with his parents as often as he is able to entice them to do so.

The choices he makes, given various options around him, are determined by ("for the sake of") his intention: "I'm going to be a major league (i.e., competent) baseball player when I grow up." As we look at him, we can see a consistent pattern to the choices he makes; in this sense "the self is a kind of 'logical thrust' . . . which organisms under our observation bring to bear as they 'come at' the world" (Rychlak, 1988, p. 350). From our aspiring young ballhawk's point of view—that is, from an introspective point of view—the self represents "that sense of orientation and *identity* in behavior which mechanists are prone to consider illusory experience" (p. 351). He has a clear sense of where he wants to go and of getting there by trying to be like Dave Winfield or Bobby Bonilla as the case may be—hence the wearing of baseball wristbands to bed and to school and the ever present baseball cap and the shirt with his hero's number on it. The point here is that the choices he is making—to get the most exposure to baseball-related things that he can—determine his activities and the skills he develops. They determine the kinds of friendships he makes—to the exclusion of other possibilities. He is actively shaping what he is becoming. Although he is conscious of his intentions—intentions that of course may not come to fruition—one does not have to assume that he is aware of the process I am describing here as such, that is, of contributing to his self-development. Nonetheless he is the product of his choices. As he affirms with pride, "I am a good baseball player," this little boy is developing aspects of his self-concept. This is a rudimentary example of what is even more true of the older adolescent or adult individual, namely, that people are active in their own creation.

In his poem "The Road Not Taken," Robert Frost (1964) captures the idea that to some degree we are responsible for our lives by how our intentions guide our choices. He describes a traveler (a metaphor for the self as I am viewing it here) who stands at a point where the path diverges in two directions. The traveler decides to take one of the paths, the one that is less worn by travel, and later comes to recognize that this choice "has made all the difference" in his life. In one sense a person's development proceeds through time in the selection of one or another "path" or option for carrying out one's life. My example was of a little boy, since we are talking of children in this chapter, but it certainly applies to people even more as they gain greater intellectual and emotional maturity and become better able to appreciate the environmental options and their own skills and to anticipate consequences. Self-concept is like the "trail" one can recognize as one turns to reflect on the steps one has taken. That trail is made of the active decisions that have brought one to this point. The trail of choices is part of the answer to the question "What am I?" The self is the particular "logical thrust" that a person's intentions give to his or her pattern of choices. To paraphrase the title of Frost's poem, self is "the road *taken*." Thus, we are the products of the choices we make—the paths we take. We are self-creating beings to an important degree.

These ideas highlight an important characteristic of human psychology, namely, the creative activity and creative potential in every human being. Now, in what sense do I mean this? As I said earlier, in imposing a conception on events, all human individuals create the "reality" for the sake of which they behave (Edelson, 1971, esp. chap. 1). Self-creation is an important example of this, too, and is a fundamental aspect of the humanistic conception. Interestingly enough, such a notion has long been implicit in Judeo-Christian thought, though unrecognized. In the biblical story of Creation, as Chein (1972) calls attention to it, all acts up to the creation of humankind are represented as being commanded simply by God and then as having been completed: "And God said, Let there be light: and there was light." The creation of humankind, however, is heralded by, "We will make Man," a statement that is a literal translation of the Hebrew text. For the first and only time, God uses the plural subject and the future tense. There is no statement in the text of the completion of humankind's creation as there was with the creation of other aspects of the world. The *we* form is seen to indicate that God took human beings into partnership, and the future tense indicates that this creation is far from completed. "What more magnificent creation, short of the creation of the universe itself, can be attributed to God than a self-creating being?" (Chein, 1972, p. 42). (While Chein indicates this as an aspect of Western thinking, such an idea is fully consonant with many other religious and cultural traditions as well.)

In drawing on this illustration I want to highlight the fact that African Americans have been very much engaged in the business of their own creation through the intentional, dialectical activity of mind. Our task in living, then, is no less than for each one of us to reclaim our creative heritage and potential in our daily living. The notion that all human beings create their worlds implies that creativity is not just a special activity reserved only for a few gifted individuals. It is true that the nature of a particular creative product is a function of the degree of self-development or special talent of a particular individual. However, the humanistic psychological tradition underscores the idea that our usual honorific notions of creativity are really a special case of what every human being does or could do to a more limited degree.[6]

It could be argued that a model that puts emphasis on choice and self-creation does not properly describe the young child's situation on two counts. First, it seems to run counter to the conventional wisdom that self is a social product, that is, that the self is the result of the influx of social experience. Second, this model may seem to be particularly inappropriate for the ethnic minority child in a hostile society. It is true that self-development is heavily influenced by the actions and attitudes of important persons toward one. "Important persons" here means family, peers, and other people in society whom one recognizes as having some authority over one. In fact, it is hard to think of a sense of self developing outside of a social context. G. H. Mead stressed this particularly in his description of self as "the generalized other," literally a self that is the reflection of the social group (1952).

It is also true that development of sense of self is a difficult task for children. This is all the more so in the early years of life when equipment for understanding the world and one's place in it is not well developed. In the face of uncertainty and openness in experience, all people, and especially children, feel the need to establish as much regularity in their lives as quickly as they can in new situations. This would seem to point to the fact that children are especially vulnerable to the influence of more knowledgeable and powerful adults.

Such notions of social influence *on* self-development and functioning emphasize a more passive and Lockean stance toward the self. They tend to de-emphasize the functioning of native personal psychological factors in the developmental process. A humanistic approach insists in complementary fashion on the importance of the active (choosing, affirming) aspects of self. To say that self-concept could not develop outside of a social milieu simply means that the social context serves as the grounds or the basis for the child's self-conceptualizing. A child is surrounded by a variety of options for self-development. All possible human options, however, are not open, and so the child is of course limited by the nature of the culture that is making the options available. Yet within these limits the child develops in ways not fully accounted for by the environment alone. The child also develops by selections made based on the personal constructions (meaning) s/he places on what is presented by the environment; that is, the social scene serves as grist for the child's mill, so to speak.

Thus, in considering the origin and development of self-concept for the purposes of this book, I would shift the focus and say that children turn to the world in search of meaningful guidelines for fashioning and patterning their sense of self. It seems likely that this is guided by what seem to the child to be effectance behaviors. While it is true that self-concept is a product of social interaction, the phrase "turn . . . in search of" implies an *active* taking on of values in the service of growth and self-development. Drive and environmental contingencies play an essential part, but the individual as affirmer is also necessarily a part of the process—usually more and more so with developing maturity.

What I am suggesting is that formation of sense of self as represented in self-concept draws on the processes of choice that are active in other areas of life. More and more as the child grows, the intentions that govern self-development become increasingly well formed (although still they are often unconscious). These of course are conceptualized within the framework of the language and materials of the child's culture. One cannot fully understand objectifiable aspects of self-concept choice without understanding the (active) intention that governs that choice. For example, it is one thing to choose a self-definition of "little ballerina" in order to fulfill the intention of being "Mommy's little girl," and it is quite another to base such a choice on fascination with the visual and rhythmic aspects of the dance itself and the intention of reproducing these by one's own activity. In self-development one tends to make choices that seem to help one to "live and grow" within one's milieu. The African-American child, like all children, brings an active orientation to his or her encounter with experience and uses the social environment as grounds—as reference points—for behavioral and conceptual choices that are adopted into the sense of self. Of course, where pleasing social interactions are few the child may develop an orientation of avoiding the anxiety of unpleasant interactions with the adults s/he needs so much by withdrawing or by stunting self-development. Drive reduction as a motive (here, the reduction of interpersonally based anxiety) becomes primary; but even so, as the individual purposefully withdraws (see Arieti's concept of "teleological regression," [1974]), s/he has an active role in "making something" of himself or herself.

Some critics would argue that a child is so constrained by the influence of parents and by his or her rudimentary equipment for understanding the world (a material-cause notion) that choice cannot be said to be a factor. The behavior "chosen" is the only one possible in the situation "as the child sees it." But the latter is just the point here. The behavior is constrained not only by the realities of the situation but by how the child "sees" (i.e., construes) them. The form of this conception, a pattern construct, governs the behavior very rigidly. As soon as one acknowledges that how one behaves is a function of how one sees things, one has to admit of a variety of possible ways of construing a given situation. Thus, one cannot rule out the active shaping by the mental process of the very young child that leads to behavior that cannot be accounted for simply by the facts of the external environment. Of course, "how one sees things" is a function of developmental maturity. The older individual will see things in ways that will allow more effective behavior. But this does not rule out the principle that, throughout life, behavior is partly dependent on how one "sees" things, that is, how one conceptualizes them.[7]

Self-Concept: A Product of Dialectical Activity

Having highlighted the active aspects of the self, let us now examine how the dialectical idea fits in with this notion of activity for a better understanding of the complexity of self-concept and self-esteem. The process of self-creation that we have discussed is guided in individuals of all ages by the striving to harmonize various facets of the self with the purpose of maintaining a sense of consistency and positive self-regard in self-conceptualization. People accomplish this at least partly by drawing on the effectance strivings that develop very early in life. In other words, human beings—children and adults—move toward activities that allow them to exercise effectance behaviors in their interaction with the world. The fact that some of the conceptions Black children may adopt reflect some of the negative experiences that the culture exposes them to is a part of the multifaceted nature of self-esteem and does not negate the positive strivings in Black children. The positive data that Taylor (1976) and Cross (1991) point to suggest that in the process of self-creation, Blacks in the United States have not simply been at the mercy of a single (unipolar) definition of themselves. Even when white doll choice reflected negative racial connotations, this did not constitute the Black child's only basis for self-evaluation. While Black children showed an outgroup orientation in some contexts, they showed considerable genuine skill and self-enjoyment when functioning in other contexts. Children have a variety of aspects of self to draw on as they develop self-esteem. A dialectical view recognizes the basic human capacity to see the alternatives that life poses, thereby making individual decision and affirmation possible. If observers recognized the existence and use of this capacity among Blacks in the developing sense of self, there would possibly be less surprise and less need to explain away either the positive or the negative side of the data on self-esteem. Thus, a child might in some contexts make a choice reflecting an outgroup preference, but that does not mean he devalues his particular friends, his ability to draw or to throw a ball, or his sense of being loved by his family. This capacity to take alternative routes in self-definition is one aspect of dialectical functioning.[8]

Another aspect of the dialectic perspective is relevant to this discussion.

Although different facets of the person may surface from time to time, the individual usually has the experience of continuity or identity in the aspects of self that are manifested. This is partly what we mean by a sense of identity. Although I recognize that I tend to be one way in one situation and another way in a different situation, it is still *I* who am that way. We are aware of a oneness in the many sides of ourselves.

One aspect of the continuity and cohesiveness of the self is the continuing striving to increase one's competence in the things that are important to one. This striving to be self-enhancing is probably so inherent a process (White, 1963) as to not require being consciously mobilized. This is a view of the person balancing the positive and negative aspects of experience to try and "come out ahead" in the sense of self as much as possible. The little boy for whom being a baseball player is the most important thing in the world right now still recognizes other aspects of self—that he is a Black child, that he is an American, for instance. He also recognizes that he is not so good at arithmetic or swimming as he is in other things. These are all aspects of himself that he recognizes. He may, at his parents' bidding, work to improve some of the things that he doesn't care so much about, but he still maintains his own hierarchy of what he thinks is *really* important. He may get into some difficulties with parents and teachers if they don't like his choices as to what is important. This may lead to psychological conflicts for him as he struggles with the problem of possibly losing his parents' love and support if he pursues what he thinks is important in self-development.

Part of the problem of measuring self-concept (leaving aside for the moment inadequate measuring instruments) stems from the fact that from one occasion to the next, when asked, the subject may come to measurement situations from a different perspective about self and abilities. From the humanistic perspective this shift does not mean that there is no internal consistency to the self.

> Much of what is called the unreliability of traits or self-concepts in predicting across different situations . . . stems from the dialectical ability of the individual to press more than simply one premise at the [choice point] in any given circumstance. . . . The extraspective theorist presumes that what must be identical across situations is the observed behavior and not some premising identity guiding even differential behaviors from circumstance to circumstance. [Rychlak, 1988, p. 352]

Viewed subjectively, there is a consistent orientation, an "identity" in the "logical thrust" that self brings to events. For Black people, then, though they have experienced themselves as having many facets, they have also experienced themselves as having a continuity of identity as individuals. For many this continuity has included the striving—the intention—to sustain a sense of competence in whatever areas of life they could. Sustaining competence involved exercising their sense of agency. Some chose rebellion and were punished; some chose escape and were successful. Others became competent farmers and artisans where they were. Many, whatever other course they took, struggled to establish stable families as havens for themselves and their children. Of course, choices were determined by available opportunities. But such opportunities did not simply force behavior in one direction or another. Opportunities were filtered through personal processes including the particular manifestation of competence strivings in different individuals.

In emphasizing self-activity in the form of competence strivings, it should also be recognized that the contributions of the self to behavior are not always positive. History gives ample testimony to the fact that the choices one makes—self-contributions—in trying to have an effect on the world too frequently take the form of wishes to dominate and destroy others. Self-contributions can be selfish. However, to note that self-contributions *can* go awry from an ethical or social viewpoint does not mean that they *must* go awry. It is almost impossible to avoid the notion that individuals make choices that govern their behavior (Schafer, 1976). (Note, too, that in the view here these processes go on at conscious *and* unconscious levels.) Self-activity exists as a function of being human. Granted, this humanistic view of people is not necessarily a more optimistic view. Whether self-activities develop to their fullest and, if so, develop as prosocial competence rather than simply skills at manipulating physical and social reality for personal advantage depends on a number of factors, not the least of which is how the social environment responds to the individual's effectance efforts.

The Black Family and Self-Concept

The Black family has always had to deal with the corrosive impact of racism on its members. Rearing children in a hostile environment has confronted parents with the particularly difficult task of giving them an opportunity to develop positive feelings about themselves, their families, and the Black community. Shielding infants and very young children from bigotry and discriminatory acts was a technique adopted by many families. But the development of positive self-images in Black children has involved much more than that. From what is known about how the family contributes to personality development—and this is far from complete—it can be said that children's attitudes toward themselves—their self-concepts—are crucially related to their experiences in the family. More specifically, it has been demonstrated that self-esteem is higher among those children who report better relationships with their parents (Bachman, 1970; Rosenberg & Simmons, 1971). It seems reasonable to expect that families that are more stably structured will provide the supportive relationships necessary to positive self-concept development. By "stable structure" I mean a household where some adults—one or two parents, a grandmother, or other relative—are consistently available and working to provide for members' basic physical and emotional needs. Of course, a stable family unit is not the only contributor to self-evaluation, nor does such a family guarantee positive self-esteem for a child. But such a setting certainly has a head start on fostering the kinds of parent-child interactions that lead to positive personal self-esteem.

Some writers have chosen to highlight the idea that disproportionately large numbers of Black families were disorganized by the ravages of both the slavery and postslavery periods. (For a review of literature on this perspective see Hill, 1990; Slaughter & McWorter, 1985). According to this view, the inability to develop the level of stability typical of other (White) ethnic groups in America made it hard and often impossible for Black families to provide security for family members and to carry out properly the tasks of socializing African-American children. However, alongside these assertions about the Black family are the findings that Black children have developed a positive evaluation of many aspects of themselves. The question arises, then, of whether or not in the main the Black family is to be discounted when we look for sources of the development of positive self-esteem in Black children. The answer, of course, is that, in spite of current difficult times for poor and working-class families, we do not have to skirt around the Black family in our search for institutions in the Black community that contribute positively to the average Black child's development.

In fact, there has been considerable rebuttal of the recently resurrected deficit view of the Black family (Billingsley, 1968; Hill, 1990). Of particular interest here is the scholarship that indicates that Blacks throughout their history in America organized their family and kinship patterns in ways that allowed them to support the development of their children and provide emotional security for family members (Gutman, 1976; Wilson, 1989). These patterns may have been similar to those they were familiar with from their African background (Sudarkasa, 1981). The research suggests that after slavery, from the end of the nineteenth century through the first quarter of the twentieth, the kinds of family organization developed by Blacks were as stable and functional as those in families of other ethnic groups. And among the comparatively larger number of female-headed households existing among Blacks in recent times there is considerable use of extended kinship networks or of nonkin who are regarded as kinfolk to support and stabilize the functioning of the family unit (Kennedy, 1980; Stack, 1974; Wilson, 1989).

This revised view of the Black family states that the Black family has long had a structure that would enable it to nurture the personal aspects of self-esteem and self-concept.[9] What Black families seem to have done historically is engender a sense of personal worth in their children by separating the personal sense of themselves from the negative perceptions a racist society has attached to racial group membership (Billingsley, 1968; Pettigrew, 1964). This separation of aspects of self-evaluation is consistent with the findings indicating that self-concept is complex and that people have varying sets of attitudes toward different parts of themselves. In the interest of survival the Black family has worked to present the Black child with frames of reference that were alternatives to those imposed by White society, thereby allowing these children other ways of evaluating their worth. W. E. B. DuBois, writing in *The Crisis* magazine in 1926, was very clear in his suggestions to Black parents about how they should go about setting up such alternate frames of reference:

> At least in your home you have a chance to make your child's surroundings of the best; books and pictures and music; cleanliness, order, sympathy and understanding; information, friendship and love,—there is not much of evil in the world that can stand against such home surroundings. [Diggs, 1976, p. 390]

Many Black families have made great effort to follow DuBois's admonitions. This has not been limited only to the literate and well-to-do in the Black community. An unlettered Mississippi woman was perfectly capable of analyzing a complex social issue when asked by her preschool age children about racial inequities. She reported her explanation as follows:

> I tell the children that it's a confusing world, and they have to get used to it. You have to try to overcome it, but you can't hide it from the kids. When they ask me why colored people aren't as good as whites, I tell them it's not that they're not as good; it's that they're not as rich. Then I tell them that they should separate being poor and being bad, and not get them mixed up. I . . . remind them that the Lord is a mighty big man, and what He thinks is not the same as what white folks do. . . . I tell them, and I hope that makes them feel satisfied, so they don't dislike themselves. That's bad, not liking your own self. [Coles, 1967, p. 64]

In this excerpt she separates being poor, which is an aspect of social role status, from the personal sense of being a good or bad person. Presumably she was also explicitly helping her children separate being Black from being bad, too. She thereby implicitly imparted the message that they have some choices in how they conceive of themselves and consequently how they approach the world. That is to say, their feeling good about themselves does not depend solely on the stereotypic evaluations of others, particularly not by others who are outside of the circle of people who love and appreciate them.

In the previous two sections we have said that even though there are pressures toward a negative assessment of self, Blacks have pursued avenues of self-definition guided by a competence theme. Consistent positive self-evaluations emerge alongside the negative ones as a result of the capacity to pose mental alternatives to those presented by some aspects of the racist culture. I said next that it is legitimate to view Black families as being strong enough historically to have made the kinds of contributions that would strengthen their children's self-concept development, even though they were not always perfect. Now the question arises as to *how* the family makes its contributions to the Black child's self-concept development.

Concerned parents and educators have always tried to influence the development of children's sense of self by making loving and positive contributions to children's experience. This is part of what is reflected in DuBois's assertion that the quality of the home can be a bulwark against the negative psychological influences of a hostile society. Providing positive models and values that the child can adopt is certainly important (Barnes, 1991). This tends to put an emphasis on the flow of good things from the environment into the child, as it were. The humanistic theorist feels the need to supplement this, however. The old saying "You can lead a horse to water but you can't make him drink," when applied to behavior and development, recognizes something else: The child must be active (intentional, at some level) in taking on the values that surround her or him.

Here, of course, is where our humanistic perspective comes in. Earlier I made reference to self-concept as a theory that the individual *has constructed* about himself or herself (see note 2). Later, in my discussion of Frost, I emphasized that the individual *chooses* his or her path from among alternatives. Both of these descriptions emphasize that the individual is active in developing himself or herself as "constructor" or chooser. A key aspect of the notion of self for the humanistic theorist is the active (conceptualizing, choosing-among-alternatives) quality of the self. I submit that what families do implicitly, that is, without always being conscious that they are doing it as such, is to stimulate children to become more active in their own development partly by becoming "aware" of their potential for active influence in their lives.

The Black Family and Self-Awareness

Most of us can appreciate the fact that we are actively involved in determining the course of our daily lives. But young children and many adults are usually not "aware" of themselves in this way—that is, while people are *conscious* of what they do, they are not necessarily *aware* of themselves in a special sense of that word that we shall use here. *Awareness* can be defined psychologically as "appreciation of the arbitrariness in experience" or, in other words, "knowing that something else might be taking place in a life circumstance" (Rychlak, 1988, p. 354). Self-awareness would imply the recognition that, although I choose to act or be *this* way in this circumstance, I could be or do something else. Many persons experience themselves as only being forced into one or another avenue by physical and social forces around them. However, when they do so they are at some level (often unconsciously) *choosing* to accept environmental factors as given rather than being externally forced to comply with them. Having done so, they find that many aspects of life become easy and automatic and fall into a pattern determined by their initial choices. To some extent such automatic responses are necessary for functioning in everyday life. We do not become aware that our patterns of behavior rest on choices we have made until something happens to challenge the premises that govern our habitual acts. However, this does not negate the fact that such habits are based on initial premises we have, perhaps long since, accepted.

As I have indicated earlier, the same is true for a person's development of self-concept. One's view of one's self is made up partly of one's selection from (and acquiescence to) environmental factors, and it is also made up of things one imagines (proposes, intends) one would like to be. (Note that even a person's acquiescence represents his or her [often unconscious] decision to go along with certain conditions.) The individual plays an essential part in the development of self-concept. When a person realizes that who s/he is becoming is composed to an important degree of choices that s/he is making, then one is *aware*, as that term is being used here. (Awareness characterizes action not only regarding self-development, of course, but all aspects of intended behavior.)

> For the person to develop . . . self-awareness, he must see the contributions he *makes* to experience, depending upon what sort of meanings are affirmed [in the given situation]. . . . In this sense the self must be *intended*—that is, the purposive meaning of *self* must be brought to life by the individual, who cultivates it and furthers it *or not*. [Rychlak, 1988, p. 355]

While self-awareness concerning all of one's behavior is not always desirable, for most people and for the developing child, broadening awareness of the degree to which s/he is an active contributor to his or her own life is a worthwhile goal. At the same time, to be truly aware of the degree to which one's conceptualizations have causal power in one's actions is a heavy burden. It reduces the degree to which one can externalize blame for one's life. It is in this sense that Schafer (1976) notes how most of us shy away from recognizing how much we are the gods in our lives—the self-creators in Chein's image.

I submit that the Black family has nurtured a sense of personal self-worth in the Black child partly by "bringing to life" a sense of self as an agent able to propose and affirm hypotheses about potential that are at variance with those White society offers. The family does this, for example, through exposure to values in the home and community that express alternatives. DuBois suggests that one can control some of the important values children are exposed to, thereby giving them choices. One can also respond to children in ways that give them choices about their affairs, small though these may be. They can in this way get the sense of having an impact on events through their choices. Thus, through contact with "the best surroundings"—including cultural information about African Americans and their historical contributions—and the recognition of the possibility for individual and group choice, "self-awareness" is enhanced and personal self-esteem is potentially improved. The family has been one institution that nurtures a sense of self-awareness—a sense of self as capable of setting its own intended goals—and the family helps expose the child to the means of carrying these goals out. (That a sense of having an impact on the options affecting one is related to academic achievement is supported by Coleman et al. (1966), who found that a sense of "fate control" was positively related to school achievement in Black children.)

Possible Selves
The humanistic notion of self-awareness relates to an area of research in cognitive psychology recently articulated by Markus and Nurius as the concept of "possible selves" (1986). This notion refers to the way people think about the potentialities for themselves in terms both of the positive as well as the negative possibilities and thus seems to reflect the recognition of alternative options for their development that people have at some level of consciousness. The idea of possible selves seems quite consistent with the concept of the dialectic as I have used it here, although Markus and Nurius do not use that term:

> Possible selves are the ideal selves that we would very much like to become. They are also the selves we could become, and the selves we are afraid of becoming. . . . An individual's repertoire of possible selves can be viewed as the cognitive manifestation of enduring goals, aspirations, motives, fears, and threats. [1986, p. 954]

These authors argue that including a sense of the possible into the self-concept gives that construct a more dynamic quality by providing specific conceptual structuring that can guide action and change: ". . . these ideas about what is possible for us to be . . . or to experience provide a specific cognitive form to our desires for mastery . . . and our diffuse fears of failure" (op. cit., p. 960).

The possible-selves notion is also quite compatible with the view advanced earlier in this chapter that by their choices people are active in their own creation: "Through the selection and construction of possible selves individuals can be viewed as active producers of their own development" [ibid., p. 955]. That is, as we develop conceptions of what is possible and try to steer ourselves toward the positive and away from the negative potentialities, we develop our particular ways of "coming at" the world. From this viewpoint, then, Black parents have worked in a variety of ways to expand the vista of their children's possible selves, thereby enhancing their self-awareness and arming them for dealing with a frequently hostile world.[10]

Social circumstances have put an extra burden on Blacks as they struggle to survive. In the service of their own and their children's self-realization, however, Black families *have* expended this energy more than is usually acknowledged. Clearly these efforts of families would be enhanced by changes in social policies and social institutions. For example, increased employment opportunity would enable persons to raise their standard of living, provide security for their families, and make tangible contributions to a sense of self-worth. A more benign social atmosphere allows more room for people's effectance motivations to guide their actions. Notice the phrasing here. There is a particular kind of interaction between social institutions and the psychology of the individual. Social conditions provide a set of environmental options and limitations. An individual with self-awareness can decide to abide by the pressures implied in a given set of circumstances or that person can act out of a different sense of self and fight even strong odds. (For example, the odds against graduating from college if you are a rural Black youth has not kept such persons, with the support of their families, from trying—and succeeding in many instances.) The environmental circumstances do not *force* the individual's choice; they do make a particular action less likely—particularly if s/he is unaware that s/he can choose. This is not to say that Blacks are primarily at fault for not having done better against the great social odds confronting them. It is rather to describe from one perspective the individual processes that have enabled them to do as well as they have. It is also to indicate how much more they could do if given a fair chance by society. In fact, the system is still very much to blame for the plight of African Americans (and the poor of various racial groups). Enhanced social opportunity would expand the arena in which natural effectance strivings could operate.

Other Aspects of Racial Self-Concept Development

I do not mean to imply that self-concept development in Blacks is simply a tug-of-war between society with its noxious pressures on the one hand and the Black family seeking to instill feelings of pride and self-worth in its children on the other. Such a view tends to imply that the family is successful when it can isolate the Black child from the larger society, which in turn implies that the Black child's problems stem from external influences alone. While it is clear that institutions in American society are structured so as to easily transmit racially prejudiced attitudes, things are not as simple as that. There are other factors in the child's life that both aid and hinder efforts to sustain and develop the sense of competence.

For example, psychoanalytic theory based largely on clinical observation of children and adults stresses bodily impulses and the way they are handled by family members as important to the development of self-concept (Kovel, 1984). During socialization normal preschool children often develop attitudes toward their bodies and skin that intertwine with racial perceptions (Harrison-Ross & Wyden, 1973; McDonald, 1970). From the perspective we have been developing here we could say that children's active efforts to make sense of the world draw on sense impressions and abundantly communicated information around them. We have seen that young children are attentive to such issues in the racial sphere. With their comparatively limited cognitive and social sophistication (which is another way of saying: with their uncertainty over the most probably correct alternative of the many that occur to them about given events), children normally develop ideas about experience that are idiosyncratic. Such notions may appear as distorted notions about themselves and social reality and may lead to personal problems if not corrected.

Ruby: "My Skin or Me?"

Coles (1967) gives a striking example of just such an interaction between developmental perceptions and racial concerns in the life of Ruby, the little girl with whom we opened this chapter. As I indicated earlier, she had to brave a mob of White protestors who formed a veritable gauntlet in front of her school each morning shouting invectives at her. At one point she developed a severe appetite loss and began to ask repeatedly whether it was "only" her skin that made her the object of such daily persecution. It became clear over the course of time that one of the picketers kept shouting a threat to choke and poison her. Of all the nasty things yelled at her this one seemed to "hit home," probably because it happened to mesh with her normal struggles in her family to control her ordinary naughtiness toward her siblings. Such behavior on her part included verbal (oral) aggression toward them; her parents on occasion punished her by withholding her favorite foods or by offering the stern observation that she might well "choke" on her hostile words. Her question "Is it only my skin?" indicated that she had become confused for a while as to whether only her skin color was what was "wrong" with her or whether she was the object of abuse for more deep-seated faults. The racial trauma had begun to confound her racial and personal identities.

How can children be helped to resolve such difficulties? In the course of children's efforts to achieve a sense of self in the larger world, many confusions and distortions can arise. Parents and educators can help children differentiate between racial perceptions about their acquaintances and themselves on the one hand and their own natural developmental lapses of the moment on the other hand. Adults can do this by dealing forthrightly with situations as they arise. For example, one little African-American child was reported to have remarked to his mother that he didn't like the brown rice served to him because it was the "color of 'do-do.'" She answered by acknowledging that the rice was brown and that this is the color of a waste product from our bodies but went on to note matter of factly that many things that he likes are brown, including the skin color of himself and his loved ones. She reminded him further of one of the books he liked called *Brown Is a Beautiful Color*, by Jean Carey Bond (1969). Here the mother dealt straightforwardly with her child's concerns and showed him the range of associations—many of them positive—that accrue to brownness.[11]

As Coles notes, Ruby's symptoms passed with time. Certainly this was partly because her family helped her in important ways. Although her parents were generally firm in their expectation that she be a well-behaved girl during the crisis, they also were supportive and loving. In addition, although she knew that the immediate family was vulnerable (her father was fired from his job because of her attendance at the desegregated school), she was given a feeling for the larger supportive clan they could fall back on. She had been told of her maternal grandfather, a Mississippi Delta farmer, who was described to her as a person who could provide a haven for them: "Momma says . . . her daddy is the strongest man you can find. . . . She says not to worry, we have a hiding place and I should remember it every day" (Coles, 1967, p. 49). This was reflected in her drawings. In contrast to her drawings of other Blacks at that time, she drew her grandfather as a large, powerful man. Thus, her family (and possibly other institutions such as the church, for example) provided a needed context in which she could work out the difficulties facing her.

Fortunately, however, there were other things working for her as well. For one thing the city began to quiet down over time as White children began to return to the schools. But in addition she undoubtedly achieved some gains in personal maturity from the exercising and developing of social and cognitive skills in the real world, as difficult as that world was. When Ruby was 10, several years after her eating disturbance, Coles, who had visited with her and her family regularly during this time, engaged her in some reflection on the nature of her growth during those years. Specifically he commented on the different and more complete quality of her drawings of Black people now that she was older. "Do you think," he asked, "there's any reason for that, apart from the fact that you're now a better artist in every way?" She answered:

> Maybe because of all the trouble going to school in the beginning I learned more about my people. Maybe I would have anyway; because

when you get older you see yourself and the white kids; and you find out the difference. You try to forget it, and say there is none; and if there is you won't say what it be. Then you say it's my own people, and so I can be proud of them instead of ashamed. [1967, p. 51]

Coles goes on to note: "Her language was so clear, so pointed; and she somehow seemed both content with herself as she was and determined to make something of herself in the future" (p. 51).

Recent research supports the notion that racial self-concept in Black children changes with age. In a retesting five years later of the children used in her Michigan and Mississippi samples, McAdoo (1977) found that the children's previous outgroup orientation had shifted significantly in a pro-"Afro" direction such that the older children, who were now 10-year-olds going on 11, were either neutral or were somewhat positive toward the "Afro" choices. To test the effect of age on racial self-concept, Williams and Morland (1976) asked a sample of Black children ranging from the sixth to the twelfth grades to give semantic evaluations of the term *Black American*. They found that among the older age ranges the rating of this term was clearly more positive than among the younger students. The indication is that as African-American children grow, they are able to apply the feelings of efficacy that they have gained from other areas of living to their sense of racial identity.

What I am suggesting is that as Black children get older, a more defined sense of self in other aspects of living helps them gain a different perspective on racial group membership. A part of this perspective comes from a somewhat greater self-awareness as we have defined that here. This feature may come not only from family interactions but also from children's recognition that as they grow and gain more skills, they are actually able to exercise more options and are able to be more independent than they have been before. Also there is growth in the ability to understand the messages coming from their own culture as well as from the dominant society regarding racial issues (Alejandro-Wright, 1985). Ruby's development was partly a function of her being older and having the skills appropriate to her age and partly a function of the ability to use some of these skills to understand her social situation better. As one of Ruby's teachers noted at this point (four years after entering school), "Ruby is an exceptionally alert child." In short, Ruby and other Black children illustrated in the research are negotiating Erikson's developmental stage of "industry."[12]

The sense of self is made up of various facets, some of which may function somewhat independently in the interests of sustaining healthy adaptation. In that sense the family's role has been seen in this chapter as helping the Black child ward off society's negative attributions regarding race by bolstering other aspects of the self. However, I am saying also that there can be an interrelation among aspects of self. One's sense of efficacy in one area of development can spread to other aspects of one's sense of the self. Thus, the efforts of the family and other supportive social contexts that work toward the stabilizing of a sense of competence in various of one's personal attributes may have a positive effect on aspects of self-concept related to racial group membership.

Attempts to Change Racial Self-Concept

The preceding summary comments suggest that one way of modifying racial attitudes of Black children is by providing good experiences for them in other areas of life. Change in attitude then would be an indirect effect—a by-product of the positive experiences in other areas. The question arises of whether or not it is possible to tackle attitude change in Black children head on outside of the family.

Since the late sixties considerable attention in the Black community has been devoted to raising the level of Black people's self-esteem. Some have claimed that this general emphasis on Black pride and in some cases the institution of specific programs have been responsible for attitude changes in African Americans (Hraba & Grant, 1970). However, direct efforts at influencing self-concept are not new in the Black community. For years many Black families have made a point of introducing their children to juvenile literature about African-American heroes—material notably absent from the established texts of U.S. history. Furthermore, it was not an uncommon experience for children raised in the segregated schools of the South in the first six or seven decades of this century to have learned a good deal about Black history. These kinds of exposures had as their purpose the effort to fill the vacuum in positive information about Blacks and to combat directly the negative information and attitudes that are a part of the warp and woof of American society. The same idea is behind many of the small "freedom schools" that sprang up in Black communities in the seventies. There was an added emphasis in these schools on African-American and African history and Swahili along with the usual basic educational skills. Another version of this effort is the recent experiment in certain school districts around the country of creating special grade schools that are targeted at lower-class Black boys. Some educators are trying to make these schools exclusively male. Black male teachers are the predominant role models in some of the schools. The primary aim of these programs is to enhance the educational achievement of a segment of the population whose academic achievement is especially vulnerable to the effects of racism (Gibbs, 1988). The specialized attention and the introduction of Black role models are seen as a way of sending messages to these youth that enhance self-esteem. (For a review of some of the debate on these schools, see Freiberg [1991].)

Such efforts as the all-male Black school relate to the question of the effect the racial mix in the school has on Black children's self-concept. Does desegregation generally enhance the self-esteem of Black children? Some researchers have argued that self-esteem may be higher in segregated school situations than it is in desegregated ones (Rosenberg & Simmons, 1971; Taylor, 1976), although others argue that the evidence is equivocal (Epps, 1975). Debate continues to rage on this point (Cook, 1988; Gerard, 1988). A crucial factor making this issue hard to resolve has to do with what one means by a desegregated situation. For example, Pettigrew (1971) argues that one must distinguish desegregated from "truly integrated" settings. In the latter kinds of situations, adults set a tone of encouraging interracial acceptance in which children can learn about and appreciate one another's cultural differences. Pejorative expressions toward one another's differences are firmly, but non-punitively dealt with—they are not ignored—and thus opportunities to respect one another and themselves are enhanced. A "merely desegregated" situation is one in which children sit in the same classroom but little attention is given to structuring the social situation. In some desegregated schools, children go to the same school but may be tracked into different classes that resegregate them anyway. There are probably few truly integrated situations in the United States. It is likely that most of the research about the effects of "integration" on children's self-esteem has been conducted in *desegregated* situations, *not* in truly integrated ones. Thus, we do not really know as much as we think we do about the effect of integration on children's self-esteem. We do know something about how to achieve truly integrated situations (Goleman, 1991), but we will not know much about the effect of such settings until we do more than simply desegregate.

There have been efforts to modify racial preference attitudes in Black children experimentally. Among these studies are those using the procedures developed by Williams and Morland (1976) using behavior modification techniques. Generally the research involved individually administered procedures in which a child's response was followed by an immediate "reinforcer"—either a reward or a punishment. Two kinds of research designs have been employed. In one type the effort was made to change racial attitude by directly changing the children's "pro-Euro/anti-Afro" bias toward photographs of people. In the other type of design the attempt was to change racial attitude—the attitude toward "Euro" and "Afro" figures—by changing the child's preference for the color white. These studies have yielded some success in moderating racial attitudes. Material rewards and punishments (winning and losing pennies) along with verbal reinforcers have been found more effective in changing children's color attitudes than verbal reinforcers alone (Reeves, 1976). There is some evidence that change persisted in follow-up measurements. By contrast, attempts to alter the pro-"Euro" bias in young children by using special curriculum programs in the classroom have not been as successful.[13]

Although we have much more to learn about effective modes of intervention, there is good reason to believe that racial attitudes in chidren can be modified (Katz, 1976). There are many things that parents and educators can do in their relating to children and in structuring institutions that can enhance the development of Black youngsters. The humanistic framework we have been developing would also suggest the specific value of helping a child become more self-aware—as someone who is an active, choosing being. To the extent this attitude is nurtured and developed, the accompanying sense of competence will lead toward effective ways of interacting with the world that will enable the child to throw off the negative connotations offered by a racist society.

Notes

1. The question has been raised as to whether or not these studies actually measure racial feeling in African-American children. The data from "racial awareness" questions in some of these studies are useful in clarifying this issue. As one method for getting at racial attitudes, one can ask a child what s/he knows about racial terms—the words *colored*, *White*, *Negro*, and *Black*—as applied to people. Or one can find out whether or not the child will sort differently colored dolls or pictures of persons into correct racially based groupings (a "racial classification" question). Further, one can find out whether the child knows what racial group s/he belongs to. These tasks would appear to tap the amount of information children have at a "cognitive" or knowledge level. Apart from their feelings about such information, the data indicate that children are aware of racial differences as early as age 3; correctness of classification increases, of course, with age, stabilizing at about age 6 or 7. Proportion of correct classifications by age and race is a function of the measure used.

The data from the "racial similarity" questions used in some studies ("Which doll looks like you?") indicate that preschool African-American children have tended less often than White children to choose figures of their own race as those that look like them (Porter, 1971; Williams & Morland, 1976). Similarly, preschool "Afro" subjects in some studies chose own-race figures less often as looking like their own parents than did "Euro" children (Williams & Morland, 1976, chap. 7). This seems not to be simply a function of faulty knowledge because even some Black children who used racial categories correctly in classifying themselves tended to label themselves as being similar to the *white* doll. African-American children made this particular outgroup selection considerably more often than did the White children.

Racial-similarity data combined with Porter's "color salience" measure seem to indicate that racial feeling is involved. *Color salience* for Porter refers to the degree to which skin color of the dolls was a more salient variable for grouping them than sex of the dolls or the similarity of the color of the clothes they were dressed in. So, for example, in the clothes-skin color control, in the course of play with the dolls a girl was presented with four dolls, two black and two white, but with contrasting clothes (a white and black doll with a red dress and a white and a black doll with a blue dress). For boys similar contrasts were made with boy dolls. The children were then asked, "Which two look most alike?" leaving them with the option of picking the dolls with similar skin color or the dolls who were similarly clothed as being "most alike."

Porter found that skin color of the dolls tended to be more salient for Black children than for White children in these comparisons. (The fact that skin color was an important variable for Black children—yet they tended to make an outgroup choice in doll preference—indicated to her that at least some Black children were making negative or at least ambivalent *affective* assessments.) Furthermore, analyzing her data on a more individual basis, she found that Black children for whom skin color of dolls was more salient were more incorrect in their racial-similarity matching of themselves. This indicated for Porter that there was special feeling about race on the part of these Black children and that the racial-similarity measure seemed to carry an important part of the weight of this feeling. As a corollary to this she found further that children who had favorable attitudes toward the dolls of their own race (high own-race preference) in the story-game procedure were the ones who were highly likely to be correct when asked to choose the doll whose color was like theirs. However, if own-race preference was *low*, correctness of racial-similarity choices tended to be low even when the children demonstrated that they knew correct racial terminology. This too was more often the case for Black children than for White children.

It seems clear that racial awareness involves affective assessments as well as cognitive (knowledge) issues for children. Porter's data led her to conclude that a specific affective issue was being tapped by the racial-similarity measure. This was that the more frequent incorrect racial-similarity choices by Black children were an index of some ambivalence or even clear discomfort with their racial group membership for some of these children. Note again that such terms as *ambivalence* and *discomfort* do not mean "self-hatred" as a global construct but do indicate a mixture of feelings and hence complexity in the self-concept.

2. Epstein has suggested that self-concept should be seen as a "self-theory." "It is a theory that the individual has unwittingly constructed about himself as an experiencing, functioning individual, and it is part of a broader theory which he holds with respect to his entire range of significant experience" (1973, p. 407). In the terms introduced in Chapter 1, self-concept is a "conceptualization"; it is one of the most central conceptualizations that an individual

develops in life. As noted in Chapter 1, the purpose of a conceptualization is to bring a sense of order and stability to a particular aspect of experience. Thus, one's self-concept is a conceptualization that stabilizes and organizes the feelings and thoughts that a person holds about his or her existence as a physical and social being. It represents the way a person has mapped out his or her psychological territory, so to speak, and represents the way a person accounts for himself or herself—it is the individual's sense of "what I am" (Keen, 1970). With this kind of map (or frame of reference, or psychological orientation point) the individual is better able to carry out a fundamental characteristic of living, which is to grow—to become ever more effective and competent in his or her milieu.

3. Cross's research suggests that Black children have available such a "reference group orientation" partly because in their homes Black parents are likely to present a dual cultural perspective to their children. "Implicitly or explicitly, the Black families seemed to be stressing the development of bicultural competence in their children" (Cross, 1987, p. 131). White parents on the other hand are more likely to present a monocultural perspective.

4. This point regarding children's sensitivity to parts of the research design that are peripheral to the researcher's intended thrust raises the question of what Martin Orne has called "demand characteristics" in research (1962). Orne found that his (college age) subjects persevered in the meaningless experimental tasks they were given long after he expected them to. When Orne questioned them later, they indicated that they stuck with the tasks because they were concerned about being "good subjects" and making a contribution to science. The typical psychological interpretation of this occurrence is that subtle but inevitable cues in the situation (such as the figure cut by an obviously earnest young student trying to complete her dissertation research or an impressive-looking older person in a white lab coat) *elicit* behavior from the subject in an efficient-cause fashion. An alternate view is that the subjects' persevering behavior was in the service of ("for the sake of") intentions they imposed on the task, not simply called out by the explicit manipulations the experimenter placed on them. The experimental situation is a "two-way street." "The subject is virtually always thinking about his role in first-person terms, asking himself questions like: What is he (the experimenter) up to? What's he trying to get me to do? What am I getting into here? What's the worth of all this? What's the trick?" (Rychlak, 1988, pp. 322-323). The teleologist sees the individual as being active in the research situation and acting for the sake of intentions of his or her own as well as those of the experimenter. Such concerns influence the way the subject responds and must be taken into account in a thorough understanding of the data.

Coming back to the racial preference studies: Young children are not as mature in the range of intentions they bring, yet they are active in similar ways. One writer, a child psychiatrist, asks:

> What is a three-year-old child to think is going on when an adult, a comparative stranger who serves no understandable purpose in his life, as parent or teacher, surprises him with a series of strange questions such as: "Which doll do you prefer? The brown one or the white one?" and then takes away the test dolls he has just given him, supposedly to play with? [McDonald, 1970, p. 31]

The child is not simply a passive object being manipulated by the experimenter—no more so than in daily life outside the laboratory. While the researcher's controls do set limits on the options for a subject's behavior, it is quite likely that even a young child is engaging in an active, if relatively unsophisticated, search as to what is going on. This search is governed by and influences his or her conceptualizations about the situation. For example, the wish to please the examiner is a relevant intention in children, particularly in view of the heightened authority relationship between the (adult) experimenter and the (young child) subject. (This doesn't mean that children are always cooperative. The Clarks [1952] report strong emotional reactions and negativism on the part of some children regarding the task presented to them. As we shall see in Chapter 3, Rychlak and his associates [1988] report that a subject's dislike, that is, negative affective assessment, of an experimental task can reliably affect performance on important aspects of that task.)

One aspect of responding to the examiner is noting his or her race. Researchers working in the area of children's racial attitudes frequently attempt to control this factor, at least partly, by having same-race examiners test the children. Porter used a Black examiner in some instances with those subjects who were from predominantly Black classrooms. Where a White examiner was used in such settings, she found that Black children tended to misidentify the doll more often than they did with an examiner of either race in a desegregated setting. Race of examiner had no effect on results with children in desegregated classrooms. Katz and Zalk (1974), however, using the Clarks' design, found race of examiner influenced doll choices of both Black and White children. Williams and Morland (1976) report not finding race-of-examiner effects and feel that such effects can be pretty much ignored with young children. But I believe that this is a premature conclusion when one looks at the variety of research designs in this area and the potential children have for attending to these and other cues. (See Milner [1983] on this point also.)

The recent emphasis on racial pride in the Black community may have highlighted certain issues for young children such that the direct questions in a forced-choice format are more easily met by children's intentions to be positive racially. (This positive change has not been a completely consistent finding, however. Powell-Hopson and Hopson [1988], using the traditional doll-test format, obtained the kinds of results characteristic of research of thirty years ago.) Porter's technique, on the other hand, which involves a more elaborate, semistructured play situation, may engage a broader range of children's feelings and has the potential for enabling an expression of feeling in greater depth. This is not to say that feelings that are more conscious are less real; rather, it is to say that feelings about self are complex, as we are emphasizing in this chapter, and they are held at many levels of awareness. Various ways of getting at them are probably necessary to get a full picture of self-concept.

5. In reaction to much of the previous work, some recent researchers have introduced a "social-cognitive developmental" model into the study of children's racial-group orientation (Alejandro-Wright, 1985; Semaj, 1985; Spencer, 1985). Briefly, this perspective takes issue with the idea that children's racial classification and awareness are similar to adult categories. These workers tend to base their critique on the ideas of the Swiss psychologist Jean Piaget, who has had a major impact on developmental psychology. In Piaget's view, "the child's thinking differs from that of the adult not only in degree, but most fundamentally in kind" (Alejandro-Wright, 1985, p. 187). The child is seen as actively constructing knowledge in interaction with the world using reasoning styles that unfold sequentially.

Alejandro-Wright, for example, argues that previous research has missed the complexity of the child's processing by focusing too narrowly on skin color as the basis for racial classification (1985). In one exploratory study she tested the hypothesis that from the perspective of the development of a child's thinking processes, knowledge of racial classification evolves "from a vague, undifferentiated awareness of skin color differences to knowledge of the cluster of physical-biological attributes associated with racial membership and eventually to a social understanding of racial categorization" (p. 186). She used semistructured interviews with a sample of thirty-two Black working- and lower-class girls, age 3–10. She presented materials to her subjects that provided variations in stimuli regarding skin color, hair texture, and facial features. These were given in a spontaneous task format that allowed children to make their own groupings and in structured formats that required children to respond to the examiner's categories.

As she expected, children's racial-classification knowledge seemed to follow a developmental sequence. The age-graded stages were: an "Idiosyncratic" level in which the children (all 3- and 4-year-olds) showed little capacity to put people into large groups and didn't use color categories consistently; a "Subliminal" level in which subjects (mostly 5- and 6-year-olds) used accurate color categories but confused skin color groupings—light-skinned Blacks and Chinese were sometimes grouped as Whites; "Preconceptual" children (mostly 8-year-olds) who were beginning to be aware that biological not just physical characteristics were involved in race differentiation; and the "Conceptual" group (predominantly 10-year-olds) who were beginning to recognize that a social dimension was involved in race classification and were thus beginning to think about race along the lines of adults. Though these results supported her hypothesis, she recognized the need for further research to validate this sequence and extend the generalizability of the findings.

A number of points emerge from this analysis. First, to the extent that this research emphasizes the "child as constructivist" (Spencer, 1985), an active participant in his or her development from early on, it is quite consistent with the theme of this book. However, Alejandro-Wright's findings indicate a complicating factor of scientific research; namely, results are often a function of the methodology used. Thus, while it seems likely that it is especially possible to elicit ways in which children's modes of thinking about race are different from those of adults, this does not mean that children do not incorporate the social evaluations of the adult world around them. The forced-choice format with proper methodological controls seems to indicate that by 5 years of age, children can reliably use such categories in ways that reflect society's (problematic) racial groupings. This does not mean that the child has full adult understanding of race or that the child does not have quite idiosyncratic ideas about such issues. Clinical studies suggest that children do—as do adults, for that matter (McDonald, 1970).

The studies that asked for feeling judgments—"nice", "pretty", "clean"—seem to invite children to put feeling judgments into their conceptualizations, which they may assume the experimenter wants to hear based on the way the latter has structured the questions. While the social-cognitive approach is making a genuine contribution to this area, what is missing from that perspective seems to be an appreciation of the intensity of the *affective* assessment of many Black and White children regarding race. (In addition, with regard to the effects of a changed societal context on this kind of research, Alejandro-Wright found that her subjects in the earlier stages couldn't use the terms *White*, *Black/Negro/colored*, or *Chinese* reliably to make classifications. [*Afro-American* and *African American* were not presented.] However, as noted, previous research had shown that preschool children did understand the terms *Negro* and *colored*. It is perhaps not surprising that for young children still trying to stabilize color concepts in general the application of the term *Black* to various-hued African Americans was confusing. Even so, as noted, this particular procedure does not rule out the idea that these young children attach racial *feelings* to their idiosyncratic racial categories.) Thus, while "early ethnic socialization has a clear cognitive component" (Ramsey, 1987, p. 72), this is not *just* an intellectual issue. The recent research has helped us to recognize that studies in ethnic socialization always should include multiple tests, such as perceptual, preference, and behavioral measures in order to see how children generalize and apply their ideas. In addition clinical interviews may help researchers to understand more clearly how children themselves see the connections among the many aspects of their identities and attitudes. [ibid.]

6. The idea of conceptualization, which is central in the humanistic approach here, can be used to further illustrate this notion of creativity. Conceptualization implies that the human individual responds to reality in terms of his or her symbolically created conception or idea of reality rather than to "real" reality as such. As Edelson notes,

> While 'real' external reality may be presumed to exist independently of its apprehension, it cannot be known except symbolically—as part, then, of psychic reality insofar as psychic reality is constituted by symbolic processes. Even the experience of simple sensations involves interpretation in a framework of meaning. (1971, p. 27)

Such constructions of reality can be illustrated in as fundamental and seemingly simple a process as how an individual begins the day. For example, when I am awakened in the morning by the alarm clock, I may have the experience of not knowing for a moment where I am. I have to actively organize, that is, conceptualize, the sense impressions around me. Doing so involves making affirmations, that is, taking a stand about my situation. I must search for the perceptual clues that will tell me what's going on. Having done so, I have meaningful anchor points ("Oh—I'm at home in bed. It's morning already!") to help determine my next steps. Note, however, that it is not finally the external fact of morning that determines my next steps; it is my mental *affirmation* of that fact with the associated feelings that determines my next moves. The process of achieving full wakefulness involves some mental *activity* on my part. As we have postulated earlier, to the extent that a situation is conceptualized, that is, organized meaningfully, it is always accompanied by a further kind of subjective judgement—an affective assessment (for example, "Darn it! It's Monday!"). Such assessments can "set the tone" for my day (as in ideas and beliefs about "Blue Monday") and affect how I cope with my day by helping to pattern the way I view events, although it is likely that events will come along that will contribute to a change in my outlook during the day. This example can be taken to characterize the many other activities of self, too.

7. An emphasis on the social aspects of self has been argued rather forcefully in the past decade (Cushman, 1990, 1991; Sampson, 1985, 1988; Sass, 1988). While we cannot discuss this perspective in detail here, we can touch on certain aspects of that point of view that are relevant to the argument being developed.

Sampson, for example, has proposed that at least two contrasting "indigenous psychologies," ways that people have developed of defining self and individualism across world cultures, can be identified (1988). One of these he calls a "self-contained individualism" characterized by *firm boundaries* demarcating the sense of self from "nonself other"; an emphasis on *personal control* and autonomy; and an *"exclusionary"*, singular conception of the self. This is a familiar character type in Western societies, especially the United States (see also Johnson, 1985, on this point).

Distinct from this is what Sampson calls "ensembled individualism," characterized by a *fluid* self-other boundary; a sense of *field* control, that is, an acceptance of being controlled by other people and external factors in the environment; and an *"inclusive"* conception of the self that is perhaps akin to Mead's "generalized other". The latter type of individualism is more prevalent in societies throughout the world. (See Roland's similar discussion of two major Asian cultures [1988].) Sampson argues that these differing perspectives have important implications for three broad cultural values—freedom, responsibility, and achievement—that he feels are achieved more completely by cultural institutions that promote the "ensembled" norm for a society.

For our purposes we can look at the value of responsibility that is targeted on the sense of agency in Sampson's analysis and consider differences between his perspective and the one being discussed here. Sampson argues that those who support a more self-contained sense of individualism promote a strong sense of the agent as the one who makes choices and is therefore responsible for consequences. Without this sense a person's experience of personal responsibility for his or her actions is compromised. But in the ensembled self, responsibility comes by virtue of having included others into the development of one's sense of self: "Who I am is defined in and through my relations with others; I am completed through these relations and do not exist apart from them. Therefore, my work on behalf of others is simultaneously work on behalf of myself" (1988, p. 20). Conceivably there are private aspects of self, but these are more easily subordinated to one's relations with others than is typical in the middle-class American ideal.

Actually the ensembled self is not so foreign to American cultural groups. Some Euro-American groups (such as Italians and Greeks) probably do not adhere as much to the self-contained norm as do others. Further, Sampson's perspective is consistent with a view proposed almost two decades ago by Wade Nobles in his characterization of the African-American sense of self (1973). Nobles had suggested that African Americans come from a cultural tradition in which the emphasis is not so much on individual self, the "I," as in Western society, but on a group self, the "we." He suggests, "The African world-view suggests that 'I am because we are, and because we are therefore I am.' In so emphasizing, this view makes no real distinction between self and others" (pp. 23–24). Nobles goes on to argue that in Western thought, self is defined in terms of the separateness and distinctness of the individual from others—in *opposition* to rather than in *apposition* to the group. However, the sense of "we" added to the "I" and "me" contributes a sense of "extended self" that is needed to fully describe the experience of the African American.

In general Nobles's and Sampson's perspectives are a contribution to the thinking about the concept of self seen cross-culturally. However, what needs to be made clear in this analysis, it seems to me, is that the sense of "we" deriving from the "extended self" or the "ensembled self" does not obliterate a sense of "I." To take the tribal society as an example, even within the "we" there were different "me's." Some group members were men with their prescribed roles and tasks; some were women with their particular roles. Though all were competent, some warriors were more expert at running, some at using specific weapons, and the society probably took note of this and made use of different warriors in different ways. Individuality and group identity can maintain a complementary relationship. To take another example, among many Native North American peoples the central importance of community identity and responsibility to the group led each individual to feel himself or herself as a representative of the assemblage: "I am the people" was typical of this sentiment (Ramirez, 1983). Yet, at the same time, the people living in this tradition were expected to educate themselves and nurture their individual skills to the fullest. They were expected to develop their free will—the capacity to recognize and choose among alternatives—by training themselves to be able to rise above selfish promptings and environmentally posed hardships so that they could make choices that were in the best interests of the group (Ramirez, 1983).

My point here is that even when groups emphasize the ensembled self, the dialectic process is not obliterated from individual mentality. In fact, group mentalities can be seen to "occur because of the *conformity* of human intelligence to the premises which all individuals in a given group take to be collectively advantageous or the 'right way' to look at things" (Rychlak, 1988, p. 306). Conformity in this sense represents the individual act of taking the group norm as the guide for the person's behavior. "The social norm is a mutual 'that for the sake of which' (premise) employed in common affirmation by all members of a discernible group . . . lending them a common sense of identity and commitment in life" [pp. 305–306]. Though in some cultural settings, people cheerfully align their expression of needs with those of others, it is being posited here that these persons have the capacity to imagine alternatives and have chosen (and, at some level of consciousness, may continuously choose) to go along with members of their cultures.

Sampson's (1988) analysis does a service as he joins those modern critics who bemoan the overemphasis on competitiveness, self-centeredness, and alienation that threatens the vitality of the American culture. However, it should be noted that cultures whose institutions have historically promoted an ensembled self have not been without their serious problems as well. In the United States, as groups become more Americanized over the generations, it appears that a greater expression of the individual "I" becomes more of an acceptable option. This does not mean that they must completely lose the sense of "we" they have but rather that they develop a multifaceted sense of self articulated differently than that of their parents and grandparents. In Chapter 5 we shall discuss research that illustrates this interplay between "I" and "we" among African Americans.

8. The psychodynamic psychologist is aware of another aspect of the multidimensionality of self, too. No one, including adults, has perfect self-esteem. All of us make judgments about ourselves as having aspects that are less desirable than we would like them to be. These negative affective assessments about ourselves represent low self-esteem. (Note that studies indicating similarity in level of self-esteem between Blacks and Whites do not imply that self-esteem is perfect for either group, though it may be at a "healthy" level.) One way of dealing with those aspects of ourselves that we do not like is to alter awareness of them, that is, withdraw attention from them or eject them from consciousness. The tendency for people to alter and in fact distort awareness of disturbing (anxiety-arousing) aspects of their experience to regain a sense of well-being is partly what psychodynamic personality theorists mean by "defense." To some extent we all must defend against certain (internal) thoughts and feelings or (external) events in order to keep anxiety from paralyzing our adaptive efforts. So we tend to shut out the more unpleasant assessments about ourselves.

The sense of imperfectness and uncertainty about self that all people harbor to some extent should be even more true of children, whose sense of self is less stabilized and developed. It should not be surprising that young Black children might manifest some effect of the highly charged racial scene in America. Depth interviews and personality assessment techniques have been able to pick up *some* degree of anger and depression regarding racial group membership. Thus, differences in levels of personality function tapped may account for some aspects of conflicting results. Porter's methodology may have tapped broader ranges of children's functioning than did some other studies.

9. There are many varieties of extended kinship organization in African-American families (Billingsley, 1968). To extol the strengths of such arrangements is not to say that they are always successful. The recession-prone American economy of the past decade along with regressive social welfare policies and other societal forces has worked considerable hardship on African-American communities (Hill, 1990; Wilson, 1989). Not infrequently an extended family arrangement must be made in a household context that was not prepared to handle it. As Boyd-Franklin notes, "It would be a disservice . . .

if we so glorified the "strengths" of [Black families] that we could not recognize problems when they appear" [1989, p. 51]. She discusses some of the kinds of difficulties that can occur in such families and gives examples. One of the reasons for correcting the scholarship and studying the strengths of African-American families is to develop models that we can use where needed in our preventative and remedial efforts with Black families.

10. The Markus and Nurius work shows ways in which modern social-cognitive perspectives are conceptually similar to the telic-humanistic approach being proposed in this book. However, there are differences. It is true that by invoking a notion of alternate possibilities for development their view puts an emphasis on the creative and constructionist aspects of human functioning. But in the last analysis, possible selves tend to be presented as heavily dependent on the effects of social inputs. Thus, Markus and Nurius note that though

> an individual is free to create any variety of possible selves, . . . the pool of possible selves derives from the categories made salient by the individual's particular sociocultural and historical context and from the models, images, and symbols provided by the media and by the individual's immediate social experiences. [1986, p. 954]

This constrains the picture of agency being presented in this book. While people often draw from the pool of possibilities offered to them, the above emphasis does not allow for variants in choice that are *departures* from the social pool—alternatives, even opposite images that are not simply derivatives from the social context.

Similarly these authors note that "because possible selves are not well-anchored in social experience" they are the aspect of the self-knowledge "that is the most vulnerable and responsive to changes in the environment" (op. cit., p. 956). Again, this is a limited conception of agency. People can tenaciously hold on to a conception of possible self—and sometimes bring that image to pass—in spite of discouraging inputs or in the absence of encouraging information from the social environment. Clinicians know that people hold on to fearful images regarding possible selves in spite of sometimes disconfirming data from the environment. On the other hand, as we shall say repeatedly in this book, to leave room for individual conceptualization of events even in the presence of social constraints is *not* to blame people for succumbing to the negative images presented by their circumstances.

11. The classical psychoanalytic point of view suggests certain inevitable instinctual drive factors that in the course of development may be expressed in racist ways. Williams and Morland (1976) have a different set of speculations about universals within the individual that can set the stage for racial attitudes. They argue that the attitudes toward Black and White as colors—distinct from attitudes toward light- and dark-skinned people—are not dependent on social learning. If they were dependent on learning, they point out, then older and brighter children would be expected to show such attitudes with greater strength than duller and younger children. This is what we would expect for a learned behavior. But, according to the Williams and Morland studies, there is no correlation between the measures of color attitudes and either age or IQ. This suggests that the light-preference phenomenon, which shows up cross-culturally, may come from an experience universal for the human species. Specifically, they postulate that the human tendency to associate pleasure and activity with daylight hours and to associate fear and withdrawal with the darkness of night may be a source of the black-white color preferences. Thus, people are primed phylogenetically for contact with American social institutions and racial mores. The feelings about dark and light that come from attitudes toward daylight and its absence are emphasized and placed in a value hierarchy in this multipigmented, status-oriented society. Of course, Williams and Morland acknowledge individual differences and the fact that differing individual experience will accent or moderate such potential. For example, a generally more fearful child might be expected to manifest the day-night attitudes more sharply. Also, darker-skinned people with positive associations to other dark people (in their families, for instance) might be less prone to transfer such negative attitudes as strongly to colors and relationships with people. This lesser degree of transfer is probably reflected in the lower amount of dark-color avoidance in African-Americans reported by, for example, Williams and Morland and by Porter.

12. In Erik Erikson's development scheme (1963) the years spent in elementary school in our culture (what Freud called the "latency" period) are a time when a child is learning a sense of "industry," a necessary feature of development toward maturity. Negotiating this phase of growth involves learning the basic tool skills of the culture and learning a sense of pleasure in work completion, as Erikson puts it, necessary for eventual adaptation as an adult in a given cultural setting. Erikson defines this phase in a way that is similar to White's ideas about competence. The child comes to take a certain amount of pleasure in being effective in the kinds of graded tasks that the society presents. Such tasks are presented in formal schooling in many cultures. Children who do not develop a healthy sense of "industry" are prone to a sense of "inferiority" as the opposite possibility. Of course, as continua, these developmental stages are conceived in terms of degrees to which an individual succeeds or fails to negotiate the tasks; this is not an "all or none" conception of attainment. In childhood, especially, successful progression through the stages depends on the social milieu providing the right balance of nurturance, opportunity, and disciplinary structure to enable the child to mature in the ways the culture sees as properly representing achievement. A sense of inadequacy or inferiority can stem from a family life that hasn't prepared a child for school or a school life that does not value what the child has learned to do well. Of course, a major social issue today is the concern in minority communities about the failure of schools to be able to enhance the potential that young Black children bring for development of a sense of industry.

13. Powell-Hopson and Hopson (1988), having found that their sample of Black and White children tended to prefer the white dolls in a Clark design, attempted to modify their subjects' attitudes with a behavior modification procedure. They modeled pro–black doll choices, they read a story to the children depicting Black children positively, and they had children recite positive adjectives while holding black dolls. They never used the terms *black* or *white* in referring to the dolls. After a fifteen-minute period, Black and White children on average reversed their preferences to the black doll. In a final session with the children—a "debriefing" session, in research lingo—they were told that neither of the dolls was better than the other one. While not expecting these results to generalize beyond the experimental situation, they felt they were a good example of what could be done for children's reference group attitudes if these and similar procedures were carried out in a sustained and natural way by parents and teachers. For example, in two classrooms where a majority of Black children had originally shown a preference for the black doll, teachers had been carrying out a variety of cultural experiences to enhance notions of Black identity. One of these teachers was Black and one was White, "indicating that the race of the teacher was not as important as attitude and commitment to teaching racial pride to Black children" (Powell-Hopson & Hopson, 1988, p. 61). Cross (1991) reviews other intervention studies on self-concept, as well.

3

The Active Intellect: Developing Competence

The assumption can be made that cultural and economic backgrounds of pupils do not constitute a barrier to the type of learning which can reasonably be expected of normal children in the elementary schools. . . . [Clark, 1965, p. 139]

The evidence of the pilot projects in "deprived" schools—odd though it may appear to many—seems to indicate that a child who is expected by the school to learn does so; the child of whom little is expected produces little. [p. 132]

The lagging school achievement of African-American children from inner-city communities persists as a major educational and social problem in America. Despite the promising educational experiments that Kenneth Clark cited in *Dark Ghetto* almost thirty years ago, inner-city schools have been unsuccessful in keeping the children of the poor from falling further and further behind in the grade levels expected of them for their age. As one Black fifth-grader observed in commenting on how little learning was going on in her classroom, "By the time we get to sixth grade, boy, we be dumb" (Gouldner & Strong, 1978, p. 64). "Dumb" is a classification now applied to many Black children—a larger percentage of them than White children have been labeled as retarded in intellectual functioning. Is this an accurate reading of the intellectual capacity of Black children?

Some educational psychologists feel sufficiently satisfied about their grasp of the facts to state that Black children are innately limited in their intellectual potential. Jensen (1969) presented this view in postulating a distinction between Level I and Level II types of intellectual ability. Level I abilities presumably consist of associative skills such as are primarily involved in the (potentially quite accurate) mental registration of stimuli and the faithful reproduction of such information. Everyone has and needs such skills. If a man wants to reach someone by telephone, he has to be able to remember the seven-digit number the operator gives him. This is rote memory. Level I ability also includes trial-and-error learning that does not necessitate sophisticated problem-solving strategies. Children do not seem to differ consistently by race or socioeconomic class in Level I abilities. If anything, lower-class children sometimes do better when tested for these skills.

Level II abilities involve the more complex capacity to pick out the relationships among stimuli. In a concept-formation test a question might be, "How are a wagon and a bicycle alike?" Another kind of Level II test might offer the possibility of using a set of relationships to solve a problem. A favorite example here is to require a child to learn a list of items presented in random order (coat, cat, teepee, dress, bear, igloo), all of which can be grouped into a smaller number of abstract categories. Noting the categories and using them (spontaneously) to group the items helps the subject to memorize them more efficiently. Those who do well on such tasks are seen as having Level II abilities. The average Black and lower-class child, in Jensen's judgment, is genetically deficient in Level II abilities—the "average" Black and lower-class child because it is not maintained that *all* Blacks are without high-level intellectual abilities. Rather, he posits that a significantly larger number of Black and lower-class persons are without such abilities and are thus limited to a Level I style of approaching intellectual problems. Looked at this way, a person who is both lower class and Black is in double jeopardy of being intellectually limited.[1]

From the humanistic perspective there is an interesting implication regarding this supposed deficit in Black intellectual capacity. It has to do with the difference between the Lockean and the Kantian conception of mental functioning. The reader will recall that the Lockean view is that mind develops primarily as a result of the flow of stimulation to the individual. The person registers it and responds to it. We have pointed out the passivity of the individual in this conception of mind. The Kantian view emphasizes that from the beginning the infant "comes at" the world with structuring activity that interacts with the reality it confronts, and so the child contributes to what it "knows."

The view that African Americans are limited to Level I, or primarily associative abilities, implies that their intellectual functioning is adequately described in a rather simplified version of the Lockean model. In other words, it implies that African Americans only function effectively in the mode of rote reproduction of what is fed into their mental systems. The concept of learning by association, with its emphasis on how recently and how frequently a particular stimulus occurs along with another, has been important for traditional psychology. In this regard, Rychlak (1988) notes, "This mechanical—often purely accidental—bonding of one item to another is what humanists consider to be a passive characterization of mental associations" (p. 333). To conceive of Blacks' intellectual capacities as being primarily associative is to consign them to a model that emphasizes passivity of intellect. On the other hand, the implication would be that middle-class White persons are properly described in the Kantian model, which posits the capacity to actively unearth and apply the dialectical options available in a given intellectual situation. (For some mechanists, more sophisticated Lockean models might be in order. See the references associated with note 7.)

Of course this book argues quite a different view—namely, that people of all races and social classes are best described by including Kantian terms. More specifically, the view is that African Americans bring into the world the kind of actively conceptualizing mental equipment that gives them the capacity to achieve intellectual competence. It is true that the performance of lower- and working-class Black children is frequently lower than that of White and middle-class children in standard testing and teaching situations. But a considerable number of researchers feel that this is not a true estimate of the basic capacity of Black children.

There is evidence to indicate that, rather than being genetically determined in the main, such disparities stem from different learning experiences that these children have had. This throws doubt on the validity of putting people irrevocably into these Level I and Level II categories. This is a basic point in Feuerstein's intriguing approach to the "dynamic" assessment of children whose intellectual functioning is below par (Feuerstein, 1979; Feuerstein, Rand, et al. 1986). He argues that such children learn to restrict themselves to Level I functioning, or at least they do not learn other ways of responding. Speaking of these children, he notes,

> [The child's] limitation to a reproductive modality of interaction with stimuli results directly from his perception of himself as a passive recipient of information rather than as an active generator of new information and ideas by inferential and constructive mental acts.
>
> [Such a child] often considers appropriate reproduction a virtue, and whatever deviation is produced by his creativity he considers inadequate. This basic attitude is reflected in a state of passivity vis-a-vis the world and the incoming stimuli. . . . He does not attempt to produce the relationships that would organize the stimuli into meaningful categories. (Feuerstein, 1979, p. 81)

The variety of factors that can contribute to what amounts to a *style* of Level I functioning will be the subject of a large part of this chapter and a portion of the next.

One of our tasks in this chapter, then, will be to review a selected sample of the evidence that indicates that Black and other minority children can think and learn in abstract as well as rote fashion. In short, we shall argue that they are potentially active in their approach to intellectual situations just as they are in their definition of self. (I acknowledge that the humanistic perspective being used to discuss the intellectual functioning of African Americans here is only one way of trying to organize this material. Many psychologists prefer not to be explicit about theoretical biases in this area. My use of this theoretical approach is an expression of my belief that the humanistic approach with its emphasis on active, coping features of human behavior provides a point of view that is quite compatible with the tenor of a certain portion of the research on intelligence in Blacks. That is the portion that stresses the equal overall intellectual capacities of African-American children with other children.)

Traditionally in psychology the term *conceptualizing* is used to refer only to the abstract, problem-solving thinking abilities, those seen as higher-level skills, associated with Level II capacities. The humanistic position, however, uses the term somewhat differently. From the beginning for all children the interaction with the world involves not only passively registering what is "there" in reality but also actively meeting experience "at the level of sensation (input) with a creative capacity to *order* it via patterns that constitute meaning and meaningfulness" (Rychlak, 1988, p. 326). This is the particular way in which we have defined the term *conceptualizing*. As we are using it here, it is a term that can be employed to subsume the various components of thinking activity, or, as thinking is often called in psychology, "cognitive" activity (see the definition of *cognition* in the section "Cognitive Components of Intelligence"). So, for example, reasoning and memory are two quite distinguishable cognitive activities, but overall they can be seen as cognitive tools by which a person structures the world. In other words, eventually the child comes to be able to mentally organize events in front of him or her into relationships and causal sequences (reasoning) and comes to reapply his or her earlier organization of a situation to a past event (memory). Psychologists have spent considerable time delineating other specific ways that conceptualizing goes on (see Rychlak [1988, chap. 8; 1991] for a discussion of learning principles interpreted from within his framework). But the main point here is that *some* rudimentary form of organizing *activity* begins at birth. We know things because of the (prior) conceptual activities, the "spectacles," so to speak, that we bring to an experience. A person is active in coming to know about the world.

In the humanistic theory adopted here, learning (which is an important aspect of intelligence) does not simply result from something falling into our mental storage bin, as it were. It involves actively extending the meaning framework that we have developed to new situations in order to make sense of them. When we have made sense of them, that is, imposed an order on them, we have learned something. What we have learned may not be correct according to some external criterion, but it does represent a mental reshaping of the situation. Of course we are required eventually to bring our learning into line with social and physical reality if we are to be effective in the world. But in principle the humanistic view is that a definition of learning needs to include what the subject understands and intends, not only what an observer sees from an extraspective point of view as behavior. So, for example, a toddler seeing a four-legged creature standing before her meowing may call it a "doggie," which is her name for the general concept of all four-legged creatures with tails. With loving interventions from parents and others the child eventually comes to make the correct distinction between dogs and cats—"Yes, good girl, that's a kitty!" In such a parent-child context, positive affective assessments can become associated both with the act of learning and specifically with the idea of approaching domesticated four-footed animals.

Throughout life, learning proceeds by extending forward the meanings of previously established conceptualizations of a situation along with some feelings about them, positive or negative. If a football enthusiast decides he wants to learn more about the rules of rugby, he probably does so in terms of his knowledge of football, which rugby resembles. He probably extends his knowledge of rugby from the similarities and differences in American football. And he develops, let's say, an appreciation (a positive affective assessment) for the game. (He would have to bring forward some other orienting conceptualization if he knew nothing about football.) Someone else attending his or her first game may also learn things about rugby based on knowledge of American football. This person might learn—that is, extend the understanding—that rugby is just as "brutal" as football and the action of a bunch of men running up and down a field and suddenly falling on one another is just as "senseless." Here a negative affective assessment is being extended from one situation to the next. This person is learning, too. A firm set of understandings is being extended and influences ways of looking at particular sports activities.

Learning, then, involves actively "bringing forward" previous conceptualizations and personal intentions in a new situation. Rychlak calls this approach to learning "logical learning theory." This name emphasizes the view that a conceptual pattern or order (a *logos*) provides the framework that guides behavior.[2] We understand a situation, and perhaps act in it, primarily in terms of our conception of it, not just because of its "real" characteristics. As we find that our conception meaningfully structures a situation that we are confronting, we apply it again the next time we seem to be in a similar situation. As we repeat this construction and the ensuing behavior, it becomes the way that we "learn" to deal with the situation (Rychlak, 1991).

One of the important aspects of this view of learning is that learning does not occur simply because a child happens to be standing there when an event—let's say the passing of a fire truck—occurs. Learning is not simply a process of automatic (passive) "bonding" of events that are accidentally present. The child doesn't learn that that thing rushing by is a fire truck, even if her mother says so, unless she is actively involved and intentional in extending forward the pattern she has developed to this noisy, bright, fast-moving object that she sees ("What's that, Mommy?"). Further, her learning in this situation involves extending the conceptualization about trucks and cars, not the ones about trees and flowers that she has developed. If she has no conceptualizations for trucks and cars, she is probably not going to learn much about the fire engine. Learning involves proceeding from where we are and extending what we have already organized to the new and (not too) unfamiliar. Included in the learning about fire trucks may be a happy excitement about the noise and flashiness (a positive affective assessment) or an aversion (a negative affective assessment) to such commotion. *Meaningfulness* in any humanistic theory, not just Rychlak's, is a very important term. It signifies that individuals decide, often subconsciously, what is important in a situation, according to their intentions and learn along lines that they have already developed and are pursuing. This of course is how we described the development of the self in Chapter 2.

This model of learning and intellectual functioning postulates that all groups of human beings bring active conceptualizing processes to experience.[3] When it is defined this way, intelligence is not a special capacity that only some privileged groups of children have, although people may indeed vary in the efficiency with which they use this capacity. This kind of conceptualizing is a part of everyone's mental activity. As we shall see later, Feuerstein has found that by using such a conception of intelligence he has been able to help many children develop intellectually who were abandoned as being unable to learn—that is, abandoned as unable to bring forward previous experience to new situations—children labeled as hopelessly retarded.[4]

In summary, then, it can be said that Black and poor children as a group bring active conceptualizing capacities to intellectual situations. Children learn best when they can see the meaningful connection between the conceptualizations they hold and the situation they are being asked to learn. If the learning situation is framed in unfamiliar ways or if the situation is associated with negative affective assessments and seems strange and forbidding, then learning and intellectual performance are likely to be hampered. On the other hand, it is known that other settings and approaches can have dramatic effects in helping children realize their intellectual potential.

Assessing Intellectual Competence

Judgments about intellectual potential are usually made on the basis of how a person does on tests of "intelligence." Our view is that a person's intellectual ability is reflected in the way s/he applies conceptualizing capacities (as just defined) to a given situation. A test provides a sample of a person's conceptualizing activities (Rychlak, 1982b). A test cannot ask all the possible questions about a given content area to see how much a person has learned; nor can it pose too long a list of problems to test a person's skill, let us say in spatial relations. So an efficient test has to select a limited number of items that presumably represent the wider domain of knowledge that is under investigation. This issue, which is fundamental to all psychometric testing, is particularly important to the testing of minorities. The accuracy of the test (its *reliability* and *validity* in psychometric terms; see Anastasi [1988]) depends on knowing what the domain being sampled actually encompasses. For example, what do we *really* mean by the term *intelligence*? What does intelligent behavior really encompass?

The accuracy of test items that are selected to measure a particular ability depends on having a good idea of what that ability involves. Further, even if one has a good idea of what is involved in a particular domain, the limited sample of questions used has to be justifiable as a representative selection of that larger domain or universe. Critics note that standard intelligence tests tend to fall down on both of these counts, especially when it comes to testing minority and poor children. We try to measure with certainty something we don't clearly understand—intelligence—and the test items we use on standard tests are not necessarily representative of "intelligence" across human groups.

The most widely used of these tests yield a score, a standardized numerical weighting, called an *intelligence quotient,* or IQ. Briefly, an IQ score is determined by comparing how one child does on the test items with the performance of a group of children who were used to provide the "norm," or the standard for the test. The test items pose differing levels of difficulty for children at a given age. This is an empirical approach to intelligence in that it lets the data from the testing of a large body of "representative" children determine what the criterion is for being more or less smart. The average IQ is set at 100.[5] If one were to give such a test to a random sample of children, the individual scores would range considerably from high to low. In this range we would find that Blacks and lower socioeconomic persons tend to score lower than White and middle-class persons on the average.

What do such results mean? Those who understand the problems of comparing intellectual functioning across cultures know that even in the United States this is a very complex question. The research group at the Laboratory of Comparative Human Cognition (LCHC) notes three problems in interpreting standard intelligence tests. First, they suggest that it is not possible to ensure that people have had equal learning opportunities for the tasks sampled on IQ tests. Not only have groups differed in direct practice on such tasks (in preschool or grade school, for example), but they differ on indirect, more informal opportunities for practice (at home or in the community). Second, since a particular level of performance on a given kind of intellectual task can arise in a number of different ways, it is not really clear what gives rise to test performance. Third, it is not clear that all cultural groups within and outside of U.S. borders share the mainstream American definition of intelligent behavior. Particularly in cultures where there are no schools, "the tasks that people routinely must accomplish to maintain themselves bear no obvious relation to the tasks that yield our basic definitions of intelligence" (LCHC, 1982, p. 644).

Nevertheless, experience seems to indicate that IQ scores are rather good indicators of potential for profiting from traditional schooling, particularly at advanced levels. The high scorers are seen as good risks in school and the low scorers are seen as poor risks. Now, there is relatively little argument over this contention when the discussion is confined to the issue of the immediate readiness of a child to profit from the standard classroom situation typical of American schools. Such tests predict academic performance in the classroom quite well. There is less argument over this point because today's test score makes a (more or less) accurate statement about what a child is ready to do in school *today*. When a score is looked at this way, the possibility still exists that providing remedial help or changing the classroom setting will trigger the learning potential of the low test scorer to improve *tomorrow*.

The real controversy begins with the insistence by some psychologists that the differences in IQ scores represent relatively immutable and fixed intellectual potential. The conclusion from such a premise is that there is little we can do to help today's low scorers become ready for higher levels of education tomorrow (Jensen, 1969). Such a perspective has a long history in our society (Guthrie, 1976; Kamin, 1974) and has been fostered by decades of a numerical measurement, or "psychometric," approach to intellectual-ability testing. It has led to a way of thinking about intellectual ability as if it were a kind of quantity. Unfortunately, professionals and laypeople alike have adopted these ideas. The IQ test score, then, is almost literally seen as an indicator of how many units of that finite substance called "intelligence" the individual has. Such a perspective seems to assert that intelligence is adequately defined and measured by IQ tests. In more technical terms, such an idea is embodied in the notion of a general unitary factor, g, heavily affected by genetic influences, which presumably accounts for intelligent performance across a variety of tasks. Such a perspective seems to assert that intelligence is adequately defined and measured by IQ tests.[6]

It is clear that such a definition has had elitist consequences and its exclusive use has led to testing procedures that have failed to take account of the potential of Black children. A more useful view of intelligence is that it is a concept, a hypothetical term, used to account broadly for what we observe about a person's potential for solving problems in life situations or creating "products, that are valued within one or more cultural settings"

(Gardner, 1983, p. x). The important consideration regarding measurement is that this potential may or may not be reflected on an IQ test. Whether or not it is depends on a variety of factors. In a multicultural society such as ours, however, differences in cultural background can influence the way intellectual potential is manifested. Thus, in contrast to the view that IQ test performance is the best measure of the potential for intellectual development, it is plausible to interpret test performance as reflecting how an individual uses his or her intellectual or thinking capacity in a given situation. Whether or not an individual has more thinking or problem-solving capacity than is used at any one moment is something that these tests, in and of themselves, are not very good at discerning for lower-class minority children. To get a clear perspective on the intellectual functioning of Black children, one has to recognize that children can have more intellectual competence than they apply to a given situation. Many factors determine whether they do in fact make the application of their capacity to the intellectual problem they are presented with.

The Anatomy of Intellectual Performance

While some people regard IQ tests as the standard way of ascertaining intellectual ability, many others do not view them as straightforward measures of thinking capacity. Those who dissent from the traditional view would probably agree with Zigler and Trickett (1978) that the standard intelligence test is actually a "polyglot sample of behavior that is influenced by three empirically related but conceptually distinct collections of variables" (p. 792), namely: (1) those that are so-called purely formal cognitive ones, (2) those that demonstrate what knowledge or information the person has been exposed to and learned—which can be called factors of achievement, and (3) a diversified cluster of motivational and affective variables influencing how a person acquires and/or expresses what s/he knows in a given situation. Looked at this way, the standard intelligence test is far from a direct and uncomplicated measure of thinking ability.

In the next sections of this chapter I shall be concerned with a selection of studies pertaining to these three sets of variables. Our focus will be on lower- and working-class Black children for the most part. My aim is to select studies that will allow us to further our humanistic theoretical perspective and show the capacity for active intellectuality in Black children. My purpose here is not to confine the discussion about intellectual ability to the arena of tests, but rather to find a way of grouping the studies about the intellectual ability of Black children that will be consistent with the humanistic perspective. Specifically the sections deal with "cognitive components of intelligence," "learning and achievement in intellectual performance," and "the impact of affective and motivational factors on intellectual performance."

Cognitive Components of Intelligence

Cognition is an important term in psychology. The developmental psychologist Jerome Kagan suggests that cognition

> refers to the processes involved in the extraction of information from both the outside world and the internal environment, the application of existing knowledge to the construction of initial representations, the storage and retrieval of that information, the integration of new with old structures, the application of structures to deal with problems, and, most important, the creation of new knowledge. [1976, p. 1]

The processes of formal cognition can also be described in such terms as *reasoning, memory, abstracting ability, speed of visual information processing,* and others that psychologists have defined.[7] For many people these components are what overall intellectual ability is really about. Such factors are often thought of as being the true representation of native ability. Even though people may be willing to acknowledge that other aspects of functioning contribute to intellectual performance, the cognitive abilities are seen as the "bottom line," as it were, of an individual's intellectual capacity. Even though the role that such factors play must be put into context, as we shall see, there is no doubt that formal thinking abilities are fundamental to intellectual performance.

Kagan notes (1976) as a principle underlying the development of cognitive or thinking abilities the idea that "the major cognitive processes . . . mature in a regular way in *any* natural environment" (p. 2, emphasis added). A "natural environment" for Kagan is one that contains people and objects—"even if the people know little of what a child requires and no object is manufactured" (p. 2). What this means is that different cultural and social class settings are not necessarily deficient in the different ways they structure the world for their offspring. At any given point in time, children from various backgrounds have arrived at different stages of cognitive development. They may also differ in what kinds of cues it takes to show that they have arrived at a certain stage of development of a particular cognitive process. But the potential for developing the process is there; that is—and this is a fundamental assumption—the basic cognitive processes are distributed broadly throughout the human family. Or, as sociologist Jane Mercer puts it, *"All ethnic groups have equal potential for acquiring any human culture"* (1979, p. 53, emphasis in original). Cognitive processes are not limited to persons of a particular race or class, although differences in background seem to affect how and when these cognitive processes are manifested (Segall et al., 1990, especially chapters 5 and 8).

Most people would agree that *some* degree of active intellectual potential is present in all human groups. There is disagreement as to whether all groups can achieve the highest levels of intellectual ability of which human beings are capable. Of course, to label Blacks and other social groups as deficient in cognitive ability is to characterize them as being inferior. It justifies a kind of racist solicitousness toward Blacks of not encouraging them to "frustrate" themselves by pursuing intellectual development that is "beyond" their abilities. It justifies tracking them into quick exits from schooling and into lower-level, dead-end occupations.

It is true that if one leaves the intellectual performance situation pretty much in its standard form, one can find ample evidence supporting the inferior functioning of minority children. What I shall maintain here is that, when one alters the form of the performance situation in specific ways without altering the basic difficulty level of the problem, one can uncover intellectual potential in Black children that is missed by standard situations. The studies in this section will be chosen to describe what some of the variables are that influence intellectual performance and how the performance of Black and poor children is enhanced when these factors are taken into account. Whether or not a child performs up to capacity depends on whether or not s/he recognizes the usefulness in a given situation of applying skills that s/he has but doesn't often use. We shall see that differences in background heavily influence such use, and we shall also see that such background factors can be manipulated or compensated for with some patient intervention techniques, perseverance, and, as Kenneth Clark says, a firm belief that these children can learn as well as any.

At this point in our level of understanding in the field there will probably continue to be disagreements about these issues. However, this research does make plausible and quite tenable the idea that basic cognitive capacities are broadly distributed across ethnic groups. It justifies helping Blacks and the poor strive for the highest levels of intellectual development rather than using their class or racial status as a sign of uneducability.

Unmasking the Potential

Let's turn first to an experimental test of the hypothesis put forward by Jensen that lower-class and Black children lack Level II thinking ability. A research team headed by Scrofani proposed an alternative hypothesis as a way of accounting for the low scores of these children on tests of abstract cognitive skills. Scrofani et al. (1973) suggest that Black and lower-class children actually possess such high-level intellectual abilities but simply fail to use them in testing situations. If these abilities are lying dormant, they might be activated by some practice or training in how to employ them on test questions.

The design of the Scrofani study was rather complicated, involving a series of steps. A short account of it follows. In the first phase they administered tests of Level I (rote) and Level 11 (abstract) abilities to a group of middle- and lower-class, Black and White fourth graders in Prince Georges County, Maryland. The children did not differ in Level I abilities and, according to expectations, the middle-class children scored much higher on the test of Level II abilities, which was an IQ test. In the second phase of the study the children were given a different kind of test—a Piagetian test of cognitive development, and on the basis of the results of this test the children were divided into three groups called categories A, B, and C.

> Category A children were middle class, almost all of whom had made perfect or near-perfect scores on the Piagetian test.
>
> Category B children were the 48 percent of the lower-class children who had also made perfect or near-perfect scores on the Piagetian test.
>
> Category C children were the remaining lower-class children who did not complete the developmental test correctly.
>
> Category A (middle-class) children were similar to Category B (lower-class) children in maturity of cognitive development according to the Piagetian test. The lower class B and C children were similar in IQ scores.

In each of these three groups, half of the children were given two 30-minute training sessions on the use of concept formation strategies. The training sessions consisted of a number of brief sorting and display exercises. In the former activity, children were given the task of sorting a group of pictures into piles corresponding to the conceptual groups they represented (e.g., food, tools, toys, and utensils). In the display exercises the examiner showed the group one or more pictures and children took turns indicating a conceptual category the picture(s) might belong to. The untrained group of children were given exercises that did not involve concept training.

Later they were tested with the kinds of free recall tasks used in Jensen's laboratory to sample Level I and Level II skills. This involved remembering as many of the items shown to them as they could in each of several trials. The items were shown in random order, but the items in the Level II task could be clustered into categories. Two of the categories were those used in the training session, but none of the pictures shown were used in training. The trained category B children showed that they had profited from the training. They performed as well as the trained middle-class children on the Level II task and better than untrained Category B children. The trained category C children did not improve very much. When socioeconomic status was controlled, there were no differences in performance by race.

What the study seemed to demonstrate was that a sizable number of lower-class children—almost half of them—actually possessed cognitive skills of a higher order but had not made use of them in the IQ test. The results of the developmental cognitive test turned out to be a better predictor of their potential functioning, for after only two half-hours of practice in forming concept categories they were able to perform as well on Level II tasks as middle-class children who had received the same training.

From the humanistic perspective we can describe the middle-class children as being able to extend forward a pattern of dealing with the environment that had been developed in previous encounters with the world. The lower-class children who scored well on the Piagetian tests did not immediately bring forward skills that they had in order to structure the Level II recall situations abstractly. They needed a couple of training sessions to help make the skills more salient. It is as if the practice sessions opened a cupboard door of skills these children had acquired but had shelved, so to speak, not quite knowing what to do with them. How the children performed in the IQ test situation was not a good indicator of their potential. Such results certainly ought to make us cautious about the conclusions we draw about lower- and working-class minority children from single intellectual tests.

Questions arise, however, about those category C children who went through the same training procedure as did some of the category A and B children. Category C youngsters were those whose cognitive development on the Piagetian tests was not on a par with the other children in the sample. Their performance even after training suggested that they did not have the cognitive skills that were available to category A and B children. This could be because they had limited genetic endowment. However, we shall look at other possibilities about these performance deficits in the course of our review of some of the research in this area.

Before we take up the category C children, let us turn to the question of why it might be that some children come to intellectual performance situations with cognitive skills they are not able to use efficiently. This, of course, was the situation with the category B children in the Scrofani study. I shall spend the next sections discussing research that describes issues influencing the readiness of children to perform cognitively at more advanced levels.

Environmental Background and Intellectual Ability
In the past fifteen years more work has emerged that speaks to the topic of children's cognitive readiness. How children think can be approached from a broad cross-cultural framework—in particular a "cultural-ecological" point of view—or we may take a more focused look at family background differences. All these points of reference make contributions to understanding the issue of influences on cognitive development and performance.

We can begin our discussion by using a broad cross-cultural perspective. Although basic intellectual skills are distributed widely throughout the human family, the maturation of specific intellectual abilities may occur at different rates. Apparently some cultural settings provide environments that hasten the rates of development. Whether by the fast road or the slow road, the children eventually reach the same destination. When urban American middle-class children were compared with various groups of rural Guatemalan children, for instance, it turned out that the American children matured in certain skills earlier than did the Guatemalan children. Urban Guatemalan middle-class children were also more advanced in some skills than were the rural children. But by the time they were 11 years old, all the children were at approximately the same level on the skills in question. If predictions of intellectual potential had been based on their scores when they were 5 and 6 years old, the rural Guatemalan children would have been incorrectly called retarded. Kagan and Klein make this interpretation: "These data have implications for America's educational problems. . . . The Guatemalan data, together with those of [studies on urban Western children], suggest that children differ in the age at which basic cognitive competences emerge and that experiential factors influence the time of emergence" (1973, p. 958).

Cultural Context Influences. Such differences highlight a more specific point being emphasized by a growing number of developmental scholars, namely, that cognitive development and performance are a function of the cultural context in which they emerge and the situational context in which they are manifest. As Rogoff and Morelli note, "Developmental researchers who have worked in other cultures have become convinced that human functioning cannot be separated from the cultural and more immediate context in which children develop" (1989, p. 344). For example, developmental milestones—such things as when a child first begins to walk or to talk—vary as a function of cultural context, and the kinds of behaviors a child demonstrates vary with the way an observational situation is structured (e.g. laboratory or "naturalistic") and with the age and gender of the person with whom s/he is interacting.

For Miller-Jones (1989), who takes a "social-cognitive ecological" point of view, this has important implications for testing cognitive ability. He argues that

> children have organized repertoires of possible responses to a question and . . . culture determines the availability or priority of access to any one of them. . . . [That is,] the child's interpretation of the *"meaning"* of a task or situation determines which reasoning processes he or she will deploy and . . . such "meanings" are the product of the interaction between the child's knowledge (i.e., his or her internal representation of past experiences) and the properties of the task (i.e., external features) at hand. [p. 364]

This perspective is consistent with the idea that children are born with a full range of intellectual capacities and that culture makes a powerful contribution to which ones are developed more quickly or more completely. As noted earlier, cognitive performance can be seen to represent a "style" of functioning to which culture contributes considerably. We shall have more to say regarding cognitive styles presently. There are similarities here also to the social-cognitive approach of Alejandro-Wright (1985) that we discussed in Chapter 2. (While acknowledging the contribution to mentality of cultural effects, we should note that social-cognitive approaches tend to put primary emphasis on the ways in which the child is shaped *by* the culture. However, the humanistic theorist recognizes that the child is not simply driven by his or her culture. In developing meaning the child brings a dialectical interpretive capacity that allows him or her to make a unique contribution to conceiving the particular situation structured by the culture.)

Family Background Influences. It seems reasonable to assume that for lower-class African-American children, differences in cultural experience significantly affect their readiness to do well in intellectual performance situations. Sandra Scarr (1977) has attempted to assess the relative contributions that family and perhaps community environment as opposed to genetic variables make to the intellectual performance of Black children. Based on a study of both Black and White twins in the Philadelphia school population, she asserted that genetic factors have less of an impact on cognitive test performance for Black children than for White; environmental factors are more influential for Black children. Many Black children "are being reared in circumstances that give them only marginal acquaintance with the skills and the knowledge being sampled by the tests we administered" (1977, p. 31). This differential access to such skills and knowledge "explains the lower performance of Black children as a group" (p. 31). As she put it in an earlier version of this work, "The Black child learns a different, not a deficient, set of language rules, and he may learn a different style of thought. The transfer of training from home to school performance is probably less direct for Black children than for White children" (Scarr-Salapatek, 1971, p. 1294).

Scarr and Weinberg (1976) made a more direct test of the possibility of influencing the environmental contributions to IQ. In order to separate genetic factors from conditions of rearing, they studied a group of 130 Black and interracial children adopted by advantaged White families. The adoptees, whose natural parents were of average educational background, scored above the mean for the White school population in IQ and school achievement. "One reason for the substantial increase in test performance of the Black and interracial adoptees," it was suggested by the researchers, "is that their rearing environments are culturally relevant to the tests and to the school" (p. 737). Later we shall see how Jane Mercer used such notions about cultural difference to try to devise a fairer method for assessing intellectual ability.

The results of a study by Moore (1985) with somewhat altered conditions support these findings. She studied forty-six African-American children who had been adopted as infants by middle-class Black and middle-class White families. When tested later, the transracially adopted children had higher IQ scores than those adopted by Black families and higher scores than White children in general. Scores for the Black adoptees in this sample were higher than for Black children in general. As with the Scarr and Weinberg research, this study indicated that Black children socialized in the White middle-class system performed on a par with their White classmates on standardized intelligence tests.[8]

The Language Matrix.   What is it about the backgrounds of young children that prepares them to do well in school? One pivotal issue in the backgrounds of the children who are ready for school seems to be a particular way of using verbal skills. I am not referring here simply to the ability to be talkative, as such. The evidence indicates that, in circumstances where they feel comfortable, lower-class Black children are as talkative as any children. The point is that children seem to differ by socioeconomic class at least in the way with which they use language internally to carry on their problem solving.

Scrofani and colleagues (1973) report as a part of the study we previously reviewed that following the experiment they asked their subjects to put the pictures used in the Level II recall test into groups of things that go together. The trained subjects regardless of category were able to do this task. Among the untrained subjects, all but one of the middle-class subjects (from category A) did so, but less than half of the lower-class subjects (category B or C) could do so correctly. Of those who did, only a few were able to come up with a precise concept or explanation for their groupings. However, most of the category B and C children grouped the pictures and verbalized the concept when prompted. The researchers note: "These observations suggest that the middle-class children may have specific skills (for example, verbal labelling skills) and know-how that the lower-SES children do not have. Perhaps the attainment of this skill was all the B subjects needed in order to actualize their potential" (1973, p. 552). Thus, although most children bring active intellectual abilities to performance situations, the backgrounds of some children teach them skills that help them use these abilities in ways more consistent with what schools typically expect.[9]

This observation concerning the way verbal skills are used is supported by other research. One study investigating intellectual performance among Black children found that social class differences in performance did not emerge until about 3 years of age (Golden et al., 1971). This was seen as reflecting the fact that between 18 and 36 months, language becomes an important way of dealing with the world, and the forms of language development tapped in standard IQ tests reflect the experiences more familiar to middle-class families. In a study of White preschool boys, Golden, Bridger, and Montare (1974) found that the middle-class subjects in the group were better than the lower-class boys at using verbal cues to find a hidden reward. The children did equally well when they had to do the task without verbal cues. The researchers concluded that the specific verbal labels—"The cookie is under the lock (or the valve, etc.)" rather than "The cookie is under this thing"—made the difference.

> These studies suggest that, in contrast to less educated individuals, highly educated adults tend to use more specific terminology and rely more on language to transmit information and to regulate their children's behavior. Children whose parents are more educated may acquire a greater set to listen when they are spoken to, to use verbal information to acquire knowledge, and to respond to verbal instructions to guide their behavior than do children whose parents are less educated. [p. 91]

It is not that lower-socioeconomic-status children come from "defective" backgrounds or even backgrounds in which there is necessarily less talking. It is rather that they may come from backgrounds where language has been used in a different way than in higher-status homes. This difference in style of language use may make higher-status children more prepared to respond to the demands of the schoolroom situations.[10]

Cognitive Style and Intellectual Performance

People from different back grounds develop distinctive approaches to perceiving the world and thinking about problems, approaches that have been called "cognitive styles." For example, a person may be either relatively "convergent" or relatively "divergent" in thinking. In the case of convergent thinkers, they use conventional reasoning processes to arrive at answers and are more likely to do better on tests that involve finding the one correct answer that, for example, is asked for on multiple-choice exams. Divergent thinkers, on the other hand, are more original and novel in their thinking and do better on open-ended questions that allow alternative ways of solving a problem.

Rosalie Cohen and her colleagues have investigated the impact of one such cognitive or conceptual style dimension on the school performance of lower-class, inner-city children. Conceptual styles for Cohen, as for Rychlak, are strategies for selecting and organizing sense data:

> The analytic cognitive style is characterized by a formal or analytic mode of abstracting salient information from a stimulus or situation and by a stimulus-centered orientation to reality, and it is parts-specific (i.e., parts or attributes of a given stimulus have meaning in themselves). The relational cognitive style, on the other hand, requires a descriptive mode

of abstraction and is self-centered in its orientation to reality; only the global characteristics of a stimulus have meaning to its users, and these only in reference to some total context. [Cohen, 1969, pp. 829–830][11]

High reliance on one or the other of these cognitive styles is not related to intelligence; both relational and analytic persons can be very intelligent. However, the dilemma is that schools emphasize the analytic approach to cognitive organization, and the ability to use that style well becomes more critical in higher grade levels in school. Thus, pupils with poor development of such skills or who develop an alternate cognitive style could be expected to do poorly in school early in their careers and do even less well, comparatively, as they advance in grade level.[12]

It is not only in relating to the curriculum—the learning of specific content and the development of problem-solving skills—that analytic abilities are emphasized. Cohen argues that the overall ideology and learning environment of the school are permeated by social and psychological correlates of the analytic style. This can be seen, for example, in requirements placed on pupils in school to sit and concentrate for increasingly long periods on impersonal learning materials and to observe and value fixed time-allotment schedules.

> So discrepant are the analytic and relational frames of reference that a pupil whose preferred mode of cognitive organization is emphatically relational is unlikely to be rewarded in the school setting either socially or by grades, regardless of his native abilities and even if his information repertoire and background of experience are adequate. [Cohen, 1969, p. 830]

Relational patterns of responding tend to be considered deviant and/or disruptive in the school setting.

Cognitive Style and African-American Children

While Cohen seems to see her work as applying to a variety of lower-class groups, others argue that the conceptual style notion is a good way of accounting for some of the learning problems of African-American children in particular (Hale, 1982; Shade, 1991; Willis, 1989). For example, Shade argues that "Americans of African descent have developed a unique culture as the result of coping with and adapting to a color-conscious society and a part of that culture includes specific and unique cognitive strategies" (1991, p. 231). This, of course, is another, more specific way of conceiving the effects on intellectual performance of environmental background differences among Black children. Hilliard (in Willis, 1989) distinguishes between an "atomistic-objective" learning style and a "synthetic-personal" style. This differentiation is very similar to that posed by Cohen. Hilliard suggests that American schools favor the former style, a cognitive orientation more characteristic of White children. The latter style, presumably much more apparent in the cognitive and learning style of Black children, reflects a preference for "experimentation, improvisation, and harmonious interaction with others and the environment" (Willis, op. cit., p. 52).

Boykin (1979) has had one of the most active experimental programs to test one set of implications growing out of a cognitive style conception. He has proposed the concept of "behavioral verve" as a way of characterizing the conceptual style of lower-class African-American children. He uses the verve idea to refer to a higher "chronic activation level" and sees it as being manifested as "an increased behavioral vibrancy and an increased psychological affinity for stimulus change" [p. 354]. He suggests that it is possible that lower-class Black children would learn better if they were taught in circumstances that provided for more stimulating surroundings.

To test this hypothesis, Boykin gave third- and fourth-grade Black and White children cognitive tasks to learn under two conditions, one of which was formal and unvaried and the other a varied one.[13] The varied or unvaried formats had no bearing on the performance of the White children (high versus low scholastic achievement was taken account of), but did make a difference for the Black children, who did significantly better in the varied presentation situations. The varied and lively context appeared to facilitate their learning, resembling more closely the crowded homes filled with people and activity presumably characteristic of lower-socioeconomic persons. Rather than being a source of distraction preventing children from acquiring cognitive skills, perhaps such lively settings have become the customary environment for learning. When these characteristics of their home environments are missing, learning may be more difficult. More recent work by Tuck and Boykin and Allen and Boykin (reported in Boykin, 1991) extends these findings somewhat. In the Allen and Boykin study, for example, the use of expressive rhythmic movement during a learning task enhanced the performance of Black children but not that of White children. Consistent with other theorists writing about the learning style of African-American children, Boykin has noted, "Schools are relatively unstimulating and monotonous places. . . . perhaps Black students are not as successful in school because they are relatively intolerant of monotony" (1977, p. 19).

The emphasis on conceptual style difference as a source of educational failure is a departure from the notion that the children have cognitive deficits. These children are seen as capable of developing high-level abstracting skills with the potential for leading productive lives as adults in fields calling for creative thinking. (Perhaps Sternberg's "experiential" and/or "contextual" perspectives on intelligence are being called into play here. See note 6.) Cohen suggests that the problem of conceptual style is not so much one of cultural deprivation as it is one of "cultural conflict." In this conception, when the relationally oriented child attempts to deal with analytically oriented schools, the child can be considerably hampered in learning. Here the educational problem is not necessarily to focus on the child and teach him or her to be like the school. Many would argue that the emphasis should be on making schools more flexible so that they can help the child function in the mode that is best for him or her while also helping the child to develop analytic skills as needed.

Recognition that there can be different high-level approaches to problem solving in different people argues for a "pluralistic" conception of intellectual ability, that is, that there are multiple equivalent high-level problem-solving styles. Such a conception challenges us to find ways of accurately measuring the talents of people from different cultures. Perhaps one of the reasons our research has not helped us get a hold on equally valid alternative methods of problem solving is that the American (Anglocentric) culture seems to favor the analytic mode. Alternate modes of approach are often associated with other, non-European cultures—by definition not as "good" as the Western one.

Intervening to Support Intellectual Activity

Studies such as those just reviewed suggest that there are differences in intellectual style and performance along lines of social class and perhaps ethnic-cultural background. Sometimes such differences may reflect gaps in early experiences. In other cases it may be that such differences reflect appropriate variations that are the result of development in a particular cultural setting. In either case such differences in intellectual functioning can interfere with children's readiness to meet the kinds of expectations imposed by the typical American school situation. Is it possible to intervene in the lives of children and their families in ways that actually enhance their readiness for schooling in a mainstream context? I think that the answer to this question is strongly affirmative. In this section we shall look at a selection of studies that discuss direct levels of intervention with children at risk and their families.[14]

As examples we can select from studies in three areas: those oriented toward intervening early in a child's school and family life to enhance readiness for school, a special approach to change the way older children address the tasks presented to them in school, and approaches that alter the structure of the classroom and school system.

Head Start Programs. In the early 1960s social scientists and educators began to design systematic educational programs for preschool children living in poverty, with the aim of enhancing their capacity to do well in school and in so doing provide them with the skills for achieving higher educational and occupational mobility. These ideas soon led to the development of national federally supported projects under the broad rubric of the Head Start program. However, by the end of the 1960s some educational psychologists began to doubt the value of these efforts. They argued that the often impressive gains in intellectual proficiency achieved by these programs did not last as the children entered the early school grades. After two decades of experience with

Head Start projects we can say that this judgment seems to have been premature.

In their recent report, Berrueta-Clement et al. (1984) review seven of the best programs of intellectual enrichment for disadvantaged preschool children. The designs of these studies compared children exposed to preschool interventions and comparable samples of children who were not. The format of the studies differed—some were twice-weekly sessions with the children, without a special program for the parents; others were half-day programs with differing degrees of parental involvement; and another, the "Milwaukee Project," introduced intensive involvement with both the children and their parents. An evaluation of all of these projects showed that preschool intervention can have a measurable short- and long-term positive impact on children's intellectual development and in some cases on youngsters' social functioning as well. For example, with respect to early development, Berrueta-Clement et al. note that "the best-documented period of preschool effects is early childhood, and the best-documented preschool effect is an immediate improvement in intellectual performance as represented by intelligence test scores" (1984, p. 101).

Of the seven programs discussed in the Berrueta-Clement et al. monograph it was the ambitious Milwaukee Project (Heber, 1978; Garber & Heber, 1981) that showed the highest level of impact on intellectual functioning. In a survey of the most impoverished area of Milwaukee, researchers found that mothers with IQs below 80 produced a disproportionately high number of children with IQs below 80—children, furthermore, whose tested intellectual functioning declined with age. A sample of forty Black families was selected from this area that seemed to have so many children who were at high risk for developing intellectually retarded modes of performance. Twenty of the families were placed in the experimental group and twenty in the control group. There were no significant differences at birth in important features of health and physique of the forty infants involved in the study. Economic status of the families and number of siblings in the household were also similar.

The program for the mothers in the experimental group included instruction in home and child care and occupational and educational training. Starting in the first few months of life the children in the experimental group were placed in daycare facilities with all-day sessions, five days a week, every month of the year through age 6. The program for the children was intensive, personalized, and focused on perceptual-motor skills, cognitive-language skills, and socioemotional development. The experimental group began to show differences at 14 months, when their growth norms were four months ahead of the controls. The controls were about at the expected levels at that time. On tests of learning and language development, children in the experimental group were not only doing better than the controls but on some tests were ahead of the test norms for their age. By the time they entered school at age 6 they were clearly ready to learn. They demonstrated the active approach to problem solving needed to do well in school.

At first there was understandable caution about how to interpret these results (Loehlin, Lindzey, & Spuhler, 1975). Some (e.g., Page, 1975) argued that these children were being trained in skills related to IQ-test taking, not necessarily in the kinds of skills that would lead to broad educational growth. However, the children were followed for four years without further intervention and continued to do well. Nevertheless, Garber and Heber (1981) noted that for those children living in disrupted family or social environments with intellectually limited parents, it is probably necessary to continue special programs for the children and supportive interventions with their families.

While this differential effect on IQ, as such, did not last through elementary school in many of the studies, a consistent finding across studies was that children exposed to the formal preschool experience showed considerably less need for placement in special education classes during grade school. In addition, the Perry Preschool project demonstrated clearly better scholastic achievement over the years—assessed at several points from ages 7 through 19—for those who had had the preschool experience. The fact that children in the experimental group did better in school even when IQ gains did not hold up again raises questions about equating intelligence with IQ. As Schweinhart and Weikart of the Perry group note:

> We can make the parsimonious assumption that quality preschool education positively affects intelligence . . . i.e. the ability to adapt, cope with, and learn from one's environment. . . . Children who attended preschool actually do function better in school, are perceived and treated as functioning better, therefore continue to function better, and so on. [1981, p. 123]

There are differences of opinion as to just what factors are most involved in the changed performance of the children in the experimental group. Some writers suggest that it is only affective and motivational factors that are changed in these programs. However, it does seem likely that cognitive factors were enhanced as well. This research is very much in line with the idea that basic cognitive processes and the capacity for intellectual competence are universally distributed in human beings, and differences in environmental opportunities are critical to determining when and how completely these abilities will become manifest.

We should also note an additional effect of preschool intervention that the Perry study has documented. The benefits of this early experience persist into late adolescence along some important dimensions of social and adaptive functioning. At age 19 the experimental group showed significantly lower rates of delinquency and crime, lower use of welfare assistance, lower incidence of teenage pregnancy, and higher rates of employment and higher rates of graduation from high school. These researchers also report a careful cost-benefit analysis of the value to society of spending money on the Perry Preschool program in particular. They concluded that "judged simply on its overall return, the Perry Preschool program was a good investment for society. . . . The present value of benefits exceeds seven times the present value of cost for one year of preschool" (Berrueta-Clement et al., 1984, pp. 89, 90). The call to the conscience of a truly enlightened nation is clear.

Dynamic Assessment of Active Potential. Granted the value of such programs, we must note that the more successful children in the Perry study were still behind the average for their school by the eighth grade. While these programs have positive effects, most of them are rather modest in design and are not a sufficient answer to educational programs of poor minority children. Generally Head Start programs make interventions on the basis of demographic features that identify children whose cognitive development is at risk. So, for example, all "children living in poverty" in a particular area become the target for a class of interventions designed to provide enrichment. While these programs are generally effective, individual children within these broad social groupings have different levels of cognitive development. In the Scrofani experiment, as we noted, category B and C children were lower class (and thus at some potential educational risk), but they differed in certain identifiable aspects of cognitive maturity. Thus, one might expect that approaches that tailor assessment and intervention to the particular needs of the *individual* child (rather than to the average level of a group of children) should have the greatest potential for making improvements in functioning. Such a perspective, couched in an abiding belief in the human capacity for intellectual modifiability, characterizes the work of Reuven Feuerstein and his colleagues (Feuerstein, 1979; Feuerstein, Hoffman, et al., 1986; Feuerstein, Rand, et al. 1986).

Let's introduce Feuerstein's work with one of his case studies:

> When first referred Joel [who had been institutionalized at the age of 8 with a diagnosis of severe mental retardation] . . . was apathetic and torpid, and only interacted with the examiner in a limited manner. [He] was illiterate, had little orientation in time and space, and lacked self-care skills. . . .
>
> Very early in our assessment and work with Joel, [however,] it became clear that he had a substantial potential for modifiability. Unfortunately, in his 8 years of institutionalization this core of potential had never been recognized or assessed.
>
> . . . we continued to work with him for 6 years. At the end of this period Joel was able to learn a vocation. He is a proficient reader and is

able to communicate his thoughts and feelings. Most important, Joel is able to function independently as a self-supporting member of society. [Feuerstein, 1979, pp. 23-24]

This vignette is presented as a representative example of many cases Feuerstein and his colleagues have worked with. It illustrates the dramatic changes they believe have been brought about by applying a different conception of intellectual potential to people whose initial test performance was strikingly below par. Feuerstein's work has been done with the many different kinds of immigrants who have poured into Israel in the last thirty-five years. The issues he raises are also pertinent to dealing with the controversies about the intellectual functioning of racial minorities in the United States.

Feuerstein's approach is based on the belief that cognitive processes involved in intellectual performance can be modified. Taking something of a "deficit" approach to substandard intellectual functioning, he starts with a belief that in many instances children do not do well intellectually because they have not developed—they lack—certain specific problem-solving skills. However, he does not believe that the deficits that lead to lowered performance stem from genetic lack or some other physiological disturbance. Instead, they are the result of reversible disruptions in the learning process. While these workers acknowledge that there is an optimal period for educational intervention in early childhood, cognitive deficiencies can be modifed through this program "irrespective of [the] level of function, the etiology of [the] level of functioning, the severity of [the] condition, or the age at which the specific intervention is offered" (Feuerstein, Hoffman, et al., 1986, p. 51).

How do these cognitive impairments come about, in Feuerstein's view? He proposes that they come from a lack of "mediated learning experience."[15] Although physiologically intact children have the potential for adequate intellectual functioning, this potential must be brought to full flower. Typically this happens as the family goes about the job of transmitting to the child the important aspects of the culture in which it is embedded. As the family does this, it teaches the child not only *what* is important to learn about the world but also *how* to learn. To put it in our terms, in focusing the child's attention on one or another pole of the dialectical world—on hunting rather than sewing for a boy child, or on weather conditions for planting rather than animal tracks for an agrarian society—the family helps the child develop cognitive modifiability, the ability to learn and use past experience. This comes from patient, repeated interactions between parent and child. (In the very earliest months and years the parent responsible for this is typically but certainly not exclusively the mother.) The basic features of intelligence emerge from this cultural transmission process in that the child comes to be modified within his or her cultural setting and develops the ability to apply prior learning to new problems within that setting.

A child for whom these experiences have been comparatively few can be said to be "culturally deprived," in Feuerstein's view. Such a person or group can be said to be "alienated *from its own culture*" (1979, p. 39). This is to be distinguished from a culturally "different" person or group in which the individual has learned content and skills of his or her own culture that may not be immediately applicable to a new setting. Feuerstein gives an example from his own experience of the "sudden change produced by the 'flying carpet' program that whisked [Yemenite Jews] . . . to Israel." It became clear that these people were not culturally deprived: "These extremely different individuals were equipped with highly developed culturally adaptive capacities—capacities acquired through their exposure to their own and very different culture" (pp. 38–39).

In emphasizing learning as basic to intelligence, Feuerstein distinguishes between two kinds of learning—direct and mediated—that are involved in the child's active coping with the world. Direct learning results from the child's own immediate contacts with the world. For example, the child swats at the rattle and comes gradually to develop conceptualizations about it. Mediated learning is defined as

> the interactional processes between the developing human organism and an experienced, intentioned adult who, by interposing himself between the child and external sources of stimulation, 'mediates' the world to the child by framing, selecting, focusing, and feeding back environmental experiences in such a way as to produce in him appropriate learning sets and habits. [Feuerstein, 1979, p. 71]

While this seems to put emphasis on the social influences on the child's development, parental mediating activity need not be seen only from a Lockean point of view. Parents not only feed stimuli to the child; they also guide the child's already ongoing conceptualizing efforts so that this activity is focused on what the culture thinks is important. Mediated learning is seen as being more important than direct learning, especially initially, because, while the child does learn from early on by direct contact with the world, the learning is not very efficient as s/he tries, for example, to grasp, suck, or bite to find the most effective ways of interacting with a new object. Thus, the parent-mediator intervenes and helps the child focus attention on the shaking of the object if it is a rattle or the grasping and throwing if it is a ball. The interactions between parent and child, of course, are not limited to visual-motor ones. The whole range of human developmental experiences is involved. Language development, learning about satisfying bodily tensions, and learning about what other people are like are all examples.

Learning from these kinds of interactions is prerequisite to engaging in effective learning on one's own through direct exposure to the world: "The more an individual has benefited from mediated learning, the greater will his capacity be to become modified through direct exposure learning" (Feuerstein, 1979, p. 71). It is important to note, too, that there is no special language of mediation. It involves the everyday activities and language used, for example, in labeling—"That's your nose," "Yes, that's a kitty"; in comparison—"That one is red; that one is green"; in locating things in space—"Where's teddy? There's the teddy bear!" and of course many other specific acts. These are daily events engaged in with infants and young children in most households in cultures all over the world. This again lends particular meaning to Kagan's previously noted assertion that parents do not necessarily have to be sophisticated in their knowledge about child development in order to provide sufficient background for the unfolding of basic cognitive skills. (It puts all the more responsibility on society for enabling people to achieve the basic living standard that will make it easier to do with their children these things that come so naturally.)

Furthermore, the important issue is not so much what children learn about themselves, their family, and their culture, important as these things are.

> Even more important . . . over and above the specific contents the child might obtain by means of mediation is an attitude toward thinking and problem solving that is actively and efficiently involved in organizing the world of stimuli impinging on the individual from both internal and external sources. [Feuerstein, 1979, pp. 71–72]
>
> Once the child has experienced mediated learning interactions and learned to focus, observe and differentiate, he or she will spontaneously continue to interact with things actively rather than passively. [Feuerstein, Hoffman, et al., 1986, p. 50]

This notion of a primary task of educating being to nurture and sustain an active attitude toward problem solving is, of course, very compatible with our humanistic point of view. In addition, Feuerstein states that the language and content of the activity are not as crucial as "the *intentionality* on the part of the mediator (Feuerstein, 1979 p. 71). The mediator has a purpose in mind that gives a special direction to the relationship between parent and child. In one sense, perhaps, children, in developing their active approaches toward problem solving, take on the active image of the parent projected to them.[16]

Feuerstein's conception is that insufficient mediated learning experience during the course of a child's development is responsible for the cognitive deficits that appear on testing. Several things can interfere with mediated learning developmentally. First, a disturbed family interaction may keep family members from attending consistently to the child. Second, the infant or child may be emotionally disturbed or physically ill and thus unable to profit from the parents' mediation efforts. Third, a child's socioeconomic conditions may narrow the interaction between parent and child to issues that put him or her at a disadvantage later in school. This may be a way of characterizing the situation in neighborhoods of the sort, in all ethnic groups, from which Head Start programs draw their samples. Finally, disrupted sociopolitical circumstances may lead to disruption of the processes of cultural transmission in the family. One can think of many recent examples of this happening to children in various parts of the world—Romania, Cambodia, Palestine, and many parts of Africa. Although children from poverty environments are at higher risk than others for experiencing insufficient mediation, such disruptions in early learning are by no means confined to poverty conditions. Children from materially privileged environments have been a sizable group for whom mediated learning has not been adequate.

In order to assess exactly which elements of cognitive functioning are impaired, Feuerstein and his colleagues developed a method of assessment that he calls the Learning Performance Assessment Device (LPAD). This is a procedure that uses developmental kinds of tasks and a greatly modified examiner-examinee relationship to observe the child carefully (Feuerstein, 1979; Feuerstein, Rand, et al., 1986). Not feeling bound by the aloof and neutral stance taken by the usual psychometrician, the examiner using the LPAD intervenes immediately when the child begins to have trouble, to see whether or not the child can moderate his or her impaired functioning to some degree by accepting the examiner's suggestions to attend more carefully to the test stimulus, pause longer to reflect on different options of proceeding, deliver the answer in more conventional terms, and so on. The assessment emphasis here is not so much on the product—whether or not the answer is wrong—but on the process—how the failure came about for this particular child. "Viewing intelligence . . . as summarily expressed in the capacity for modifiability or learning, implies that assessment procedures used for educational and social intervention should not be primarily concerned with interindividual differences. Rather, they should enable a full, independent study of each particular individual" (Feuerstein, 1979, p. 50).

From the perspective of mediated learning, Feuerstein's approach involves presenting brief task situations in the form of test items to assess the individual's ability to profit from learning experiences. The test items are flexible enough so that finding out about specific cognitive skills can be tailored to an individual child's particular style. On the basis of the assessment a training plan is worked out. The examiner and eventually the educator serve as the mediators for learning what the child lacked in his or her previous educational experience.[17]

Feuerstein and his colleagues attempt to make up for the effects of the missing mediated learning experiences through an "Instrumental Enrichment" (IE) intervention program. The aim of IE is to enable the learner to profit from direct exposure to new experiences. It seeks to provide individuals with "the prerequisite functions that equip them for active, productive, representational thinking that leads to higher mental processes" (Feuerstein, Hoffman, et al., 1986, p. 51). The program achieves its purposes through implementing six goals, which include: identifying the nature of the cognitive deficiencies, helping the student acquire the tools (concepts, strategies, vocabulary, etc.) for completing specific tasks, helping the learner generate intrinsic motivation through forming appropriate habits, and changing the learner's self-perception to that of one who is an active and competent generator of new information. (See Feuerstein, Hoffman, et al., 1986, pp. 52–55 for a more complete discussion of goals.)

The goal of identifying the nature of cognitive deficiencies is worthy of particular attention since it is relevant to both assessment and modification interventions. Though the nature of impairments resulting from inadequate early mediated learning experiences will vary among individuals, the deficiencies tend to fall into categories that can be grouped into three phases of the mental act—the input, elaboration, and output phases. The *input* phase concerns gathering of information. Deficiencies include, for example, unfocused, amorphous perception; unplanned and impulsive exploration of stimulus items; poor precision and accuracy; and inability to deal with more than one source of information at the same time, among a number of others. The *elaboration* phase is concerned with processing gathered information. Here deficiencies include inadequate definition of a problem, inability to focus on relevant cues, lack of use of logical evidence, no strategies or poor ones for hypothesis testing, and lack of planning behavior, to name a few issues in this domain. The *output* phase involves the individual's capacity to express the products of elaboration. Here presenting problems might be egocentricity, blocking, inability to engage in precise responding, trial and error behavior, and the like.

The IE program consists of fifteen paper-and-pencil instruments of content-free exercises presented over a two-year period. This 400–500 pages of material is spaced over several hours a week in conjunction with the regular curriculum. Specially trained teachers fit the instruments and sequences to the learners' needs. The instruments can be used in group settings permitting peer interaction or they can be used with individual students. "The teacher seeks to become an effective mediator by intentionally using the given tasks to attain the various subgoals of the program, endowing them with significance and a transcendent quality" (Feuerstein, Hoffman, et al., 1986, p. 56). The phrase "endowing them with significance" has a familiar ring to the logical learning theorist. Remember that learning in logical learning theory involves "predicating," that is, developing a *meaningful* or significant (to the subject) way of organizing new things that are presented to one (Rychlak, 1991). Similarly, the emphasis in Instrumental Enrichment is on helping the learner become aware of how to bring a more organized pattern of meaning to intellectual problems that will enable him or her to deal with them more effectively. This focus on changing the learner's process is another aspect of bringing to life the individual's potential for agency. For purposes of consistency with his language I have continued to use Feuerstein's term "mediator" to describe the nature of the good parent's and/or educator's interventions with the child. However, from a humanistic view the mediator is better seen as a "participative conceptualizer," one who engages and then expands the child's capacity for conceptualizing activity.[18]

Thus, Feuerstein and his colleagues claim to have been able, by applying principles of structural cognitive modifiability, to assess the difficulties of children and offer them learning experiences that have helped them develop their intellectual capacities in dramatic ways. He has case examples of persons who have become unusually bright and productive adults by any criterion. Probably most of the children he worked with lived modest lives but capable and contributive ones, considerably beyond the level of retarded functioning predicted for them by standard testing procedures. Fifteen years of evaluative studies on IE indicate that it has been applied in a variety of settings (Feuerstein, Hoffman, et al., 1986). It has been used not only with persons functioning at below average levels intellectually, but with gifted and adequately functioning persons as well. The method has been used in a variety of countries around the world and with persons spanning the age range from elementary school children to the elderly. The authors acknowledge that small sample size in many of the studies has made it difficult to conduct an adequate test of the effects of IE. A recent review of the empirical literature on IE, while acknowledging a considerable enthusiasm for this method in educational settings, argues that available data do not offer strong scientific support for this technique (Savell, Twohig, & Rachford, 1986). This is not to say that IE is invalid. Rather, these critics contend that the evaluative studies have not been well designed. Savell et al. offer a number of suggestions for how to conduct better tests of IE that will advance our understanding of cognitive enrichment programs such as this one.

The relevance of the Feuerstein material to this book is the belief in the principle that the various cognitive skills involved in intellectual problem solving are not simply carved into the granite of the child's constitution at birth. What a child develops in the way of thinking abilities depends on how his or her structuring activities are met and mediated by the cultural environment. The variety of populations to which Feuerstein's methods have been applied puts a somewhat different light on his use of the terms cultural "deprivation" and cultural "difference." With regard to some African-American lower-class children who have "deficits" with respect to functioning in the standard classroom (perhaps the category C children in the Scrofani study), background differences related to culture may well contribute to performance differences (Boykin, 1991; Miller-Jones, 1989; Rogoff & Morelli, 1989). However, it may also be that all children suffer some degree of deficit in that probably few families of any social class generate a perfectly mediated learning process for their children. In other words, possibly not even middle-class White children come as close to the ceiling of their abilities in school as they would if each child's learning style were addressed individually by an attentive evaluator assessing each child's learning potential.

To underscore the logical learning theory view here, we understand that certain kinds of environments provide children with opportunities for building conceptual skills that mesh with the expectations of educational settings. It is not that the environment determines intellectual development in a mechanical (efficient-cause) way. Social and physical environments do make important material contribution to development. But "enriching" environments do so to an important degree by providing an arena in which effectance activities, dialectic options, and the development of intentions can have a fuller expression. J. McVicker Hunt's observation fifteen years ago still seems relevant: "Development doesn't come just from exposure to environment. It comes from the child's attempt to cope with his environment—from his *experiences* in acting on the things and people around him and getting a response from them" (in Pines, 1979, p. 59). Furthermore, enrichment does not come only from the material facets of one's environment. Through exposure to books, television (not to mention trips to the "other side of the tracks" for an inner-city youth), and loving mediators (parents and family), one may facilitate a child's imaginative processes such that (dialectic) alternatives, new intentions, and a wider range of "possible selves" (Markus & Nurius, 1986) emerge.

Whether or not such new developments emerge depends on the nature of the organization of the mental patterns. As children develop their conceptualizations (and the actions that these patterns generate) along certain lines, they become more able to form further conceptualizations along those lines, particularly as the accompanying affective assessments about these experiences are positive. Effectance strivings become channeled through such patterns and children become competent in particular areas. Thus, as young children are supported in developing mental patterns that generate an interest in books and reading, in familiarity with a pencil and with writing, with counting their blocks, and with talking about their activities to other children and to patient, attentive adults—to name a few kinds of things—they find themselves more ready for classroom activities. In other words, readiness for new experiences is a function of the kinds of mental organizations that have developed heretofore in the individual. Whether or not exposure to new experiences "takes," so to speak, depends on whether or not these experiences do in fact fit in with existing conceptualizations and thus allow a child to change existing conceptualizations "meaningfully." Thus, the form of a child's conceptualizing activity and the way s/he manifests that activity on behavior samples called tests is influenced by the kind of environmental background in which s/he has grown up. The fact that a child does not show the expected level of conceptualizing activity in a particular situation does not mean that s/he does not possess such ability or the potential to develop such ability. It is of interest that Kagan and Klein (1973) interpret their data from the Guatemalan study using a perspective that is explicitly critical of the predominant Lockean influence on Western psychology. Their support is for "the idea that the child carries with him at all times the essential mental competence to understand the new in some terms and to make a personal contribution to each new encounter" (p. 960). This is to be taken to apply to children from *all* cultures.

Changing the System
Some kinds of interventions to affect the intellectual functioning of poor children approach the problem from another direction. It can be granted that stable cultural and family background features make contributions to intellectual performance. However, this should not be taken to mean that the child and his or her family are always the primary points for intervention. As we suggested earlier in our discussion of Boykin's work, perhaps the school setting needs to be changed to accommodate the child.

Some educational scholars take a strong position on change in the schools. For example, Edmonds (1986) has argued, based partly on his experience in the New York City public school system, that school performance is primarily a function of the "effectiveness" of the school, not home background factors. That is to say, achievement differences among school age children in the United States derive from the *"variability in the nature of the schools to which they go"* (p. 95). An "effective" school is one in which the same proportion of lower-class children as middle-class children in a given school are performing at a basically adequate level. The features of such a school are, for example, strong instructional leadership from the principal; a climate of orderliness, cleanliness, and safety; and the use of standardized pupil achievement scores for the school's self-evaluation. This puts the major burden on the school system for instituting the kind of change that produces results.

Cooperative Learning Methods. One fairly recent kind of classroom innovation, the "cooperative learning" technique, takes up this challenge to some extent. In his review article on these methods, Spencer Kagan (1986) notes that three urgent problems currently face the American educational system: "(1) failure to hold and educate minority students; (2) failure to successfully create positive race relations among students; and (3) failure to socialize students toward prosocial values and behaviors such as respect and care for others, and knowledge of when and how to cooperate and help" (p. 231). He notes that this last problem, which reflects how modern pressures have undermined family and community life, is particularly ominous for this country's future.

This is so because increasingly in the American workplace social skills and interdependence in problem solving will be required. With respect to the healing contribution that the schools can make, Kagan believes that cooperative learning methods speak to all three of these problem areas.

A variety of these methods have been used around the country. We can look briefly here at the "jigsaw" method, which puts particular emphasis on interdependence among children and has more than one format. In the basic form of this method the curriculum materials on a particular topic are specially rewritten and divided into separate individually comprehensible parts. The teacher divides the class into teams structured to be heterogenous as to race, gender, ability level, and possibly personality characteristics such as assertiveness. Ideally there are five or six children in each team. Each team member has responsibility for mastering a specific assigned portion of the total lesson. When the students return to the group, each member is responsible for teaching his or her portion of that lesson to the other members of the team. Thus, in order to do well, team members are dependent on one another for getting the whole lesson. Teachers must work diligently with the children to develop communication skills and to help them initially in group organization and team building. In addition, in order to aid their mastery, students meet in "expert" groups with those from other teams who have been assigned the same portion of the total lesson. In the basic method individual students are evaluated on their own test performance; in other methods, students may receive a common grade based on progress of individual members, or there may be some other form of group evaluation.

Kagan reports that results using one or another of the cooperative methods indicate, first, that on the whole such techniques enhance academic achievement. Of particular importance is the fact that the medium and low achievers—usually poor and minority students—gain most from cooperative methods. However, at the same time, high achieving students learn *as much* if not more in cooperative as compared to traditional settings. In one study in which Black children had gained twice as much as any other group it seemed as if "the Black students were not motivated to learn in the traditional competitive/individualistic classroom structures, whereas they were highly motivated to learn when their learning contributed to the team score and was associated with peer approval" (Kagan, 1986, p. 246). With respect to interethnic relations and fostering of prosocial behavior the trend also favors the cooperative classroom. It is of interest to note further that "under the traditional class structure, both minority and majority students were more cooperative to majority than minority students, giving them more. In contrast, when cooperative students teams were employed, both minority and majority students were more cooperative toward the minority students" (op. cit., p. 253). Students seemed to be more cooperative generally after having been involved in a cooperatively structured learning setting.

The question arises as to how cooperative learning works. The available research seems to suggest that a number of factors are involved. These bear on the different and more rewarding kinds of academic activities the children engage in and the salutory changes in teachers' and students' roles and behaviors (Kagan, 1986). In light of earlier discussions in this chapter two other points are worth mentioning. For one thing, in cooperative learning contexts, students seem to begin to experience themselves as having more control and responsibility for their learning. They become more "origin-like instead of pawn-like" in the classroom (op. cit., p. 262). In addition, it appears that cooperative classroom structures are particularly compatible with the cultural backgrounds from which many minority children come: "There is evidence . . . that Black, Asian, [Mexican-American], and Native American students . . . are relatively more cooperative than Anglo students" (op. cit., p. 268). This also seems to be true of low-income children regardless of their cultural background. With respect to this issue, then, cooperative learning methods are an important intervention because, as Boykin (1991), Hale (1982), and others have indicated, "the exclusive reliance within public schools on certain kinds of classroom structures can have the effect of systematically undermining core cultural values and the psychological stability of certain minority students" (op. cit., p. 271).

Cooperative structures speak to the challenge issued by Edmonds (1986) noted previously. As Kagan (1986) points out, "Schools cannot choose . . . [whether they will] affect race relations and prosocial development[;] the only question is what kind of impact they provide" (p. 275). Cooperative learning methods provide interventions that can be used *now* to make a difference without requiring that we "fix" families and children first before the students enter the educational system. The prosocial orientation to ethnic and interpersonal relations is very much in the spirit of Pettigrew's notion of "true integration" as we discussed it in Chapter 2.

The School Development Project.   The work of James Comer and the Yale New Haven Prevention Program (also referred to as the School Development Project) illustrates some aspects of these ideas applied in selected Black communities (Comer, 1980; 1985). Comer's belief has also been that schools in poverty neighborhoods can make an independent contribution to reversing the impact of social disadvantage on the achievement potential of African-American children. This does not require waiting for social oppression to be lifted. Intervening in the schools does not mean starting in the classroom, however. It requires beginning with change of the school as a system.

In 1968 Comer and his group began their work in two New Haven schools where the enrollment was almost totally African-American and predominantly lower class. These schools had the lowest achievement scores and pupil attendance records in the city, along with frequent and severe behavior problems (Comer, 1985). The children in these schools were in the primary grades, kindergarten to fourth grade, so there was the opportunity for catching them at the start of their educational careers. One key feature of the intervention process was the creation of a group responsible for management and governance. This twelve to fourteen-person "School Advisory Council" (SAC), chaired by the school principal, was made up of teaching staff, parents, and a mental health team member. The SAC was responsible for planning and monitoring all phases of school activity, including development of staff, resources, curriculum, and the structuring of parent involvement. In addition, the School Development Project provided opportunity for differing levels of parent participation such as serving as half-time classroom assistants and involving themselves in the yearly calendar of social activities in the school (Comer, 1985).

It was within this broad context set by the SAC and furthered by broad parent activity that classroom interventions tailored to the needs of individual children and the broader curriculum issues were developed. In this kind of overall intervention, change was instituted at the top with the goal of "creating a desirable climate or social environment in schools through the application of mental health principles in a way that affects a coordinated management, curriculum and staff development program, teaching and learning process" (Comer, 1985, p. 155).

By the mid-1970s all the schools involved in the project were reported to have made gains in academic and social functioning. Data reported on the first school that the Project entered, the King School in New Haven, indicated that by 1976 King began to rank among the top five in the city in attendance, with a dramatic drop in behavior problems. Further, by 1976 fourth-grade children were performing at grade level in reading and math. Regarding longer-term effects, a group of seventh-graders who had been in the King School program compared favorably with a matched group of children who had not participated in the program. The participants had higher achievement test scores, math grades, overall grade point average, and a greater sense of school competence and total competence (Cauce, Comer, & Schwartz, 1987). A similar intervention was made in selected schools in Benton Harbor, Michigan in the 1980s. Gains in academic achievement were noted as compared to other schools in the district, and absenteeism and the need for corporal punishment decreased (Haynes, Comer, & Hamilton-Lee, 1988). Thus, Comer believes that organizing a "systems approach" in which "decision making is shared and parents are permitted to play key roles in the activities of the schools" can work efficiently and effectively to produce change in public schools (Haynes, Comer, & Hamilton-Lee, 1988, p. 20).

It is not fully clear *how* the SDP works. Perhaps strict attention to curriculum and teacher beliefs that the children can learn in this new program have more effect than the various levels of parent participation. It may be that various components of SDP are so intertwined that it is hard to tease apart meaningful individual effects. The results from various evaluations suggest that the program has had at least a modest positive impact in different school settings. Further, SDP's structure embodies very laudable educational values: emphasis on a challenging and interesting curriculum, development of a sense of competence in the children, and meaningful participation by parents.[19]

It is clear from these studies that low-performing Black children cannot be lumped together in a single group. There can be many reasons why minority children do not perform well in standard educational and testing situations. A child's background may not have helped him or her use language to cue himself or herself into employing the thinking strategies that s/he has already developed. Or the background may not have helped to develop the needed thinking strategies for effective problem solving that s/he could develop. Or, again, background may have fostered the development of an approach that is at a conceptually high level but that is not geared to the task demands of the given situation. Broad stereotypes about the uneducability of Black children for higher thinking is refuted by these ideas. One generalization that is supportable is that these children have the capacity for competent self-expression in the intellectual sphere, and if we take the time we can help them to fulfill it.

Learning and Achievement in Intellectual Performance

The standard intelligence test tells us something about what the person's thinking abilities are and also what s/he has learned. It is difficult if not impossible to separate the contribution of cognitive skills per se from achieved knowledge in the final test score. But it is important to appreciate the distinction in principle between process and content in intellectual performance. So, for example, when one reasons (a cognitive process), one does so with certain ideas and information (content). Achieved knowledge is obviously influenced by a child's particular set of experiences. For example, the test question "How are a bus and a cable car alike?" does not fairly test the reasoning powers of a young child who has never heard of that prime San Francisco tourist attraction or seen a picture of a cable car.

This example touches on a particular bone of contention for many critics of the testing of minority groups, namely, the negative effects of the "cultural bias" of tests on minority children. *Cultural bias* refers to the idea that the poor performance of minority and economically disadvantaged children stems from their unfamiliarity with the content and format of the tests rather than their lack of the thinking processes needed for high-level problem solving (see Feuerstein [1979], Garcia [1981], Modgil & Modgil [1987], and Reynolds & Brown [1984] for a further discussion of issues regarding bias in testing). It has typically been thought that tests emphasizing verbal skills are the most biased or unfair to minority children. Many of the efforts to develop so called "culture-free" tests of intellectual ability have attempted to de-emphasize verbal factors. However, it is not a matter of verbal factors alone. Halpern (1973), writing of her experience working with southern, rural Black children, noted that even nonverbal portions of the widely used Wechsler children's test proved a challenge to her subjects. What is often not recognized is that

> subjects who do not have books or magazines in their homes, whose walls are without pictures, often find pictorial representations of common objects a strange experience. In fact, in many instances, they do not recognize what the picture is intended to represent . . . and so the Black subject is at a decided disadvantage when compared with most White subjects. [p. 93]

Robert L. Williams (Williams, 1975; Williams & Mitchell, 1991) has argued in essence that poor performance is a matter of lack of familiarity with the culture that serves as the reference base for most intelligence tests. His Black Intelligence Test of Cultural Homogeneity (BITCH) has 100 verbal items geared to sampling knowledge about Black American culture.[20] As expected, Blacks do considerably better than Whites on this test, and Williams has argued that a high score by Black children may very well indicate learning potential that is not revealed by more conventional tests. Whether or not one must be as culture-specific as Williams in attempting to offset the one-sided effects of mainstream culture, the influence of acquired knowledge is clearly an important aspect of intellectual performance.

A Multicultural Approach to Bias

Rather than focusing on changing the content of IQ tests, Jane Mercer took an alternate route (1973, 1979). Assuming that the test is biased, Mercer kept the test but found out what differences from the cultural norm in the child's background made that test biased. She gave those factors a score in a prediction formula by which the child's learning potential could be estimated.[21]

Mercer championed the view that all "intelligence" tests are in fact tests of achievement, since intellectual functioning can only develop in a cultural context. Insofar as intelligence tests measure the degree of exposure to the "American" culture, understanding the problems of testing of minority children requires some appreciation of the cultural history of the United States. In this vein, Mercer (1979, 1984) has made one of the most searching current critiques of the influence of culture on standard IQ tests.

The molding of this nation culturally has involved inducing or coercing all immigrant groups to shed their particular cultural backgrounds and conform to the dominant "Anglo" cultural model. In its milder forms, Anglicization has involved insisting that non-Anglo immigrants learn the English language and adopt Anglo ways. "In its more virulent forms, Anglicization rested on a belief in the superiority of the English language and culture and of the 'Nordic' and 'Aryan' races" (Mercer, 1979, p. 15). School systems in America have been entrusted with the task of developing in non-Anglos a set of Anglo values—Protestant religious values, White Anglo-Saxon social values, and Puritan economic values.

The standardized tests used to determine who can profit from schooling have always been culture-specific to the Anglo American core culture. The tests, Mercer argued, tend to be heavily loaded with questions requiring "progressively more advanced verbal skills in the English language and knowledge of the history, values, customs and institutions of the Anglo core culture" (p. 19). The tests assume that most non-Anglo cultural groups have had the opportunity and the desire to become assimilated and have indeed absorbed the essentials of American (Anglo) culture. Therefore, when non-Anglo children do not perform well on the tests, it is assumed that they *cannot* do well—that is, they do not have the ability to do well, even though they have lacked exposure in their daily lives to what they need in order to do well. If, on the other hand, it is admitted that different ethnic groups are being reared with different degrees of exposure to the kinds of materials used in standardized tests, it means that no single set of norms can fairly assess the learning potential (i.e., the intellectual abilities) of the varieties of children from different ethnic and class backgrounds. It means, further, that children's intellectual performance should be compared with other children who have similar exposure to the experience needed to do well on the test, similar motivation to learn the material in the test, and similar test-taking experience. Hers is clearly a "cultural-difference" approach to assessment.

The procedures that Mercer used to try to do a fairer job of evaluating the ability of lower-class minority children are included in what she called the System of Multicultural Pluralistic Assessment (SOMPA). It is made up of some previously standardized procedures and some that she devised based on her research with Black, Chicano, and White children residing predominantly in California. The SOMPA consists of scales to tap the child's physical health history and sensory-motor intactness; visual and auditory acuity; physical dexterity; ability in simple geometric design copying; a measure of the child's social behavior (the Adaptive Behavior Inventory for Children—ABIC) to provide information on how the child functions at home, in the neighborhood, and in extracurricular aspects of school life; a standard measure of intellectual ability, to assess academic readiness (the Wechsler Intelligence Scale for Children [WISC–R], which is a widely used individually administered test); and a set of scales to determine the degree to which a child's socioeconomic circumstances approximate the Anglo pattern.

This latter set of scales (called Sociocultural Scales) is particularly important to the pluralistic approach. Such an approach takes the issue of cultural difference quite seriously and tries to build it into the assessment procedure systematically. These Sociocultural Scales assess qualities of family structure, family size, socioeconomic status, and urban acculturation (Mercer, 1979). They are used to determine whether to interpret a child's IQ score according to the norms appropriate for children from the standard American cultural background or whether to use another set of norms to determine learning potential. Mercer's research has shown that, provided a child is physically well and shows adaptive behavior appropriate to his or her age, the less a child's sociocultural background fits the "core culture" (Anglo) profile (core-culture children on the average have IQs of 100, of course), the more likely this child belongs to a cultural group whose average performance on the test is less than 100. In other words, a measurable degree of sociocultural difference from the Anglo standard means that children who in fact actually have average intellectual ability score lower on the WISC–R. Mercer advocated using formulas derived from her research to determine what the predicted average score would be for a particular child. For example, consider a girl whose WISC–R score is 90 and whose scores on the Sociocultural Scales indicate that the average IQ for children from such a background is 80. The score she achieved indicates an above average degree of learning potential even though her attained score puts her barely at the lower limit of the average intellectual ability range according to the standard norms for the test. The standard set of norms used with this girl gives an index of her *school functioning level* (SFL), and it may be a fairly accurate estimate of how well she will do in the standard classroom without some individualized attention. But the measure derived from the use of the sociocultural norms gives an *estimated learning potential* (ELP).

Mercer would describe such a child as a "bicultural" child—one from a background in which there may be familiarity with standard English and some degree of limited participation in the core culture. There is considerable internal heterogeneity in ethnic groups, and degree of biculturality can range from recent immigrants who barely speak English but wish to acculturate somewhat to those almost completely Anglicized. Mercer's work with her California sample showed that a bicultural child can be from any ethnic group—Latino, Black, or White.

On the other hand, some minority children are raised in social circumstances characteristic of the core culture. For a Black child, for example, this might occur in a family where, among other things, the parents were reared outside the South and had attained at least a high school education, the father provides the income for the wife and two or three children, and the parents speak standard English and participate actively in community affairs. For such a child the standard norms might well be a fair yardstick of learning potential because the background is likely to have exposed the child to the kinds of things on which this test is based.

There is a third group of children for whom the standard IQ test is seen to be totally inappropriate. This group, the "monocultural, non-Anglicized" children, are those "being reared completely outside the White core culture, who are not familiar with the English language, know nothing about the values, lifestyle, or culture of modern America" (Mercer, 1979, p. 134). The families of these children may be recent immigrants or they may choose to keep their cultures apart from the core society. Mercer advocated not using the WISC–R with children whose predicted Verbal IQ average is lower than 75—and great caution should be used in the 75–79 IQ range. These might be the kind of children for whom Feuerstein's approach would be particularly apt.

The implication of Mercer's work is that the evaluation of whether or not a lower-class minority child is "slow" intellectually should not be made from a single assessment perspective. Children whose socially adaptive behavior is adequate but whose intellectual performance is low when compared with the core-culture standard probably need to be evaluated with a different set of norms. Minority children should not be labeled retarded or subnormal intellectually unless both adaptive behavior and intellectual functioning as compared with culturally similar children are also subnormal.[22]

Affective/Motivational Factors and Intellectual Performance

The third set of factors affecting intellectual functioning involves a child's feelings about the school or test situation as well as attitudes toward the (possibly White and/or middle-class) examiner. No educational psychologist would disagree that these factors play some part in performance. The question is *how much* of an impact do they have? The centrality of such issues might best be illustrated by research from the logical learning theory laboratories that places affective factors at the heart of human functioning.

Affective Assessment

As the reader will recall, the term *affective* has a special meaning in the humanistic approach adopted here. It is used in the term *affective assessment*, which refers to an inborn dialectical aspect of mentality. Conceptualizations, meaningful affirmations about the world, are always accompanied by a "like-dislike" judgment, thus lending a clear dispositional tone to their meaning. This meaning is determined by the person's intentions and standards, not by those of the environment (see Chapter 1, note 6). Much of Rychlak's research has been devoted to demonstrating the effect of such assessments on the learning process and to showing that humanistic concepts can be rigorously investigated.

Rychlak called his operational measure of affective assessment "reinforcement value" (RV). It is one kind of "subject variable" that persons bring to every experimental situation (see the discussion of subject variables in Chapter 2, note 4). The RV measure is derived by asking subjects to rate whether or not they like materials that they are going to be asked to learn or deal with in some way in the experimental situation. A rating of "liking" is presumed to reflect a positive affective assessment; negative assessment is reflected in a rating of "disliking."[23]

While the learning of nonsense syllables was the original domain of investigation for testing his humanistically oriented theories, Rychlak and his coworkers have extended their methodology to a number of other areas including studies on the interaction of RV effects with personality factors and some aspects of psychopathology (1988, chap. 9). Of particular relevance to our discussion here is the research by the group on RV learning styles in minority and lower-socioeconomic-status (SES) groups. Several studies have established that Black subjects (both junior college and junior high school students) were more influenced by RV considerations in their learning of lists of trigrams than were their White counterparts, and lower-SES adolescents were more influenced than were middle-class subjects. However, class differences did not eradicate the influence of an RV learning style for Black subjects. Reliance on an RV style may reflect strong tendencies within the African-American culture to emphasize the basic human affective assessment propensities. (Garza [reported in Rychlak, 1988] found a similar RV preference in Mexican-American as compared to Anglo-American subjects.)

It is also of interest to note that "clustering" kinds of measures in free recall tasks have been used in some of the RV studies. Rychlak and his colleagues have found that subjects cluster more frequently on liked trigrams than on disliked ones. In other words, people use a more high-level thinking style on the tasks they like. Having established that Black subjects learn more easily along RV lines than AV lines, Rychlak hypothesized that Blacks would cluster significantly more—that is, show more of the high-level kind of thinking along RV lines than White subjects. A study designed to test this with a college age sample found this indeed to be so. Although all subjects showed preferences for clustering liked trigrams more than disliked ones, Black subjects showed this RV-phenomenon even more than did White subjects.

This does not mean that the RV capacity is learned. Rychlak notes:

> Just because we have added a sociocultural theme in these experiments on minorities, it does not follow that affective assessment is itself a sociocultural product. . . . It is possible, of course, for cultures or subcultures to encourage their members to behave spontaneously and act on impulse. This in turn could lead to a pattern of relying upon affective factors in ongoing learning. But this does not mean the affective evalu-

ations *per se* are cultural products. . . . A subculture in which individuals are encouraged [for example] to perfect their ability to retain experience in memory would probably influence its members to develop mnemonic techniques to facilitate recall. It is the same for affective assessment. Culture influences but does not create such native human capacities. [Rychlak, 1988, pp. 382–383]

Rychlak is also careful to point out that he is not suggesting that a genetic (efficient and material-cause) factor is involved in these racial differences. The fact that non-White minority groups may retain RV modes of approaching situations as a salient value does not mean that other modes are not available to govern conceptualizing. In one study comparing Whites and Blacks of middle and lower SES, Rychlak found that middle-class Black males tended to be among the *least* sensitive to RV factors.

To the extent that any group in the culture identifies with the language discriminants, accepts the demands of school-like tasks (memorization, time pressures, etc.), and ascends the economic ladder, to that extent will AV considerations play a greater role in the group's learning proclivities. In the process, the relative influence of RV will be reduced. [Rychlak, 1988, p. 383]

The Scrofani et al. study (1973) suggests that such AV modes are available to some degree and presumably have been taught in some homes and perhaps absorbed somewhat from the broader mainstream culture. By contrast, it may well be that groups excluded from participation in most aspects of society's educational and occupational structure come to emphasize less the conceptual modes (such as AV style) that would be useful in advancing within that social structure.

Just as learning and formal cognition are hard to separate in practice, Rychlak's research suggests that affective assessments and cognitive factors are also hard to separate. Affective assessments help determine how an individual's conceptualizing activities are brought to bear on a situation. Rychlak's data provide a broader basis in humanistic theory for understanding the susceptibility among lower-status minority children to affective issues in intellectual situations.

With this research as a background, Rumsey and Rychlak (1978) carried the affective assessment line of investigation directly into the area of IQ testing. They considered the possibility that the cultural differences in the salience of an RV style might extend to performance on IQ tests. In addition to the previously-cited work with minority groups, such an extension also derives from several studies from Rychlak's laboratory that had indicated that a subject's positive (or negative) assessment of a task can influence the subject's performance in that task (Rychlak, 1988). Rumsey and Rychlak predicted that subjects would score higher on intelligence test tasks reliably prerated as positive in RV than on tasks rated as negative in RV. More specifically, they predicted that the positive-RV effect would be stronger for lower-class than middle-class subjects and stronger for Black than White subjects.

They showed seventh- and eighth-grade subjects a film depicting tasks modeled on the subtests of the WISC. After the demonstration of each subtest the children, who were Black and White youngsters from lower- and middle-class backgrounds, were asked to express their like or dislike for doing a task of the type presented (the RV assessment). Here, as in others of these experiments, subjects' RV ratings were taken twice, with twenty-four hours separating. Several days later the students took the actual WISC. The researchers found that, in general, subjects scored about 5 points higher on their liked as compared to their disliked subtests. Black and lower-class children did not increase their score more than White or middle-class subjects as the authors had predicted. Nevertheless, the substantiation of the notion that a positive affective assessment has a salutory effect on a standard intellectual performance task is noteworthy. "An implication of this finding might be that education should cultivate positive interest value for academic tasks and learning, as opposed to merely supplying information" (Rumsey & Rychlak, 1978, p. 424).

With respect to the failure to find racial and class effects, it may have been that the *entire* IQ test situation was negatively assessed by Black and lower-SES subjects, thus overriding the RV effect. Therefore, it is still an open question as to whether or not a more careful design might show the effect predicted by Rychlak. It should be noted that IQ differences on liked and disliked subtests, while statistically significant, amounted to only about 5 points. The traditionally oriented psychometrician might well dismiss such a small absolute difference as being unimportant. However, this as well as other work from Rychlak's laboratory suggests that affective assessments in intellectual situations are a part of inevitable processes that operate broadly in human behavior. As such they are not factors to be dismissed or "controlled out" of situations but rather factors to be accounted for in all human behavior. Now let's look at the influence of affective factors in other educational and assessment contexts.

The Test Situation and Motivation

Zigler (1974) maintains that the minority child's failure to function adequately can often be traced to "a negative self-image, to a 'can't do' philosophy and to a wariness and/or hostility toward others, that in all too many cases has been honestly come by" (p. 158). Children's cognitive abilities can be masked by these negative attitudes. While recognizing the need to establish rapport with the examinee, some psychometrically oriented psychologists tend to overlook the fact that a testing situation can hold a broad set of anxieties for minority children. For example, Zigler describes asking a child the test question "What is an orange?"

> The child replied that he did not know and then went on to do everything in his power to maximize the social interaction. This was a child residing in an institution, and what was conveyed was that, given the child's need system and motivation, he was much more interested in obtaining a warm human interaction than he was in playing some game of little interest to him concerning oranges. . . .
> Why exactly do children insist on engaging in what our value system tells us to be such self-defeating behavior? . . . Our best hunch is that they are fearful of [examiner and testing situation] and therefore behave in an adaptive manner having as its goal the termination of an unpleasant experience. [Zigler & Trickett, 1978, p. 793]

This anxiety-based behavior can be compounded if the child is Black and the examiner White. Watson (1972) suggests that the test situation can then come to represent to the Black child something of the tension-ridden atmosphere of the wider society, lowering the child's expectation of succeeding and hence his or her motivation to perform to his utmost.

Various studies have shown that when the motivational setting of the test situation is enhanced, intellectual performance is significantly improved (e.g., Bortner & Birch, 1971; Flynn & Anderson, 1976; Terrell, Taylor, & Terrell, 1978; Thomas et al., 1971; Zigler & Butterfield, 1968; Zigler, Abelson, & Seitz, 1974). (The Terrell, Taylor, and Terrell study [1978] is of particular interest because it reflects the different angle on traditional problems that Black psychologists can bring to issues of cultural pluralism. In showing that social reinforcement enhanced performance on the Wechsler Intelligence Scale for Children [WISC–R], they found that in a sample of second-grade lower-class Black children, receiving a "culturally relevant" reinforcer—"good job, blood," "nice job, little brother"—obtained significantly higher IQ scores than two other groups: a control group receiving no reinforcement and a group receiving the typical kind of verbal reinforcement—"good," "fine".)

These studies tend to use "optimizing" procedures as the way of influencing performance. Optimizing procedures are things the examiner does in the individual testing situation to try to elicit the child's best motivation to perform. They may consist of altering the item or subtest sequence of a standard test to enhance the child's interest and to try to prevent long sequences of failures or making a more liberal use of encouragement than is customary in the standard setting. These procedures do not involve a permissive atmosphere that sets few performance standards, however (Vosk, 1966). For example, the tester may refuse to accept a silly answer that a child might give just to finish the testing ordeal quickly. In such a situation the examiner might state the expectation for the child to try again and do better if it were felt that the child could do better. The examiner's encouraging firmness is a way of expressing respect for what the child can become. Some of Feuerstein's procedures clearly fall within this "optimizing" rubric, although he uses tests that are more likely to elicit examiner-child interaction and makes these interactions rather than the final score the primary basis of his evaluation. Optimizing procedures are effective with working- and lower-class children but seem to make no difference in the performance of middle-class children.

The effect of motivation and affect on intellectual performance is not confined to the test situation. Rosenthal and Jacobson's (1968) investigation of the effect of teacher attitude on pupil achievement in the classroom indicated that when teachers had been given (false) information about differential learning potential of their students, the pupils' achievement at the end of the year matched the information given the teachers. In this so-called "Pygmalion effect" the data seemed to support the hypothesis of teachers treating their students in accordance with their prior expectations of them. The Pygmalion effect involves identifiable components of interpersonal interaction. When people expect their students, clients, or whomever to do well, they "[1] create a warmer social-emotional mood around their 'special' students (climate); [2] give more feedback to these students about their performance (feedback); [3] teach more material and more difficult material to their special students (input); and [4] give their special students more opportunities to respond and question (output)" (Rosenthal, 1973, p. 60). There is enough evidence about the stressful nature of performance evaluation situations for Blacks and the existence of deleterious middle-class attitudes toward the poor to take the Pygmalion effect seriously. Zigler, Abelson, and Seitz put it this way:

> Once one recognizes that the performance deficit in disadvantaged children, instead of being invariably due to a cognitive deficit, may be due to a variety of motives, attitudes, general approaches to tasks, and even to psychological defenses that tend to be defeating in the school setting but are generally adaptive to the child's life, then one is ready to seriously entertain the proposition that disadvantaged children are brighter than their test scores indicate. [1974, p. 213][24]

Test Format and Motivation
In our discussion of the cultural biasing of tests we noted that children do not do well with material with which they are not familiar. We can extend these concerns into the section we are considering now to say that children are less motivated to perform well on test content or tasks that they find less interesting to them or less pertinent to them.

Kagan (1976) points out, for example, that in testing memory span, 3-year-olds were able to recall a sequence of only two or three items when these items were numbers to be orally reproduced. But when the task involved reaching to find a toy, the children could recall under which one of four or sometimes five different receptacles an item was placed.

In another study (Franklin & Fulani, 1979) Black high school drop-outs demonstrated high-level thinking strategies (clustering) in a free recall task when materials were included that drew on ethnically relevant themes such as types of dancing and different "soul foods" as well as themes familiar to both Black and White subjects (called "universal themes"). Under these circumstances the Black youths showed a considerably greater use of concept formation than did White adolescents. This was contrary to the level of performance usually anticipated for Black youngsters. Rather than concluding that the White students were cognitively deficient, the researchers suggested that the White students were stymied by their unfamiliarity with themes relevant to the Black culture. "The seemingly miscellaneous nature of many of the Black items for the White students apparently contributed to the overall poor performance in categorized recall" (Franklin & Fulani, 1979, p. 237). The Black students used categorizing strategies on both Black and universal items, suggesting that when the task was interesting, they applied their abilities across the board to all materials. The unfamiliarity of a significant portion of the content seemed to freeze the capabilities of the White youth.

It is of interest to note here that Franklin and Fulani's finding fits in with Rychlak's data on clustering, which we discussed earlier, which showed that Blacks tended to make use of a clustering strategy more than White subjects under certain conditions. This suggests again that when opportunities that are meaningful are presented, Black youngsters can respond in the active conceptual mode. It may be that in the Franklin and Fulani study, and in Boykin's work (1979) as well, there are RV effects that are accounting for at least some of the findings.

A hypothesis worth investigating here is that it was not only prior associations to the Black community that made for ease of clustering in the Franklin and Fulani study. Perhaps in addition to prior familiarity the Black subjects' positive affective assessments helped to trigger an active involvement with the word list and thus facilitated extending a sense of meaningfulness into the materials. Prior familiarity would not necessarily mean "liking" the materials. It is conceivable that Black persons striving to escape association with Black culture might have assessed the Black list negatively, resulting in detrimental effects on learning those words. For the White subjects the sense of "meaninglessness" they experienced with the Black cultural list may have been accompanied by at least mildly negative affective assessments that diminished their inclination to learn them. In Boykin's study Black children may have assessed varied stimulation formats positively and unvaried stimulation negatively, making for the better performance in the varied situation. Such a hypothesis would make fewer assumptions about the varied format being like the homes of the Black children, although the reason for liking that format could be similarity to the home. In any event, both studies seem to exemplify the idea that children learn better in situations they like.

In the interests of trying to find alternate ways of assessing intellectual and personality characteristics of children, Yando, Seitz, and Zigler (1979) used a variety of behavioral problem-solving tasks selected to minimize the predominance of academic achievement in the outcome. The tasks used were designed to investigate creativity, self-confidence, autonomy, curiosity, frustration threshold, and dependency. The sample consisted of Black and White second- and third-grade children, half of whom were economically advantaged and half of whom were disadvantaged. They found that the groups performed equally well across the variety of tasks; the group differences that did emerge reflected stylistic rather than capacity differences. They noted also that disadvantaged children were particularly able on tasks requiring creative thinking. They state: "The present results add to the argument that a better understanding of children in our society who are not middle-class White children can be gained only if we attempt to devise measures and define situations that allow their competencies to emerge" (1979, p. 107).[25]

Cole and Bruner (1971) concur in these assessments: "When we systematically study the situational determinants of performance, we are led to conclude that cultural differences reside more in differences in the situations to which different cultural groups apply their skills than to differences in the skills possessed by the groups in question" (p. 874). In other words, persons do not manifest cognitive skills in situations that are not meaningful to them, and they differ in the kinds of situations in which they bring forward the conceptual patterns they have developed. Or, as another set of cross-cultural researchers put it, differences across groups in the way persons interact with the world often represent "differences in the way basic cognitive processes are applied to particular contexts, rather than [the] presence or absence of the processes" (Segall et al., 1990, p. 184).

Motivation and Home Environment
The child's affective and motivational set is not only a function of the structure of the intellectual performance situation. As one might expect, the affective and motivational climate in the home also makes an important contribution. As DuBois suggested, " . . . sympathy and understanding; information, friendship and love" pay important dividends (Diggs, 1976, p. 390). For example, Slaughter and Epps (1987) review literature on low-income African-American pre-schoolers showing that the mothers of successful school achievers set clear and firm guidelines for behavior but also were "warm, accepting, and flexible enough to consider the child's viewpoint and to communicate this understanding" (p. 7).

In a similar vein, Scheinfeld's research (1983) seems to support the notion that "the mother's propensity to recognize the child's interests, motives and feeling states" has a definite effect on the child's achievement (p. 128). His study is particularly interesting because some of the descriptive dimensions he used to categorize parents' attitudes are relevant to central notions in this book. Selecting a group of Black families from a low-income Chicago neighborhood, he conducted rather extensive, open-ended interviews with thirty-three randomly selected families who had children in the local sixth grade. In a pilot study he had found that parents of children who were higher achievers in school wanted their children to learn to get satisfaction from active engagement with people and things in the environment. Scheinfeld called this an "appetitive aim." Parents in that pilot research who expressed a value that children should be more isolated from people and things around them—an "aversive aim"—had lower-achieving children. In the main study, Scheinfeld coded his interviews on nine different dimensions of parental attitudes; the data he presents are for the *mothers'* ideals for their *sons*. (He found that parents' discussion of the girls was less detailed and reliable, because "a considerable number of parents simply said, 'The same for girls as for boys,' or otherwise truncated the responses" (p. 130). In addition, since the number of father interviews was small, they were dropped from the analysis, although "father-absence" from the home was not significantly related to the mothers' interview scores or to the boys' school achievement as indexed here.)

Maternal attitudes as expressed on all of these dimensions (and on a factor score derived from the dimensions) were significantly correlated with the boys' school achievement. Among these dimensions was one Scheinfeld called being a "Purposeful Agent" and another called "Competence-Gaining Activity." The former expressed the parental value that the child should develop "an interest in something, a goal, a desire—some internal sense of direction that leads the child to focus on the environment in an active way" (p. 130). The latter dimension, Competence-Gaining Activity, is influenced by Robert White's (1963) notions. It expresses more than the wish that the child be competent; it is concerned with *how* the child is to become competent. "It involves, implicitly or explicitly, the development of *mind*; i.e., an increased understanding of the people and things one is dealing with and how to deal with them" (p. 131).

The results indicated that parents who tended not to espouse such values for their children turned out to be less effective in contributing to their children's academic progress. In the emphasis on purpose, competence, "mind", and activity (vs. passivity), Scheinfeld touches on issues that are obviously at the heart of the notion of psychological agency. His results suggest another concrete way in which parents bring this capacity to life in their children. In this regard we might note results indicating that parents of *both* low- and high-achieving children had a similar belief in the importance of schooling for their youngsters. The difference here seems to have been in the way children were encouraged to make use of their school and other life experiences. The fact that these were lower-class parents underscores again the idea that successful parents need not be highly literate, nor need the family setting necessarily be the standard nuclear one. As a further note, it may be that beneath their apparent belief in schooling the parents of the low-achieving children held a "folk theory" that did not support genuine engagement with the school experience (Ogbu, 1986).[26]

Competence Motivation and Intellectual Performance

The thrust of the argument in this chapter has been to portray intellectual functioning as being subject to a number of influences that can provide entry points for intervention. Much of what looks like a ceiling on the child's ability in fact represents the performer's failure to recognize how to use dormant skills in a given situation. One can capitalize on the child's naturally active mentality and tendency to learn things in the context of positive affective assessments by structuring the educational interaction appropriately. There is considerable room for enhancing the performance of the developing minority child, and the role of psychology should be that of enabling children to make the best use of their abilities. In this regard, let us turn to a group of recent articles in the psychological literature that argue for enhancing competence motivation by a particular kind of emphasis on the cognitive "conceptualizing" abilities of children as a way of bringing intellectual competence to life.

In the preface of their edited book, Sternberg and Kolligian (1990) note their "guiding premise that at all points in the life cycle it is one's construal of reality, rather than reality itself, that most accurately predicts self-concept, goals, academic performance, and overall mental health" (p. ix). This, of course, is fully compatible with the logical learning theory emphasis that behavior is guided by the active *conceptual* constructions that one makes about the situations one confronts rather than being simply driven by the "objective" nature of circumstances. Thus, an individual's conception of ability in a given situation—the sense of competence—is a critical determinant of performance. This is consistent with the logical learning theory emphasis on an "introspective" view, a consideration of how the actor's perspective lends meaning to a situation.

Many of the modern writers in this area who take this conceptual, or "cognitive," point of view note that the *kind* of conceptualization about the self that individuals tend to bring to intellectual tasks affects their performance. For one thing, this emphasis on the conceptual strategies that people use to negotiate academic situations is related to Sternberg's (1985) interest in "implicit theories" of intelligence. Such conceptions are guiding notions that people harbor about what intelligent behavior on intellectual tasks involves. Such notions vary with age and social status, and they influence motivation and behavior on academic tasks. Different researchers come at these implicit theories in different ways.

Learning versus Performance. The work of Carol Dweck (1986) and her colleagues on motivational processes that affect learning is an example that is relevant to our concerns here. Her work suggests that developing adaptive motivational patterns is essential to academic performance. She distinguishes between helpful and detrimental patterns:

> Adaptive motivational patterns are those that promote the establishment, maintenance, and attainment of personally challenging and personally valued achievement goals. Maladaptive patterns, then, are associated with a failure to establish reasonable, valued goals, to maintain effective striving toward those goals, or, ultimately, to attain valued goals that are potentially within one's reach. [p. 1040]

Research indicates that these motivational patterns can be identified in two kinds of achievement goals. "Learning goals" are reflected by persons who seek to increase their competence through understanding or mastering new things. "Performance goals" reflect individuals' attempts to get favorable judgments of their competence and avoid negative judgments. These goals stem from different implicit theories of intelligence that the child has learned. Children motivated by learning or "mastery-oriented" goals tend to have an *incremental* view of intelligence. They see ability as being malleable, and they use their efforts to *enhance* their ability, by learning from and overcoming their errors. In experimental situations when given the opportunity to choose tasks on which to perform, these children tend to prefer tasks that challenge them and foster learning. They take pride in the effort that they expend in grappling with a task.
Performance goals, on the other hand, are associated with an *entity* theory of intelligence. Such a view holds that intelligence is a fixed quantity and manifests itself in one's performance. In this view bright people do well; if one does not do well on a given task, it means that one is not so bright. These children use their effort to *demonstrate* their ability. Research shows that to ensure this result they tend either to select tasks that are easy for them or ones that are so difficult that failure is not a sign of low ability. Successful outcomes are more gratifying to these children when they have come with *little* effort, since that shows they have the "right stuff," so to speak. Further, ability is not related to motivational patterns. That is, children with high academic ability are just as likely to have a motivational orientation characterized by low confidence and avoidance of academic challenge (Dweck, 1986). Nicholls et al. (1989) report a similar distinction between an "ego-oriented" and a "task-oriented" approach to academic motivation. The former refers to children concerned with establishing their superiority over others in academic ability,

as opposed to children having the goal of increasing their understanding and mastery on the task. These orientations have not been found to be related to academic ability.

Clearly a learning-goal orientation is a preferred one in academic situations. Then, what is it in a child's history that contributes to the opposite style—motivation by performance goals? Dweck (1986) suggests that one source of such an orientation is the prevailing tendency on the part of educators to use "positive reward" strategies incorrectly as ways to motivate children's behavior. This theme is picked up by Boggiano and Katz (1991) in their review of an extensive body of research related to this point. In this view maladaptive achievement patterns, particularly the "helpless response pattern," characterized by "performance impairment, lowered motivation, lowered quality of hypothesis-testing strategies, and reduced pursuit of mastery," are fostered by "controlling" management styles by teachers (p. 36). Such teacher strategies—for example, using evaluation, terms like "should" or "ought to," and externally focused incentives—lead to an "extrinsic" motivational orientation in learners. In such an orientation, children become more interested in the reward or praise than in mastering the task. Since factors most salient to them are outside their control, they are more susceptible to helplessness deficits in the presence of a challenging task. By contrast, intrinsically motivated individuals "pursue activities for the pleasure inherent in the activity and for the satisfaction gained from mastery over task components" (Boggiano & Katz, 1991, p. 39). The person can see control as deriving from internal factors because the acquisition of skills stems from the person's self-initiated and self-regulated activity.

Teacher strategies that encourage a sense of autonomy in children's problem-solving activities and an intrinsic motivational development enhance a mastery orientation in children. (As noted earlier, cooperative learning methods would seem to fit into the classroom techniques that enhance the student's sense of personal involvement and control in the educational process.) Considerable research reflects the various detrimental effects of extrinsically oriented methods on the child's motivational style and approach to learning. However, paradoxically, research suggests that parents tend to prefer that teachers use controlling strategies because they seem to believe that tangible, externally based rewards are the most effective way to promote children's academic achievement (Boggiano & Katz, 1991). But, as the research suggests, this is likely to lead to children whose attention shifts from developing their own interests and intellectual skills to trying to understand how to please the adults who seem to have control over them. These results are consistent with the work of Deci and Ryan (1985), who note that external controls, including rewards, must be used very carefully in the classroom. Such strategies tend to limit intrinsically motivated performance and also lower the flexibility and creativity of children's functioning.[27]

Such research does not suggest that children should not be made aware of the relation between academic achievement and certain results in the real world (ideally, getting a good job, getting into college, etc.). What it does remind us of is that a child's active use of his or her conceptualizing (cognitive) ability is central to adaptive achievement behavior. As we noted earlier, the effectiveness of a person's behavior depends partly on his or her conception of the situation and the sense of competence s/he brings to the situation. These points suggest that more attention should be paid to helping children develop effective conceptualizing strategies.

When we look at the conceptual processes that seem to accompany achievement efforts, we find that both children and adults tend to make use of various kinds of cognitive strategies to mediate and evaluate their performance (Norem & Cantor, 1990). Frey and Ruble (1990) suggest that the form of these strategies can be expected to change over the course of the life span. Langer and Park (1990) in their "conceptual reconsideration" of the notion of "incompetence" argue that, within limits, rather than being a stable psychological attribute, incompetence is how a particular performance is perceived and in that sense is socially defined rather than simply being a stable characteristic of a person. They note different categories of incompetence, each with different origins and different implications for intervention. For example, in some circumstances what appears to be incompetent behavior might better be seen as "precompetent" functioning; that is, the individual may (as a function of age or background) not have yet learned certain skills or may still have a limited and rigid conception of possible ways of approaching a task.

So, rather than being allowed to conceive of themselves as simply incompetent on a task, it might be better for children to be seen by others and helped to see themselves as being precompetent with respect to adequate performance in a given arena. What would be called for in such a case in the academic setting is enriching the child's conceptual strategies for handling a problem (Feuerstein's IE approach, for example), that is, increasing the spontaneous active mentality—the child's "mindfulness"—and helping the child see the alternative ways of conceiving the situation (Langer & Park, 1990). (In Dweck's terms, perhaps "learning"-oriented children more easily see themselves as precompetent on challenging tasks and persevere. Children who are "performance"-oriented are perhaps prone to see themselves as incompetent on difficult tasks and so retreat from grappling with the challenge.) The "mindfulness" notion is consistent with another one of the basic themes of our humanistic approach. That is, competent functioning draws on the capacity to conceive alternatives, to see the dialectic nature of events.

Possible Selves. This latter point brings us back to the possible-selves notion discussed in Chapter 2, which draws on the cognitive (or in our terms, "conceptualizing") model in psychology. We can recall from our earlier discussion that the notion of possible selves refers to imagined possibilities about what an individual might become. They serve as a guide to an individual's action, helping the person to bring the desirable potentialities into being and avoiding the negative ones. In their recent writing, Markus and her colleagues (Markus, Cross, and Wurf, 1990) link this idea directly to intellectual competence. They argue that competence in a domain requires ability, but it also requires a *conceptualization* about one's ability in that domain and a sense of the importance of that area to one. That is, one not only has to have an ability, but one has to *know* that one has it and want to do something with it. Markus, Cross, and Wurf call such conceptual structures "self-schemas," which are made up of cognitive and affective components—the latter being affective assessments in our view. Presumably the various self-schemas are important functional aspects of the self-concept:

> With the development of a self-schema comes a base of knowledge about one's abilities. The individual who knows that she is "smart" or "good in school" will be enduringly sensitive and responsive to issues relevant to intelligence or school achievement. . . . It is the self-schema—the representation and articulation of a given ability—that allows an individual to use his abilities instrumentally and to have a sense of control over them. [Markus, Cross, & Wurf, 1990, p. 207]

Important to the self-schema are the possible selves that focus the individual's intentions on what s/he can become in the future. By practicing in imagination what it would be like to function in a particular targeted domain, one can work at narrowing the gap between the actual and the not-yet-realized potential. Research suggests that when people have access to stable conceptions of themselves—and thereby the potential of engaging in particular kinds of future actions—they are more likely to actually engage in those actions. Anecdotally, Markus, Cross, and Wurf (1990) noted that "Greg Louganis, the Olympic champion high diver, described how he envisions every feature of an upcoming dive, mentally rotating his body through time and space" (p. 210). Bringing a desired possible self into being leads to an energizing affective state. This supports conceptions and activities that stabilize competence in the area one is focused on. Such self-schemas bias the individual toward stimuli that enhance growth in that domain. (Consider again the little boy discussed in Chapter 2 who delightedly concentrates his interests around people and information that enhance his abilities in baseball.)

If we put some of the perspectives of the cognitive theorists into the context of the theme of this chapter, we would say that many African-American children, particularly of lower-class background, do not recognize that they have scholastic abilities. The intellectual thrust of these cognitive researchers is consistent with Feuerstein's idea that many poor and minority children have learned to restrict themselves to an intellectual style that does not let them deal adequately with school tasks. One aspect of bringing to life a sense of agency in the sphere of academic competence is enhancing the kinds of cognitive strategies that these children employ in intellectual situations. This includes helping them develop images of themselves that include the possibility of being academically capable. The emphasis on developing active imaginal structures about desired possibilities focuses the child on aspects of the future and lets the child see that s/he can exercise control over self-development. The general emphasis on active conceptualization is fully consistent with placing a value on an incremental theory of intelligence and a learning orientation toward achievement (Dweck, 1986). These emphases are all quite consistent with Feuerstein's emphasis on structural modification of the child's cognitive skills, thereby enhancing control over performance in the academic situation.

As Ogbu (1986) suggests (see note 10), the social situation of African Americans, which places a ceiling on achievement opportunities, works against Black children developing a possible self as "good student." Doing well in school seems to make relatively little difference for them in occupational status. Educators have the task of working against any underlying community "folk theory" that suggests to children that academic success is of no value (Ogbu & Matute-Bianchi, 1986). In addition, Dweck (1986) notes ways in which the assumption of a performance orientation toward achievement by bright girls hampered their learning. Though the research has not been done with African Americans, it seems likely that they are at a similar disadvantage. It is probable that much in society fosters a "fixed-ability" notion of intelligence among bright Black children with a consequent performance goal orientation that hampers their achievement striving. This is possibly augmented by teachers and parents who have, in some instances, a well-meaning but traditionalist extrinsic-reward orientation to pedagogy. Ogbu would insist on recognizing the degree to which the larger culture sets the tone for academic results. Comer's approach, which recognizes that an effective school must be a system that articulates with its community, begins to speak to some of Ogbu's concerns.

Conclusion

The theme of this chapter has been that intelligence involves the ability to learn how to bring forward patterns (actively) developed in one situation to adapt to new problem situations. This is consistent with a Kantian view of mental functioning and is seen as being distributed throughout the human race. To some extent individual differences in the efficiency and speed with which one learns are probably a function of genetic contributions, but the ability to extend prior patterns into new situations is very critically dependent on the quality of developmental experiences—the opportunity to apply one's abilities actively in a variety of situations and the opportunity to develop verbal mediation skills to help in the problem-solving process. When such developmental experiences have been lacking, there is strong evidence that deficient conceptualizing performance can be considerably improved, even in adolescence. For some children, special attention to cognitive functioning is what is necessary to set them on the right track toward intellectual competence. For others, what is of primary importance is giving consideration to the affective and motivational context in which intellectual learning takes place. All children would benefit in a classroom context in which issues of competitive or cooperative classroom structure are attended to and supportive involvement of parents is included. Often, when the child realizes that intellectual problem-solving situations involve interesting and pleasing challenges posed by supportive adults, s/he decides that the academic situation at hand is the kind of situation to engage actively.

What is called for is a recognition on the part of our educational system of the need to adapt to the pluralism of cognitive styles and cultural backgrounds that children bring. We must also recognize children's readiness to learn *something* when they come to school. Just because children are not learning what the teacher wants in inner-city classrooms does not mean that they are not actively conceptualizing the situation. Learning is going on. "Since the advent of behaviorism learning has been conceptualized as occurring only when there is an alteration of overt performance, which means that some experimentally preconceived criterion of performance has been attained by an animal or human being" (Rychlak, 1988, p. 325). It is the meaningful ordering of the situation (conceptualization) with or without some expected external performance that constitutes the learning. The children may well be learning not to learn what the teacher presents. Many minority children come to learn that in the average school situation it is hard to develop feelings of efficacy and fulfill the general effectance strivings that they bring. Negative assessments color the learning situation and are extended to more and more aspects of the school setting. As Steele (1992) puts it, they learn to "disidentify" with school. The child begins to learn to express competence strivings in nonacademic situations or in street-game pursuits. It is little wonder that minority youth show intelligence in the extraclassroom pursuits. They are using the same active (native) conceptualization processes that have been thwarted in the classroom! The burden is on society then—not on the children—to make the changes in techniques and attitudes that will help all children make competent and socially contributive use of the considerable skills they already possess.

Notes

1. Jensen's 1969 paper brought to a full boil the long-simmering controversy concerning the intellectual level of Black and lower-class children. Jensen stated that low-IQ children are genetically as well as environmentally handicapped and that genetic factors account for differences between ethnic and socioeconomic groups as well as within such groups. Jensen concluded that low-IQ children can be taught if one de-emphasizes learning through the use of abstract (Level II) abilities and instead emphasizes learning by rote methods. The idea of genetic inferiority of Blacks was not new with Jensen. However, there has been much debate centering specifically around this article, because it is one of the most sophisticated presentations of the argument of racial inferiority to date. For most social scientists the current resolution is toward emphasis on interaction between endowment and environment. Interesting recent commentary is provided by Lewontin, Rose, and Kamin, (1984); Loehlin, Lindzey, and Spuhler (1975); Mackenzie (1984); Modgil and Modgil, 1987; Ogbu (1986); Segall et al. (1990); and Weinberg (1989). For this writer, in addition to the weakness of the strong nativist point of view, the particular tragedy of the way this issue has been raised is that it deflects attention away from the many things that can be done to enhance the intellectual development of African Americans.

2. Rychlak's recent writing expands the importance of the *logos* notion (1990, 1991). To stress the centrality of the *logos* in determining learning and behavior is to emphasize the fundamental activity of "predication" in human mentality: "Predication involves the cognitive act of affirming, denying, or qualifying broader patterns of meaning in relation to narrower or targeted patterns of meaning" (Rychlak, 1991, p. 7). In learning something new we move from broad meanings that we have previously affirmed or that are generally known and we apply them to specific circumstances or objects that we are now considering. So, in describing his friend, Stella, to another person who does not know her, Jack might say "Stella is a kind person." He is taking the term *kindness*, which is relatively broad and inclusive and which refers to attributes he assumes his friend already understands, and he is applying it to a specific person (relatively unknown to his friend), Stella. In this case there is probably also a positive affective assessment associated with his comment. We should note that, consistent with our humanistic conceptions, Jack's predication of Stella is not "driven" by the facts of her behavior and thus the only possible view of her. Rather, it is a (basically arbitrary and therefore "freely willed") conception of her that reflects the meaning to Jack of his experience with her. Someone else who is equally familiar with her style might say of her in a disparaging tone, "Stella is weak."

3. Feuerstein's definition of intelligence centers on learning: "We define intelligence as the capacity of an individual to use *previously acquired experiences* to adjust to new situations. The two factors stressed in this definition are the capacity of the individual to be modified by learning and the ability of the individual to use whatever modification has occurred for future adjustments" (1979, p. 76).

4. This is not to deny that some children are indeed retarded, that is, actually limited in their intellectual ability. However, we shall maintain here that the proportion of children who are really hopelessly retarded is small, far smaller than the numbers of minority children now being labeled as retarded.

The term *retardation* has generally been applied to persons who score below the IQ range of 70–75. It is more appropriate to use the term *mental subnormality* for the broad group of persons falling into that range and then to distinguish between two kinds of mental subnormality (Sarason, 1966, and Zigler, 1968). One kind of subnormality involves a group of persons who on the average have mental scores that are extremely low—on the average about 35 (Zigler, 1968). This group comprises persons with known physiological defects, such as Down's syndrome, congenital rubella, and phenylketonuria (PKU), to name but a few. This group of persons, which is often identified as the "mentally defective," is a small percentage of the subnormal.

The far larger proportion of the subnormal is a group labeled the "sociocultural retarded." By and large they fall within the 50–70 IQ range and have no identifiable physiological basis for their retarded performance. It seems reasonable to assume that social environmental factors (poverty, lack of access to educational opportunity, etc.) make an important contribution to their subnormal performance. On the other hand, some see limited genetic endowment as making an important contribution to their subnormality. Even with such an assumption, education for some degree of usefulness in society would not be ruled out for these people. What is sometimes forgotten is that people can achieve scores in the retarded range for different reasons. The retarded are a quite heterogeneous group. Some may have limited genetic endowment, but a great many others score low for reasons of environmental history during their development. (For an updated conceptual overview of mental retardation, see Mercer, 1992.)

5. There is considerable disagreement in psychology about the appropriateness of the IQ conception of intelligence. One major alternative that has been very influential for some time is the developmental approach to cognition taken by Jean Piaget. Rather than taking the rather blindly empirical approach to functioning that characterizes the IQ orientation, he begins with a conception of the child as a being from birth trying to make sense of the world. In Piaget's conception the child's abilities to grapple with the world cognitively emerge over invariant developmental stages. Piagetian theory was derived by

careful, intensive observation of the ways that children of differing ages go about solving intellectual problems posed to them. Rather than trying to derive a measure of intelligence level from how many right or wrong answers to specific standardized questions a child gives, the score on a developmental test represents the degree to which a child shows that s/he has in his or her own way achieved mastery of a particular cognitive task.

One of the more familiar tasks is the mastering of "conservation," an aspect of that cognitive level achieved in middle childhood called "concrete operations." *Conservation* is the ability to recognize that a given quantity of a substance, let's say a liquid, remains the same even when transferred to a different-shaped container. Thus, two pints of water looks like more to the 5-year-old when it is in a tall, slender beaker than when it is in a short, wide beaker. The younger child does not conserve the quantity even when it is shifted from one container to the other right in front of him or her. Many of the original Piagetian tasks were designed to be presented in an individualized, clinical style allowing for different ways of getting to the answer. Though the Piagetian view is still highly regarded, criticisms of this perspective have begun to surface more and more (Gardner, 1985). Writers are questioning the universal applicability of these notions across cultural contexts (e.g., LCHC, 1982). We shall consider other ways of conceiving intelligence presently.

6. The perspectives that psychologists take on intelligence are not mandated by the "facts" but are interpretations—conceptualizations—of the data. These include the traditional theory that generates the idea of IQ. More and more, however, researchers have come to question the usefulness for any people— minority or otherwise—of the view that posits intelligence as primarily a global general ability (Garcia, 1981; Gardner, 1985; Kagan, 1989; Miller-Jones, 1989). Two prominent researchers, Howard Gardner (1985) and Robert Sternberg (1985), have recently proposed that intelligence as a human process is more complexly structured than the way it is traditionally presented.

Sternberg (1985) has proposed a "triarchic" theory of intelligence that posits three "subtheories" to characterize intelligent behavior. His "componential" subtheory tries to characterize the mental structures and mechanisms that underlie analytical functioning. The "experiential" subtheory addresses the individual's capacity to use insight to deal with novelty in situations confronted. The "contextual" subtheory refers to the individual's ability to excel in dealing practically with his or her particular environment. The latter presents the idea that to an important degree the sociocultural context in which the behavior occurs helps define what is intelligent behavior. Everyone has some capacity in each of these dimensions, but for various reasons people tend to emphasize one or another of them in their intellectual style. It is Sternberg's aim to be able to assess a person's standing within each of these areas in order to be able to help people maximize their abilities.

Gardner (1985) takes a more radical approach to the variegated structure that he sees in intellectual potential. He argues that "there is persuasive evidence for the existence of several *relatively autonomous* human intellectual competences" (p. 8). The distinctness and importance of these seven basic "frames of mind" are drawn from neuropsychological, psychometric, and cultural evidence. The IQ, venerated in Western culture, tends to depend heavily on logico-mathematical and linguisitic abilities, which are only *two* of Gardner's "human intelligences." Thus, in his view, people have different profiles of intellectual strength in which they are better at some than at others, though effective functioning in a variety of the intellectual areas is desirable. (So, for example, we expect a gifted musician to be able to read music, but we also expect that she will have a certain level of competence in other intellectual areas as well.) The patterning of a person's particular strengths, in Gardner's view, is a function not only of native talents but also of the way the cultural environment has provided opportunities for developing such potential.

Gardner does not shut out the idea that additional basic intellectual competences may be discovered, and he acknowledges that considerable empirical work remains to be done to fully substantiate his ideas. While we shall not be concerned with the details of Gardner's approach, his view helps us appreciate that, even with respect to the linguistic and logical abilities, relying on the IQ test alone is a risky procedure for assessing the potential for intellectual development in minority children. While the work of these two researchers is not ready for widespread application in clinical and educational settings, it seems to have promise for a more useful characterization of the potential of African-American and other minority children.

7. Rychlak feels that the term *cognition* has been too much associated in psychology with a passive characterization of thought processes. Such connotations can be seen in the term *mediation*, which is now popular with social learning theorists and cognitive behaviorists, researchers who while having rejected a strict environmental contingency approach still are basically mechanistic in persuasion. From their view, individualized cognitive or thinking processes are seen to mediate or filter an incoming stimulus so that a response to that stimulus may be relatively unique and perhaps unexpected. Thus, they agree that the response cannot always be accounted for by the present stimulus. But Rychlak argues that cognitive theorists describe mediation in a way that makes it clear that mediation occurs because psychological structures have been developed in the individual through his or her exposure to *previous* stimuli. Mediation, then, is only the process of applying previous input to the present situation. The person never in principle brings a unique response to the situation *de novo* as a truly dialectic option would propose (see Chapter 1). The humanistic approach allows for previous stimulation as well as the truly original response—what Rychlak (1979) calls a "telosponse" —to influence

behavior. Thus, modern cognitive approaches are still mechanistic in that they try to account for a person's behavior on this day in terms of yesterday's (efficient-cause) stimulation (see Rychlak, 1988, especially pp. 154 and 217–218; and Rychlak, 1991, especially p. 9, for further discussion of this idea). Granted that the terms must be used carefully, I shall use the terms *cognition* and *mediation* from time to time here but fully within the humanistic spirit.

8. Of course, such studies raise social and political questions. Scarr and Weinberg (1978) note that they are not advocating the adoption of Black children by White families. They took the opportunity available to investigate the effects of a different environment on a sample of children. Both of these studies demonstrate the broad potential for competent intellectual development that Black children share with all human beings. The assumption here seems to involve the desirability of trying to see what could enhance IQ-test performance and possibly thereby school achievement in Black children. These studies do not argue against changing the system so that Black families can help their own children. In fact, it suggests that allowing Black families the opportunities to help their children will do some good; these children are able to profit from changed environments. It is also important to note that from the perspective of recent approaches to intelligence the superior IQ scores of the transracial adoptees is not necessarily a pure advantage. In Sternberg's (1985) terms, while the transracial adoptees may have excelled in componential, or analytical, aspects of intellectual functioning, we do not know about their creative (experiential) or practical (contextual) intellectual potential. We also do not know about the quality of their social competences, which may be even more strained for the transracial adoptees, who will still be seen as "Black" by this race-conscious society no matter who their adoptive parents were. Moore (1985) also addresses some cautions in a study of this sort.

9. No one, including highly educated adults, uses abstract modes of thought all the time. In fact, abstract thought probably makes up a relatively small percentage of waking thought. Some writers even question whether abstract thought is always the best way of thinking (Rohwer, 1980). It is different from more concrete modes, but given a particular social circumstance the concrete mode may be more adaptive. The trick is knowing when it is appropriate to institute an abstract mode. Kagan (1976) argues that this kind of sophistication is governed by the presence of "executive processes" in our cognitive arsenal. Executive processes are superordinate cognitive processes that appear later in a child's development and that control the use of the more discrete cognitive functions such as memory, perception, generation of hypotheses, and the like. He lists a number of such executive processes. Among these are appreciating the level of complexity of a problem and adjusting one's effort accordingly, flexibility of approach—the ability to shift from ineffective solution hypotheses and search for better ones, and searching for ways of organizing a problem

situation so as to deal with it better. In some cases the strategies that an older child will use are ones that younger children already know but do not use. The younger child's "deficit" is in the activation of or use of the knowledge. Executive functions allow the older child to use what s/he already has.

As an example, Kagan analyzes Piaget's stage of concrete operations in this way. In this stage younger children are presumably more influenced in their reasoning than are older ones by the more superficial and apparent aspects of a situation. Thus, pouring a pint of water from a low, round dish into a tall, slender beaker influences the child to think there is more water in the beaker. Kagan suggests that coming to understand, as older children do, that the quantity of liquid remains identical, does involve cognitive maturation. But perhaps what changes is the executive process of understanding the nature of the problem and the nature of the question being asked. So, for example, a 5-year-old, when asked a class-inclusion question related to this stage such as "There are ten red beads and four green beads here. Are there more red beads or more beads?" responds typically, "More red beads." It may be that he understands the question to be: "Are there more red beads or green beads?" It doesn't occur to him that the examiner would ask the question that he does. Important to rising above an apparently concrete response is the growing ability of the child to understand what adults are after.

> As with answers on intelligence tests and the replies of schizophrenics, very few answers to examiners' questions are irrational, although they are scored as incorrect if they are not the answer intended by the questioner. What happens in cognitive growth, in large measure, is coming to appreciate the mind of the questioner and knowing at once the [meaning] implicated by the question. [Kagan, 1976, p. 28].

The particular point for our consideration is that children achieve executive processes at different speeds depending partly on the history of their experiences with the environment. These are probably associated with social class to some degree and possibly with ethnic group differences. Kagan cites research to suggest that exposure to varied stimulation enhances the development of these processes. It may well be that inner-city children do use such processes in contexts outside of the school. We shall have more to say about this idea later in this chapter and in the next one.

10. Ogbu (1985, 1986; Ogbu & Matute-Bianchi, 1986) suggests there is another social background influence on the educational progress of Black children. He suggests that achievement for any group in society is to an important degree a function of that group's perceptions of the opportunity structure based on its history of experiences with that structure. These experiences lead to a collection of beliefs about "status mobility", about what one has to do to get ahead. He calls these community beliefs a "folk theory of success" (Ogbu & Matute-Bianchi, 1986).

Writing particularly about people of color in the United States, he distinguishes "caste" minorities from "immigrant" minorities. The former are descendants of those brought to America through conquest, slavery, or colonization, e.g., African Americans and Mexican Americans. Immigrant minorities come to America more or less voluntarily to find better opportunities, with a clear grasp on their ethnic heritage that they initially, at least, work to sustain intact as much as they can. One thinks particularly here of various Asian groups who have come to America. The "immigrant minorities" have made use of high academic achievement as a route to success. However, according to Ogbu, caste minorities have discovered that academic success does not lead to occupational advancement because their status seems to be dependent more on society's racist social manipulations of the opportunity structure than by caste members' academic capabilities and achievements. Such attitudes in the community and the family filter down to the children, who may then become actively oppositional to traditional educational involvement. They become a part of a community subculture that develops competencies in nonacademic pursuits and alternate ways of surviving. Ogbu (1986) classifies these responses to oppression by African Americans in a variety of ways. To the observer, the caste minority's attitude toward education may appear to reflect lesser academic ability. However, Ogbu argues that socially oppressed, lower-caste groups all over the world produce lower IQ-test results. This suggests that the low academic performance of American Blacks is motivational and in fact represents the purposeful channeling of energies away from formal schooling and into what seem like more productive avenues, considering the socially constricted opportunities for self-development.

Ogbu has been criticized for, among other things, failing to make necessary social class distinctions within the ethnic groups under consideration and failing to note the complexity of "ecological" issues that affect Blacks (Bronfenbrenner, 1985; Trueba, 1986). While some of the criticisms of Ogbu's work seem apt, he does provide an interesting set of concepts for characterizing the broader social and historical context in which Blacks have struggled to express their aspirations and the strain this has placed on the families' efforts to promote their children's educational development.

11. In one test example, subjects are asked to find which pair of pictures out of a set of three pictures of objects belong together. Two answers are possible for different reasons. One picture is of a simple wood chair with one leg missing; the second is of a plain wood table with a leg missing; the third is a picture of an intact, overstuffed arm chair. The relational subject with a more global style is presumably more likely to pick the chairs as belonging together. The analytic subject with a "parts-specific" style is more likely to pick the chair

and table as going together—because each has a leg missing (see Cohen's appendices, 1969, for detailed comparisons from the measures used in research in this area). There is considerable overlap among tests of cognitive style (Rice, 1979), and research has not gotten a clear handle on these issues. Yet it is interesting that personality theorists have observed for some time that people tend to adapt to the world by emphasizing thinking and ideation on the one hand or by responding to a situation in terms of the emotions aroused about it on the other. Thorough personality description is much more complicated than this, of course. However, such styles, which we might loosely call thinking and feeling types, adopting terms used by Carl Jung, seem to correspond loosely with Cohen's analytic and relational types.

12. Cohen (1969) notes further that the studies from her laboratory raise questions about the rationale for "culture-free" tests. Such tests presumably reduce the culture-bound characteristics of assessment procedures by reducing the verbal and informational aspects of such tests that are felt to carry much of the cultural loading. Cohen suggests, however, that the resultant "culture-free" tests require the use of an analytic conceptual style. She notes that such tests, in the effort to emphasize reasoning skill in the nonverbal sphere, are composed of items requiring a parts-specific, stimulus-centered mode of abstraction. Bright students who achieve higher levels of abstraction through relational means are particularly penalized by these higher-level analytic tests. Cohen found that on concrete tasks bright relational and bright analytic students do equally well. It is only when high-level analytic abstraction is involved that the former pupils are no longer competitive. Thus, not only the mode of conceptual organization but also the level of abstraction is a factor in performance. It is in this sense that nonverbal tests have not freed themselves from their culture-bound features. (We shall note another example of this presently.) The possibility of a culture-free test seems impossible in principle.

13. There were four types of tasks and five tasks in each type, making twenty tasks in all. Presenting all five tasks of one type to the subjects and going on to all five of those of the next type, and so on, represented an unvaried format. Mixing the four types of tasks across the twenty presentations represented a varied format.

14. The argument will continue to rage among behavioral scientists and policy planners as to whether it is better to focus on changing the larger social and institutional context that creates poverty as opposed to emphasizing programs for rehabilitating those most heavily affected by poverty. To some the latter position seems to blame the victims by implying their inadequacies to cope. These need not be mutually exclusive alternatives, however. We recognize that human behavior must be viewed from a multicausal perspective. In order to enable the "truly disadvantaged" to channel their competence

intentions in the most productive directions, certain "formal cause" factors, that is, larger economic and political realities, have to be changed (Wilson, 1987). However, at the same time, help can be given in the form of educational and occupational skill training to learn to negotiate the system and eventually to participate in changing it. Thus, for example, one needs programs that provide job training for people and *along with these* a properly managed economic system in which jobs are available for the trainees. Assuming the necessity of concomitant social system changes, this section of the chapter focuses further on the modifiability of individual children's intellectual potential.

15. As pointed out in note 7, the humanist is not comfortable with the term *mediation*. While adopting Feuerstein's terminology here, we shall reinterpret that concept within our Kantian perspective.

16. It is of interest to note how these ideas regarding the importance to cognitive development of mediated learning fit with certain psychoanalytic ideas. Psychoanalysis places particular importance on the effects of the mother-child relationship on personality development. In one sense what Feuerstein postulates reflects Ekstein and Motto's (1969) notion that development proceeds from "learning for love to love of learning." In other words, from early on the child begins to learn in order to gain the love and acceptance of the adult, who is acting as mediator, and then the child grows to love the active pursuit of learning on his or her own.

Other data bear on this. Blatt, Wild, and Ritzler (1975) cite data showing that the quality and speed of early cognitive development depend to an important degree on the quality of the early mother-child relationship. For example, more rapid development of conceptions about the physical object world occurred where mothers had a more accepting relationship toward their babies and expressed more availability to their child. This supports the idea that the quality of the interpersonal mediation experience between parent and child affects the quality of cognitive development.

Some even more dramatic results have been reported recently using a method developed by Silverman (1983) for investigating unconscious ideation called "subliminal psychodynamic activation." In this method a number of carefully controlled experimental studies have shown that one can influence behavior by showing subjects particular messages subliminally. This involves showing subjects messages at speeds faster than they can register them consciously. All that subjects are aware of seeing as they look into the machine showing them the messages are flashes of light. However, there is considerable experimental evidence from Silverman's research that subjects respond in predictable ways to the presented messages. The theory is that this is so because the messages register at subconscious levels. (See the excellent recent review of this work by Weinberger and Hardaway [1990].) The studies that are particularly relevant to our concerns, and that have produced the most robust results, have to do with the use of the stimulus "Mommy and I are one." This stimulus is designed to evoke fantasies of being united in a "symbiotic-like" relationship with a loving and all-providing mother, fantasies that derive from the normal psychological situation in the early months of life, according to psychoanalytic theory (Mahler, 1974).

Silverman's research has shown that the "Mommy and I are one" stimulus has had an adaptation-enhancing effect on various kinds of behavior, presumably because residues of these yearnings remain in the unconscious fantasy of all people. It is as if stimulating the symbiotic fantasy decreases an individual's customary levels of anxiety, making better psychological functioning more possible. In one study using this paradigm, Parker (1978) found that subliminal presentations of the symbiotic stimulus over a several-week period to a group of students were associated with better grades in a college course. This was in comparison to a control group in the class who received a neutral stimulus. Even more relevant to our discussion in this chapter, Bryant-Tuckett (1981) found that the symbiotic stimulus was associated with improved school performance (reading and math scores) for emotionally disturbed adolescents with learning problems. Almost all of these subjects were Black and Hispanic. Thus, from a different vantage point, these studies seem to bear on the quality of the mediation experience. The results suggest that stimulating the fantasy of closeness with a maternal (mediator) figure enhances learning. We have only theoretical speculations as to the exact way this works, but for one thing it does indicate that while cognitive and affective factors can be differentiated in principle, they are very much related in actual learning situations. We shall have more to say about this later when we discuss affective assessment as a factor in learning.

17. The individually tailored administration is of course an expensive process. Feuerstein and his coworkers have devised group procedures for administering the LPAD (Feuerstein, 1979, chap. 5). In those procedures typically two examiners, possibly with an assistant or two, work with a group in a modification of the "test-train-test" situation. The test materials provide the gradual modification in the test stimuli from simple to more complex that assess the child's ability to be modified. Some children are able to show learning potential in the group situation where the individual interpersonal feedback from the examiner is minimal. Such children are good candidates for being placed in school settings. Other children who have more serious problems in cognitive ability and lowered motivation often need the support of one-to-one interaction with an examiner. The group procedure can be something of a screening device to find those who do not need close personal attention in the training process. This implies that the children able to profit from the group administration are more developmentally advanced than children unable to profit. To go back to the Scrofani et al. (1973) study, this may be something like the difference between the category B and C children. Perhaps the category C children, although not retarded, need more individually tailored assessments of their learning ability. The group procedures are used when, for example, people want to know about the learning capacities of homogeneous groups of children in order to make educational decisions.

18. The thrust of IE is very similar in some ways to the perspective of the Russian psychologist L. Vygotsky (1978). Vygotsky's point of view is becoming more popular with American cognitive psychologists who emphasize the importance of the socio-cultural context in learning (Belmont, 1989; LCHC, 1982; Rogoff & Morelli, 1989). The most obvious connection between Vygotsky and Feuerstein centers around Vygotsky's notion of a "zone of proximal development" (ZPD). This is an index of a child's learning potential, and it is different in principle from the IQ approach to intellectual functioning. Central to Vigotsky's conception is that learning is very much an interpersonal enterprise and thus cannot be separated from social and cultural activities (Rogoff & Morelli, 1989). The ZPD is to an important degree for Vygotsky, therefore, an interpersonal phenomenon. It is established through the examiner's creatively interacting with the child ("participative conceptualization," in our terms) so as to determine a higher level of potential function for the child. A particular child's ZPD is ascertained by the use of both "static" and "dynamic" testing procedures. A static (standard IQ) test assesses a child's current level of independent functioning on a given kind of task. A dynamic test assesses what a child can do when "strategic"—that is, carefully designed assistance—is given by the examiner. The difference between the levels of performance achieved by the two methods is the ZPD. "The zone of proximal development defines those functions that have not yet matured but are in the process of maturation, functions that will mature tomorrow but are currently in an embryonic state" (Vigotsky, 1978, p. 86). (That "embryonic" quality seems particularly clear with Scrofani's category B children.)

A zone derived from a particular set of operations does not pertain to all cognitive domains (e.g., verbal reasoning) but is relevant to that range of activities (e.g., abstracting ability) in which it was established. Having established a zone, the adult intervenor's aim is to work with the child so as to increase the level at which the child can function independently in that domain. The central mechanism describing how this is achieved is the "transfer of responsibility." Through interacting with the child in the ZPD, the educator, who initially takes responsibility for finding and providing cues for handling more difficult tasks, helps the child to be able to use those cues independently, thus transferring responsibility for solving the more difficult problem from intervenor to child. While the terminology is somewhat different and the emphasis on the *social* aspects of cognition is not as explicit in

Feuerstein's approach, essential similarities between Feuerstein and Vigotsky are quite apparent here.

19. Steele (1992) feels that the data are rather clear as to how programs such as these work:

> Research involving hundreds of programs and schools points to the same conclusion: [B]lack achievement is consistently linked to conditions of schooling that reduce racial vulnerability. These include relatively harmonious race relations among students; a commitment by teachers and schools to seeing minority-group members achieve; the instructional goal that students at all levels of preparation achieve; desegregation at the classroom as well as the school level; and a de-emphasis on ability tracking. [pp. 76–77]

20. The test items are in a multiple-choice format; the subject's task is to choose the one alternative for each item that represents the "correct definition as Black people use the words and expressions." Among examples that Williams gives are the following (1975, p. 124):

1. Black Draught
    (a) Winter's cold wind
    (b) Laxative
    (c) Black soldier
    (d) Dark beer
2. Blood
    (a) tire
    (b) worthless
    (c) an injured person
    (d) a brother of color

21. Mercer's work emerged in the atmosphere of a 1970 suit by a group of Black children in the San Francisco School District. In this action, *Larry P. v. Wilson Riles,* the plaintiffs were seeking to stop the use of IQ tests as the primary basis for placement in classes for the mentally retarded. They noted that a disproportionate number of minority children were being placed in these classes on the basis of IQ tests. After two temporary injunctions in the mid-1970s, Judge Robert Peckham in 1979 banned the use of such tests for Black pupils for placement in special educational classes, and he required the use of nondiscriminatory assessment techniques for such purposes. This decision was upheld on appeal in 1982 by the Ninth Circuit Court in San Francisco, and a settlement was finally reached with the State in 1986. (For a good, succinct review of the history of this case see Figueroa and Sassenrath [1989]).

22. Whatever its merits, Mercer (1992) acknowledges that the cultural pluralism model on which the SOMPA is based has not received wide acceptance in the psychological communuty (e.g., Poteat, Wuensch, & Gregg, 1988; Reschly, 1982; Sandoval, 1985). The WISC-R has recently been revised—the Wechsler Intelligence Scale for Children-Third Edition (WISC-III)—and the indications are that the SOMPA will not be marketed for use with that revision. With regard to some of the criticisms, Reschly (1982), for example, presents data to indicate that the norms used for developing the Sociocultural Scales, based on California samples, may very well not be applicable to minority samples in other regions across the country. In addition, he and other critics argue that Mercer's dismissal of standard achievement measures for cross-cultural comparisons overlooks the fact that *some* "real-world" index of a child's learning ability has to be used to assess the validity of a new measure such as the SOMPA. Reschly acknowledges Mercer's belief that the proper criterion for the ELP is how well it predicts children's ability to learn new material, not its correlation with prior learning as measured by an achievement test.

Evidence that would speak to this issue would be data from longitudinal research. Figueroa and Sassenrath (1989) report just such a study on a subset of the original 1972 normative sample for the SOMPA. Of the original group of 2100 children these researchers were able to test 1184 youngsters ten years later. (Although the normative sample had consisted of equal numbers of Black, Latino, and Anglo children, in this follow-up group there were somewhat more Anglos than Latinos or African Americans.) Achievement levels were assessed by a standard achievement test and by the students' grade point average (GPA).

For our purposes we can focus on just a few of the many results reported. First, the WISC-R scores were moderately good predictors of later achievement, as has been reported elsewhere (Poteat, Wuensch, & Gregg, 1988). Further, IQ scores correlated with achievement test scores better than they did with GPA. Using the ELP, for Blacks who fell in the lowest 25% on an index made up of two of the Sociocultural Scales, the Verbal IQ-ELP predicted their school achievement better than did their standard WISC Verbal IQ (an SFL index, in effect). A similar trend, not statistically significant, was found in the other two ethnic groups in this quartile, as well. The Verbal IQ-ELP index did not predict as well as the standard Verbal IQ for those in the upper 75% on this sociocultural index. Although the results with the lowest quartile group were modest, it is consistent with Mercer's rationale: Those who least met the presumed cultural norms for the standard IQ test had their learning potential predicted somewhat better by an alteration of the standard IQ.

Figueroa and Sassenrath go on to note: "SOMPA's Estimated Learning Potential comes from a long-standing historical tradition of 'adjusting' IQ tests when these are used with minority populations. . . . [and it] is, perhaps, the most elaborate attempt in this enterprise" (1989, p. 17). The fact, however, that for most of the sample the Verbal IQ-ELP was a less sensitive predictor of achievement than was Verbal IQ alone supports those who argue against using ELP to "declassify" children who have been labeled as retarded, that is, take these children out of special classes for the mildly retarded. These critics say that the SOMPA is not yet suitable for use in educational settings (Reschly, 1982). Sassenroth and Figueroa also suggest some psychometric issues that possibly limit the contribution that ELP could make in prediction.

However, it should be noted that the criterion in the Figueroa and Sassenrath study was how well the pupils were handling the *traditional* academic experience ten years later. One of Mercer's primary aims is to identify those pupils whose academic potential may be masked by the standard IQ score. Having identified children whose ELP is higher than their standard IQ score, the implication is not to deny such children special educational intervention by simply "dumping" them back into the regular classroom. Children in the Figueroa and Sassenrath study whose ELP index was higher than their WISC–R score in 1972 might have done better if given an Instrumental Enrichment experience or had extensive exposure to cooperative learning methods or been in something like the Yale–New Haven Prevention Project—or had been given a specially tailored combination of these and similar strategies.

The critique of Mercer's work occurs in the context of the broader ongoing debate as to what constitutes test bias. Though more empirical work probably needs to be done to strengthen the SOMPA as an assessment device, Mercer's approach to test bias draws attention to the cultural factors that may well impact on a child's test and classroom performance. Indeed, noting the modest, even if stable, correlations between IQ and academic performance, Figueroa and Sassenrath comment that in California, at least,

> particularly with respect to Black children, school psychologists and special education personnel may have to learn to do diagnostic assessment without IQ. The technology may be more theoretical . . . than psychometric, but it is there. As in any other radical shift in paradigm or job description, however, the challenge will be in the human factor. [1989, p. 18]

That is, the challenge will be for professionals to change the mental frames that guide their conceptions of minority children's intellectual potential and look for new ways to help children develop their skills. Recently Mercer has become persuaded that the general rejection of traditional tests by some Black psychologists is valid and that the presently used tests (such as the WISC) should be abandoned (personal communication, Jane R. Mercer, May 14, 1994). However, I believe if one understands their limitations a standard test included with other assessment procedures can make a contribution to understanding a child's performance ablities.

23. In a large number of carefully controlled experiments, Rychlak and his coworkers (Rychlak & Ingwell, 1977) have shown that the reinforcement value (RV)—the subject's reliable rating of liking or disliking the sound—of so-called "nonsense syllables" (consonant-vowel-consonant trigrams such as *SAJ, COV, BIK*, etc.) influences the learning of such syllables. Subjects tended on the average to learn more readily the trigrams they had independently rated as liking than those they did not like. (Similar results have been obtained when the stimulus material was words, abstract designs, and names to faces.) He and his coworkers have shown that RV defined in this way is independent of the association value (AV) of the trigrams in two ways. It is independent of the number of familiar associations for the subject aroused by the trigram, and it is independent of the general familiarity of the syllable in terms of the number of people who recognize the trigram as being wordlike. The particular RV choices an individual makes are probably related to his or her personal history. In this sense they are mediated by experience. However, Rychlak posits that the propensity for making affective assessments of some sort is native to the individual.

24. Zigler, Abelson, and Seitz (1974), as well as other researchers we have discussed in this chapter, feel that the IQ as the prime index of problem-solving ability is greatly overemphasized in our society. Zigler and Trickett (1978) feel that we should be educating and assessing for "social competence"—how well an individual uses his or her abilities to live a productive life. We all know from our own experience of very "bright" persons unable to do this. Social competence, though not easily defined, is seen as comprising a number of facets. In addition to the three factors of cognition, achievement, and motivation, some index of a child's physical health and well-being should be included and some index of how well a child is meeting societal expectancies. Seen from a different perspective, this is very much like what Mercer (1979) attempted to accomplish in the SOMPA.

25. The idea that lower-class Black children are able to express intellectual ability when freed from the constraints of the standard IQ situation is illustrated in an interesting study by Gerstein, Brodzinsky, and Reiskind (1976). They administered the Rorschach ink blot test to children being seen for emotional and learning disorders in their outpatient clinic. The Rorschach stimuli are ambiguous in shape and force the subject to structure the material visually in answering the question "What does this (blot) look like?" (A similar job of imaginative structuring is involved in the game we have all played of finding shapes of real things—animals, ships, faces—in clouds passing overhead.) The Rorschach is used to assess the unconscious strivings and thought styles that make up personality structure. One way of scoring responses yields an approximate measure of how mature a child's perceptual style is. It is one

way of getting at formal cognitive ability and is similar to the developmental approaches to intellectual assessment.

Low-IQ Black children were found to be developmentally more mature in cognitive ability with this measure than were low-IQ White children. These authors took their results to mean that "standard IQ tests may not adequately tap the cognitive capacity of some Black children and that use of the Rorschach from a developmental-structural perspective may provide a useful adjunctive measure of intelligence that would more realistically assess children's cognitive competence" (Gerstein, Brodzinsky, & Reiskind, 1976, p. 760).

26. Scheinfeld gives proper attention to the dangers of making strong causal statements about correlational data. That is, from a methodological viewpoint the high correlations here do not *necessarily* mean that parents' attitudes influenced their boys' achievement, though that is highly plausible. To the contrary, it *may* be that the low-achieving boys' poor performance could have influenced their parents' attitudes toward *them*. It is also worthy of note that only the boys in the upper 25% of the achievement range in this sample were doing rather well by national standards. The next highest 25% had a reading level that was almost a year and a half behind the national norm and a math test average that was eight months behind. Parental attitudes certainly do not account for all that is involved in children's school achievement. Thus, we cannot rest responsibility solely on parents for their children's receptiveness to schooling. It is still society's responsibility to create the social circumstances that support parents' making the best contributions they can.

27. We should note that these critiques of extrinsic reward are not in contradiction to the earlier discussion of Rosenthal's work on appropriate teacher strategies to influence children's achievement. As Dweck points out (1986), Rosenthal was advocating an "incremental" theory of intelligence in which the emphasis was centered around presenting challenging material to children in order to develop their abilities.

4

The Black Speaker: Cherishing Pluralism

This story bout three lil pigs. One day, the lil pigs went out to play. They made lil house. One made a dog house an one made a hog house. One made a pen. . . .

[The wolf] came to the big house. And the wolf say, "Let me in!" And [the pig] say, "No, no, no, my shinny shin shin!" He huff, and he puff, and he tough, and he rough, but he couldn't knock the house down. . . .

And ol wolf say, "I'm a jump down you chimney!" And that ol pig put some water on the fire till when you could jump in it, and the lil pig had cook [some] greens. Yeah, he fool him! He jump in the hot water, and the pig, he had greens and wolf! Greens and wolf! [Houston, 1973, p. 46]

The above is an excerpt from an 11-year-old southern Black child's oral rendition of the familiar story of the "Three Little Pigs." It is told in a vernacular form of the English language called the Black English Vernacular (BEV), which this boy probably speaks much of the time.[1] Many lower- and working-class Black Americans frequently use this style of speech or variants of it. It could even be said that such speech represents one distinctly observable way in which some Black Americans are different from many White Americans, and this in turn reflects some of the differences in cultural history between Euro- and African-American peoples. To some extent the consistent and unique features in the language of some African Americans provide evidence of the existence of cultural pluralism in America. The language spoken by Black Americans not only can be distinguished from the so-called standard American English spoken by many White Americans, but Black Americans themselves speak the language in various forms. In other words,

Blacks as a group represent a pluralistic speech community. They differ, for example, by region and by social class in terms of the styles of speech they use. Whereas the speech of some Blacks is indistinguishable from that of White people living in the same region, other Blacks, particularly in the northern United States, are clearly identifiable as being African-American by their speech patterns. Since differences are so frequently viewed with hostility in America, it is important to understand what some of the implications of using "nonstandard" speech styles are for Black Americans.

Black English: What Kind of Dialect?

The fact that there is considerable overlap between Black and White individuals in speech styles raises the question of just how different Black and White speech variations really are. After all, these speech styles are forms of the English language spoken by people living in the same nation. Actually there is difference of opinion among linguists as to how similar or how different "Black English" (BE) is with respect to the other dialects of the English language spoken in the United States. "The term *dialect* refers, strictly speaking, to differences between kinds of language which are differences of vocabulary and grammar as well as pronunciation" (Trudgill, 1974, p. 17). From this perspective, because "standard" English differs lexically and grammatically from other forms of English, it can be considered to be a dialect, too. The reason we think of it as being standard is that it is "that variety of English which is usually used in print, and which is normally taught in schools and to non-native speakers learning the language. It is also the variety which is normally spoken by educated people and used in news broadcasts and other similar situations" (ibid.). Nonstandard forms of English do not differ from standard English along the dimension of formal versus colloquial. Standard English has colloquial variants as well as formal ones. Nor does more "bad language" appear in nonstandard dialects; "standard English speakers swear as much as others" (ibid.).

The definition of *standard English* is what could be called a "stipulated" definition rather than an operational or factual definition arrived at by observation. In other words, the definition of standard English is an arbitrary one that a group of people (educated speakers of English in this case) agree is an acceptable range of styles for speaking the English language. It is not standard in the sense of being purer or better than nonstandard versions in any absolute or factual sense. It follows then that *nonstandard* English refers to those dialects that are not the (arbitrary) standard of English. Nonstandard means different from standard—not worse than standard. What used to be called Nonstandard Negro English, which in its purest form can be referred to as the Black English Vernacular, is not sloppy English. It is another dialect form of the English language (Labov & Harris, 1986).[2]

Some linguists argue that the separate history of African-American people has made a unique contribution to Black language forms. William Stewart (1970) is one of a number of scholars who advance the idea that the distinctiveness of BE stems from its African origins. This view proposes that BE derives from a creolized English that historically drew partly on West African pidgin forms and thus is different from other English dialects. (When a linguist refers to a "creole" language he refers to a dialect that derives from a "pidgin" language—a simplified form of a complex base language by which nonspeakers of the language communicate with the speakers of the language and other nonspeakers with whom they do not share a common language. Over the years a language may develop from the pidginized language, a creole, which becomes the native tongue for the group in question. The creole may become as complex grammatically as an unpidginized language over time.) Although BE has lexical and structural similarities to the dialects used by both uneducated and educated Whites, in the vernacular form in particular there are syntactical differences between British-derived dialects and those dialects deriving from speakers of West African tongues. What needs to be noted, Stewart suggests, is that BE is a language form governed by rules, that it has a specific historical derivation, and that it has been passed on within a subculture through legitimate processes of socialization. Above all, it is not just careless or ungrammatical English, as it is so often regarded, but it has separate origins in Africa for some of its roots and a grammar and syntax of its own as well.

Other social scientists disagree with the claim that BE is a dialect separate and distinct from those spoken by other Americans. They argue that Black speech patterns have resulted from a blending with other nonstandard English speech patterns. For these writers, whatever African linguistic influences there may have been, and these are not always granted, they have not survived sufficiently to make for any real distinctiveness of the Black dialect (see Trudgill [1974], pp. 73–76, for a brief summary of these opposing views). Rather than using a single dialect of their own, it is argued, Blacks speak a variety of forms of the American language, the dialect used depending on the region of the country they come from and the social situation in which they find themselves (Williamson, 1975). In both the past and the present, so this argument goes, there has been and still is much borrowing of speech patterns cross-ethnically. Thus, Blacks and Whites actually speak variants of a common American language rather than, to any significant degree, distinctly separate ethnic dialects. Based on this interpretation BE is more accurately viewed as any language form that Black Americans speak according to where they live and what social class they belong to.

While it is still possible to debate the origins of Black speech forms, a number of social scientists find it meaningful to identify BE, particularly in its vernacular form, as a distinct linguistic entity, which, while sharing characteristics with other American English language forms, also has a "core of linguistic features . . . which are found in none of the American or other language systems . . . [and] which . . . are sufficient to make most Black speakers ethnically identifiable" (Taylor, 1975, p. 35). Other linguists seem to agree (e.g., Hall & Freedle, 1975; Labov, 1972; Labov & Harris, 1986; Trudgill, 1974).

Among the frequently cited features of BEV that differ from standard Anglo English are its phonological characteristics (pronunciation) and its grammar. Although many features of BEV are shared by speakers of British-derived nonstandard styles, some linguists argue that these forms occur with greater frequency among Black speakers or that there are fairly exclusive variants in BEV. For example while the deletion of *r* in such words as *car* and *cart* is common in many English dialects, the deletion of *r* after initial consonants—as, for example, *p'otect* = *protect*, *f'om* = *from*—may be restricted to BEV (Trudgill, 1974). In respect to differences in grammar, a frequently cited form in BE is the use of "invariant be" to indicate "habitual aspect"—referring to an event that is repeated but that is not continuous, as in, "Sometimes she be late," which in standard English would be, "Sometimes she's late." Trudgill (1974) suggests that this is strongly reminiscent of creole language: "In Caribbean creoles, verb aspect—the distribution of an event through time (whether it is repeated, continuous, completed, and so on)—tends to be of greater importance than tense—the actual location of an event in time" (p. 72).

Varieties of Black English

It is typical to equate all BE with the vernacular form. Since the varied and distinct speech forms of Black people are identified exclusively with the vernacular, there is a tendency for the public to regard all deviations from standard Anglo English by Black people as lower class and uneducated. This view stems from an ignorance of the variety and complexity of BE forms and the wide range in the verbal repertoires of African Americans (Hoover, 1978; Wright, 1975).

As Claudia Kernan notes in her ethnographic study of speech within a west coast African-American community, even among vernacular speakers, "as one moves from household to household and indeed within households one is impressed by the amount of individual variation among speakers with regard to the use of non-standard variants" (1971, p. 36). Moreover, many Blacks who are relatively better educated and/or maintain contacts outside as well as within the Black community speak what could be called a standard BE (Taylor, 1975), which is like standard Anglo English in certain characteristics and different in others. The speaker of standard BE, unlike the vernacular speaker, uses standard English syntax; however, in vocabulary, phonetics, and intonation his or her speech contains features similar in varying degrees to vernacular Black English.

> The speaker of standard Black English will tend to weaken final consonants, simplify consonant cluster, and exhibit general *l*-lessness and *r*-lessness; where the weakening of final consonants affects grammar, however, as in lack of possessive *s* or loss of *l* in the future, or the *ed* past tense, standard Black English speakers will retain the ending. [Hoover, 1978, p. 69]

In other words, BE is far from a monolithic entity.

Sociolinguistic Issues

The use of particular BE forms has social as well as linguistic significance. To give just one illustration of this, the speech employed by Black Americans affects the way they are allowed to function as workers in the White society. How a person speaks also has meaning within the Black community. Standard BE, for example, tends to be seen as good English when it is used in appropriate settings and when discussing certain topics. These "good" speakers are distinguished from what some would call the "ultra proper-talking" Black speakers who characteristically strain to adopt the Anglo dialect in phonetics and vocabulary. (Of course, there are many Black speakers whose standard English style has practically no detectable vernacular features. This is characteristic of their normal, unaffected speech.) In the presence of Black listeners, they may be ridiculed for their attempts to make an impression by creating social distance from their Black audience (Hoover, 1978; Kernan, 1971). Sometimes, of course, a Black speaker will switch into such "proper" talk as a way of teasing or "sounding on" a friend about, for example, his unusually neat attire, as in, "My goodness, Mr. Jones, don't you look elegant today!"

For Black speakers, then, whether they use a nonstandard vernacular form of the language, standard BE, or any one of the other linguistic categories that a Black speaker may fall into, there are social consequences resulting from how they speak. Two of these consequences are, first, how language functions in establishing social relationships, and, second, what role language plays in conveying information about the speaker (Trudgill, 1974). To say that people in a national society speak different dialects of the national language, or even different languages, is a statement of linguistic fact. But the fact itself has the potential for eliciting value dispositions or affective assessments about the speaker.

People use information they get from others' language styles to make social judgments about them. Cataloguing people by their speech is a way of expressing either positive or negative social preference. On the one hand, people can feel pleased and intrigued to hear the different variations of language in their society and feel that they live in a richer cultural milieu on account of it. On the other hand, such differences from established speech can elicit negative affective assessments. The habitual use of one or another speech form can open or close doors to privileged society, as Shaw pointed out so masterfully in "Pygmalion." This phenomenon has operated with telling effect not only in societies in which the British influence is strong but in every culture. Speaking of the relationship between the French and their colonies, Fanon (1967) wrote:

> The colonized is elevated above his jungle status in proportion to his adoption of the mother country's cultural standards. He becomes whiter as he renounces his blackness, his jungle. . . .
> The Negro of the Antilles will be proportionately whiter—that is, he will come closer to being a real human being—in direct ratio to his mastery of the French language. [p. 18]
>
> Yes, I must take great pains with my speech, because I shall be more or less judged by it. With great contempt they will say of me, "He doesn't even know how to speak French." [p. 20]

This tendency to stigmatize the speech of conquered people has probably characterized most historical instances of one society imposing its culture on another. As with many other aspects of their differences from Euro-Americans, many African Americans have reacted to the stigma attached to BE by feeling a considerable ambivalance toward the way they speak. Even though Black speech styles derive from a legitimate linguistic form, many Black people feel that BE represents "incorrect" and deviant speech rather than different and legitimate speech (Taylor, 1975). The negative evaluations of their speech styles illustrate the difficulties created for Black Americans in various aspects of their lives as they try to sustain positive racial self-concepts. Thus, speech style becomes one of the dimensions on which Blacks may experience conflict about themselves.

Simply put, speaking involves using a certain syntax; but it also entails considerably more: "It means above all to assume a culture" (Fanon, 1967, p. 17). People who assume the culture that is involved in Black speech styles not only communicate with words but also use the gestures, vocal intonations, postural adjustments, and facial expressions that go along with the words. These accompanying features provide a context for and augment the meaning of the communication. In addition to the formal grammatical distinctions from textbook English, Black speech styles are rich in the structured use of nonverbal communications to convey specific social meanings. Majors (1991) reviews literature on "kinesic" or "body language" styles among African Americans. Included are a discussion of various hand gestures, facial expressions, and styles of standing and walking that men and women use to communicate various messages. He has identified a particular set of such expressive behaviors among some African-American males "in their demeanor, gestures, clothing, hairstyles, walk, stances, and handshakes . . ." that he calls "Coolpose":

> To cope with the "invisibility" and frustration resulting from racism and discrimination, many African Americans . . . use such nonverbal behaviors to accentuate the self, appear urbane, suave and charming . . . and also . . . to keep whites off guard about one's intentions, to exercise power and control, [and to] express pride, dignity and respect for themselves and their race. . . . [p. 270]

Thus, a people's speech and communication style are ways they express and develop their conceptualizations of the world.[3] On an individual level, when the person achieves the capacity for language in the course of psychological development, s/he has a powerful way of shaping a sense of self by applying tentative labels to aspects of self and using these labels and a myriad of other ideas to guide action in the world. Language is a powerful tool for framing and carrying out intentions. Language gives an important boost to the process of developing a sense of identity. In logical learning theory terms, it is a way of giving expression to developing conceptualizations and a way of extending meaning about oneself—in one's cultural context as well as in wider arenas of activity. Trying to do away with children's cultural language variations—as opposed to simply teaching them additional language styles—tends to stifle the way they are extending the meaning of themselves. It is like saying this (ethnic) part of yourself expressed through your language is not acceptable. By using the language—assuming the culture—of a particular group, an individual can also solidify his or her group membership, which is an aspect of identity. However, having to confront a dominant norm in this society that says that the only respectable language style is a narrowly defined Anglo-American one, some African Americans are confronted with a challenge to one aspect of how they define their cultural identity.

Black English: Difference or Deficit?

Some psychologists and educators have assumed that failure to use language in the standard grammatical way implies the presence of cognitive deficits in the user. According to this traditional view, speakers of BE are speaking English *badly* rather than simply speaking it *differently*. The difference is considered negative because it is interpreted as evidence of deficiencies in the overall language development of speakers of BE. It follows, according to this assessment, that a change of language habits is required before intellectual skills can be taught to users of BE. Remedial measures are essential because, it is maintained, speakers of BE are linguistically and hence cognitively deficient.

A trenchant critique of this position is made by William Labov in a classic essay entitled "The Logic of Nonstandard English" (included in his 1972 volume), in which he counters in several ways the notion that BEV puts limits on the intellectual development of the speaker. Differences in grammatical expression of an idea, that is, in the "superficial structure" of a language, says Labov, do not imply differences in meaning or "deep structure" of a language form. There is, according to Labov, more than just *one* grammatical way to express a concept. When a person learns a grammatical form, s/he uses it to communicate in a particular cultural context, but it is not necessarily the best way or the only logical way of expressing an idea. The French are not illogical for expressing the negative in a double form (*ne . . . pas*); by the same token neither is the speaker of BE illogical when s/he uses the double negative. Thus, the sentence "Don't nobody here have any common sense," communicates the speaker's scorn quite clearly, and the addition of a triple negative—"Don't nobody here have *no* common sense"—makes it even more emphatic, without any loss of logic.

An incident from a language session will further illustrate the point:

Student: (*reading from an autobiographical essay*): This lady didn't have no sense.

Teacher: What would be a standard English alternate for this sentence?

Student: She didn't have any sense. But not this lady: *she didn't have no sense.* [Gumperz & Hernandez-Chavez, 1972, p. 102]

This student had an understanding of differences in superficial structure but still had a preferred way of expressing the deep structure—meaning. Whether to use or not to use such forms is governed by arbitrary conventions that have linguistic and historical derivations. Speakers of the regularized BEV dialect are therefore not conceptually weak because they use conventions that are different from "standard" English usage.

Because learning standard grammatical form is necessary for functioning in a complex technological society, Labov thinks it is important for inner-city children to acquire some of the language characteristics that are often associated with middle-class speakers. This will allow the children to communicate adequately in more formal public settings when they need to, but it does *not* mean that middle-class speech patterns are necessarily better ones than their own. There are, in fact, qualities of middle-class speech, such as verbosity and circumlocution, that are nonfunctional for clear expression. To illustrate this point, Labov compares the transcript of a lower-class inner-city adolescent's discussion of his conception of God with that of a college-educated, middle-class Black speaker's presentation of his views on witchcraft. In the course of the discussion with the inner-city resident, the interviewer (JL) poses a hypothetical question:

> *JL*: No, I was jus' sayin' jus' suppose there is a God, would he be White or Black?
>
> *Larry*: . . . He'd be White, man.
>
> *JL*: Why?
>
> *Larry*: Why? I'll tell you why. Cause the average Whitey out here got everything, you dig? And the nigger ain't got shit, y'know? Y 'unnerstan'? So—um—for in order for *that* to happen, you know it ain't no Black God that's doin' that bullshit. [Labov, 1972, p. 217]

Though ungrammatical by standard English canons, the lower-class speaker's discussion is direct and shows sophisticated logic in grappling with the problem.

The middle-class speaker (Charles M.), interviewed by CR, presents a contrast:

> *CR*: Do you know of anything that someone can do, to have someone who has passed on visit him in a dream?
>
> *Charles*: Well, I even heard my parents say that there is such a thing as something in dreams, some things like that, and sometimes dreams do come true. . . . I don't particularly believe in that, I don't think it's true. I do feel, though, that there is such a thing as—ah—witchcraft. I do feel that in certain cultures there is such a thing as witchcraft, or some sort of *science* of witchcraft. . . . I do believe that there is such a thing that a person can put himself in a state of *mind* (Mhm), or that—er—something could be given to them to intoxicate them in a certain—to a certain frame of mind—that—could actually be considered witchcraft. [Labov, 1972, p. 218]

This middle-class speaker is vague, rambling, and repetitive. Familiar stylistic devices in the latter's speech mark him as an educated person but, in fact, he does not necessarily think through the problem presented him any more effectively or deal better with abstractions than does the speaker of BEV.

The comparison of the two speakers illustrates the need for more careful study of linguistic behaviors in the speaker's cultural context before making generalizations about the relative merits of language employed. In fact, Labov found in his studies that a majority of people used well-formed, complete sentences in their everyday speech, but, surprisingly, working-class speakers did this more frequently than middle-class ones. The precision of expression associated with technical and scientific writing is not so frequently found among middle-class speakers whose "accumulating flow of words buries rather than strikes the target. It is this verbosity which is most easily taught and most easily learned, so that words take the place of thoughts, and nothing can be found behind them" (Labov, 1972, p. 222). Actually the explicitness attributed to middle-class forms is often a function of the test situation and limited to it. Indeed, contrary to what might be expected, Labov found that not all aspects of the middle-class style are optimal for communication. He suggests that ideally what we should do is discover the features of middle-class speaking style that actually help us express ideas clearly and separate them from those that do not. This will then let us say which standard grammatical rules should be taught to young nonstandard speakers.

Black English in the Classroom

The implication of the Stewart and the Labov work is that BE has legitimate status as a language form. It is a position that is consistent with a pluralistic view of American society. But such a perspective does not resolve some central educational and political issues. The problem is that children from lower- and working-class backgrounds who speak BE are usually not skilled in the language of instruction used in the schools. However, they are skilled and efficient speakers of the language they bring to the school.[4] Granted the linguistic legitimacy of BE, what should the educational system's attitude toward this speech be? Attempts to deal with this question have generated much controversy in the Black community.

Everyone recognizes that the language function is a central one for human beings. The command of language skills is essential for people to be able to achieve the full potential of their humanity. Some Black parents and educators relate this fact directly to its presumed effect on academic achievement, feeling that language styles used by some Black children are a detriment to their educational progress. They emphasize that children must learn to speak "properly" to succeed in American society. These critics argue that giving legitimacy to BE speech styles is just another way that White society has of keeping Black children from attaining competence in the standard language forms necessary for achieving in America. They emphasize the fact that if the children don't master standard speech forms, they will not be able to read, will consequently fall behind or drop out of school, and will be unfit to be hired in good jobs. In short, these critics continue, the promotion of BE in the classroom is just another racist ploy for keeping Blacks out of competition for the good things in this society.

Acting on another aspect of this issue, a group of Black parents brought suit in 1979 against the public school system of Ann Arbor, Michigan, for what they alleged were the teachers' pejorative attitudes toward the children's BE and the school's attempt to obliterate their ways of speaking. The purpose of the suit was to have their children's speech styles recognized as legitimate ways of talking rather than being interpreted as indicators of subnormal academic ability. Although the parents very much wanted their children to learn to read, write, and speak the standard English taught in school, they did not want this learning to be carried out at the expense of the children's self-image and the language spoken by their own people. A sympathetic court ordered the school system to accommodate the children's BE while it taught them the standard curriculum. (See a brief review of this case in Smitherman [1991], pp. 249–251.)

Those who would celebrate the kind of diversity represented by Black speech patterns have to deal with the possibility that the use of BE forms may actually interfere with learning classroom English. This possibility has arisen not only with respect to the linguistic format of educational tests but, perhaps even more important, also with regard to learning to read.

Black English Vernacular and Learning to Read

Some linguists have suggested that children who speak nonstandard dialects may have difficulties learning to read in school systems that provide instruction in standard English. This may be an explanation for an important part of the low reading achievement found in inner-city schools. Most of the research on this issue of dialect effect on reading is directed at questions of phonological or grammatical interference (Hall & Guthrie, 1979a; Simons, 1976). Phonological interference would arise presumably because certain written words are pronounced differently by Black dialect speakers than by standard English speakers:

> The results of these differences are words that have a pronunciation unique to Black dialect, e.g., "ness" for "nest," "ress" for "rest," and "han" for "hand." In addition, there are words whose Black dialect pronunciation results in a different word, e.g.; "tess" for "test," "men" for "mend," "walk" for "walked," "coal" for "cold," etc. The latter result in an extra set of homophones for Black dialect speakers. These differences in pronunciation presumably could interfere with the acquisition of word recognition skills even though the precise way they interfere has never been spelled out. [Simons, 1976, p. 61]

However, in a variety of studies using different kinds of designs, Simons notes that Black dialect phonology was not found to hamper the reading of standard English passages by Black elementary school children.

Regarding grammatical interference, it has been advanced that the mismatch between the Black child's syntax and standard English texts would produce difficulty in reading passages. For example, the form of standard sentences would not be equivalent in the Black dialect. The sentence "He will be working" might be interpreted by the Black dialect speaker as habitual action because of the meaning in dialect of the word *be*. Or the reader might fail to interpret *ed* as a past tense marker because it is not pronounced in BEV. But on testing this hypothesis, Marwit and Neumann (1974) found that presentation of passages of the reading comprehension section of the California Reading Test in standard or dialect form did not change the comprehension of them by Black children. However, according to Simons, there is evidence that the failure to pronounce "ed" in singly presented sentences can often lead to failure to recognize the past tense. Thus, in the sentence "When I passed by, I read the posters," the word *read* is pronounced in the present tense because the "ed" is dropped from the pronunciation of "passed" by the BEV speaker (Labov, 1972). In contrast with single sentences presented out of context, passages composed of several sentences probably provide sufficient cues to the intended meaning and thus offset the possibility of interference due to differences in pronunciation.[5]

The Sociolinguistic Hypothesis

All in all, the research does not support the idea that structural linguistic interference is the source of reading problems of inner-city children (Hall & Guthrie, 1979a). What seem to be a more fruitful source of hypotheses are sociolinguistic factors in the reading instruction or talking situation. For example, educators have reported that many Black children in inner-city schools do not speak fluently in the classroom in relating to educational materials. Rather than using this as an indication of a lack of verbal abilities in the child, such a fact may be attributable to the way the social situation is structured. Labov (1972) notes that much of the sampling of the verbal facility of inner-city children has failed to take into account how much the response of the subjects was affected by the circumstances and surroundings they were in when tested. The result is that the testing situation has contaminated the results. Attacking the notion that the inner-city child's language capacity can be adequately measured in the typical testing situation, Labov cites the meager output of speech often secured from the children by researchers. However, when the language assessment situation is changed from a "vertical" one (in terms of the structure of the status relationship between the examiner and child) to a "horizontal" one in which the social situation is more egalitarian, the verbal abilities of these children are abundantly demonstrated. For example, in a testing situation a research associate of Labov's was unable to get Black lower-class children to say much to him even though he was from

Harlem, spoke BEV, and was from a working-class background. But when he altered the situation by getting down on the floor with his young subjects, encouraging them to speak about taboo topics, and bringing them party snacks to eat, their reticence changed into a verbal flood.

The work of other scholars supports the idea that a speaker's fluency changes according to the situation (Cazden, 1970; Hall & Nagy, 1987; Houston, 1971, 1973). Houston suggests that lower-class Black children actually have two speech "registers" available to them. There is one register that they use in the formal classroom situation and perhaps other situations with unfamiliar adults. In this mode their speech is likely to be sparse and rather inhibited. The other register is the one they use at home and in surroundings that they experience as being friendly and socially gratifying. Speech in this latter context, which may be filled with BE forms for children who have them available, is likely to have a great deal of what Houston calls "flair"; that is, it shows originality and liveliness while at the same time being quite communicative of meaning and logic. The speech of children using the more informal register definitely "makes sense." One can see all of these things in the "Three Little Pigs" excerpt.

The operation of flair can be seen in responses to storytelling tasks that Houston has presented to Black and White children. Middle-class and White children tend to report details more accurately than poor Black children, but the latter children as a group insert more original elements into their stories without losing the overall theme of the story. If the task had been considered a test of memory, the Black children would have failed. But if it were an index of active conceptualizing ability, they came off quite well.

These children heard and understood the directions clearly, but they took "the given instructions as a base line upon which to demonstrate individual imagination and creativity" (Houston, 1973, p. 48). They responded differently in other ways, too.

> They generally interacted with other children far more often than did the other groups. . . . They frequently attempted to help their partners, prompting them nearly twice as often as the other groups did. They also made greater use of nonverbal behavior, and their gestures often involved the whole body, unlike the more confined gestures of the White children. [p. 48]

They tended to do this whether their partner was White or Black. The picture that Houston draws is one that sounds very much like Boykin's (1979) concept of "verve" discussed in Chapter 3. Again there is the implication that the standard school setting is not geared to helping lower-class children capitalize educationally on what they bring to the learning task.

But the disjointedness between child and school may have to do even more with the dynamics of teacher-pupil relationships. With respect to the question of reading failure in particular, some sociolinguists have suggested that there are additional social consequences of speaking BE. One thing about "nonstandard" speech is that it signals that the speaker is different. Research has been reported that indicates that teachers from inner-city schools are sensitive to deviations from what they consider correct English and they sometimes respond negatively in their evaluations of it (Williams, 1970). Some teachers assume on hearing a child speak Black English that s/he will be a low achiever. Teachers have been observed to structure the seating arrangements in their classrooms to distance themselves from these kinds of students, ensuring that the children, who probably need more attention, in fact get less of the teacher's time (Gouldner & Strong, 1978). While this is a rather straightforward expression of bias, culture clash in the schoolroom is often more subtle than this, though just as telling. Teachers and students may "turn off" to one another to the detriment of the learning process, because of the different ways they use language even when they *are* trying to talk to one another. This may stem partly from the fact that people from different cultural groups use language and accompanying nonverbal cues of gesture, intonation, and facial expression differently to express themselves. People may misunderstand each other because of these differences.

While dialect interference may not be involved when a child is reading to himself or herself, it may occur when the teacher is giving instructions in reading (Simons, 1976). For a listener to understand a speaker, the listener must understand the speaker's specific intent in the context of that particular social situation. Calling this the "situated meaning" of an utterance, Gumperz suggests that the parties in the situation must share an interpretive framework regarding the meaning of the cues emitted, both linguistic and nonverbal (Gumperz, 1974; Gumperz & Herasimchuk, 1972). But differences in cultural background can lead to differences in the ways people understand and interpret the cues in a communication context and may lead to a communication breakdown.

One study that illustrates some of the potential pitfalls in communication describes teachers and their pupils working together on reading exercises (Piestrup, 1973). In one instance a teacher is trying without success to get a pupil to pronounce the word *they* in the standard fashion, instead of as "dey." Analyzing this interaction, Simons (1976) hypothesizes that the teacher's failure to change the student's pronunciation is at least partially due to the fact that (1) the participants do not share background information about standard and dialect pronunciation, and (2) the teacher uses only indirect cues to communicate her disapproval of the child's pronunciation (e.g., by getting him to start the sentence over repeatedly and by pointing to the incorrectly pronounced word without being specific as to what is wrong). Commenting on the interaction, Simons notes:

Indirectness is an effective strategy when there is a great deal of shared background knowledge. In the case of Black children there is probably less shared background knowledge than teachers assume, because, in addition to adult-child differences, there are cultural differences in communicative background experiences. . . . Also in everyday conversation where there is a great deal of indirectness when someone does not understand the meaning of an indirect speech act s/he can ask the speaker to explain in a more direct way. In the tapes under study this does not happen very often. It may be that it is not encouraged or accepted in school discourse. If this is the case, then the child is put at a further disadvantage in interpreting indirectness than s/he would be in everyday conversation because s/he cannot use his/her normal repair strategies when s/he does not understand something. [p. 25]

Of course such an inappropriate communication strategy is not the only factor affecting the success of reading instruction. There are many other conditions in the students' lives, such as peer group relations and verbal play styles, that are significant. However, it is agreed that one of the most critical factors is the teacher's belief in the child's ability to learn. What the teacher's attitudes are and how the teacher communicates with the child are particularly important.

Homegrown Language in the Classroom

When we see the differences in language style that some African-American children bring to school, there is a tendency to view them as having been disadvantaged by their backgrounds. Of course, for some children impoverished backgrounds in which contact with supportive adults is lacking do hamper their readiness to profit from schooling. But children from stable working-class communities are at a disadvantage only to the extent that those in the school system are limited in their understanding of these communities and remain inflexible in their approach to these children. The sociolinguistic perspective makes useful contributions to knowledge in this area.

We cannot discuss in detail here the various psychological and educational factors impacting on literacy. However, we can continue to look at one aspect of this issue: the effects on learning of language mismatches between teachers and pupils. As a way of analyzing classroom interaction, the anthropologist Shirley Heath made observations in classrooms and homes of Black children and their middle-class teachers in a small city in the southeast United states. The section of the city that these Black families lived in she called Trackton (e.g., Heath, 1982).[6]

A former elementary school teacher herself, Heath noted that traditionally classroom teachers often try to elicit answers from their pupils about the facts of a given topic by a series of questions. The problem is that this well-meaning interaction often contrasts with the way the children of that community are talked to by the adults who take care of them. "In Trackton, children did not hold high positions as information-givers or question-answerers, especially in response to questions for which adults already knew the answer" (Heath, 1982, p. 116). Rather than ask a child, "What color is that crayon?", a Trackton adult might say, "Isn't that [color] like your shirt?", thereby making a comparison to something the child is already familiar with. These children, being unused to queries for specific labels or features, were not responsive to the teachers' typical questions—"What is the name of the boy in this story?", "What color is his dog?", et cetera. One exasperated third-grade boy in response to such questions about the elements of a story the group had just read finally said, "Ain't nobody can talk about things being about theirselves" (Heath, 1982, p. 105). That is, [he and his] people can't talk about things in and of themselves—outside of the meaningful context in which they are embedded.

The middle-class teachers did not use such methods with hostile intent. They were interacting with their pupils the way they did with their own children at home—trying to get them to comprehend and produce language about the world with specificity and precise elaboration. Teachers thought of this as the standard way for all children to develop their cognitive and linguistic abilities: "In their interactions with Black children in the classroom, teachers invariably assumed they would respond to language routines and uses of language in building knowledge, skill and dispositions just as other children did" (Heath, 1982, p. 114). This was as natural a style for the teachers as the alternative style was for the residents of Trackton. But it did not fit the children's expectations, because, as one resident said to Heath, "We don't talk to our chil'un like you folks do; we don' ask 'em 'bout colors, names, 'n things" [Heath, 1982, p. 117]. (Recall from Chapter 3 that Golden et al. [1971] discovered much the same thing in their work with middle- and lower-class children.)

Show, Don't Tell. The point, of course, is that this does not mean that these Black children lived in an impoverished verbal environment. They were surrounded by the rich verbal traditions of their community. Commenting in a later article, Heath (1989) noted about many such Black families that, like all stable families, they socialized their children "so that they [would] learn the forms and functions of language that [would] help them achieve some self-identity as group members and also meet the needs of everyday interactions" (p. 367). Speaking particularly about Black communities outside of inner-city settings, Heath goes on to note that as a result of the language interaction in such environments,

> children take adult roles, issue commands and counterstatements, and win arguments by negotiating nuances of meaning verbally and nonver-

bally. Adults goad children into taking several roles and learning to respond quickly to shifts in mood, expectations, and degrees of jest. Adults expect children *to show* what they know rather than *to tell* what they know. . . . [Heath, 1989, p. 369]

Heath (1982) gives a delightful illustration of the ability that even young children have as they learn to negotiate their way through different cultural experiences. She described Lem, a 4-year-old whose first institutional experience away from home was in a middle-class cooperative nursery school. Lem's participation in school was characterized mostly by a silent and watchful attitude. He preferred manipulative toys and tended to become restless when adults presented him with talk-centered activities. Traveling home in the car after his first nineteen days of nursery school, Lem saw a fire truck. He came out with the following sequence of questions:

What color dat truck?
What dat truck?
What color dat truck?
What color dat coat?
What color dat car?
What color . . . [p. 120]

Heath was caught off guard by this patter of questions until Lem's laughter led her to realize that he was playing a "teacher" game with her. He had all along been quietly internalizing the style of teacher-initiated talk he was being exposed to and had now become able to use it in his banter with Heath. In school he continued to have little interest in tasks that centered around words and talking about things, but he was enthusiastic and very adept compared to the other children in activities that involved learning how to *do* things.

In this episode we can see that Lem had developed a capacity for "awareness" as we discussed that term in Chapter 2. He demonstrated that he *could* play the traditional verbal school games that he was being exposed to, but he was deciding that he *wouldn't* play them. His positive affective assessments were directed toward other ways of coming at the world based on his experiences in his community.[7] Of course, this was shortly going to pose problems for him and other Trackton children as they progressed into the primary grades. More and more their later schooling was going to center around the kinds of verbal interplay that the nursery and kindergarten teachers were trying to engage them in. Such eventual classroom exercises were going to emphasize the use of questions that required students to take objects out of their context and name their attributes—"What color is the queen's crown?", "Where is the policeman's badge?"—or the use of questions that had an interrogative form but had a directive intent—"Would you like to pick up your coat?" = "Pick up your coat" (Heath, 1982, pp. 121–123). (The indirect command style in the latter example is similar to what Simons [1976] described.) Learning to use language in Trackton had not prepared children for important characteristics of talk in their classrooms. Their consequent unresponsiveness to it was going to affect their educational careers.

Of course, the fact that people in Trackton used language differently did not mean they didn't value literacy. The need for mastery of written language by community members was fully recognized as important in dealing with various kinds of bureaucratic and commercial matters as well as for functioning in school and church. However, in communities such as Trackton it is not necessarily expected that everyone in the community, though literate, would be equally effective in all communicative skills. Thus, some members become prized for their skills in helping individuals negotiate interpersonal issues within the community. Others might be relied on for their abilities in organizing records, telling the community's history, or planning events. Heath goes on to suggest that as a result of their participation in their communities, African-American and other minority children develop wide-ranging language skills that could, in fact, be useful to all youngsters: "[sharp] listening and observational skills, quick recognition of nuanced roles, rapid-fire dialogue, hard-driving argumentation, succinct recapitulation of an event, striking metaphors, and comparative analyses based on unexpected analogies . . ." (p. 370). (The reader might want to compare this description to Larry's justification of why God must be Black, p. 145).

However, mainstream schools tend to deny that such abilities make any major contribution to literacy in the broadest sense. Instead they "tend to deal with literacy skills as [mechanical] abilities that separate out and manipulate discrete elements of a written text, such as spelling, vocabulary, grammar, topic sentences, and outlines, apart from the meaning and interpretation of a text as a whole" (Heath, 1989, p. 370). So, "classrooms' narrow focus on only certain kinds of literate behaviors typically discourages Black children's positive transfer of adaptability, keen interpretive talents, and group collaboration to either academic life or employment" (p. 372). Such children are likely to come into the classroom speaking with "flair", as Houston termed it. However, there is the tendency to label them as being basically incompetent rather than as having skills that need to be augmented.

The Assets of Language Difference. In her discussion of language differences in Black communities, Heath notes the implication of such differences for the changing needs of the American workplace. Her observations extend a point we touched on in our discussion of S. Kagan (1986) in Chapter 3. She notes that the traditional American school setting that trained students to work efficiently on their own as individuals was a good preparation for the typical workplace setting earlier in this century, where workers tended to function in isolation carrying out the directions of their bosses. The work arena in the technological world of the approaching twenty-first century, however, has evolved into one in which key skills are those of collaboration, communication, and negotiation within and among work teams. Heath (1989) suggests that this is true for jobs ranging from minimum wage to positions at the highest managerial and professional levels.

In that light, schools that set up competitive contexts encouraging individuals to find the single "right" answer are becoming much less functional. Many problems being faced in today's world have alternate possible solutions and call for more information and expertise than any one person is likely to have. Thus, "the most valued oral language habits include giving directions, asking clarification questions, offering rapid and on-the-spot summaries, laying out short-term as well as long-range plans, and giving effective and nonthreatening assessments or recommendations to fellow workers" (Heath, 1989, p. 371). By these criteria the children that Houston (1973) describes, who demonstrate flair, already have a head start on certain rudiments necessary for successful adult functioning as a result of the kinds of language communities they come from.

Artful Teaching
Granted that children do need certain specific skills that their backgrounds have not provided for them, a major problem is helping teachers see that they have other valuable skills that literacy training could build upon. How do we adapt the children and the school system to one another? Several kinds of suggestions flow from the literature we have reviewed.

Teachers of the Trackton children felt concern over the fact that many of their students were not making progress. Heath (1982) recognized that "traditionally, education research has emphasized the need to train parents of children who are not successful in school achievement to conform to school practices. Knowledge had proceeded along a one-way path from school to " 'culturally different' communities" (p. 125). Her intervention goal was to set up a *two-way* process between the school and community and to try to avoid the development of a "we-they" split. She supplied teachers with ethnographic data about normal language use in the community and encouraged teachers to develop curriculum materials and ways of talking about them that were more natural for the children. At the same time, students were helped to become proficient in the typical school talk as well. Done gradually, over a period of time, it seemed as if this could be done in a way that was not threatening to the teachers and not superficial or condescending to the children. Such a two-way process seems very consistent with what Comer advocates in his intervention project (Chapter 3).[8]

Returning to the inner-city context and the issue of Black English specifically, the study of Ann Piestrup (1973) sheds further light on sociolinguistic issues involved in the language used by teachers and pupils in the classroom. The subjects of the classroom observation were fourteen first-grade teachers and their approximately 200 pupils selected randomly from predominantly Black inner-city schools. Under investigation were the effects of the teachers' classroom style on children's reading performance and on their tendency to use BEV in the classroom.[9] The researchers identified six different styles used by the teachers during reading instruction. These were called the Vocabulary Approach, the Decoding Approach, the Standard Pronunciation Approach, the Interrupting Approach, the White Liberal Approach, and the Black Artful Approach, each of which was characteristic of no less than two and no more than three of the teachers.

The Vocabulary Approach teachers focused on explaining the meanings of unfamiliar words, emphasizing especially the distinctions in meanings between homonyms. Teachers who used a decoding emphasis spent time helping children sound out words, often at the expense of meaningful reading. However, these children did less wild guessing at words than did children in other groups. The teachers employing the Standard Pronunciation Approach insisted that the children always employ formal standard English during reading classes. These teachers would sometimes stop a child who was reading aloud and instruct the class to repeat the correct sounds—a practice that the researchers thought was quite distracting for the children. In the Interrupting group there was an even greater emphasis on stopping children to correct their BE, and although the standard pronunciation was presented to the children, the teachers did not necessarily see to it that the children repeated the correct forms accurately. The teachers using the Interrupting Approach used a good deal of unfamiliar materials without explaining the content.

The White Liberal teachers accepted the use of Black dialect by their pupils in their writing and speech, and they used it occasionally themselves in communicating with the children. Although they seemed to engage the children's interest in reading more successfully than did teachers using some of the other styles, their emphasis seemed to be more on friendly communication than on the task of learning to read.

Black Artful teachers used BE during reading instruction and spoke it fluently in class. While they accepted use of dialect by their pupils, they also made sure that the children learned standard English forms as well. While making use of the vernacular to establish good rapport with the children, the Black Artful teachers also set high learning standards for them. These teachers appeared to be the most successful at involving the greatest number of children in the reading task.

> The label Black Artful is used to describe teaching which incorporates a form of rhythmic play unique with Black dialect speakers. It is not the

surface features of phonology or grammar that are important, but the rapid interplay with intonation and gesture familiar to Black children as one of the art forms of Black culture. [Piestrup, 1973, p. 103]

Unlike the White Liberal teacher's brief, imitative phrases, the Black Artful teacher's dialect seemed familiar and comfortable. [p. 105]

In comparing the effects of these teaching styles on the children's reading performance and dialect usage, Piestrup's results seem to show that the Black Artful teachers had the most positive effect. Children exposed to this approach had the highest mean reading scores of any group—significantly higher than those exposed to either the White Liberal Approach or the Interrupting Approach. The latter group had the lowest reading scores. Children experiencing the Black Artful style also had the lowest dialect usage scores on the sentence repetition task, significantly lower than the Vocabulary or the Interrupting groups. In fact, there was a tendency overall for those children with higher reading scores to have lower dialect usage scores. It appeared that the adeptness in BE of the Black Artful teachers added to their success in involving the children in the reading instruction, whereas the Interrupting teachers created just the opposite effect on their pupils:

Some children from this group tediously worked alone at decoding without reading as if they understood; others seemed to guess at almost as many words as they were able to read. Some children withdrew from participation in reading, speaking softly and as seldom as possible; others engaged in ritual insult and other forms of verbal play apart from the teacher. [pp. 131–132]

Since an exploratory observational study of this kind could not account for the many factors contributing to the outcomes, it would be premature to jump to any firm conclusion about effects of the six teaching styles on reading achievement. The results are consistent with research indicating that a primary emphasis on decoding and interrupting approaches in reading instruction has deleterious effects on comprehension (Brown, Palincsar, & Purcell, 1986). At the least, however, it appeared that the use of BE in certain classroom contexts did not hamper learning standard reading skills. This represents a different kind of example in which the school attempts to make use of language skills that the child brings in order to make a bridge to new learning. In fact, it turned out that the use of dialect by students was lowest in those classes in which the teachers not only emphasized BE while giving reading instruction but also permitted their students to use it without interrupting them. In these classes the children learned how to switch from the vernacular to the more standard form as the situation warranted and in the process gradually became able to use BE less.

It may have been that the pupils paid better attention to the reading instruction because they felt more at home in the classroom in which their speech was not constantly under criticism. According to Piestrup, there was good reason to believe that it was not the structural conflict between BE and standard dialect forms that interfered with the learning in these classrooms. Rather, she thought a functional conflict was primarily responsible for the deterioration of the communication between some of the teachers and pupils to the point that they no longer tried to "reach" each other when they talked. This occurred "when teachers did not listen carefully to children, as if they were interested only in a correct answer and did not expect to hear it, or when children did not attend to the lesson, as if they gave up on its making sense or being of interest" (p. 65).

Labov makes a similar point regarding functional conflict in the classroom. Among the inner-city youth whose language he studied, those youngsters who were most alienated and frequently truant from school were the purest speakers of BEV. Some of them were quite bright and verbal, with good learning potential. Although they were most intensely involved in gangs and the peer group culture, they not only understood the values of the mainstream society but also had a good grasp of how the system operated. It was Labov's (1972) conclusion that reading failure among this group of boys was to a large measure a consequence of political and cultural conflict in the classroom rather than linguistic difference as such.[10]

Although accepting Black English in the classroom may be one method of improving communication between teachers and students, it is evident that it does not in itself substitute for teaching the standard dialect features in reading instruction. It was possible to be a reasonably effective teacher of students speaking BE without using the vernacular in the classroom. Students of some of the teachers who used no BE had scores that, though not equal to, were not significantly worse than those in the Black Artful groups.

Thus, we end with the common thread of observation that has been running through the material of this and the previous chapter: Teachers who understand and believe in their students will not be hampered by background differences in teaching them the academic skills needed to succeed in life. Most children come to school with many of the cognitive-linguistic processes they need in order to learn.

In this regard, with respect to reading and writing readiness, Teale and Sulzby (1986) emphasize the idea that literacy development in young children begins even before children are exposed to more formal training. It begins in the child's very early interactions with his or her social environment. As we have been saying throughout this book, in these settings even preschool youngsters are "active participants in learning—hypothesis generators and problem solvers—rather than . . . passive recipients of information" (p. xv). Thus,

> Literacy develops in real-life settings for real-life activities in order to "get things done." . . . Children learn written language through active engagement with their world. They interact socially with adults in writing and reading situations; they explore print on their own, and they profit from modeling of literacy by significant adults, particularly their parents. [p. xviii]

Heath (1986) amplifies this further in an interesting way. She suggests that preparation for developing rich communication skills in standard English can come from a background of rich language use in one's own native language or dialect.

> Retail and service institutions [in their communities] give children the opportunity to interact and watch their parents communicate with individuals who are not intimates. . . . Whether in English or in their native tongue, children need extensive practice in having to explain themselves to those who do not share their specific home experiences, assumptions about meaning, and expectations of outcomes. [p. 176]

Later in their education, children will presumably be better prepared for transferring these various types of language use into the English they need to learn to do well academically and vocationally. When children come to school, they may not be reading well, but even when they come from stable backgrounds that are not middle class, they have often experienced interactions that provide skills from which literacy can emerge.

Cherishing Pluralism

The effect of making use of indigenous language forms in the school while teaching standard English to Black children may well be to maintain the use of some form of BE in their extracurricular life. Is this a good thing? One value of sanctioning the use of Black language forms in school may be to provide institutional support outside of the home for an aspect of self associated with ethnic identity. It is a way that young people can know that their uniqueness is included in the American mosaic, thus strengthening positive affective assessments about themselves and their cultural identity. (The bolstering of a sense of identity in Black children is probably one of Smitherman's intentions in insisting that BE is a language. See note 2.) This need not be done at the expense of membership in the larger "American" culture; rather, it is possible to conceive of it as being concomitant with such participation. In a study of attitudes toward BE, Hoover (1978) found that Black parents in two west coast communities wanted the schools to teach their children to master standard English—standard BE was preferred. (Standard Anglo English was not presented as a comparison to the BE forms in this study.) At the same time, they wanted their children to be able to speak or at least understand the vernacular so that they could maintain contact with Black culture and feel comfortable with Black people of all social strata and varying age groups.

In a society still hostile to cultural differences the use of the vernacular may also promote a tie with positive memories and supportive relationships in one's community. Black vernacular forms are rich in the ways they are used to define and carry on social intercourse—in conveying a particular relationship between the dialect users. In informal circumstances, with family and friends who are Black, dialect forms tend to be used by those African Americans who have some command of them. The use of BE is a way of signaling a greater sense of intimacy and camaraderie in these close social relationships. In addition, the dialect serves as a connection to sources of creative vision or at least to alternate and meaningful perceptions about experiences that might otherwise be lost. Such perceptions might, for example, allow a storyteller to savor a meal of wolf and greens in fantasy or might encourage the development of a more sophisticated literary talent.

An example of the latter, worth presenting at some length, is provided in a moving autobiographical essay by the noted West Indian novelist and poet Paule Marshall (1983). She notes that a major influence in her development as a writer was her daily exposure to the group of "poets" who gathered for a cup of tea in her family's kitchen at the end of the workday and talked as she and her sister sat in the corner doing their homework. "Now they didn't look like poets—whatever that breed is supposed to look like. Nothing about them suggested that poetry was their calling. They were just a group of ordinary housewives and mothers, my mother included. . . ." (p. 3)

These women, who had regular jobs as housekeepers or hired themselves out daily, would take this time in her family's kitchen to briefly unburden themselves at day's end before going home to cook for their families. Their talk ranged from the world, national, and racial politics of the day to gossip about their acquaintances and fond memories of home. They bitterly resented the racism they found here, but they acknowledged America as a place where economic opportunity existed.

Marshall noted that it wasn't so much the content of what the women talked about, but the *style* they used to express themselves that was so remarkable:

> They had taken the standard English taught them in the primary schools of Barbados and transformed it into an idiom . . . that more adequately

> described them—changing around the syntax and imposing their own rhythm and accent so that the sentences were more pleasing to their ears. They added the few African sounds and words that had survived.... And to make it ... more in keeping with their expressive quality, they brought to bear a raft of metaphors, parables ... [and] sayings.... [p. 34]

Their metaphors were unforgettable: " 'The sea ain' got no back door', ... meaning that it wasn't like a house where if there was a fire you could run out the back ... meaning perhaps [further] ... that man should treat all of nature with caution and respect." Their observations were pointed: "God ... don' love ugly and He ain' stuck on pretty." In using everyday, commonplace speech "with imagination and skill—they gave voice to the most complex ideas" (p. 34).

For her part, Marshall soon became an avid user of the local public library. She read widely in English literature and then discovered with delight a variety of African-American writers, including the Negro dialect poet Paul Lawrence Dunbar. Eventually she herself began to harbor "the dangerous thought" of becoming a writer someday. And while she acknowledges the formal teachers and famous writers whose influence helped shape her craft, she insists that prior to such mentorship was that of

> another set of giants ... the group of women around the table long ago. They taught me my first lessons in the narrative art. They trained my ear.... [T]he best of my work ... stands as testimony to the rich legacy of language and culture they so freely passed on to me in the wordshop of the kitchen. [p. 35]

This example of a West Indian experience adds a component that is different from the main thrust of our discussion. Nevertheless, it is an eloquent example of the larger point, which is that the majority of African Americans grow up familiar with some form of BE from early childhood.[11] This is particularly true of persons from lower- and working-class backgrounds, some of whom have achieved middle-class, professional status in adulthood. The latter group are still familiar with the dialect even though their daily work situations may demand that they communicate in the more standard language forms. If more standard and "proper" forms are used in the home, most Blacks still have some exposure to relatives and neighbors who speak the vernacular. For those African Americans who were surrounded by a good deal of BE during their formative years the vernacular is a kind of "mother tongue." These speech forms have mediated social experiences that have become a part of the self. For some African Americans, having BE language forms available enables them to "come home" psychologically and culturally. The ability to use different language forms for different social situations allows for the bipolar or multipolar (dialectical) definition of self that we have been discussing in this book.

Yet we have to recognize that there are costs as well as benefits for African Americans trying to maintain speech pluralism. Although preserving the language forms of BE strengthens ties with the racial group, their use also meets up with the bias in the mainstream society against cultural differences associated with Blackness (J. Jones, 1991b; Kovel, 1984). For all its liberal veneer, the Establishment does not take kindly to reminders that its participants have backgrounds different from the European and especially the "Anglo" norm in cultural style. Consequently African Americans live with the psychological dilemma of trying to sustain an aspect of self, their racial linguistic style, in the face of disapproval from the dominant society. Although this may be somewhat easier to handle for those Blacks who have relatively little contact with Whites, others in both middle-class and working-class jobs must make the decision to keep their language style within a standard range, at least some of the time, if they expect to advance within White institutional structures. In his critical appraisal of the Black middle-class, Frazier (1962) argued that the typical members of the "Black bourgeoisie" attempted to model their behavior and institutions as much as possible after the White norm. But having expunged as many of the vestiges of cultural Blackness and lower socioeconomic status from themselves as they could, they found they were not fully admitted into White society. Since in fact Whites were not prepared to accept Blacks as equals on any terms, middle-class Blacks, according to this analysis, had worked themselves into a cultural "no man's land." The moral of the Frazier analysis would seem to be that Blacks will have to sustain a dialectical relationship with the Anglo-American cultural standard, because Whites by and large are still not ready to join in a truly integrated effort to create a cultural mosaic for the American society.[12]

Let us return to the metaphor used earlier—that dialectal pluralism allows a person to "come home" culturally. A majority of Blacks learn to function relatively well on the job even though this involves being away from "home" in certain respects. (This is so even though Blacks have historically made continual contributions to American culture that have been woven into the fabric of the society. Whites take such contributions to speech and various aspects of popular entertainment and art so much for granted that they are oblivious to the sources.) Maintaining Black communicative styles side by side with using standard forms permits them to commute psychologically from a personal cultural home to the common world of work and culture shared with other ethnic groups in America. For them, switching codes may be a useful way of sustaining multipolar aspects of their identity. There are other Blacks who are not comfortable commuting linguistically and who prefer to remain in one cultural setting or the other; that is, their speech styles are geared either to an Americanized or to an African-American orientation. Among the former are some Black Americans who grow up in social class or geographical settings where they speak only "standard" English forms in all speech contexts and consequently never feel homesick. Another large group never leaves home at all. As Kernan (1971) notes:

> The bi-cultural status of Black Americans makes the socialization process a time when each individual attempts to find some viable personal reconciliation to cultural patterns, values and attitudes which do not cohere or intersect in any consistent fashion. Some solutions find individuals essentially submerged in things Black, rejecting outside standards and valuations across the board. Others look outward toward the wider culture and still others straddle the two, selecting from either as the needs of the moment require. Language is an important reflector of these various positions. [p. 83]

The thrust of this chapter points toward an ideal of cherishing pluralism in speech styles. Pluralism should imply that people will feel free to retain a variety of options and will learn to fit them to various occasions. Between Blacks and Whites this ideal implies that although Blacks learn to handle standard speech forms competently—and it is essential that Blacks have that skill in this society—they should be able to feel comfortable using Black forms as well for the psychological and cultural gratifications that come with such usage. By the same token, Blacks should be able to feel perfectly at ease about never using BE forms and associated communicative styles if they choose. But, when opting for one or another stance in their own use of speech, Blacks should not disparage other Blacks for making different choices.

Notes

1. The term *vernacular* refers among other things to the "normal spoken form of a language" (Webster's, 1988, p. 1310). It can also refer to a "nonstandard" form of a language. Consistent with the definition of *dialect* to be presented shortly, the term *vernacular* does not refer to a "substandard" form of a language but to a variant form.

2. The linguist Geneva Smitherman (1991) argues the case for Black English (BE) being a separate *language*, not simply a separate dialect. She believes that, in addition to the structural differences that mark BE as an African-derived speech form, BE serves distinct and important social purposes in the Black

community. In her view, it is spoken by a people who have shared social norms and a shared social reality. The fact that many Black people perceive it to be a language uniquely expressing their experience further qualifies it to be more than a dialect form. Linguists recognize that, strictly speaking, it is difficult to distinguish between a language and a dialect (Trudgill, 1974). Indeed, Smitherman (1991) notes: "Linguistics, as a science, cannot and does not offer the definitive word on language-dialect differentiation in general, nor in the case of Black English in particular." She goes on to note, however:

> The point is that differences between Black and White English create barriers and points of unintelligibility and have significant impact on African Americans in the American political economy....
>
> Is Black English a language or a dialect, then? Ultimately, it comes down to who has the power to define. As the linguist Max Weinreich once put it, the difference between a language and a dialect is who's got the army. [p. 256]

In one sense the distinctions Smitherman is making are those between the formal *structure* of language and what we shall address in the next section as "sociolinguistic" issues. Her definition of language seems to lean heavily on the latter kinds of concerns. I shall continue to make the dialect/language distinction here since I am taking the position that no dialect form of a language, including the "standard" dialect, is inherently superior to any other form. However, I fully agree with Smitherman that the various issues regarding BE as a social phenomenon, which most of this chapter deals with, are the ones of critical importance to African Americans.

3. This phraseology touches on an issue raised in the so-called "Sapir-Whorf hypothesis" (Cole & Scribner, 1974; Trudgill, 1974). This view states that a person's native language constrains how s/he perceives the world and contributes greatly to differences in world view between speakers of different languages. The direction of influence in this view is from language to society. The alternative directional view is that language and thinking reflect the structure of the physical and social environment. Differing from both these perspectives on language and society, the logical learning theory point of view would be that language reflects the ordering activity of mind. Words give expression to conceptualizations.

4. In fact, what research shows is that Black children who are dialect speakers tend to switch standard English sentences read to them into dialect form when repeating them to the experimenter (Baratz, 1970) and even tend to use dialect forms consistently in sentences containing nonsense syllables (Marwit, Marwit, & Boswell, 1973). Story recall has been found to be better in the preferred dialect form, too (Hall, Reder, & Cole, 1975).

5. The British sociolinguist Basil Bernstein (1970) has described another set of differences that affect educational performance. Arguing that language development is related to social class, he has described language styles in terms of two different "codes"—"restricted" and "elaborated." Very briefly, a restricted code comes into being in more intimate or familiar social relations where there are "closely shared identifications . . . [and] a range of common assumptions" (p. 32). Understanding one another rather readily, people in such social relations do not feel the need to depend on precisely delineated verbal forms to spell out their intentions. As a result, they tend to rely more on implicit and nonverbal modes of communication. An elaborated code, by contrast, arises in social relationships where it is not easy to take others' intentions for granted. In elaborated codes, speech forms are more differentiated and precise, presumably permitting expression of a wider and more complex range of thought. There is greater extension and explicitness of meaning, with an emphasis on objective intelligibility.

In his studies of some speakers of British English, Bernstein sought to demonstrate a relationship between social class membership and the use of the two codes. His findings seemed to show that the middle-class children in his samples used both elaborated and restricted codes, whereas the children from working-class backgrounds tended to use only the restricted code. Parenthetically, it should be mentioned that this relationship did not have to do with social class differences in dialect. Since some of these findings have been used by others to support positions that Bernstein felt the need to disavow, he has taken pains to say that elaborated codes should not be seen as inherently and in all ways better than restricted codes. Nor did he think that the restricted code implied either linguistic deprivation or an innate tendency: "What we have here are differences in the use of language arising out of a specific context" (1970, p. 27). Restricted code users were not nonverbal, Bernstein went on to say; rather, the speech that they used was "of a different order from that controlled by an elaborated code" (p. 33). In fact, the restricted code, he pointed out, was more suited for communicating the affective meanings that enriched human life and promoted group solidarity, while elaborated codes, however affectively barren, were necessary for acquiring the educational and technological skills needed to participate in a complex industrial society. Those who brought elaborated code skills with them to school had a head start on educational achievement because the schools prized such skills.

Although it was not clear to Bernstein exactly how the association between language style and social class came about, he proposed that the language codes developed at least partly from different styles of family structure and family social control. Distinguishing between family structures that are "person-oriented" and "positional," Bernstein proposed that in person-oriented families, decisions and judgments are based on the person's individual psychological characteristics rather than on his or her formal status. These person-oriented structures encourage open communication systems. In positional families, decision making rests on the person's formal status in the family according to age or sex, for example, making for a more "closed" communication.

> In person-oriented families social control is likely to be realized through verbally elaborated means oriented to the person, while in positional families social control is likely to be realized through less elaborated verbal means, less oriented to the person but more oriented toward the formal status of the regulated (i.e. the child). [Bernstein, 1970, p. 41].

Such habitual interactions within the family presumably contribute strongly to the verbal style the child adopts.

Some British and American educators have been impressed with this kind of sociolinguistic view as an explanation for some of the academic difficulties of the lower- and working-class child (Olim, 1970). Research has been somewhat supportive of the usefulness of these categories (Cook-Gumperz, 1973; Ward, 1971). But there has also been considerable criticism of Bernstein's conceptualization (Rosen, 1974).

Trudgill (1974), for example, has suggested that some interpretations of Bernstein's work have led to biased views of lower-class children—from which Bernstein has explicitly disassociated himself in his later writing. If one does not take the two proposed language codes as hard and fast social class distinctions and if one recognizes that language performance is a function of the context in which language behaviors occur, then, according to Trudgill, the following reinterpretation of Bernstein's findings might be in order:

> In many contexts some working-class children are less willing or less used to employing a more formal style than are middle-class children. This, of course, by no means suggests that they are in any way linguistically deprived . . . although it may mean that working-class children have a narrower range of stylistic options open to them. (This . . . may well be compensated for by the fact that in many working-class groups verbal skills of particular types, such as joke-telling, narrating and insulting are very highly valued: there are probably certain options open to them which are not available to middle-class children.) [p. 56]

Of course, this interpretation of Bernstein still leaves open the question of exactly how social class differences have contributed to the development of restricted and elaborated styles. As we have mentioned earlier, other researchers have also come across class differences in language behavior and cognitive performance. In Chapter 3 we noted Golden's finding that children of different socioeconomic status demonstrated a differential readiness to use specific verbal labeling skills in problem-solving tests. Although performance in structured experimental situations was not a foolproof measure of capacity, nevertheless schools tended to seize upon and augment these different initial levels of performance. The Golden work suggested that there was indeed something about the preschool child's normal home experience that led to differential readiness to use certain verbal styles. Although we are a long way from being certain about what specific mechanisms influence these developments, the area of the child's interaction with the mother and probably with other family members appears to be important. The work of William Hall and his colleagues, which included observations of speech behavior of young children in a variety of naturalistic settings, has attempted to elucidate some of these issues further (e.g., Hall & Dore, 1980; Hall & Guthrie, 1979b; Hall & Tirre, 1979).

6. Heath's characterizations of Trackton children bring to mind the descriptions of working- and lower-class African-American children made by Boykin (1991) and Shade (1991). There is the suggestion in this sociolinguistic work that cognitive style differences in the children develop partly from the language practices of healthy loving adults with one another and their offspring.

7. Heath used an "ethnographic" research method. That is, over a period of several years she intermittently lived with and observed her subjects in the everyday settings where they carried out their lives. She describes the goal of ethnography as being "to describe the ways of living of a social group, usually one in which there is in-group recognition by the members that they indeed must live and work together to retain group identity" (1982, p. 105). Ethnographic research is a method for getting at people's "introspective" point of view—the subjects' lives as they see them—which is at the heart of the humanistic approach discussed in this book. Other examples of the use of ethnographic research to study schooling can be found in Gouldner and Strong (1978) and Spindler (1982).

8. In a similar vein, Tharp (1989), based on his experience with the much cited Kamehameha Early Education Project (KEEP) in Hawaii, notes the need to "contextualize" education with lower- and working-class children from minority communities. As we have seen, in its emphasis on language mechanics *first*, the traditional teaching style lifts learning about things out of meaningful contexts. As Tharp notes, "schools teach rules, abstractions and verbal descriptions . . . *by means of* rules, abstractions, and verbal descriptions. Many cultural communities do not" (1989, p. 355). Such school practices baffle these children.

For many students from minority communities, schools must promote learning by relating the rules and abstractions that they want to teach to the everyday world with which the child is familiar. Tharp (1989) identifies three levels of contextualization. The first, or technical, level is one in which the teacher repeatedly calls up a child's existing conceptualizations in the form of relevant personal experiences, for example, as they are related to material being taught. At a second level cultural materials and community-based experiences make up the core of the curriculum that is used to teach reading, writing, and arithmetic. The third level is that of policy planning, and it is one in which parents and community members are encouraged to participate actively with school officials in developing and supervising educational program.

9. A standard reading test was used to measure reading performance, and a sentence repetition exercise was used as a measure of the amount of dialect a child was prone to use. This latter task presented the subject with standard English sentences they had to listen to and then repeat aloud. The sentences contained words that had a high potential for eliciting Black dialect forms. For example, one sentence was "My brother *is* f*i*ve *year*s *o*ld becaus*e his* bir*th*day pass*ed*" (Piestrup, 1973, p. 179). The underlined portions represent parts of words where omissions might be expected in the vernacular.

10. Labov's observations shed some light on data reported by Robins (1968). Her studies indicated that Black adolescent youngsters who had a history of school problems and truancy were highly likely to become involved in violence leading to their deaths at an early age. Dropping out of school based on such school problems was a better predictor of later violence than was socio-economic status or having come from a broken home. In fact, low-income Black youths who finished high school had a *lower* chance than equivalent Whites of suffering early and violent death. It seems quite possible that the truancy of these lower-class youths is a result of the kind of cultural and political conflict in the classroom to which Labov refers. These data are consistent with the findings of Hare and Castenell (1985) and with Gibbs' (1988) argument that young Black males are an "endangered species."

11. Another excellent literary example of the richness of Black speech forms is found in Alice Walker's (1982) *The Color Purple*, written in what she has called her "beautiful first language: Black Folk-English" (in Rosenthal, 1984).

12. Recent research by Labov and Harris (1986) has called attention to another danger of trying to maintain speech pluralism. This work, done in Philadelphia neighborhoods, led them to the conclusion that dialect patterns in a number of urban American communities may be diverging sufficiently so that Black and White people are becoming *less* able to understand one another's speech and communicate with one another. Labov and Harris suggest that a major cause of this phenomenon is that urban Black Americans increasingly

live in segregated situations. They note that there are a considerable number of exceptions to this development, of course, with many Blacks able to speak standard English and tending to shift dialect use according to the setting in which they find themselves. One of the negative potentials of speech divergence is that Black children may have increasing problems in dealing with the language of the standard classroom, as we have been discussing it in this chapter. Labov and Harris do make a brief reference as to how some of the effects of this trend toward divergence might be mitigated without compromising the cultural integrity of the participants. In my view, though it might hold certain dangers, to promote language pluralism is not necessarily to advocate cultural separatism. I support African Americans knowing and speaking their native dialects if they wish to do so, *in addition to* having a full command of standard American English, *not* instead of it.

5

The Assertive Self: Emerging of a New Identity

In the late fifties and early sixties, African Americans began to make changes in their style of public demeanor. Individuals became more assertive in stating forthrightly their own sense of self-worth. As a group, Black Americans became more aggressive in opposing discrimination through organized militant action. Many White people, startled by this straightforward behavior, saw Blacks as simply becoming more hostile toward members of the White society (Cheek, 1976). But this view on the part of Whites missed the point. The primary goal of the changed behavior of Blacks was not so much to put other groups down as it was to try to move to a new plane of Black identity development. This was to be achieved not only by acting less conforming and submissive to the expectations of the White society but also by putting forward their own intentions boldly and insistently. A particular hallmark of this new assertiveness, as we shall see in this chapter, was a deliberate effort on the part of African Americans to link a good personal sense of self with a prideful sense of racial identity.[1]

Assertion and Aggression

Assertion, like affirmation, involves an *active* structuring of the world—an active "coming at" the world. In this sense the concept of assertion can be taken as another perspective on effectance and competence strivings. But assertive behavior is also related to aggressive behavior, the wish not simply to act on and change an object but to actually destroy or harm something or someone.[2]

When people are blocked from being normally assertive, they frequently respond with angry feelings and angry behavior. It is a common clinical observation that persons who feel neurotically conflicted about expressing aggressive feelings not only inhibit direct expression of hostile behavior but also restrain appropriately assertive behavior, too.

Angry feelings—rage, in fact—have been a continuing issue for Blacks since being in America (Grier & Cobbs, 1968; Lester, 1968). Historically Whites have tried to suppress Blacks' rebellious anger as well as assertive (and possibly competitive) self-expressions. Whites have done this by being extremely punishing toward Blacks. This has led partly to responses of *adaptive inferiority* (Pugh, 1972), a term that is akin to the notion of psychological "defense."³ In a hostile, White-controlled society, then, one of the major adaptations Blacks were forced to make was controlling the overt manifestations of their aggression.

Defenses are ways of responding to and viewing the world that reduce a sense of psychological threat and allow a person to proceed with the task of living with a sense of relative inner security. Blacks have had to defend against direct expression of anger against Whites. Since aggression is such a ready response in human beings, such feelings could not have disappeared from within Black persons, although they were not frequently manifested frankly and overtly. Forced to minimize direct hostile expressions toward Whites, Blacks have used the defense of displacement by frequently directing aggression at one another (*displacement* refers to unconsciously shifting the expression of a troublesome impulse to an object [person] other than the one originally intended). In some instances, of course, overt hostility and destructiveness did emerge. Riots in twentieth-century urban Black communities are examples of such aggressive discharges.⁴

Aggression in Blacks: Selected Studies

There have been a number of efforts to study the effect of bottling up aggression on the personality functioning of Blacks. In one often cited study the psychiatrists Kardiner and Ovesey (1951/1962), using a small sample of subjects most of whom were patients in psychotherapy, concluded that Blacks in general were hampered in their personality functioning (for criticism of this study, see, for example, Thomas and Sillen [1972]). Their view was that the anger aroused by the discrimination and hostility of Whites was often handled in a variety of maladaptive ways. Thus, some of the anger not directed against Whites was directed at themselves, leading to self-hatred, low self-esteem, and hostility toward other Black people. Another effect was that, while holding White middle-class aspirations, they blocked the assertive behavior that would have enabled them to be successful in the White-dominated society. Laboratory studies have demonstrated that Blacks did not express hostility toward Whites where frustration was induced experimentally. But in the same laboratory situation they expressed hostile feelings toward other Black participants (Winslow & Brainerd, 1950).

The hypothesis that the segregated American society has inhibited effective personality functioning and thereby reduced social achievement in African Americans was tested in a large sample of northern urban Blacks (Crain & Weisman, 1972).[5] One of the important consequences of segregation and racial oppression, Crain and Weisman suggest, has been the loss of the capacity by African-Americans to express assertion and legitimate anger effectively.[6] We noted in Chapter 1 Crain and Weisman's view that racism had stunted the personality functioning of Blacks, thereby blocking the effectiveness of their achievement strivings. Some of the data that illuminate this issue come from their analysis of responses to a brief form of the Internal-External Locus of Control (LOC) Scale (Rotter, 1966) in combination with a short measure of self-esteem that they developed. Briefly, the LOC Scale describes people's perceptions about the degree of control they have over that part of the world they are trying to master. Those who have a low sense of internal control feel that planning and hard work are of little use since what one gets in life is determined by chance or luck. The person with a high sense of internal control tends to feel that diligence and personal effort mark the road to success.[7]

With respect to the handling of aggression, Crain and Weisman found that persons high in internal control tended to inhibit their aggression more. ("Inhibition" was defined in this study by whether or not individuals could recall being angry recently and whether reading or hearing about discrimination made them angry as opposed to sad. Those who could not remember a recent incident and who reported becoming sad rather than angry were seen as being inhibited in expression of aggression.) Of those men who were better educated (high school graduates), the ones who expressed a high sense of internal control were less likely to have been arrested or to have been in fights. Although it is a problematic measure in a number of ways, lack of arrests or a history of fighting were the authors' measures of ability to control overt hostility. In this sample of men and women, being high on internal control was also strongly related to expressing a relatively small amount of anti-White sentiment, especially among those women who were employed.

The self-esteem measure used asked respondents to rate themselves as to whether they were "above average, about average, or below average on some things that you do and some things that you are" as compared to other people (Crain & Weisman, 1972, p. 71).[8] Crain and Weisman view this measure as being one of "self-pride," not primarily one that gets at the reflected view of oneself in the eyes of "significant others." "Self-esteem, as we have measured it, has a tone of competing against others, rather than merely accepting the views of others toward oneself" (p. 76). Thus, this measure seems clearly slanted toward personal self-concept rather than racial self-concept. Further, the implied meaning was that this measure of self-esteem taps assertiveness, a kind of neutralized or sublimated aggression. "Assertiveness refers to competitiveness and the tendency to manipulate the environment to one's advantage. Assertive people are socially aggressive: they seek self-improvement and actively take steps to assure their well-being" (p. 77). Their data show that this index of self-esteem was correlated with various reports by respondents of being more socially assertive and upwardly mobile: oriented toward looking for a better job, having participated in civil rights demonstrations, being better prepared educationally, and the like. However, high self-esteem as measured here was also found to be associated with "dysfunctional" expression of aggression; that is, with a higher incidence of getting into fights, being arrested more, and being separated or divorced.

When the subjects' orientation on the LOC Scale was combined with their level of self-esteem, four different reaction styles emerged: "drifters," "militants," "accepters," and "achievers" (see Table 5-1). "The different combinations of self-esteem and internal control represent alternative strategies in two ways: (1) they depict a choice between externalizing anger (system-blaming) and internalizing anger (self-blaming), and (2) they represent a choice between assertive behavior and deferential or passive behavior" (p. 81). The situations of persons in groups A and D were relatively straightforward. The so-called "drifters" in group A had a sense of low personal control over their lives and low self-esteem, seemed to be nonassertive and less effective in the larger world, and expressed a good deal of hostility. (The four groups are identified by letters in Table 5-1, with Crain and Weisman's descriptive terms being put in parentheses to help minimize the tendency to take the labels as being real entities rather than suggestions as to what the data may mean. Reported relationships involving these variables are low, accounting for small amounts of variance, and hence any conceptual characterization would best be an approximation of the richness of the actuality of the respondents' lives. For example, the characterization "drifter" for group A does not necessarily imply marital instability for this group, although this is not an infrequent connotation of the term. Group A's reports of their divorce and separation history is essentially no different than that of persons in group D ["achievers"].) The group D subjects, the "achievers," were quite assertive and tended to act as if they believed they could control their destinies. (These are the two categories—groups A and D—that have typically been found among Whites, according to Crain and Weisman, and they are usually positively associated with socioeconomic status, group D being middle class and group A being lower class.)

Persons who were in group B, the "militants," and those in group C, the "accepters," are particularly illustrative of the personality dilemma that racism has imposed on Blacks. While persons in group B were assertive, they had less of a feeling that they could control their lives and so they were

TABLE 5-1 Locus of Control and Self-Esteem Styles

	Internal Control	
	Low	High
Low self-esteem	A ("drifters")	C ("accepters")
High self-esteem	B ("militants")	D ("achievers")

Source: Adapted from R. L. Crain and C. S. Weisman, *Discrimination, Personality, and Achievement: A Survey of Northern Blacks* (p. 81), New York: Seminar Press. Used with permission of Academic Press.

presumably less inclined to rein in their hostile behavior. Group C persons, being high on the internal control variable, were quite "responsible" and muted in their expression of aggression. But, lacking the buffer of a sense of self-worth, they were self-blaming and nonassertive.

Crain and Weisman's depiction of the group B person (the "militant") is somewhat similar to the descriptions of those persons more likely to be actively involved in ghetto riots of the 1960s. Caplan (1970) and Forward and Williams (1970) characterized these individuals as seeing themselves as capable but blocked by racism and the faults of the social structure rather than feeling alienated and hopeless (Caplan's review of the studies that paint this picture are in an article he titled "The New Ghetto Man"). The group C person (the "accepter") has behavioral qualities reminiscent of what Grier and Cobbs (1968) described as the "postal clerk syndrome":

> This man is always described as 'nice' by White people. . . . He is passive, nonassertive, and nonaggressive. He has made a virtue of identification with the aggressor, and he has adopted an ingratiating and compliant manner. . . . This man renounces gratifications that are available to others. He assumes a deferential mask. He is always submissive. He must figure out "the man" but keep "the man" from deciphering him. [p. 66]

The Crain and Weisman study found mixed consequences of being in groups B and C. Those in group B, who were higher in self-esteem, tended to have somewhat higher incomes than those in group C. However, the latter group described themselves as being generally more content with their lives. Thus, higher self-esteem, defined here as assertiveness, did not necessarily bring "happiness." Which of these choices was more dysfunctional—"overexternalization" or "overinternalization"—would be partly a matter of the observer's political values. There clearly were personal costs and gains in both styles. For those Blacks able to combine assertiveness and control of hostility, that is, group D subjects (the "achievers"), the highest degree of social achievement was possible. So lack of aggressiveness on the surface was not always accompanied by low self-esteem and a diminution of assertiveness.

The complex ways that Blacks have handled their aggression historically were analyzed by Powdermaker (1943). She pointed out that, although victimized by certain aspects of the culture, Blacks have also found subtle ways to resist and have been able to ventilate otherwise problematic aggressive feelings. Blacks displaced angry feelings onto safer targets (other Blacks, for example) and also dealt with aggressive feelings by attempting to withdraw socially from or deny the impact of contact with Whites ("I just don't let it bother me"). In some cases they defended themselves by attempting to identify with and become like Whites in order to minimize persecution.[9]

Much of Powdermaker's article was devoted to trying to understand how the great majority of Black people remained meek and unaggressive and at the same time were able to maintain sufficient identity and dignity to survive as human beings. She suggested that the superficial meekness dating back to slavery helped first to defend against conscious and perhaps less conscious awareness of anger at Whites. Being meek and "turning the other cheek" helped appease the guilt feelings of persons who believed with Christian conviction that it was wrong to hate. In the racial situation that constantly stirred their rage and consequent guilt, presumably meekness helped them atone. But equally as important, she argued, meekness achieved a moral victory as well in which Blacks could experience feeling more righteous in their forbearance than racist Whites and thus earning a place for themselves in heaven. They even contributed to their oppressors' eventual punishment by "heaping coals of fire" on their heads; that is, by returning good for evil, they magnified even more the moral affront of the oppressors' crime.

Furthermore, there was the continuing moral victory in this world of fooling Whites by making them think that they (the Blacks) *believed* the role they were playing. As noted earlier, many Blacks probably never fully identified with the racial role assigned to them by Whites. Blacks had the intention of using the disguise of meekness to assert themselves covertly. As the old folksong says, "Got one mind for White folks to see, got 'nother for what I know is me" (Ames, 1950).[10] The victories they gained helped Blacks maintain some psychological balance in an oppressive situation. But while not provoking retaliation, it also tended not to promote social change because Blacks maintained outwardly subservient roles and did not threaten Whites.

With respect to overt expression of aggression, Powdermaker predicted that as Blacks became increasingly urban they would be less willing to deal with their anger in the traditional ways. The historical events of the 1960s and early 1990s in Los Angeles have of course borne her out. The mood in the Black community seems to have moved more toward approval of Crain and Weisman's pattern B, the "militants," over pattern C, the "accepters." Group B persons were more openly anti-White on interview items than either group C or D people (Crain & Weisman, 1972). Other survey data (Schuman, 1974) and experimental data indicate that such inhibition and displacement of aggression away from Whites have been changing. As we saw earlier, experimental work has demonstrated that Blacks were reluctant to express hostility toward Whites (Winslow & Brainerd, 1950). More recently, by contrast, Wilson and Rogers (1975) found in an interracial laboratory situation that Black subjects were quite retaliatory toward Whites who were perceived by them as insulting. The measure of hostility used was the intensity of shock that subjects thought they were delivering to a "victim." While their reactions toward other Black subjects showed a considerable residue of the traditional in-group hostility, it was the overt expression of anger toward Whites that had changed.[11] However, even prior to such changes there have always been persons who represented militancy in the Black community and a large number of persons who silently identified with them, at least in part.

Evolution of Identity

The research just discussed focused on the emergence of a more forthright assertiveness and aggressiveness in at least some segments of the Black community. The Crain and Weisman study in particular looked primarily at factors that influenced *individual* achievement. The perspective seemed to be the traditional one, namely, that social advancement for African Americans as a group would come from the aggregate effect of individuals having bettered themselves as individuals.

But even as Crain and Weisman were collecting their data, different notions were surfacing in Black Americans about the ideological basis for self-worth and about the best route for achieving group advancement. We can look at these issues in two separate lines of research. We shall first discuss William Cross's description of the personal psychological road, *nigrescence*, that many African Americans took as they developed a changed racial group orientation, and then we shall examine the growth of assertive group action on Black college campuses as investigated by Patricia Gurin and Edgar Epps.

Nigrescence

In Cross's view, nigrescence is an outgrowth of the second phase of the "Black Social Movement", the Black Power phase, which began to develop in the Black community in the late 1960s. (The first phase of the Black Social Movement had been the civil rights phase, extending from the mid-1950s to the late 1960s.) *Nigrescence*, the process of becoming psychologically "Black," refers to the attitudinal and behavioral changes associated with Blacks' identification with the concept of Black empowerment (Cross, 1991). Nigrescence involves developing a sense of self and personal worth that explicitly includes central reference points taken from perspectives of African-American history and consciousness, rather than primarily from the frame of reference toward oneself and Blacks dictated by White society. In his recent book, Cross (1991) notes that there have been a number of psychologists over the last twenty years who have attempted to describe the nigrescence phenomenon. Cross's model (which is similar to one developed by the late Charles Thomas [Thomas & Thomas, 1971]) is probably the most elaborated of such paradigms and the one that has inspired the most research. His work is partly a reaction against the effort to describe African Americans' reactions to race in terms of static "profiles" or "types" of behavior (as do Crain and Weisman or Pettigrew, 1964; see note 9). The nigrescence process emphasizes the changes a person undergoes as a function of confronting the continuing issues of race in the United States. The model tracks the individual through a series of specific steps in the conversion from being "Negro" to being "Black" psychologically. Cross's original description (1978) of the five stages of this conversion process have not changed basically. However, in the ensuing years he has developed some of the implications of his paradigm with particular respect to the idea that the personal identity and reference group orientation aspects of self must be kept relatively distinct. We shall first look at the original model.

Stage 1 is that of "Pre-encounter," in which the "person's world view is dominated by Euro-American determinants" (Cross, 1978, p. 17). In this stage those features of the individual that characterize his or her Black racial identity are denied or downgraded in the interest of accepting the Euro-American view. Such a person's cultural orientation is a "deracinated" one. Stage 2, "Encounter," follows next and consists of a disrupting confrontation with a new way of viewing the African-American situation. "The 'Encounter stage' describes a shocking personal or social event that temporarily dislodges the person from his old worldview, making the person receptive (vulnerable) to a new interpretation of his identity and his condition" (p. 17). This stage ends when the person becomes convinced that a change of perspective is in order and s/he makes the decision to "become Black." This involves a highly energetic search for Black identity.

In the third ("Immersion-Emersion") stage the individual works to get rid of all traces of the Pre-encounter frame of reference in the self and explores the implications for himself or herself of the new point of view. The person acts the way most converts to emotionally involving ideologies do. There may be "glorification of African heritage, dichotomous ('either-or') thinking, Blacker-than-thou attitudes, unrealistic expectations concerning the efficacy of Black Power, and the tendency to denigrate White people and White culture while simultaneously deifying Black people and Black culture" (p. 17). As an individual emerges from the emotional heat of this period, s/he begins to be able to step back and look more critically at the strengths and weaknesses of his or her new identity and be less intensely involved in the search.

At this point the person is ready to enter stage 4, a phase of "Internalization," in which s/he takes on the new values in a less defensive way. There is a decreased need for rhetorical posturing as a way of impressing others, but rather a "calm, secure demeanor" characterized by "ideological flexibility, psychological openness, and self-confidence about one's Blackness. . . . While still using Blacks as a primary reference group, the person moves toward a pluralistic nonracist perspective" (p. 18). As Thomas put it, "You lose your hangups about race, age, sex and social class and see yourself as a part of humanity in all its flavors" (1970, p. 78). Optimally, when this has been accomplished, the individual moves on to stage 5, "Internalization-Commitment," in which s/he finds activities through which to manifest the new identity in ways that will further the progress of the group. "This 'ideal person' has not only incorporated the new identity but is struggling to translate personal identity into activities that are meaningful to the group" (Cross, 1978, p. 18).

Shades of Black

Clearly the description embodied in the Cross model is one of active identity change and self-creation. At any point in time different people will be at different points along the dimension of racial identity evolution. But even during the relatively brief or extended period that they are in a given stage, people have different ways of adapting to the issues involved at that phase. Thus, as implied in the title of his book, *Shades of Black,* Cross (1991) does not underestimate the complexity and variegated nature of racial identity dynamics among Black people.

For example, the fact that the personal sense of competence is not necessarily related to racial group orientation makes for a variegated picture even at Stage 1. Thus, a racial outgroup or "Eurocentric" preference on cultural dimensions by African Americans does not mean "self-hatred"—rejection of other aspects of self not related to race. It appears that there are at least two styles among African Americans who are at stage 1. Recent research (reported in Cross, chap. 5) suggests that many such persons are quite stable, self-accepting people who feel connected to Blacks and generally positive toward them. However, their cultural orientation is a European-based one and they are concerned with being good "Americans" in an assimilationist sense. They may be quite active in social organizations that are not primarily centered on Black political or social issues. They maintain their sense of racial identity at a level of low emphasis or *low salience.* When such people move through the nigrescence process to stages 4 and 5, their *racial* priorities change, not their personality features: "The shift [is] not so much from negative to positive, [but rather] from low salience to high salience, apolitical to political, Eurocentric to Afrocentric, positive and healthy involvement in organizations that [do] not stress Blackness to healthy and positive activism in organizations that [give] high priority to being Black" (Cross, 1991, p. 174).

On the other hand, in what Cross describes as a smaller group of the African Americans who hold a Eurocentric point of view, two other attitude clusters tend to be present that do reflect negativity in personality functioning. These two features are (1) a sense of "alienation" from Blacks, a feeling of being cut off and not supported by other Blacks; and (2) "anti-Black" perceptions, the tendency to see Blacks in the same stereotyped way that racist Whites do. The addition of such attitudes to an out-group, assimilationist orientation "has been linked to depression, low self-esteem . . . aggressive as opposed to nurturing social attitudes, a propensity in asocial behavior to commit violent crimes, . . . hypersensitivity, [and] anxiety" (Cross, 1991, pp. 185–186). Presumably, though, if such a person works his or her way through the nigrescence process to an appreciation of Black racial identity, s/he will not necessarily have changed the prior personality difficulties along with this change in racial self-concept. Change in personality would require other kinds of interventions such as counseling or psychotherapy. Thus,

> the price of a stage 1 identity—having an "out-group perspective"—is not necessarily poor mental health but the development of a world view and value system that can inhibit one's knowledge about and one's capacity to be an advocate for, the political and cultural interests that flow from the nonassimilated, more "ethnic" Black frame of reference. [p. 187]

Thus, even though the nigrescence process can be outlined in terms of stages, with different behavioral and experiential features characteristic of each, people reflect different adaptations within these phases. To exemplify this further, we can move to the end of the nigrescence model, stage 4. Cross argues that three general personality functions are available at this stage. A maturely internalized African-American orientation helps to develop appropriate defensive attitudes for dealing with a racist society, it enhances affiliative contacts with one's own reference group, and it serves as a base for reaching across ethnic and racial boundaries to those in other groups. However, granted these rather broad potential functions, the Internalization stage can manifest a range of different personal expressions.

For example, at one end of the dimension that defines high salience are nationalist positions. What Cross calls the "vulgar" nationalist position tends to espouse beliefs in the biological superiority of Blacks. Less radically, the "traditional" nationalist perspective emphasizes the importance of African culture to the exclusion of other cultural influences, but without using biogenetic constructs. On the other end of the high-salience continuum we can find African Americans who reflect a "bicultural" point of view, which we have commented on at different points in this volume. From this frame of reference, the stage 4 individual develops a style that attempts to blend what are personally acceptable aspects of European American culture with his or her sense of Blackness. A further variant of such a stance is a "multicultural" approach, in which persons' discovery of the richness of African culture opens them to a genuine appreciation of and interest in becoming familiar with a still wider range of cultures as well. Thus, the "cultural identity of the stage 4 person can vary from that of the monocultural orientation of the extreme nationalist to the identity mosaic of the multiculturally oriented Black" (Cross, 1991, p. 213).

Recycling
Parham (1989) has made a thoughtful contribution to Cross's work with his postulation that people "recycle" through some of the stages of nigrescence in the course of their lives. We are inclined to think of the effort to establish a clear sense of identity as the primary psychological task of the late adolescent–early adulthood phase of life (Erikson, 1963). Implied in this view is a sense of self that presumably becomes solidified by the time of one's mid- to late-twenties.[12] But more attention has since been given to the fact that psychological development, including the evolution of identity, continues to occur throughout the life span. Important aspects of people's personalities and sense of themselves can change as a function of the different life events they encounter—, establishment of an intimate relationship with another, usually through marriage; birth of children; the adjustment to one's middle years; and so on. Parham proposes that the nigrescence process is a lifelong one also.

He suggests that three modes of adaptation characterize the way an individual develops racial identity. A person could begin and remain at a particular nigrescence stage throughout life—"stagnant," as it were, and relatively unresponsive to life experiences that might help racial identity evolve. (In this view, one's early sense of Black identity need not necessarily begin at Pre-encounter. It is possible, for example, that, having been reared in a home environment characterized by the parents' enduring Immersion-Emersion attitudes, an adolescent's racial attitude development might initially crystallize at that period rather than at stage 1.) The second mode of racial adaptation is the standard "stagewise linear progression"—succession through stages in the sequence described in the nigrescence model. This is usually thought of as a single process occurring across time facilitated by inherent strivings toward personal growth. The individual stabilizes this evolution presumably by achieving and sustaining some form of Internalization (stage 4).

However, Parham suggests that, as with other important aspects of life history development, the process of nigrescence is probably not best thought of as a once-in-a-lifetime event. People often recycle through the various stages of this racial identity development as a function of the life span issues that they confront.

> *Recycling* is defined as the reinitiation of the racial identity struggle and resolution process after having gone through the identity development process at an earlier stage in one's life. In essence, a person could theoretically achieve identity resolution by completing one cycle through the Nigrescence process (Internalization) and, as a result of some new experiences that stimulate identity confusion, recycle through the stages. [Parham, 1989, p. 213]

This could be illustrated by a person who achieves a multicultural, or what Parham calls a "humanistic" approach, to the Internalization stage, perhaps leading him or her to value the experience of connectedness to people generally. By this very openness, however, s/he may be vulnerable to recycling if "confronted by one or several racist or oppressive incidents that shatter his or her belief in idealistic relationships and social experiences" (p. 215). This person might go back through the Encounter phase and proceed into Immersion-Emersion before coming back to stage 4. While the individual might conceivably return to this stage with a more "nationalist" orientation, recycling would allow the person to confront new challenges in living. Recycling and moving through the linear progression to a new resolution in the Internalization stage would clearly seem to be preferable to becoming rigid and stagnating.[13]

It is worth noting again Cross's longstanding position that the nigrescence model is not one intended to describe a change in total personality style. While he proposes that important values are represented in these stages and these values change in some Black people, many other features of personal style may well remain the same. As he suggests, it is likely that "people who began the conversion as 'neurotic Negroes' emerged from the experience as 'neurotic Blacks'; likewise, fairly well adjusted nonneurotic Negroes were well adjusted nonneurotic people with a new Black worldview at the completion of their conversion" (1978, p. 29). Likewise, a fairly well-adjusted person—who before the conversion approaches the world through modes of emotion and action rather than primarily through thinking and ideation—will respond in similar ways afterwards. What some personality theorists would call "basic personality structure" is not necessarily postulated to change in this "process of becoming Black."

Malcolm X

Although many of these changes in ideology have been described in higher-status persons, there are clear examples of how this model applies to persons of working- and lower-class background as well, notably in the case of such leaders of the Black Revolution as Malcolm X. His life as reflected in his autobiography (1965) can be seen to reflect many of the issues that have been discussed in this chapter. Any conceptualization about a personal history or biography is somewhat arbitrary. But for our purposes here I think we can see five periods in Malcolm's life from the perspective of a struggle to achieve greater self-realization. In the first period, during his days as a youngster in Michigan, although wanting to achieve and be accepted by Whites, in early adolescence he became more clearly aware of racial conflict and began to develop a heightened color consciousness. His father, a follower of Marcus Garvey's movement for African-American liberation, was lynched presumably for his outspokenness. Racial identity was further emphasized through his mother's open ambivalence toward him because of his light skin color. He felt the racially tinged derision of the welfare worker toward his poverty-stricken family. But his sense of self was never so flattened that he could not see the anomaly of having achieved in school only to have his teacher counsel him not to aspire to a high occupational level. When his eighth-grade teacher told him that his ambition to become a lawyer was "no realistic goal for a nigger," he noted,

> It was a surprising thing that I had never thought of it that way before, but I realized that whatever I wasn't, I *was* smarter than nearly all of those white kids. But apparently I was still not intelligent enough, in their eyes, to become whatever wanted to be. It was then that I began to change—inside. [Malcolm X, 1965, p. 37]

In response to the bruises he received from trying to integrate, Malcolm withdrew from Whites and went to the east coast, where he immersed himself in the world of lower-class Black culture. In this second phase of his life he became part of an underworld culture and also made contact with a large segment of much of the vitality of Black culture, some of it outside the law and some not. The thread of identity here was still one of assertive "resistance," in Lester's (1968) terms, resistance to working a "slave" (a menial job with meager material returns) and accepting the White society's definition of him as being second class. He bent all his effort toward becoming a successful hustler partly because he found a subculture that supported his sense of competence as a Black and as a person. Being outside the "law" was irrelevant; Malcolm could see that the law operated primarily to support White upper- and middle-class privileges. "I have no mercy or compassion in me for a society that will crush people, and then penalize them for not being able to stand up under the weight" (p. 22). He came to see the humanity of the outcast and saw that many of the pimps, hustlers, and prostitutes he encountered were intelligent, spirited men and women like himself who had been defined out of the human race before having had a chance to develop and prove themselves. His rejection of a "dignified" menial job within the system was his recognition that he, like many other Blacks, was potentially far more competent than such work implied. He chose one of the few avenues of exceptional individual achievement available to him. This phase does correspond to the Pre-encounter stage in the Cross model from a Black consciousness political perspective. But from a perspective of active self-creation, Malcolm was even during this period busily working on the process of self-definition.

The third phase was a transitional one that corresponds to Cross's Encounter stage and the beginning of the Immersion-Emersion phase. In the first part of his prison career, with his customary assertive avenues in society blocked, Malcolm's rage mounted and his negativism toward White society reached what he himself described as its peak. He spent considerable time in solitary confinement because of his rebelliousness to the prison system (which had put him there not only for burglary but probably even more, he felt, because he had involved White women in his illegal activities). Even though he was in some ways like a dangerous, caged animal, his aim was a very human one—to resist the prison's effort to subjugate him and rob him of an identity. He expressed his selfhood in the only way he knew how at the time.

In the fourth phase, beginning in prison and extending through most of the rest of his life, he turned to Elijah Muhammad's definition of the religion of Islam. He described his conversion as being fueled by his sense of guilt and his recognition of the errors of his past life, but it is likely that his willingness to submit to the Black Muslim discipline stemmed to a significant degree from its allowing him to continue his development of himself through the avenue of assertive resistance to racist America. As a disciple of the religion he could turn his intellectual talents and both hostile and assertive energies not only to individual achievement but also toward group advancement. In terms of personal dynamics, it seems quite plausible to postulate further that Elijah Muhammad also represented a paternal figure for Malcolm, perhaps allowing him to reunite symbolically with his beloved father, who had also preached both the dignity of Blacks and the necessity of a separatist solution to the racial situation.

In a last phase before his death, after his trips to Mecca, it seems as if he were taking further steps toward self-development by narrowing his scorn to certain segments of White society rather than the White race as a whole and concomitantly broadening his concept of brotherhood. At the time of his death he seemed clearly to be manifesting Cross's fourth and fifth stages.

A <u>central theme illustrated</u> by Malcolm's life is <u>that of dogged self-creation, constantly moving toward greater competence</u>, frequently in dialectical opposition to an oppressive "Other's" definition of him—a White "Other" and sometimes a Black "Other." This sometimes led him into the position of being an "outlaw" in White society's eyes or a dissident in the view of his Black colleagues in Islam. Malcolm did not change his personality style. He remained a forcefully assertive and often an aggressive person trying to persuade people to his point of view and standing up to his antagonists. His effort at self-development did not begin with what Cross would call the Encounter phase. An active orientation toward self-realization marked his entire life—from his days in Michigan up to his final hours—notwithstanding that some phases of his development were destructive to himself and to his race. To some extent his life illustrates my earlier statement that self-contributions to behavior, the choice processes that one brings to the world, are not always positive from a socioethical or a personal point of view. Yet they are an expression of a person's effort to take hold of life, have an impact on it, and make something of oneself and the world. (Milliones [1980] interprets Malcolm's life more strictly in accordance with the Cross stages.) In the eventual overall thrust of his life, in spite of negative periods in it, Malcolm wedded his striving for individual development to a drive for group advancement, and in the merger a new sense of identity emerged.

Malcolm said that he laid bare the intimate details of his life not to titillate but as a guide to others and an illustration of a central problem in American society—its treatment of its colored minorities. In doing so he made clearer how many adequately competent Blacks, though perhaps less talented than he, turned to socially marginal and less productive activities because they were not able to express and develop a sense of competence within established American social structural boundaries. The subjective view of an autobiography clearly has its biases, and there will be disagreements about some of the historical facts. (Recent biographical discussion presents other perspectives on Malcolm's life [e.g., Coughlin, 1992; Frady, 1992; Lester, 1991].) However, the thread of consistent intentionality that can be seen in Malcolm's life, even in the many unflattering moments, supports the view of his as a self-creating spirit. The point is that much creative energy is and has been available in the Black community for generations and generations. Much of it has been suppressed or forced into other channels. The need for social change among minorities is not just that of teaching Blacks how to make use of opportunity and engage in self-development but, rather, making available to them in the first place the same range of social opportunities that have been provided for Whites of upper socioeconomic stratas. Given this, many Blacks will "take it from there." Indeed, in some cases there *is* a need for special training to participate in the technological aspects of society. And these needs must be addressed fully—in technical detail. However, it is equally important to realize that Blacks in general have the wish to be competent and infinitely self-developing, and they have continually expressed this striving against great odds with sometimes remarkable results.

Expression of a Collective Voice

Let's look now at an empirically derived view of identity change in the college context. Though Cross has argued persuasively that personal identity and reference group aspects of self-concept are not necessarily correlated, he did not say that this *never* happens. His point is that in important ways these different facets of self come from different aspects of experience that do not necessarily develop together. Those (previously) well-adjusted persons who reach the stage of Internalization are examples of persons who combine positive personal identity with positive reference group identity.

In *Black Consciousness, Identity and Achievement,* Gurin and Epps (1975) described some of the factors that contributed to some students putting together a positive sense of personal competence with a positive sense of racial (group) identity. Their study was done at ten historically Black colleges in the south during the 1964–1970 period of ideological ferment on campuses. (On southern campuses, the activity involved participation in the civil rights movement in local communities; later it shifted to activism for changes on the campuses themselves.[14]) Many of this generation of college students, like those before them, had come from families that had had to struggle to get these youth to college in order to give them a better chance for personal status in the American society. This had been the time-honored way of advancing "the race." In the first set of data collected, students tended overwhelmingly to believe that good academic preparation by individuals was the best strategy for breaking down the barriers of discrimination for Blacks as a group. But during their college years many of them were also beginning to believe in the need for a different route to group achievement as a way of supplementing individual effort. Students sampled in their senior year in 1968 and 1970 had come to the view that collective action was the way of furthering progress for African-Americans.

Personal Achievement and Social Involvement

The task taken on by some of these students was to try to combine individual achievement with collective action for group advancement. In essence these modes of behavior represented two different avenues for the expression of assertion. However, the job of balancing these dimensions was not an easy one. Some were successful at doing this, while others couldn't do both at the same time. Of those who were most involved with social activism, particularly early in their college careers, a greater proportion had difficulty keeping up their motivation to study and dropped out of school. (They may have attended other colleges later on.) Those who remained, however, employed a variety of ways of using (or not using) the opportunities for personal achievement and group action. In order to sharpen some of the issues these students struggled with, Gurin and Epps (1975) described their data in a kind of typology based on whether students were high or low in their commitment to group action and high or low in personal achievement aspirations. (Data for this part of the study came from two sources: [1] a follow-up investigation of seniors at one college who had been in the research as freshmen, and [2] a body of data collected from a sample of seniors at six of the originally participating colleges.) Four groups emerged in this typology: "Committed Achievers," "Individualistic Achievers," "Activists," and the "Unengaged" (Gurin & Epps, 1975) (see Table 5-2). These students did not differ much in their academic performance during college—their grades and standard test scores were, more or less, equivalent.

The students who were able to combine a high sense of personal efficacy with a strong positive sense of commitment to group identity were the "Committed Achievers." They were the ones who expressed occupational aspirations for high professional and/or academic status and were "committed" to action, that is, had engaged in social action throughout their four years of college. (Seniors who had never engaged in civil rights or student power activities were classified as "Uncommitted.") It was this "Committed Achiever" group that was most successful in blending individual and group modes of assertion. Other groups in one way or another were less oriented toward combining these two dimensions. (More specifically, the criteria for high individual aspiration were: [1] intent to pursue the Ph.D. or a graduate professional degree, and [2] holding aspirations for jobs whose nontraditionality for Blacks or ability demands were in the top 25% for this student population. This last was determined for each occupation by asking a random sample of students to judge "what percent of their college class, ranging from only the top 1% to almost everyone, would have the requisite ability for the job" [Gurin & Epps, 1975, p. 47]. Being classified as high in achievement orientation came from meeting either one or both of these criteria. Seniors failing to meet either criterion were seen as having a lower achievement emphasis in their future goals [p. 355].)

"Individualistic Achievers" were those who had personal goals for achievement that were as strong as those of the Committed Achievers but had

TABLE 5.2 Occupational Aspiration and Social Activities

		Achievement orientation	
		High	Low
Commitment to Action	High	Committed Achievers	Activists
	Low	Individualistic Achievers	Unengaged

not participated in collective action at all during their college years. The "Activists" were differentiated from the Committed Achievers on the other pole. They had been just as involved in group participation as the Committed Achievers during college, but they had low occupational goals for themselves at graduation. The "Unengaged" had taken part in no collective social action during college and did not have particularly high personal achievement goals either.

The Implications of Different Choices
There were some further specific differences in postcollege plans among these groups of students that set them off from one another. Committed Achievers more than any other group spontaneously expressed the intention of choosing an occupation that would directly benefit Black people. In joining their high personal aspirations with their commitments to collective action, the Committed Achievers were overwhelmingly headed toward professional schools. They seemed to focus themselves rather narrowly on a small range of occupations—predominantly law and medicine—as ways of trying to carry out their social action goals. Individualistic Achievers had career goals that were not particularly tied to engaging in social action. They were planning to turn their high aspirations into a broader range of options spanning the spectrum of academic and research degrees. Most of them had the aim of pursuing the Ph.D. degree in various fields.

The Activists, who had been just as involved with group strategies as the Committed Achievers, also aspired to jobs that might provide them outlets for their social idealism, but at a lower prestige level. The Activists in many instances did not expect to go beyond the B.A. degree. Even when envisioning such a possibility, they tended to have rather remote plans to get Master's level training in such areas as social work, guidance and counseling, public administration, and the like—in areas related to human service.

Motivational and ideological differences between the groups were particularly illuminating. Over their college careers the Committed Achievers developed more of a feeling of academic self-confidence, a greater expectation of being able to succeed in their chosen occupations, and a greater sense of personal efficacy than any of the other three groups.[15] None of the others gained in these areas by the time of their senior year. And this gain occurred even though the four groups had not differed on those variables as freshmen; only the Committed Achievers made such gains. (The groups also had a similar mixture of precollege social backgrounds and levels of occupational aspiration in the first year.)

A particularly interesting set of group comparisons was that between the Committed Achievers and the Activists. As we have seen, these two groups were similar in having been actively involved in promoting collective strategies for Black advancement. They were also similar not only in activity but also in their ideologies concerning the Black situation. They both espoused a "System Blame" point of view—a belief that factors in the social system rather than in Blacks as individuals were primarily responsible for Blacks' social plight.[16] Committed Achievers and Activists also tended to agree with one another more than with other groups in holding politically nationalist views—for example, favoring political self-determination, community control, and the use of violence if necessary to attain political ends. But—and this is of particular interest—the differences between Committed Achievers and Activists on the self-confidence and efficacy measures was as great or greater than between any other group. In fact, the Activists experienced a *decrease* in their level of occupational aspiration more than any other group through their college years. In other words, in gaining a greater sense of competence through their college years, the Committed Achievers left their compatriots in the struggle far behind with respect to self-confidence.

How did this come about? The Activists as a group seemed to come to the conclusion that they had no right to pursue high personal goals once they were acquainted with the hardship and poverty of the lower-class Black community. The idea was almost that individual and group ambitions don't mix. As one female Activist put it:

> I've come to feel that you can't think about what's best for you and ever make the choices that help other people. If you think about personal advancement, there'll always come a time when you rationalize taking a better job that makes you leave the people you've been working with. It just always happens. [Gurin & Epps, 1975, p. 376]

But were the Committed Achievers somehow "selling out" by sustaining high personal ambitions? The data did not support this. In fact, of all four groups the Committed Achievers seemed to have a particularly sensitive "race consciousness"—even somewhat more so than the Activists. They felt more than any other group that discrimination affected Blacks in all occupational and status levels—that no Blacks were exempt. But their strong views about the nature of the racial situation led them to be even more demanding of themselves with respect to the occupational level at which they planned to enter the struggle for human rights.

It is interesting to note that, while most of the students in the overall sample became more system blaming and external in their control ideology, the Activist group changed along these lines most of all. Recall that this group dropped the most in their level of occupational aspiration. Their differences from the Committed Achievers may be accounted for by the different ways in which they used their college experience. For example, commitment to action had to be embedded in a broader set of positive campus experiences for the student to sustain high individual aspiration. There were specific dimensions on which the Committed Achievers could be differentiated from the Activists:

> The Committed Achievers, but not the Activists, stood out for having had contact with more faculty outside the classroom, turning to faculty specifically for help in planning their future careers, finding these faculty contacts more helpful, belonging to more campus groups, holding more leadership positions on the campus, having had more experience in campus governance committees and groups concerned with educational policies, and having taken advantage of more campus events with a distinctively Black political perspective. Activism alone did not promote the integration of collective and individual achievement. Activism in a particular context did. [Ibid., p. 389]

Many of the same kinds of issues separated the Individualistic Achievers from the Committed Achievers. They had tended not to form supportive relationships with the faculty as the Committed Achievers had. They had not been particularly active, even in the more conventional kinds of collegiate activities. In terms of friendship patterns they seemed more to be loners. "Overall, they seemed less integrated into campus life, less touched by the experience of going to college" (p. 390). While the Committed Achievers were most sensitive to racial issues, the Individualistic Achievers were least sensitive to such concerns. The latter group tended most of all to hold to the belief that race was irrelevant to Blacks getting ahead; they believed talent and effort alone would carry the day. The Individualistic Achievers were the group that remained outside of the trend of the total sample away from individual blame toward external explanations regarding the racial situation. Thus, they remained where they had come in as freshmen, both ideologically (conservative) and in aspirations (high). "What they did in atypical numbers reinforced their conventionality rather than shaking them up. They needed what colleges ideally can do best: they needed to be challenged, personally and ideologically" (p. 390).

The value of having counselors and faculty attuned to the need for supportive contact with students is apparent. The Gurin and Epps data also make clear that having meaningful opportunities on campus to take leadership and planning roles is a requisite for students. Such values are not newly discovered in this study, of course. However, these authors do see their data as supporting the value of the Black college for some Black youth, especially those from rural and poverty backgrounds, who often thrive socially and intellectually in the more compatible milieu they find there. As we shall see next, such a college environment is valuable for a broad group of Black students, not just for economically disadvantaged ones.

In ending this brief discussion of the Gurin and Epps material, it is possible for us to draw some parallels between their Committed Achiever who was a college student and the Black youth seen as "the New Ghetto Man" (Caplan, 1970) who participated in ghetto riots. Basing their protest on a system-blame perspective, the young rioters had a sense of being blocked from achieving what they could in a fairer society. They were a group that decided they were not willing to give in to a sense of hopelessness and simply take discrimination "lying down." The Committed Achievers embody a similar feeling of personal worth and system blame, but with the opportunity to get to college they made use of their opportunities to try to achieve things for the group as well as themselves. In Caplan's idiom they perhaps represented a "new college man and woman" in the Black community, persons who came out of the turbulent years of the civil rights and student activist movements of the south.

Unfortunately we do not have follow-up data on what this particular group of young people actually *did*, although we shall soon look at some data on Black college students in general. While the Committed Achiever group had laudable ambitions, their career solution was not necessarily perfect. They restricted themselves by electing to become lawyers or doctors in the effort to carry out their sense of social mission. It was as if they failed to appreciate that they could contribute by training in other professions. Researchers trained with Ph.D. degrees in the social sciences, for example, can be in the vanguard of knowledge and action about the racial scene. Even if a Black person's choice seems to be unrelated to African-American issues, such as in natural science or humanities careers, there are a variety of ways that one can be of use. The individual can take direct action within the profession and be a visible role model in nontraditional (for Blacks) occupational areas. The problem for the Activists was that many of them lowered their goals below what they might have accomplished had more support been given to sense of self-esteem and other achievement values. To the extent that a "less prestigious" career is chosen with a genuine sense of potential fulfillment and as offering opportunities for self-development, then there could be little quarrel with the choice. The point in this study was that the drop in aspiration was accompanied by a drop in self-confidence. That should be the alerting cue for the educator's and counselor's concern.

The Gurin and Epps work brings us back to a point raised in Chapter 2, note 7. There we discussed the Nobles and Sampson notions of the importance of an "extended" self—a sense of "we"—in the self-concept of non-Western people. These and other authors have been critical of the Western emphasis on the individualized "I" in the sense of self. It is interesting to note that the Gurin and Epps work seems to indicate that the Committed Achievers were able to blend elements of individualized striving with a strong sense of commitment to group action. They pointed themselves toward occupations that they experienced as rewarding and in which they could potentially make significant contributions to the community, such as law and medicine. These would seem to be the people who blended a clear sense of "I" with a sense of "we." Those who were "activist," who had an equally strong sense of "we" but who had developed less of a sense of personal competence, were less effective in college and not prepared to move on to more influential professional positions. These data support the idea that for group advancement an emphasis on "we" can usefully be a strong supplement to, but not necessarily a replacement for, a clear sense of self that guides personally meaningful life choices. They seem to embody the ideals of those in some Native American groups that "I am the people." In the ideals of the Committed Achievers there is an emphasis on recognizing and developing one's individual talents for use in advancing one's people.

In addition, the Cross model suggests that too narrow a definition of "we" is also not necessarily the most desirable solution. The final stages describe a sense of "we" that is more broadly defined. Malcolm X came to a sense of "we" that included people who were not of Black African heritage.

Blacks in College: An Update

The Gurin and Epps study documents different ways that young people took advantage of the chances for self-development offered by their college experience. In this increasingly sophisticated technological society, college is one important way for young people to develop skills for channeling assertive energies in constructive and rewarding directions. As we saw, some used these opportunities to blend strong personal achievement aspirations with an activism associated with strong racial group identity. For all of the groups, except for the Unengaged, the college experience seemed to promote some aspect of their assertiveness at a personal and/or group level. While the Gurin and Epps observations are encouraging in many ways, we must remember that their study was conducted in predominantly *Black* college settings. It was on such campuses in the south that the assertiveness of college student activism in the 1960s began and was particularly strong. But by the mid-1980's three-fourths of African-American students were attending predominantly White colleges and universities (Allen, Epps, & Haniff, 1991). The picture we have from the Gurin and Epps study is of a rather small sample of the total Black student population. How are African-American young people faring more recently as they attempt to avail themselves of the college experience?

When we address this important question, we confront a troubling scene. As Jonides et al. (1992) have noted, higher education for African Americans

is beset by a host of problems. African-American students . . . are more than twice as likely to drop out of college than Caucasian students. And this trend exists even among African-American students who perform outstandingly in high school. Because African Americans are unlikely to begin college in the first place, the cumulative effect of these problems of recruitment and retention is that there are deplorably few African Americans on our college campuses. To illustrate the problem, there are currently more African-American males in prison than in college. [p. 2]

It is not so much that African-American young people are unaware of the value of a college education. It is that the young people and the educational establishment are unable to connect with one another.

Supporting Academic Identity

Recent research indicates that the failure of American higher education to serve African-American youth is not a uniform phenomenon across all kinds of colleges. A widely cited study by Jacqueline Fleming (1984) indicates that Black students, especially Black men, do better on predominantly Black college campuses than in White university settings. Fleming's sample consisted of approximately 2600 African-American students and nearly 400 White students on fifteen Black and White college and university campuses located in Georgia, Mississippi, Ohio, and Texas. Her subjects were selected from the freshman and senior classes and tested once. Controlling for scholastic aptitude scores and socioeconomic status, she used a variety of instruments to assess intellectual development and psychosocial adjustment. (Appendix A in her book gives a detailed description of the tests used.)

With regard to one set of southern campuses she concluded:

> [Black] students exhibit stronger personal attachments to faculty, enhanced involvement in the career process, greater satisfaction with their academic lives, improvement on measures of academic performance, more enterprising vocational interest patterns, and maintenance of higher occupational aspirations. Black students in white schools, however, show quite the opposite, with increasing dissatisfaction with academic life, negative attitudes to teachers who use unfair grading practices, little return on time and effort invested in schoolwork, and no net improvement in academic performance. [p. 166]

With regard to campuses in the northern setting she noted that the Black schools were "twice as likely to encourage improvement in academic functioning and gains in intellectual self-confidence" (p. 183). When Blacks tended to do better in White college settings, the success seemed related particularly to supportive faculty-student interactions. In addition, her research indicated that Black seniors from a southern Black university were better able to perform competitively in an interracial experimental situation than were Black seniors from a White university in the same city.

One of the guiding ideas in Fleming's project was her belief that the college years are a time when all young people are working to solidify a sense of identity (Erikson, 1963). This includes combining emotional and interpersonal growth with the intellectual development that will be the basis for a rewarding career. Though the White campus setting provides rich educational resources for academic development, Black students do comparatively less well on those campuses because the socio-emotional context is not experienced as nurturing. It is often either coolly oblivious of the Black student or actually hostile toward him or her. By contrast, the Black college environment seems to provide students overall with a context in which they can develop both personal and intellectual resources for later adult functioning. The picture is more complicated for women, whose socioemotional development seemed not to be quite as positive as was that of men on Black campuses (Fleming, 1984).[17] The overall findings are consistent with the Gurin and Epps observations about the value of the Black college for many Black students. Is this, then, a prescription for trying to reverse the trend of the last few decades and direct Black students, men in particular, back to Black colleges? Not necessarily, as the next study shows.

Reversing "Stigma Vulnerability"

Recent work by a team of researchers (Carter & Steele, 1992; Steele, 1992) suggests that interventions can be made that empower the relatively larger numbers of Black students on White campuses. Steele (1992) has suggested that underachievement and attrition by Black students in White colleges are primarily a function of what he calls "stigma vulnerability."

Stigma vulnerability refers to the sensitivity Blacks feel concerning their perception that White people devalue them because they are Black. Such devaluation on the part of Whites does not always emerge in openly racist behavior. In fact, Whites may not be conscious of what they are doing. In many contexts, especially academic and occupational ones, such behavior is often reflected in a simple failure to affirm and support the talents and aspirations of Blacks with the same vigor that the interests of Whites with comparable ability are affirmed. Such behavior is more that of slighting than of slandering a Black person. While frequently it is clear to Blacks what is happening, it is likely that in some instances Blacks have a subconscious awareness of such repeated subtle encounters with White authorities but are not able to develop a clear conscious sense of what they are responding to. As this happens repeatedly in school—for example, in the problematic classroom interactions we discussed in Chapter 4 and in other ways—the student begins to disengage from academic pursuits and fails to use his or her talents. The student begins to direct negative or ambivalent affective assessments toward school.

Research has shown that such underachievement does not stem from socioeconomic status issues, from a failure to value education, or from a lack of academic preparation (Brown & Steele, 1992; Steele, 1992). African-American students at high ability levels show the same degree of academic underachievement and attrition from college as do those from lower ability levels. A more powerful explanation of poor performance is the hypothesis of students "disidentification" with the university setting. This refers to not being invested in one's studies and the academic life of the campus. So far this sounds much like the experience of Black students in White institutions that Fleming details in her study. However, recent research suggests that efforts need not stop there.

A research group at the University of Michigan developed a project to demonstrate that stigma vulnerability in Black college students can be mitigated and that this can have good effects on their achievement (Carter & Steele, 1992). The Michigan group set out to create what they called a "wise environment." They wanted such a milieu to be guided by a specific perspective: They were concerned that students should feel that they were being invited to participate in the program on the basis of the university's belief in their ability to succeed and that their risk of failure was linked to the difficulty of the academic work, not to their ethnic minority status. Too often, well-meaning intervention programs in prestigious universities communicate a message to participants that they are seen as an academic risk simply because they are minority students. This weakens such programs from the outset because the participants often feel subtly stigmatized as potential "losers."

This experiment involved 235 first-year students, Black and White, recruited from the 1991 entering class and 127 nonparticipants who served as a control group, selected to match the participants as much as possible. Program participants lived in a select section of university housing and in that sense were like other "college within a college" programs at Michigan. There were several other features of the Wise Environment Program aimed at countering racial stigma vulnerability.

- There was a freshman seminar that covered a wide range of topics allowing students to learn about one another as persons in their various dimensions.
- Regular subject mastery workshops, led by upperclass sudents, helped participants discuss difficult assignments, prepare for exams, and discuss concepts at levels that went beyond course requirements. This last was aimed at preparing them for more advanced coursework and perhaps

future careers. An active ingredient here was to focus concerns about failure not on racial status but on the difficulty of the work.
- Participants were encouraged to enroll in particular sections of courses that allowed them the further opportunity of working on concepts and difficult material together.
- A strong overall emphasis on community was fostered by their common living situation and by events that they were encouraged to become involved in together.

It is of interest to note that the emphasis on group interaction in the program is similar to themes that Heath (1989) and S. Kagan (1986) stressed, as we have seen in Chapter 3.

Initial results from this project suggest that the Wise Environment Program is meeting with success. In the general student body, at all levels of academic preparation, European-American students had higher GPAs than did African-American students (Carter & Steele, 1992). However, after one semester high-ability African-American students who were in the program had GPAs equivalent to high-ability European-American students. Further, it should be noted that *both* White and Black students profited from the program: High-ability European-American program participants had significantly greater GPAs than equally capable European-Americans who were not participants. In addition, though Black and White students in the experimental group did better, the degree of improvement among high-ability African-American participants was greater than among European-American participants.

Kleinsmith and Johnston (1991) report another project at the University of Michigan to boost the performance of minority science students. This effort emerged specifically from the senior author's observations of the poorer performance of these students in the large introduction to biology lecture, a gateway course to the study of medicine. He devised a rather extensive computer program that allowed students to become actively engaged with the course material. This supplemented the more passive learning activities of attending lectures and reading the textbook. Special workspace was set aside in a Biology Study Center, and a number of microcomputer workstations were provided. It was advertised as an extra resource available to anybody in the class who wanted to use it.

The beneficial effects seemed to be clear. Minority students as compared to other students used the software considerably more, and they uniformally rated it as being very valuable. Most important was exam performance. The mean exam score for the class as a whole improved noticeably over the three years of data analyzed. Scores for minority students improved dramatically over these years such that at the end of this three-year period their scores, which had been 20 points below the class average previously, were virtually equivalent to those of their European-American classmates. During this period it did not seem as if the difficulty of exams or the content and perceived effectiveness of the lectures had changed. The results clearly seemed attributable to the study center. Of further importance in combatting stigma vulnerability, this computer resource was not billed as a minority student facility; it was made available for all students. "Hence, minority students [were] not subjected to the indignity of being sent to a special facility for remedial help. They [were] simply taking advantage of a general facility whose overall goal was to provide all students . . . with the opportunity for achieving a roughly equivalent understanding" of basic course material (Kleinsmith & Johnston, 1991, p. 246).

The authors of both sets of studies indicate that these are preliminary data; continuing to follow both the experimental and control students is necessary. But these early results do suggest what can be done when the environment is structured to allow for positive affective assessments to be associated with learning. It is quite consistent with the statement quoted from Kenneth Clark at the beginning of Chapter 3 to the effect that children who are believed to be capable of learning do learn.[18]

Life After College: Adulthood

College and university education provides a means of preparing for competence in adulthood—that span of life during which one continues the never ending process of self-creation. African Americans confront these issues of adulthood in their work, family, and community life (Bowman, 1989; Harrison, 1989).

Though societally imposed limitations continue to exist, Black men and women are increasingly entering the workplace at high levels of responsibility. A recent book, *Children of the Dream* (Edwards & Polite, 1992), presents examples of African Americans who have, with considerable personal effort, turned the long struggles of their parents and relatives into their own personal success. This book contains a set of succinct narratives of the lives of Black men and women who have achieved upper-middle-class status and positions of leadership in various aspects of the business and professional world. The sample of forty-one persons that Edwards and Polite discussed in the book were born in the thirty years between 1935 and 1965. The stories of their success illuminate the special strengths and skills it takes to prevail in the face of persistent racism. Never trying to deny the fact of their racial group membership, neither did they let other people's conceptions about race determine their fate. A number of them succeeded by taking what we have described here as a dialectic attitude toward their situations.

California Congresswoman Maxine Waters, for example, commented to a newspaper reporter on her collection of Black memorabilia—which included Aunt Jemima images: "Aunt Jemima is very special. . . . She symbolizes the strength of our people and the strength of black women. . . . And if I'm ashamed of Aunt Jemima—her head rag, her hips, her color—then I'm ashamed of my people" (Edwards & Polite, 1992, p. 98).

Waters later said to the authors:

> What they [Whites] did in creating Aunt Jemima as a stereotype . . . was try to make fun of my people—my mother and my grandmother. And I can take what they attempted to make derogatory, to poke fun at, and see something positive. And I can say, You can't make me ashamed of my past. That tells white people something about who you are. That they don't describe the world for me—I describe it. [p. 99]

A successful entertainment executive learned early on that the world presented a variety of possibilities for choice: "My father always said there's a difference between being poor and being po'. Poor has an 'or' in it, which means you always have a choice. Po', on the other hand, means you got no mo'—no more choice. I never believed I was po'" (p. 137). Here is an excellent example of a family background that nurtured a sense of "awareness" as we defined it in Chapter 2: "knowing that something else might be taking place in a life circumstance" (Rychlak, 1988, p. 354). Taking such a dialectic stance was a fundamental factor in this man's success.

Edwards and Polite affirm that dealing with anger and rage over the injustices of racism is one of the major stumbling blocks that African Americans face in trying to "make it" in a nominally desegregated world. Based on their material, Edwards and Polite derived three styles of coping that seem to mediate Blacks' ability to succeed or not. The first is the "knee-jerk reaction." In this style the person angrily assumes that every critical or negative response from a White person is motivated by racism. This person is unable to be open to learning and lives constantly on the defensive, with considerable stress. Chances for success in a White work setting are the least in this mode.

The second mode is that of "the measured response," in which the individual withholds judgment, examining each interaction on a case-by-case basis, recognizing that every possible slight cannot be answered. But a considerable amount of energy is spent on evaluating what should be responded to and what should be ignored. The third and healthiest mode for getting along in the White workplace in the authors' opinion is "the operational trusting mode." Here the Black person assumes that Whites may have racist feelings but is prepared to ignore those if coworkers are prepared to be civil and not let their hostile feelings interfere with the Black person doing his or her job. "Blacks who operate with 'operational trust' tend to be most successful, for their attitude regarding white racism is usually, 'That's their problem, not mine' " (Edwards & Polite, 1992, p. 228).

The Edwards and Polite work, only briefly highlighted here, brings us back to the theme of this chapter regarding the development of healthy assertion in Blacks. While these reaction modes are presented in a kind of typology, to the extent that they reflect strong components of racial group orientation, these styles might also be seen from the perspective of nigrescence. The "knee-jerk" mode may be one heavily weighted with issues of Immersion. The "measured response" may characterize the person who has gained more distance and has moved to Emersion. The mode of "operational trusting" has more of the quality of Internalization or, in Harrell's terms, "aware cognitive flexibility." It may be that Black colleges have been more successful on the whole than White colleges in helping Black graduates develop an operational trusting mode. If so, all the more reason for predominantly White schools to develop projects like the Wise Environment Program described earlier if higher education is to fulfill its promise. But the fact that some Blacks are quite successful at prevailing against the odds does not mean that the majority of African Americans have access to educational, occupational, and other opportunities to aid them in dealing with the demeaning challenges to their self-image.

Conclusion

We began this chapter by noting a shift in the way African Americans have come to handle their assertion and aggression. The Crain and Weisman data suggested that the racial situation historically had forced too many Blacks into less productive ways of expressing their aggression—either by overinhibiting or by not channeling their assertion judiciously. Cross's paradigm describes the process by which many Blacks, after the Black Social Movement of the 1960s, began to take a new tack in self-creation. It was one that raised the "salience" of racial group identity, thereby opening up new aspects of self-awareness and new avenues for self-expression. Gurin and Epps and Fleming showed how African-American students on Black campuses have used the support they found there to develop their capacities for more effective assertion. To the extent that predominantly White universities in this country are willing to catch up with Black schools in their capacity to serve African-American youth, it appears that the methods for doing so can be developed.

One of the hallmarks of the assertiveness that has characterized the psychology of the African American, beginning particularly in the late 1960s, is the unabashed linking of sense of self as a person with the sense of oneself as being Black. Throughout their history in the United States, African Americans have had to struggle with the angry feelings stirred by the "obstacles and meannesses imposed on them." This struggle has been made particularly difficult by the limited opportunities for giving vent to their hostile impulses. While becoming more frank about their hostility toward Whites in recent times, many African Americans have not let themselves simply be consumed by the fires of their own rage. They have continued to turn much of their energy into efforts at more effective expression of assertion and competence strivings. Such strivings have included for Blacks an increasingly self-conscious effort to assert both individual and group pride.

Notes

1. The shift in preference for the term *Black* from *Negro* was a defiant insistence by African Americans that *they* decide what to be called, that is, that they define their own identity. It involved taking a word that White culture had attached primarily negative connotations to and (dialectically) focusing on the contexts in which Black is "beautiful" (black is the color of rich, fertile earth; precious oil; valued ebony; etc.). The current preference among many Black Americans for the term *African American* over *Afro-American* is meant to express more explicitly an ongoing cultural connection with the mother country, Africa, and with people of the African diaspora. The latter term refers to people who live in various parts of the world who have a (Black) African heritage.

2. Traditional psychoanalytic theorists have argued that aggression is innate, an instinctual force that must be channeled properly to ensure the individual's survival (and ultimately that of the human species, of course). A differing classical position regarding the source of aggression is that it is the result of the *frustration* or blocking of some goal the person is striving for at the moment. The instinctual theory would not preclude frustration as a source of aggression, but the frustration-aggression theory does intend to exclude the innate drive notion. A more recent psychoanalytic position that is quite consonant with the ideas we are developing in this book is expressed by Kovel (1984). He suggested that aggression is best conceived as

> a raw striving, relatively undifferentiated, able to undergo any number of transmutations, and able to direct itself to any number of objects . . . aggression is in the most basic sense an impulsion to act upon an object, and to alter the object of its activity. Thus its range of expression extends from a "healthy" sense of mastery to the most unbridled and seemingly gratuitous aim of destruction. Seen in this light, aggression loses its connotation of badness and becomes instead a basic propulsion to act

upon the world. What is "bad"—i.e., destructive—is reserved to a particular outcome of aggression, one all too universal, to be sure, but not so much a biological given as it is the consequence of the human situation. [1970, pp. 257–258]

Aggression expressed as mastery is similar to assertion as we have described it here. In Kovel's view, when that "raw striving" is expressed as *hostility* it has different aims. (Classic psychoanalytic theorists would probably account for "mastery" as a "neutralized" expression of the aggressive drive, that is, a drive that has the same source but aims that are not associated with destructiveness.) Robert White (1963) indicates his belief that the problems with the usual drive notion, some of which we discussed in Chapter 1, make it unwise to put mastery components, at least those conceived as competence, under the umbrella of the aggressive drive. It does seem plausible that an impulsion to act on and change the world, as Kovel conceives it, might contribute to many constructive kinds of acts. This would not preclude effectance behavior from emerging independent of a more traditionally acting drive such as aggression in its various forms. This is not the place to try to resolve the longstanding controversies regarding the origin and nature of aggressive behavior. I shall assume that assertion and mastery in some forms can conceivably be expressed in part through the aggressive drive as it is more broadly formulated by Kovel, for example, and that some efforts to act on and change the environment stem from the independent competence motive. (See also Kovel [1981], especially pp. 237–241, and the preface to his second edition of *White Racism* [1984], especially pp. xlii–xliii, for some of his further thoughts on aggression.)

3. Although competence strivings are ubiquitous in all groups, it cannot be denied that African Americans have developed some chronically self-defeating behavioral styles. Many of the behavioral attributes that Pugh (1972) referred to as "adaptive inferiority" are descriptive of such styles. Rainwater (1966) made a similar point. Reporting on his investigation of life in an urban slum, he suggested that the suffering of lower-class Blacks in such settings is not only a function of oppression by Whites and their institutions but also is a function of the personal adjustments and adaptations to such situations that Blacks have made. For example, the pressures on the lower-class family are such that interaction patterns develop among family members that limit the performance of emotionally supportive functions in the family. This leads to negative impacts on the socialization of children.

Rainwater expressed this as a kind of paradigm. He argued that it is an oversimplification to see the suffering in African-American inner-city communities as coming about only from White oppression. He suggested that such suffering comes about also because White oppression leads to chronic personal reactions on the part of Blacks that keep them from advancing socially. This is the traditional view of problems in the inner cities. Breaking the equipment and disregarding the punctual starting time are ways of actively expressing "resistance," but they also get the worker fired and keep him or her from advancing economically. Rainwater argued that Blacks' behaviors—perhaps most importantly those toward one another in their families and communities—do the work of caste victimization for the White society. The specific misfortunes of a Black person are, then, not necessarily the direct result in every case of a racist act.

Not only does this kind of emphasis overlook the continuing positive features of a great many Blacks—the loving sacrifices made for their children's benefit, the work at more than one low-paying job in order to make ends meet, the sustaining of an essentially humanitarian perspective toward the world—it tends to blame the victims for their plight, a tendency to which social science is prone (Caplan & Nelson, 1974). While cataloguing the kinds of maladaptive reactions that can legitimately be seen among Blacks and in their families we must also keep a clear focus on the overbearing social context in which these behaviors occur. If this pathological institutional and cultural context were corrected, in some cases behavior would change, and in the other cases the effort to correct the chronic self-defeating habits would be an easier task.

4. Are Blacks more aggressive than Whites? This is a question that some have felt deserves serious consideration (Baughman, 1971). The longstanding evidence of intragroup hostility and crime within Black communities and the rioting that has erupted with some frequency in the last twenty-five years seem to make this a legitimate query. Some White people may see hostility in Blacks where none is intended due to failure to understand Black cultural styles (Cheek, 1976). However, beyond such considerations one cannot look at the history of some 400 to 500 years of colonialist and racist exploitation of native populations in Africa and North and South America and justify the contention that Blacks are more aggressive than Whites. In fact, there seems to be considerable *projection* (the defense of unconsciously attributing to others the unacceptable impulses that exist in oneself) by Whites involved in such an indictment of African Americans.

5. Recent large sample studies of African-Americans (Gurin, Hatchett, & Jackson, 1990; Jackson, 1991) have updated the picture of the modern Black American community. Although the Crain and Weisman study is somewhat outmoded, the data still provide some useful insights about certain historical trends in the Black community.

6. Related to the issue of unique effects on Blacks, Crain and Weisman (1972) wrote: "We have argued that Blacks have more personal problems than Whites" (p. 26). The ethnocentric bias in this statement is striking. To the extent

that "more personal problems" refers to the fact that Blacks proportionate to their numbers in the population suffer more effects of poverty, there could be some merit to the statement. But the fact is that it has been the White mentality and personality that have created the conditions from which Blacks suffer. This implies a striking number of problems in White people. A statement such as Crain and Weisman's does not address this issue. At best, then, it could only be said that Whites have different personality problems from Blacks—certainly not fewer personal problems than Blacks (Kovel, 1984).

7. The scale used by Crain and Weisman consisted of five items, three used by Coleman et al. (1966) and two from Rotter's original twenty-three-item scale. On the Coleman items the subject was asked to express agreement or disagreement with a statement, for example, "People like me don't have a very good chance to be really successful in life." On the Rotter (1966) scale a person is to select one of a pair of statements that s/he agrees with: "Being a success is mainly a matter of hard work, and luck has little or nothing to do with it" (Internal) versus "Getting a good job depends mainly upon being in the right place at the right time" (External). Blacks have been seen as being more externally oriented generally—that is, low in Internal Control. Banks et al. (1991) in their recent essay see this as an inaccurate characterization, however. In the Crain and Weisman study, subjects scored as External on three of the five items. We shall look at other interpretations of Blacks' performance on this scale later in the chapter.

Of particular interest to us is the notion that Internal-External Control can also be related to Rychlak's causal constructs, which we discussed in Chapter 1. Having a sense that one is the master of one's fate involves confidence about being able to impose one's own intentions as a frame or pattern on events in one's life and thus be able to determine the direction of things. Rychlak and Barna (1971) have developed a Causal Construct Scale that attempts to operationalize some of the implications of the causal principles and show their impact in human functioning. The scale consists of seventy-two statements, each of which attempts to express the sense of one causal idea. Thus the statement "A man is about as good as the stock he comes from" expresses a Substance construct. "The great minds of all time have risen above misfortune to shoot for better things in the future" expresses an Intention construct. The scale consists of thirty-six items that pair the various statements with each other, requiring the subject to choose the one s/he prefers. As they predicted, Rychlak and Barna found that preference for Intention constructs tended to be associated with emphasizing Internal Control statements; Impetus meanings were associated with External Control. This picture was clearer for men.

8. A list of ten items covering three areas was read to the respondent. The first area dealt with the roles related to being a family member—as child, parent, and spouse. The second group dealt with aspects of character—"trust-

worthiness" and "willingness to work hard." The last few items tapped the subject's assessment of his or her ability in five areas such as intelligence, mechanical ability, and athletics. The same scale had been given in a different study to a large national sample of White men and women and so comparison data were available. Results indicated that overall the Black sample rated themselves as above average on fewer items than did the White sample, thus presumably indicating lower self-esteem. However, when results were considered by region of birth, it was found that southern-born Blacks (raised in the North) scored considerably lower than Whites, but northern-born Blacks scored at least as high and in some cases higher than Whites. It's not clear what the reference group for comparison here was for the Black sample, but it is again in opposition to the Kardiner and Ovesey notion of uniform low self-esteem in the Black population. In her dissertation, K. White (1977/1978), using a semantic evaluation measure, also found that the self-esteem ratings were equivalent in degree of positiveness in a sample of northern urban Black and White adults.

9. We noted in Chapter 1 the three styles that Pettigrew proposed to characterize historical reaction tendencies among African Americans. In his formulation he drew on Karen Horney's tripartite description of human personality to propose abstractions about reaction tendencies among African Americans, recognizing that no such conceptualization does full justice to the complexity of individual human behavior. He proposed that general tendencies can be identified for (1) "moving toward the oppressor," that is, seeking acceptance through integration; (2) "moving against the oppressor," conscious experiencing and open expression of hostility toward Whites at an individual or group level; and (3) "moving away from the oppressor," ranging from avoidance of contact with Whites to avoidance of contact with problematic racial situations.

Taking off from Pettigrew's perspective, Gibbs (1974) identified four styles of adaptation of Black students to predominantly White universities based on her counseling contacts with a sample of students at the Stanford University mental health service. The modes of relating are called "assimilation," "separation," "withdrawal," and "affirmation." Assimilation corresponded to moving toward the oppressor, with the student being conforming and desirous of acceptance and approval by the dominant group and tending to be an overachiever to prove his or her worth. These persons tended to be anxious socially and quite sensitive to ethnic references and cues. The mode of separation, corresponding to moving against the oppressor, was characterized by hostility, anger, interpersonal conflicts, and rejection of White middle-class values. Such persons tended to be active protestors against White institutions and customs. In the withdrawal mode, moving away from the oppressors, apathy, depression, and alienation were some of the primary feelings leading to the students wanting to pull away from contact with troubling academic and social situations. Gibbs suggested that a fourth adaptive mode could be seen among Black students also, an affirmative mode. This designation refers to those oriented toward moving *with* the dominant culture, not simply toward it or against it; that is, such Black students accepted their own culture and were trying to "merge [their] minority identity with the broader American identity" (Gibbs, 1974, p. 731). Gibbs described the students operating within this mode as showing "self-acceptance, positive ethnic identity, hyperactivity, high achievement motivation, and autonomous self-actualizing behavior" (p. 736). They tended to run into trouble when they were unable to live up to their own standards because of conflicting pressures from Blacks and Whites. Gibbs discussed the incidence of these patterns in terms of their relative frequency, especially as related to class backgrounds. Although statistical analysis of results was not performed and although this was an analysis of behavior of students presenting themselves for counseling, suggestive trends seemed to emerge. The withdrawal mode, which seemed to be accompanied by the most serious psychological symptoms, was the most frequent one regardless of class, and it was characteristic of those who rated themselves as feeling inadequate. A large percentage of those who rated themselves as feeling adequate were in the affirmation category. Among results related to socioeconomic status there were no separationists among the upper-middle-class students and no assimilationists or affirmationists among the students in the lowest of the socioeconomic backgrounds. Further, whether or not the student had attended an integrated high school seemed to have a bearing on the mode of adjustment to college: "Twice as many students who attended integrated high schools compared to those attending predominantly Black schools developed the mode of affirmation, while four times as many were assimilationists and one-fourth as many were separationists" (p. 738).

10. These role behaviors in interracial settings can be seen to be an aspect of the "persona" of Black individuals, in Jungian terminology. The persona is a concept Carl Jung used to describe the fact that we all have a social facade that we adopt in playing our socially prescribed roles. While this may be a consistent way of being in certain situations and hence a part of personality, a person is usually aware of this aspect of himself or herself as being different from other aspects of self. The danger to the individual comes when s/he comes to accept the persona as the real personality. It may be possible to see the group D persons in the Crain and Weisman analysis as persons able to maintain a distinction between certain role behaviors and self, whereas the accepters, with low self-esteem (group C persons) may have come to believe in the role imposed on them. For them the mask had come to "stick to the face," as the saying puts it.

11. In the light of the growing political activism among African-Americans in the 1980s one might think that Jesse Jackson's bids for the Democratic party's presidential nomination would have galvanized some of this more open anger toward Whites. Gurin, Hatchett, and Jackson (1990) analyzed Blacks' response to Jackson's 1984 campaign. Among the various dimensions of their results their data indicated that while his candidacy did allow assertive expression of Blacks' political aspirations, only a small portion of Jackson supporters could be described as expressing clear anti-White feelings.

12. Much of the empirical work done to evaluate the nigrescence concept has been done with college age and young adult populations. This would tend to restrict the generalizability of findings to a somewhat more privileged group socioeconomically. However, Cross (1991) cited studies that suggest that the issues discussed in his model apply to a wide range of African Americans. We shall illustrate that point with respect to the life of Malcolm X.

13. The continuing development of the nigrescence model by Cross and his colleagues (Cross, Parham, & Helms, 1991) answers at least some of the concerns about the general usefulness of a linear developmental model of racial identity adaptation. Harrell (1979) had rejected the idea of using a sequential-stage approach to characterize the adjustment of most Blacks to the racial situation. His criticism is of the implicit idea that there is a single albeit broad psychological process through which Blacks *should* be moving, with the presumption that the last stage is the most mature and desirable. He argued that different circumstances for African Americans have led to different ways of adapting to racism and that Blacks have not simply chosen one way to respond, even though they have had similar perceptions about the fact of social oppression. Harrell proposed six "coping styles" that Blacks have developed in recent decades in response to their situation. His six styles are labeled "continued apathy," "seeking a piece of the action," "obsession with counter-culture alternative," "the Black nationalist alternative," "identification with an authoritarian solution," and "historically aware cognitive flexibility."

An important aspect of each style is that it is seen as having both positive and negative possibilities for personal and social adjustment; that is, no style is seen as being without its problematic aspects. For example, the "Black nationalist" orientation promotes a positive view of Black people and Black culture but, as in the Immersion phase, a person with this orientation may become too narrow and rigid in his or her approach to White institutions. Or in "identifying with an authoritarian solution" such as Marxism or the Nation of Islam the individual gains direction and discipline in his or her behavior but may lose contact with personal perspectives in the overdependence on the authority. Even what seems like the most sophisticated adaptation, the "aware cognitive flexibility" style, is not without problems. It is a position in which the Black person is aware of the ambiguities and complexities of the racial situation. This fits our humanistic definition of awareness—a consciousness of alternatives (see Chapter 2). This orientation to life recognizes that "the struggle against racism is not over, and indeed, there are presently no comforting or even familiar answers to the issues facing Black people today. This individual stands poised and processing—creating new theory, practice, ideology, and consequently, new hope" (Harrell, 1979, p. 105). This position sounds very much like the final stages of the Cross model. On the other hand, Harrell sees this style, though embodying maturity—relative openmindedness, nondefensiveness, and a readiness to generate creative strategies for dealing with racism—as also potentially having pathological effects. Psychological awareness leaves one open to pessimism and despair: "This emotional state is not inconsistent with the recognition that after protracted struggle an unfamiliar and uncertain road lies ahead" (p. 105).

It is likely that most African Americans would be best described by several of these categories at once. For any style to be sustained, it has to have some features that the individual feels are positive even though there are also imperfections and personal costs in the way the adaptation works. It is quite conceivable, for example, that a person might show the achievement orientation of the "piece of the action" style in a competitive interracial work situation and at the same time support organizations that have a Black nationalist ideology and have an aware cognitive flexibility about the position of the African American in this society. As we have been saying, people use more than one frame of reference to structure the world for themselves. The styles that Harrell describes in many instances are probably modes that an individual can call upon at different times depending on the situation s/he is in or at various points in his or her life. Furthermore, and this is an important point, it is quite likely that people develop a number of such simultaneous facets in their coping style during the course of their lives.

Harrell's critique was an attempt to challenge the narrowness of options implied by a fixed-stage notion. Cross, on the other hand, developed his perspective to counter the static quality of personality types and describe the process of change in racial identity. His recent thinking recognizes the plurality of adjustments within the stages. Thus, as we have seen, there can be quite healthy features of the Pre-encounter adaptation and there can be rigid aspects of an Internalization identity resolution. Parham adds to the recognition of this complexity by his notions of stagnation and recycling. (People who are identifiable as primarily at one or another of Harrell's coping styles may be exhibiting stagnation.) Combining Harrell's notions with the Cross kind of model, it may be that development from Pre-encounter to Internalization kinds of phases corresponds to a person's opening up a wider range of options for conceptualizing and coping with the world, not just the change from one single stage to another. Further, consistent with Parham's notion, people who have passed through Encounter and Immersion-Emersion phases may develop a sensitivity—an awareness—that makes them more susceptible to the recycling process.

14. This study yielded considerable data about patterns of student achievement and motivation in college, students' precollege backgrounds, and development of their ideologies and political action during college years. There were findings discussing characteristics of the various college institutions as learning environments and information on the different kinds of contexts the campuses provided for students' social action interests. This provided a representative picture of the heterogeneity of these Black colleges. There is a far larger body of data here than can adequately be reported, and much is not relevant to our main theme. We shall select for discussion that relatively circumscribed though central set of findings that discusses how students linked aspects of individual and group identity.

15. Gurin and her coworkers have used the internal-external control variable as a measure of personal efficacy and competence. As we have seen, *internal control* refers to the degree to which an individual believes that his or her own efforts are the determining factors in gaining rewards in life. The thinking about this variable has traditionally placed a strong positive value on the internal end of this dimension and tended to associate that pole with a masterful conception of the self. However, in their extended program of research (e.g., Gurin et al., 1969) the Gurin team found that for Blacks only some of the Rotter items get at the individual's belief that s/he can control factors directly affecting his or her life. They have identified these five items as a "Personal Control" factor; all five of them are phrased in the first person. An example of the internal end is "What happens to me is my own doing"; at the external pole would be "Sometimes I don't feel I have enough control over the direction my life is taking" (Gurin et al., 1969, p. 37).

Other items in the scale, only one of which is worded in first-person terms, are seen to refer to the respondents' belief in the Protestant work ethic as a general social value irrespective of their application to the individual himself or herself. This factor has been labeled "Control Ideology." An example of the internal orientation on this variable is "Some people just don't use the breaks that come their way. If they don't do well, it's their own fault" (as opposed to the external version: "People who don't do well in life often work hard but the breaks just don't come their way"). The reasoning behind the distinction is that African Americans may grow up accepting the value of hard work in general, but their experience in American society is that hard work does not pay off in their lives, because factors in the social system keep them from reaping the benefits of hard work. Thus, many Americans have worked their way to the top of the economic ladder, but a disproportionately large number of Blacks have been kept on lower rungs, no matter how hard they have worked. It was the belief in one's personal efficacy (high on Personal Control), not a belief in the general work ethic alone (Control Ideology), that was associated with higher academic performance and aspiration variables in the Black college student sample (Gurin & Epps, 1975).

Gurin and Epps (1975) and Gurin, Gurin, and Morrison (1978) note the finding from their studies and those of other workers that the distinction between Personal Control and Control Ideology holds also for Whites who are highly liberal. Thus, for many such persons and many Blacks it is the first-person (Personal Control) items that carry the weight of sense of personal effectiveness. Third-person items (Control Ideology) are interpreted in political terms; these people tend to take an external orientation on these items, indicating their recognition that the system doesn't always work for people, even when they do work hard. Gurin, Gurin, and Morrison assert that an important point for prediction with Black and liberal White populations especially is that the Personal Control items reflect sense of efficacy in those arenas in which these individuals actually feel they can have an influence. Their political ideology, however, leads them to feel that the individual alone cannot have an influence on social system issues, and hence collective action is necessary. For politically conservative people the distinction is not made between Personal Control and Control Ideology.

16. While it is supposedly preferable to be internal, it is presumably not so good to be external in one's locus of control orientation. In other words, the locus of control theorist looks with a jaundiced eye on one who believes that random luck or chance rather than effort is what pays off in life. However, again Gurin et al. (1969) pointed out that the racial situation forces a different view of life on Blacks: "The operation of the labor market which can lead to layoffs over which individuals have no control, poor transportation facilities which reduce their possibilities in the job hunt, the tendency of employers to hire within the social network of those already on the payroll, etc." (p. 33) operate quite systematically and reliably in the lives of the poor and non-White minorities. (Acknowledging such issues is what Ogbu and Matute-Bianchi [1986] felt to be important, too.) For persons experiencing such events an external orientation is not just a belief; it fits the facts of their lives all too well. In their research with the internal control variable, Gurin et al. administered items worded to get at how Blacks might view the way the racial situation affects opportunity. They derived an individual versus system-blame factor indicating people's feeling about the extent to which factors external to the individual are responsible for Blacks' racial plight as opposed to the degree to which the failure of individual Blacks to work hard enough to prepare themselves accounts for their situation.

For example, the statement "The problem for many Negroes is that they aren't really acceptable by American standards. Any Negro who is educated and does what is considered proper will be accepted and get ahead" represents an individual-blame response—an internalization of responsibility by directing blame back at the group (and by implication, at the self). The alternative choice, "The attempt to 'fit in' and do what's proper hasn't paid off for Negroes. It doesn't matter how 'proper' you are, you'll still meet serious discrimination if you're Negro," rests responsibility on factors outside the individual (Gurin et al., 1969, p. 49). It blames the system and is an externalizing response. For most Black people and for the group as a whole, taking an "external" stance on this scale squares with the facts of life in America and therefore would seem a more realistic response. Of particular interest here is the fact that in their college student sample, Gurin and Epps (1975) found that men who took a system-blame stance ranked higher on some performance and aspiration variables than men who took an individual-blame perspective. This was true even among men with an equally high sense of personal efficacy (high Personal Control).

17. Critical discussion of Fleming's work can be found in Sedlacek's review (1986). Allen, Epps, and Haniff (1991), reporting data from the large-scale National Study of Black College Students (NSBCS), gave a more recent view of the situation of Black students on Black and White campuses across the country. Though the methodology of the NSBCS was not the same as Fleming's and certain features of the results were somewhat different, the Allen, Epps, and Haniff work presented a rather complementary picture to that of Fleming.

18. Other kinds of interventions approach the problem of underachievement from a somewhat different direction. Both the Gurin and Epps and the Fleming work indicated that the availability of supportive and understanding faculty contacts, while probably important to all students, is essential for Black students if they are to find an intellectual home on college campuses, especially White campuses. Faculty and administration of predominantly Black campuses seem to have readily understood this.

Again, a University of Michigan research group has taken an approach used at many colleges, individual research mentoring of undergraduates by faculty and graduate students, and used such a program to counter the trend toward academic disidentification among minority students (Jonides et al., 1992). The academic goal in this five-year University Research Opportunities Program (UROP) is to teach the minority student participants about research and/or a particular academic topic. But a further goal is that of facilitating "the identification of minority students with the university . . . through the regular interaction between faculty and student participants in an atmosphere that is focussed on learning, [and] is . . . highly social and personal . . . as well" (Jonides et al., 1992, p. 3). It is thus the central idea here that identification with the college, fostered by UROP, will lead to better academic functioning.

The UROP program involves pairing students and faculty on the basis of mutual interest. Participants, who are first- and second-year students, serve as research assistants to their faculty advisors and join in the lab groups and team meetings as well as meeting with more advanced student assistants. The principal outcome measures are improvement in GPA, increase in the tendency to select advanced-level courses, and staying in college. The program also is using several attitudinal and behavioral measures as an index of changes that will facilitate academic progress (Jonides et al., 1992). UROP students are to be compared to a similar group of minority students and to a group of Caucasian students.

The project is in its initial phases and so only preliminary data are available. At this writing the researchers indicate, first, some positive motivational changes. UROP students reported a greater interest in going on for advanced training and more confidence in their research skills than did controls. They showed higher levels of personal self-esteem than did minority controls and similar levels of collective self-esteem. (The latter contradicts some reports in the literature that African Americans who show high performance and interest in academic areas manifest a lower degree of ethnic identification.) In the sphere of behavioral changes, UROP students showed a greater likelihood than did controls to seek help when they needed it. (Fleming had found a tendency for Black students on White campuses to keep things to themselves when they were having difficulty; students on Black campuses seemed more readily able to talk over their problems with others.) It may be that UROP participation has personalized the faculty and made them seem more approachable and genuinely interested in their progress. Finally, data on GPA did not indicate an unequivocal positive effect. However, after one year, sophomore UROP students were opting for more upper-level courses, thus possibly enhancing their academic chances during and after college. This increased courseload was not at the expense of their GPA, perhaps reflecting more interest in their academic work. There was the indication here that a greater number of these minority students were becoming more *identified* rather than disidentified with the school situation.

Again, the researchers caution that it is too early to conclude that this project has met its goals and that we are justified in making firm recommendations about such programs. Furthermore—and this is an important point that is often overlooked in the consideration of the "average" African-American student—this research design, and that of Carter and Steele discussed previously, does not tell us much about the Black students who are doing well on the White campus without such a program. We need to understand how this comes about, too. Nevertheless, these data are certainly encouraging for the large numbers of students for whom it applies. Note, too, that the UROP program is not presented as a "remedial" program but is offered as an opportunity to see a side of the academic enterprise that (even as bright high school students) they might not have been able to imagine existed.

Some might argue that the academic effects of stigma vulnerability come from the racism of American society. Thus, it is wrong to develop programs to change the attitudes and behavior of Blacks. That is, this focuses mistakenly on the victims of oppression; what is needed is change in the oppressor. From that view, the main thrust should be on programs to change the attitudes of White students, faculty, and administrators. There is merit to such a notion. Firm guidelines for respectful behavior should be made conspicuous in the college community, and these could be reinforced by structured orientation procedures for new arrivals and by other programs as the need arises. However, Black students come to college with an ingrained set of survival responses based on prior experience that include negative affective assessments that interfere with their studies, in many instances. Using trained and relatively enlightened faculty and students, the aim is to expose Black students to broader *human* processes such as faculty mentoring and peer support that will engage their competence strivings and help them develop their "awareness"—that is, come to the recognition that the heights of scholarly accomplishment are an option for them. Such a restructuring of the university environment also gives Black students a more useful set of choices between Black and White college environments for deciding what is best for them.

6

The Wayward Self: Distortion and Repair

Some argue, and with good reason, that much of the personal stress people feel in modern times can be attributed to societal disorder and social pressures. An unstable peace in an age of rising nationalism, racial strife in beleaguered cities, job scarcity for the unemployed and job dissatisfaction for many of the employed, declining certainty about ethical standards—these among other things, symptoms perhaps of a "sick" society (Fromm, 1955), contribute to chronic tensions that can be the seedbed for severe emotional upset. With problems such as these surrounding us it would seem we don't need to look within the individual for explanation of mental disorder. But not everyone thrown out of work becomes unusually morose and begins to hear voices telling him he is bad, or withdraws from and neglects her children, refusing to talk to anyone. While many of our formulations about mental disorder must take the external conditions of living into account, concepts of disordered *personal* reactions cannot be eliminated.[1]

As we look at the psychological problems that Black people may have, it is tempting to rest all the blame on the oppressive social conditions to which Blacks are exposed. And this is an understandable and sometimes quite justifiable perspective (Akbar, 1991b). Racism does put an added burden on the psychological adaptation of Blacks by presenting direct assaults on the sense of self and the self-activity of African Americans. Since the earliest days of slavery, racist practices and ideology, extending beyond the individual behavior of White persons into the institutional structure and cultural mores of the United States, have worked to dehumanize Black people (Kovel, 1984). Dehumanization involves first forming an idea of another living person as a "thing" and then acting on that person "so as to sustain one's dehumanized conception of him" (p. 36).

Although slavery as such is long gone, many of the attitudes toward Blacks that grew out of that period of American history remain. Developing the belief out of their own psychological and economic needs that Blacks are "no better than animals," White people have treated Black people in ways that make it harder for the latter to develop their humanity (in fact, Whites also stunt their own growth by the efforts they sustain to keep Black people down). In the terms of this book a dehumanized view implies that Blacks are seen as not being capable of or entitled to a full sense of self-worth and competence or to an independent sense of agency that would help promote a sense of self-esteem.

Our concern here is particularly with some of the issues involved when the conceptualizing process goes so much awry that people find themselves unable to decide on or make satisfying and effective choices about which road of self-development to take experiencing along with this considerable anxiety, despair, and confused, sometimes strikingly bizarre thinking. Obviously there are many ways of looking at the facts and theories about mental and emotional disorder. Our goal here is not to catalogue disorders and their treatment like an abnormal psychology text. Rather, our purpose is to speak to issues of abnormal personality functioning from our humanistic perspective as these issues pertain particularly to racial group membership for African Americans. In this chapter we shall use such terms as *mental/emotional disorder* instead of the more familiar term *mental illness* for disturbed psychological reactions. My preference for these terms derives particularly from Thomas Szasz's rejection of the term *mental illness* (1974). For one thing, Szasz's ideas agree with our basic humanistic position that behavior is guided by the person's conscious and sometimes unconscious *intentions*. This puts an emphasis on the degree to which the person is an *agent* in the circumstances of his or her emotional disorder. (See Wakefield [1992] for a critique of Szasz's views and of other modern notions about psychopathology.[2])

A legitimate call in recent years for innovations in mental health service delivery is geared to taking account of the cultural diversity of people in minority communities (Smith et al., 1978). The task of helping people choose more effective paths of self-development in life requires making available to people a variety of techniques and even different conceptual viewpoints. Fitting such techniques and perspectives to the individual client involves a clinical approach, the recognition of the uniqueness of the individual that exists along with the similarities of that person to other people. In other words, besides cultural diversity there is also a considerable degree of individual diversity among peoples of the same cultural background. A clinical approach is tailored to the individual's needs and uses theory and research about human personality generally, along with data about cultural group membership, as an orienting point from which to reach out to understand the particular person. We shall be concerned in this chapter with some of the implications for emotional disorder and its amelioration that derive from the humanistic view we have adopted here. I shall argue that humanistic perspectives in some of the traditional clinical approaches are a necessary though not sufficient part of understanding disturbed psychological behavior in African Americans. In discussing psychopathology, traditional terms will be used as a way of raising issues that are consonant with our humanistic orientation. Although there are codified ways about how to categorize people's behavioral difficulties, notably the revised third edition of the *Diagnostic and Statistical Manual of Mental Disorders* of the American Psychiatric Association (1987), there is considerable controversy about the adequacy of such categories for *anyone,* let alone for minority group persons (Menninger, Mayman, & Pruyser, 1963; Schact & Nathan, 1977; Smith et al., 1978).[3]

Anxiety and Defense

The process of daily living involves harmonizing needs and intentions with the limitations and opportunities posed by "reality." Defenses, what the noted psychiatrist Harry Stack Sullivan called "security operations," are of particular use in preserving a sense of equilibrium in one's life. When a person's personality organization seems to be threatened, for example, when a cherished aspect of a person's view of self seems to be under attack or is being called into question, perhaps through the potential emergence of conflictual feelings, that person is likely to experience anxiety at some level of awareness. *Anxiety* is the "state of apprehension and dread cued by threat to essential personal values, [to] the integrity of the personality, or to life itself" (Korchin, 1976, p. 57). At such a point, taking the cue that danger is imminent, the individual may resort to a psychological defense. As noted earlier, defenses operate to change one's awareness or behavior so that a disquieting external stimulus or a potentially conflictual thought or feeling is avoided. Such a solution usually lowers the sense of danger so that the person no longer experiences the anxiety.

Let's take as an example a man who, since early childhood, rather than become aware of forbidden angry thoughts at his younger brother, has come to *repress* such thoughts—keep them out of consciousness—and unconsciously to replace them with kindly, friendly thoughts and actions toward his brother and *all* men younger than himself all of the time. Adopting his parents' prohibitions in this regard, he has developed his personality in this way so as not to run the risk of tarnishing his sense of self with fratricidal fantasies. Or, to take another example, suppose that a policeman speaks to a Black man in what the latter perceives as a racially demeaning way. The man has a choice of retaliating directly or, for example, suppressing his anger and perhaps even forgetting for a while that the event ever took place. Taking one of the latter courses makes it more likely that he will be able to get on with other important tasks in his day and allows him to perhaps direct his simmering anger into social action groups working to improve police-community relations.

From one perspective, defensive activity of this sort is another example of the kind of dialectical activity that is inherent to the human individual. We have described the dialectical mode, the capacity to consider a variety of other options in a given situation, as a part of human creative potential and an important mode by which Blacks have sustained their sense of competence in a racist milieu. Through the act of defense an individual tries to reduce the sense of threat to manageable proportions by acting as if certain impulses did not exist or that they have other sources than their true ones, for example. In essence the individual imposes a (dialectical) alternative on the situation that attempts to resolve it, at least temporarily. This too is a part of the everyday creative activity of the human being. (Freud had many case examples and theoretical formulations illustrating the ingeniousness of people's defensive compromises. See G. F. Mahl [1969] for a thorough discussion of the classic psychoanalytic ideas about defense.)

However, this capacity can be a mixed blessing. The trouble with defenses is that if they work too well, they may make a person's behavior in the world less flexible and adaptive. For example, it might be appropriate sometimes for the man mentioned earlier to be stern and irritable with his younger brother's not infrequent cheekiness, both for his own and his brother's good. But his defenses won't allow that, and so his interpersonal relations and his personal development are less effective than they might be. Regarding the man who walked away from the policeman, because of the strength of his personal character overall (what psychologists call "ego strength"), he may well be able to function effectively on his job and be amiable with family and friends. On the other hand, it may be that his anger is so great that, although he did not show it very much to the policeman, he "displaces" the expression of the anger to the form of irritability and hostility toward his boss and family. Or perhaps, although he "forgets" about the incident (represses it), his encounter adds to the general level of tension he feels about the racial and social class conditions that affect him, and his propensity for psychosomatic reaction—perhaps hypertension or an ulcer—may be aggravated significantly.

Sometimes a person's energies are so caught up in trying to control behavior and keep anxiety out of awareness that adaptive efforts are noticeably strained and even distorted. Then we are talking about psychological disorder. The particular behavior patterns manifested are a result of a person's life history combined with the particular set of stressful circumstances. Different people would respond differently to the same stress; one person often responds differently to different kinds of stress. One might ask why a person would use behavior patterns that are socially maladaptive or seemingly personally distressing, patterns that don't seem to work adaptively. The answer is that such patterns usually do work, at least temporarily, in shutting off the experience of potentially severe anxiety—and that is what is crucial. In a choice between not being obviously socially awkward or not being so anxious, not being anxious usually wins, even at the expense of, for example, crippling phobias or time-consuming obsessive-compulsive rituals. *Psychopathology*, or mental disorder, then, can be defined as disproportionate or inappropriate reactions to anxiety.

Throughout the book we have described the individual as being active in creating the conceptual frames that are crucial to determining the understanding of experience. From the perspective here the same is true for psychopathology. Mental and emotional disorder also stems from an active conceptual structuring of events. However, when it is designed primarily to ward off anxiety at all costs, it becomes maladaptive. The mentally disturbed individual is still actively trying to cope even though caught up in the tangle of disturbance. From one view, the individual's behavior, even though objectively we call it "disturbed," seems to him or her to represent the best choice s/he can make under the conditions as s/he sees them, that is, as s/he (actively) conceptualizes them. (Compare the discussion of this point in Chapter 2, pp. 38–39.)[4]

Mental Disorder as Disturbed Self Activity

People in need of psychological help are not always the first to know it. However, when the individual does have insight into the need for assistance, the psychological state experienced is one that Jerome Frank calls "demoralization." Persons in such a state are

> conscious of having failed to meet their own expectations or those of others, or of being unable to cope with some pressing problem. They feel powerless to change the situation or themselves and cannot extricate themselves from their predicament. . . . Some severely demoralized persons feel unable to control even their own feelings, and this gives rise to the fear of going crazy. . . . {Frank & Frank, 1991, p. 35]

In previous chapters we have proposed that people have as a basic goal the maintenance of a positive self-esteem, a feeling about themselves that the organization of attitudes and strivings called self is in good order. Another way of putting the term *demoralization* is to say that people in a state of demoralization have exhausted the options they can see for sustaining a positive sense of self-esteem—or at least they feel they have exhausted such options.[5] Racism certainly operates to make it harder to find such options.

This characterization is like saying that people experiencing emotional disorder have a diminished sense of being able to meet their intended goals. Rychlak has applied his Causal Construct Scale to the analysis of such issues. In an earlier study, Rychlak and Barna (1971) had shown that scores indicating emotional abnormality on the Minnesota Multiphasic Personality Inventory (MMPI) were strongly associated in a positive direction with endorsement of "substance" and "impetus" constructs. "Pattern" and "intention" constructs tended to be associated negatively with abnormality; that is, the more the endorsement of such proverbs, the less abnormality in the personality test scores.

In another study he and a colleague found that a sample of men hospitalized with the diagnosis of schizophrenia tended more often to endorse proverbs representing "material-cause" themes than did a group of men hospitalized for nonpsychiatric disorders (Rychlak & Ingwell, 1977). The latter group tended to endorse "final-cause" proverbs. The greater preference for the intention-oriented proverbs among the nonpsychiatric subjects was taken to reflect their greater sense of being agents—active in their own lives, more in control of their affairs. The schizophrenic subjects, on the other hand, expressed a sense of being constrained by things around them with little sense of a reciprocal influence on the world.

This supports Frank and Frank's description of the demoralized person as one experiencing a sense of powerlessness. It is not so much that people suffering from various degrees of disturbance do not have intentions. From a psychodynamic view, it is that important and pressing intentions, some held at unconscious levels, are in conflict with one another. The individual is not able to impose a kind of order and harmony on conflicting tensions for the purpose of achieving adaptive goals. All of us experience conflicts among our strivings; "ego strength" partly involves the capacity to concentrate our energies on a select set of goals and keep others subordinate. Such an organizing focus, embodied in a person's experience as a sense of self, is either missing or not in effective control in psychopathology. Perhaps another way of describing psychological disorders from our perspective here is to say that the individual has lost the capacity to generate adaptive alternative modes of handling the problems s/he experiences.

Racial Differences in Mental Disorder

To an important degree these issues are relevant to both Black and White people; American Blacks are prone to the same disorders that other groups are. What does their special racial situation add to this? It is conceivable that some kinds of disorders will be more emphasized than others among Black Americans as a result of their collective cultural experience. Although the striving for some more effective level of self-expression exists everywhere in the Black community, there is no question that this flame burns lower, and sometimes flickers out, for persons trapped in degrading social circumstances or victimized over generations by social and family pathology.

If there are special stresses such as racism that have an impact on Black Americans, it is reasonable to wonder whether or not Blacks, especially working- and lower-class Blacks, are more susceptible to mental/emotional disorder than are Whites. Are the rates of serious psychopathology different across racial groups? Although this sounds like a straightforward question, the answer is not so simple. Such kinds of queries are the province of epidemiology, which is the discipline concerned with whether or not certain aspects of the population are more prone to certain diseases because, for example, of their gender, their occupation, their social grouping, or their geographic location. Having established such descriptive differences, one must then analyze the patterns to determine the often multiple causal factors involved. For example, the historically greater appearance of chest diseases (heart and lung disorders) in men can be associated with differential smoking rates and probably the stresses associated with differential occupational pressures. The increasing rates of such disease for women are being associated with increases in smoking and their increased entry into hitherto exclusively male executive professions. The epidemiologist seeks to establish the "incidence rate" of a disorder, that is, the number of new cases in a specified time, and the "prevalence rate" of the disorder, the number of cases present over a specific interval of time.

The reasons for asking questions about the incidence and prevalence of mental disorder ought to be to find out where mental health services are most needed, for one thing. Also, such information could presumably be useful in identifying ways in which cultural groups respond differently to life situations and thus contribute to our knowledge of the human condition. However, another possibility is that establishing differences can contribute primarily to stigmatizing Black people. For example, some writers have noted the contradictions in epidemiological descriptions of African Americans (Thomas & Sillen, 1972). Some studies have found Blacks as having more disorder than Whites, others as having less mental disorder than Whites. In either case a pejorative inference is drawn. In the former instance, African Americans are seen as having inferior ego strength; in the latter, Blacks are seen as being too simple to appreciate and be bothered by the stresses of life in a technological society: "In short, you're damned if you're ill, and you're damned if you aren't" (ibid., p. 124). Some prominent psychiatrists have stated their belief that slavery, and later segregation, provided a stable situation for Blacks. Desegregation and the consequent competition with Whites, according to this notion, led to greater stress and mental illness. The fact that Blacks streamed out of the "happy" south of the early twentieth century was explained by their being the "unstable" Negroes.

It isn't easy to do unbiased epidemiological studies (Fischer, 1969; Kramer, Rosen, & Willis, 1973). One major problem has been that epidemiological studies were based on state mental hospital records, and people in different social groups have different access to the different kinds of treatments available in society. Thus, if there are more Blacks in a given state hospital population over a period of time, that doesn't necessarily mean that more Black people were seriously disturbed than Whites. Lower-class Blacks ordinarily do not have as many treatment alternatives to state institutions as Whites do. It's likely, then, that illness rates based on state hospital data are spuriously inflated.

Further issues cloud the process of identifying the incidence and prevalence of mental disorder among Blacks. Racial stereotypes on the part of community officials and even misunderstanding on the part of a person's peers and family can determine who is counted in the mental illness census. For example, Brody, Derbyshire, & Schleifer (1967) investigated the case histories of a sample of thirty-eight young Black men, first admissions to a Maryland state hospital. It became clear that many of these people had been candidates for psychiatric treatment—psychotic or chronically antisocial—for several years prior to admission. One of the principal agencies that had previous and often repeated contacts with them was the police. Even their families, confronted by frightening and aggressive behavior, often saw them as being more in need of control or needing discipline of their withdrawn and "lazy" behavior than in need of psychological help. At times the family and friends, aware of the realities of prejudice, were inclined to accept the complaints of the troubled person when he spoke of specific social injustices done to him. To the extent that socially striking symptomatology is an aspect of a cry for help, this delayed identification of mental disturbance typically required that Black males had to "shout" louder and longer than did a White person.

> In a crude sense it seems likely that the police (as do other social institutions, e.g., schools, hospitals, employers, etc.) applied different standards to the behavior of middle class Whites than of lower class Negroes. . . . The apparent tolerance of the urban policeman to psychiatrically disturbed behavior in lower class Negro men may also be coupled with a tendency to view it as the naturally expected consequence of the "lack of responsibility" of members of a simple or inferior race. [Brody, Derbyshire, & Schleifer, 1967, p. 215].

Thus, accurately determining the presence of mental disorder among Black people in White society is a complex matter (Gary & Weaver, 1991; Neal & Turner, 1991; Snowden & Cheung, 1990). It does seem that a greater amount of psychopathology exists among the most disadvantaged social classes than among the more well-to-do (Belle, 1990). Blacks have seemed to receive a larger share of the more serious psychiatric diagnoses (Baker, 1988; Geller, 1988). But this may be due to their being disproportionately represented in the lower social classes. Two decades of research seem to support the idea that actual mental health differences between "advantaged" and "disadvantaged" groups reflect differences in socioeconomic status rather than racial group membership (Fischer, 1969; Neighbors, 1984; Robins et al., 1971; Warheit, Holzer, & Arey, 1975; D. H. Williams, 1986).

Recognizing that people's use of mental hospitals is not a particularly valid measure of the prevalence of mental disorder, some researchers have gone into the community to assess people's sense of subjective distress. Neighbors (1984) notes:

> [T]he best available data from community surveys indicate that blacks are no more likely than whites to have higher rates of average distress . . . [and] there is no strong evidence that blacks react more strongly to stress than whites. Such results are intriguing because blacks are known to be disproportionately exposed to social conditions generally considered to be antecedents of psychiatric disorder. . . . If it is true that blacks lead more stressful lives than whites, then we need to know more about the cultural strengths and coping resources that may account for the comparable or lower rates of morbidity among blacks in comparison to whites. [p. 174]

In regard to this latter point, it is likely that intraracial comparisons rather than between-race comparisons will be more useful in obtaining an accurate understanding of the mental health picture in the Black community. Gary and Weaver (1991) report several studies that take account of the differential effect of such factors as age, income, and marital status. For example, in some of this research they found that "depressive symptoms were lowest for men, married individuals, middle-to old-aged persons, employed persons, individuals with a college background, and persons with a household income of $25,000 or more" (p. 738).

Diagnostic Understanding

The question of the identification of mental disorder in the Black community leads naturally to the more person-focused question of diagnosis, that is, how one goes about determining that a given individual is disturbed or, granted that a person's behavior is disordered, what the nature of that disturbance is. This is the process of trying to "understand . . . eccentric symbol performances" in Sullivan's terms (1925–26/1962, p. 32). Diagnosis is a difficult and fallible activity. It rests on the skill and training of the diagnostician.[6] It depends on his or her ability to encourage the client to be open enough to be willing to reveal things that are painful and that indicate that s/he can't handle life at this time or that might lead to the client being hospitalized. It depends on the interviewer's empathic attitude and ability to establish rapport with the patient. (We shall have more to say about factors involved in establishing a helping relationship later in the chapter.) Under such conditions the client will begin to reveal himself or herself and allow the interviewer access to his or her mental life so that help can be given. This is difficult enough when client and mental health worker are of the same social class and ethnic background. It can be considerably more difficult when the two are of different backgrounds.

Over thirty-five years ago Hollingshead and Redlich (1958) pointed out the differential distribution of mental health services by social class—longer and more intensive talking therapies to the middle and upper classes, somatic and brief supportive therapies to the poor. Frequently being poor, Blacks have perhaps been more likely to fall victim to this trend. But there is the added dimension of ethnic difference that many White professionals have had trouble bridging. Tomes (1976) has cited studies indicating differential attitudes toward Blacks who presented themselves for treatment. In one such study Black men tended more than others to be denied access to a university-controlled inpatient treatment facility, usually a more prestigious kind of treatment unit (Weiss & Kupfer, 1974). Foremost among the reasons for these men being barred were that they were not seen as fitting the service's treatment model (for being verbal and insightful, for example), and they were also seen as being physically dangerous and sexually threatening.

While one kind of bias has been to see Blacks as disturbed than traditional services can handle, Lewis, Balla, and Shanok (1979) report an opposite kind. In their clinical and epidemiological studies they found that there was a tendency to underdiagnose disturbed behavior in Black delinquents, attributing aberrations to cultural factors:

> Many Black delinquent children referred for psychiatric evaluation to clinics, private psychiatrists and psychologists, and mental hospitals, were dismissed as characterologically [less severely] impaired in spite of what appeared to us to be clear evidence of psychotic or organic disorders. Symptoms that would have been recognized as pathological in White children or their parents, were ignored in Black children. [p. 54]

In one striking case a Black child, described as intelligent and quite paranoid, was admitted to a private psychiatric institution where his aggressive and bizarre behavior was diagnosed to be the result of an epileptic disorder. (Paranoia is a disorder in which an individual experiences himself or herself as being victimized, persecuted, sometimes under attack from hostile outside forces or agents. The individual's response tends to be one of hostile defensiveness, vigilance, and sometimes combativeness.) However, the youngster was transferred out of the hospital, eventually winding up in a correctional facility without clear mention of the neurologic disorder. He was not given continuing therapy for that disorder or the concomitant psychological problems. It is likely that both disorders were controllable and deserved primarily a psychiatric rather than a correctional response. Thus, too often the problem for Black clients experiencing severe personality difficulties is that such persons, youngsters and adults alike, are caught as it were between the Scylla of being seen as too disturbed for more prestigious interpersonally oriented therapies and the Charybdis of being seen as not really meriting psychological treatment—as simply manifesting "culturally appropriate" behavior or meriting incarceration. (One of Lewis's students [Bernhard, 1987/1988] found that by using carefully delineated psychological characteristics and case-history features it was possible to differentiate between boys who were prone to delinquent acts and those who were not. A majority of the boys in his sample were African-American. Ethnic background did not hamper diagnostic acuity in this study.)

These examples are raised to further the notion that if one has a clear conception of human behavior, empathic sensitivity to people, and a recognition of how cultural differences for a particular group tend to be expressed in interview or test situations, the process of coming to understand "eccentric symbol performances" can be carried on in ways that are helpful to African Americans and relevant to their personal and clinical troubles.

An example of sensitivity to this issue is a study by Haimo and Holzman (1979). They used a scoring system developed for assessing the presence of "thought disorder" in the test records of a sample of persons including Black and White schizophrenic patients and a psychiatrically normal control sample. The procedure involves evaluating thinking processes through the quality of the verbal productions on the Wechsler Adult Intelligence Scale (WAIS) and the Rorschach test.[7] The authors were also especially interested in whether differences in language style of lower/working-class Blacks made them more vulnerable to being diagnosed as manifesting thought disorder on these tests. They scored the protocols of Black subjects in the standard way and in two other ways that explicitly took account of African-American speech styles. They found that there was a significant tendency for the standard scoring system to overdiagnose thought disorder on the intelligence test but not on the Rorschach. However, all measures of thought disorder, whether corrected for language style or not, significantly differentiated schizophrenic subjects from normal controls in the predicted direction—the schizophrenics showed more thought disorder. Thus, the thinking disorder of the disturbed Black subjects could be discerned. It indicates that relatively accurate diagnosis is not necessarily confounded by this aspect of cultural difference in Blacks. Of course this does not mean that present systems do not need refining or drastic overhauling for people in general and minorities in particular. (Jones and Thorne [1987] suggest directions for such changes that involve making greater use of what I would call an "introspective" point of view in assessing minority groups rather than relying solely on "objective" measures standardized on the majority culture. Such a point of view is consistent in various ways with the humanistic view here.)[8]

In sum, the implication is that careful study shows no good evidence that the amount of mental disorder differs between Blacks and Whites when social class is controlled. It does suggest that the racial attitudes that poison our society in so many spheres can hamper the efforts of Black clients to make themselves understood and get help in regaining a productive course of living. The tendency to see Blacks as "too sick," or culturally inappropriate for talking therapies, or not really psychologically disturbed may be a way not only of avoiding their own race and class attitudes on the part of White professionals but also of avoiding exposure to the intense feelings that Black clients may want to vent toward them concerning their social and racial as well as personal concerns. Black professionals can be as much a target for such resentment at first as White ones. But the mental health establishment must turn and face such feelings, helping clients to resolve those that are unrealistic and dealing straightforwardly in personal and in institutional practices with those that are accurate (Geller, 1988; Krebs, 1971). Actually the individual, group, or family treatment relationship and a secure well-run hospital setting when needed can be a marvelously therapeutic social and personal experience freed from the multiple pressures of the external world. This happens when the professional makes the office or community setting a place where the minority client can feel well understood and fully able to express himself or herself. We shall look further at research bearing on this issue in our discussion of treatment.

Self Disturbances and Race

In this abbreviated discussion of race and mental health issues we shall focus on problems in sense of self. As has already been stated, the impacts of racism, though perhaps manifested somewhat differently according to social class and regions of the country, have placed a special psychological strain on the sense of self of the African American as a capably active agent. Consider again the example of that psychologically normal man who had the encounter with the policeman. It may well be that this man's situation in life enables him to be a good and loving provider for his family. Yet at some level of awareness perhaps not fully conscious, perhaps within his conscious awareness for a brief period at least, he is very likely to experience a blow to self-esteem at this incident. Perhaps the history of what armed Whites—whether police or not—

have done to Blacks, and periodically continue to do to them, momentarily becomes vivid for him. For a fleeting moment, along with his anger, he is likely to experience some self-doubt, some sense of inadequacy, some sense of vulnerability—the sense that he will be at the mercy of others and unable to exercise independent control over his own existence. At one level this is an example of the "acculturative stress" that Blacks must deal with in their daily lives (Anderson, 1991). From a clinical view, one that is not confined to any single racial group, the chronic intense experience of such feelings is central to pathological developments in the self (Kohut & Wolf, 1978). In the extreme, some of these disorders emerge in what are called narcissistic character problems.[9] In this terminology, racism is an assault on the healthy egocentrism—a sturdy sense of self—in Black Americans. As I have said before, doubts occasioned by negative reflections from a racist society are usually kept in check. (Normal people experience such doubts in occasional fleeting thoughts or in dreams and nightmares giving evidence that such issues are indeed part of the psychic system.)

However, when a person's individual history has been troubled and/or when the weight of events becomes too crushing, s/he may develop clear psychological symptomatology; that is, the person becomes psychologically disordered. Then some of the things that the person ordinarily keeps out of the way come to the surface psychologically. Thus, to the extent that the psychological symptomatology of those Black persons who become mentally disordered has admixtures of damaged narcissism, these may be exacerbated by racial pressures.[10]

Depression

What kinds of psychological experiences might trigger disturbances in a functional sense of self? Depression is one major source, derived from the experience of feeling in some ways unwanted and unacceptable.[11] A number of writers have suggested that, along with the experience of anger and rage discussed last chapter, a widespread feeling of sadness, a kind of "cultural depression," is a part of the Black individual's response to historical and current conditions in America (Comer, 1972; Grier & Cobbs, 1968; Poussaint, 1972). Florence Halpern, commenting on her clinical work with rural Blacks in Mississippi in the late 1960s, felt that "reactive depression was almost universal" (1973, p. 124). Crain and Weisman (1972) reported data from several studies that asked the question "Taking all things together, how would you say things are these days—would you say you are very happy, or not too happy?" (pp. 86–87). The indication was that Blacks were twice as likely as Whites to say they were "not too happy."[12]

When Halpern indicated the extent of "reactive depression" in her rural population, she was referring to the responses of Blacks to the oppressive external circumstances under which they lived. A particularly worrisome problem is that of sorting out the meaning of White people's behavior. Is the White personnel officer's iciness toward the Black applicant a habitual personal style? Is it due to the fact that she "got up on the wrong side of the bed" this morning—an attitude that she would display toward anyone today? Or does it reflect her racially prejudiced attitudes toward this Black applicant? These kinds of issues have long been a problem for Blacks living in some northern settings where racism was not always so blatantly expressed. In the south, for example, where Whites pride themselves on cordiality and warmth, a harsh response toward a Black had a clearly racial meaning. As the frank expression of personal racism becomes more muted in the south, perhaps the African American's dilemma regarding how to interpret White behavior will apply there too. Such issues are not only depressing but can contribute to the suspicious, self-protective style in interpersonal relationships that was noted earlier and is a quite understandable stance for a person to take (Grier & Cobbs, 1968). This can be seen sometimes in the problems that a Black person brings to therapy.

One 19-year-old Black woman of working-class background presented herself to a psychology clinic with marked feelings of depression and loneliness, continual feelings of anger toward people generally that she had trouble justifying even to herself, and problems with identity and lack of sense of purpose in life. Her personal history included strong feelings of having been neglected by her family, especially by her mother, leaving her with considerable anger and unfulfilled dependency longings. Her sense of mistrust of others and her expectation of not being treated kindly led her to look for racial insults from White coworkers where it was not really clear that such animosities existed. Being able to be clear about how much of her rage could be justifiably applied to her interracial contacts and how much was referrable to sources in her own particular family history was quite difficult and in and of itself depressing to her. The dilemma was even more difficult because she was frightened and saddened to acknowledge how furious she was at her mother, whose approval she still craved. Further, the shame she felt at revealing these things to her Black female therapist made it difficult for the therapist to help her since she kept the therapist at arm's length, as it were, with her hostility, her missed appointments, and lateness to sessions, all of which helped her to avoid getting involved in psychotherapy.

Her sense of self was like a sensitive wound, bruised easily by events that had even a trace of reference to race or her personal worth, and this very problem for which she came for help kept her from letting herself get closer to her therapist. One illustration of her personality-based dilemma was that she was being seen in a clinic whose fees were extremely low. She was able to afford the fees but felt she wanted to take a vacation trip to the Carribbean soon—something she had long wanted and felt she owed herself. She couldn't afford both to do this and pay for therapy, and she recognized a need for therapeutic help. She was angry with her therapist for not agreeing to see her for nothing. The therapist was seen by the client as not being sufficiently giving or sufficiently understanding of what she saw as real deprivations in her life (although she was earning a living wage currently). It seemed as if racial sensitivity had added to her more basic sense of fragility as a person to make her difficult to reach, even for a Black therapist.

Depression as Hopelessness

Let's look further into the literature to try to understand depression and self disturbance in African Americans. Classical psychoanalytic theory originally described the general psychological source of depression as anger at a loved one seen as abandoning the subject. This anger turned defensively against the self is the experience of depression (Freud, 1915, 1917/1957). Anger turned against the self may be an element in clinical depressive episodes for many African Americans.[13] However, such a formulation does not seem fully relevant to the *social* dysphoria of the African American. What is called for is a perspective that recognizes that racism represents a psychological assault on the sense of self. Another point of view, a more recent contribution to the psychoanalytic thinking about depression, is that of Edward Bibring (1953/1968). Though we do not have to be concerned about all of the implications of Bibring's formulation, it provides a more useful perspective for minorities. In his view, clinical depression represents a feeling of helplessness and hopelessness with respect to achieving healthy, self-affirming goals. He suggests that all persons normally strive to achieve at least three interrelated but conceptually separable aspirations in their personal growth. Expressed as central strivings or "wishes," these are:

> (1) the wish to be worthy, to be loved, to be appreciated, not to be inferior or unworthy; (2) the wish to be strong, superior, great, secure, not to be weak and insecure; and (3) the wish to be good, to be loving, not to be aggressive, hateful and destructive. [p. 163]

Making progress toward such goals at least partly mirrors the process of achieving competence as we have defined it in this book, and it does so in interpersonal spheres, not just in relation to the material world.

Depression in this view stems from the individual's perception that s/he is unable, helpless, to achieve one or another of these cherished goals in psychological development. Depth of depression could be related at least partly to the degree that any of these achievements in personal living is seen by that individual to be beyond reach. (The idea that the experience of helplessness is basic to depressive conditions has received a considerable amount of supporting experimental investigation from an experimental psychology perspective [Seligman, 1975].) Now, racism in its personal and institutional forms in American society operates intentionally and perhaps sometimes unintentionally to thwart the achievement of such psychological goals for Blacks where it can. In the effort to dehumanize Blacks, American society has portrayed them as being unlovable and unworthy. By intimidation and by limitation of social opportunity, society has attempted to keep Blacks from establishing the kinds of family and other institutional settings that would provide loving contacts and help them provide strength and security for one another. Society works directly to make Blacks feel competitively inadequate by abridging educational opportunities and relegating them to dead-end menial jobs, for example. (In this regard see Bowman's discussion [1989] of "role strain" processes as they effect hopelessness in Black men.) The frustrations in African Americans stemming from these unfair hindrances have generated the kind of rage and despair that have made it harder for Blacks to experience themselves as being good and loving. These are ways of characterizing the uphill struggle that Blacks and other minorities have experienced psychologically. There are a number of variations in theory about how clinical depression comes about in general (Blatt, 1990; Gaylin, 1968; Scott & Senay, 1973). Some of these may apply to incapacitating clinical depression in African Americans. Although greater helplessness among Blacks does not show up in clinical depression, the milder, more pervasive cultural depression related to race may perhaps be best understood in terms of a formulation that emphasizes the degree to which society engenders a sense of helplessness and hopelessness regarding the achievement of basic human strivings. Since Blacks do persist in their competence strivings, these feelings are relatively milder where personal and social circumstances allow a Black person to overcome obstacles. Where circumstances are chronically defeating, the chances are that socially generated experiences of hopelessness come to be taken as meaningful at a personal level. Negative experiences that become associated with aspects of self related to racial group membership can spread to other aspects of self, and one begins to believe them to apply to one's personal self. The individual then begins to develop conflicted feelings and ideas about the self and develops maladaptive reactions to protect the self.

The Family as Buffer
This casts another light on the role the family has in trying to provide the Black child a sense of self as agent, one who is loved and who can find ways of making itself adequate and skilled ("strong and secure") and thereby feel able to be worthy, loving, and giving to others. Thus, the quality of the "mediation" experiences in the family are important, to call on a term we used in Chapter 3. In this chapter the emphasis is more on emotional than on cognitive aspects of the mediating activity. The development of a cohesive core or "nuclear" self, one that provides the base for healthy personality functioning, comes about

only in the context of parenting that is "empathic," that is, parenting that anticipates the child's needs and responds to them appropriately (Kohut, 1977). (We shall have more to say about empathy later.)

Typically the prototype of this kind of relationship is established in the interaction between the mother and newborn child in the feeding situation. The task of the minority mother is made more difficult because she has to help the child develop healthy facets of self and self-esteem in important areas related to racial self-evaluation as well as in broader aspects of personal self-esteem. The mother's (or parents') ability to take on these extra tasks depends on her own well-maintained sense of self. Where this is minimal or lacking, the parent may feel affronted by the child's healthy efforts to establish an independent sense of self. The family can become a punishing place where the child may have his or her sense of self torn down by the other family members (Gouldner & Strong, 1978; Rainwater, 1966). A number of writers tell of Black parents feeling the need to teach children early to curb their verbal and physical assertiveness so that they will not endanger themselves in interracial situations. Often this is done out of love for the child but sometimes it may stem from a projection of the parents' own sense of worthlessness onto the child. To the extent that the Black mother is aware of the potential effects of racial prejudice on her children, she can offset much of the impact of racism on a healthy sense of self. Kohut and Wolf (1978), in discussing early personality development in general, make a comment that applies to the situation for the Black child and the parents coping with the racial situation. Granted that the child will be exposed to traumatic events, "these events leave fewer serious disturbances in their wake than the chronic ambience created by the deep-rooted attitudes of the [parents], since even the still vulnerable self, in the process of formation, can cope with serious [traumas] if it is embedded in a healthy supportive milieu" (p. 417).

When an individual's family background and early personal history have not provided a stable core of experiences from which a solid sense of self can develop, the individual, spurred by competence strivings, frequently can compensate to some degree for early experience, with supportive experiences later in his or her development. Many theorists feel that early experience does set some limits to personality development, but even with such limits, many people using later remedial contacts with lay or professional people are able to do remarkable things in turning their lives into more productive channels. It is likely that sometimes, when help is not available to Blacks to support their compensatory efforts, the way in which the social system routinely hinders a person's efforts at self-development may begin to reawaken in him or her the memories of a painful family setting in which s/he grew up. Thus, the person may come to identify past injuries with present ones and react with psychological disorder. (Granted the importance of supportive early experiences, this is not to deny that some social stressors, such as involuntary unemployment, tend to have an impact on even well-adjusted persons. In his study in a southern Black community, Dressler [1986] found that unemployment was associated with depressive symptoms independent of other risk factors for depression such as chronic stressors and other noneconomic life events. Further, the depressive impact of unemployment occurred even in the presence of "resistance resources" in the subjects, such as an active coping style, religiosity, and family supports.)

Emotionality in African Americans

In our consideration of disturbances in self-activity let's turn briefly to a topic that bears on our previous discussions in this book regarding affect. Halpern ventured the impression from her clinical contacts with southern rural Blacks that "a tendency to hysteria was prominent" in those persons she saw with emotional problems (1973, p. 124). Hysteria is a neurotic disorder with a long and important history in psychodynamic psychology (White & Watt, 1981). The most striking of the manifestations that have been focused on in hysteria were bodily symptoms—for example, paralyses, anesthesias—which did not seem to have somatic origins but rather appeared to have origins in psychological conflict. Modern interest in hysteria has broadened beyond these kinds of "conversion" symptoms to a concern with the more pervasive response style, the "hysterical personality." This pattern tends to be characterized by reacting to the world through emotional and impulsive responses rather than primarily by ideational or thinking responses (see Chapter 3, note 11). In its more extreme form, one cluster of traits that has been identified clinically as typifying this style is that of a "fluid change in mood and emotion, excitable, episodically flooded with feelings" (Horowitz, 1977, p. 5).

It is not surprising that Blacks might tend to develop a style that emphasizes emotional response to the world. Certainly much happens and has happened to them to justify sharp emotional response. (In considering Halpern's use of this category to describe Black reaction styles, we must remember that she worked with people from a certain geographical region—the rural south. The tendency to see Blacks as hyperemotional and impulsive has been used to stereotype them diagnostically. In wider samples of African Americans that include urban and middle-class persons, a different picture might well be expected. Yet, without assuming that hysteria as a neurotic style characterizes Blacks, her observation may be instructive.)[14]

The picture that some Blacks present of emotionality and "impulsivity" may also reflect a cultural value placed on being able to manage life stresses actively. Block (1981) suggests that "the Black culture stresses early in life the ability to 'do it.' Emphasis is placed on the active—managing difficult situations without showing stress" (p. 179). This observation is of course in line with the basic philosophical considerations of this book regarding active mastery strivings being present in the personality functioning of African Americans. When a Black person whose circumstances over the years have taught a coping style emphasizing physical activity and intense feeling stumbles psychologically and is at a loss as to how to proceed, the symptom picture s/he shows may have "hysterical" (or as the current *DSM-III-R* manual phrases it, "histrionic") components.

Conversion hysteria, in which bodily or somatic symptoms are predominant, has been seen as a reaction pattern in lower-class groups (Temoshok & Attkisson, 1977). Such styles have been attributed not only to lower-class Black but also to Latino groups. From a broader psychosocial perspective it has been suggested that conversion reactions have long been one way in which persons who experience themselves as having little social power in Western society can have influence and be attended to personally (Szasz, 1974). If hysterical disorders are somewhat more prevalent in Blacks, it may partly be a class-linked phenomenon.

There is an issue here that is relevant to our considerations of affective assessment. We noted in Chapter 3 that a tendency to bring personally based affective assessment to learning situations characterized Black and Latino subject groups as compared to Whites. This reflected a tendency of minorities to rely more than Whites on the universal ability to conceptualize situations in terms of their positive or negative valence toward them. One is tempted to speculate that normally functioning persons with hysterical personality features, or, beyond this, persons who are neurotically burdened hysterically, might be persons who rely more on responding to situations in terms of their affective assessments about them (in logical learning theory terms) and hence may have come to develop this facet of their response potential more. One implication would be then that emotionally or hysterically oriented persons in general will be more RV (reinforcement value) oriented than are "obsessive-compulsive" or ideationally oriented people. Such a notion could be tested rather straightforwardly in a research study. The implication would be, then, that Blacks may carry the RV propensity with them into a number of situations as a personality style.[15]

Special Disorders in the Black Community

The mental disorders we have discussed are a selection from the traditional disorders, and they pertain to persons in probably all ethnic groups in this country. Various writers call attention to some of the special health problems in the Black community such as drug addiction and alcoholism (Redd, 1989; Wallace, 1991) and hypertension (Harburg et al. 1973; Harburg, et al., 1991; Myers, Anderson, & Strickland, 1989). However, the raising of these topics of special, though certainly not exclusive, interest to African Americans brings up another diagnostic issue that is relevant to Blacks. This is the notion of "masked depression" proposed by Lesse (1974). He points out that sometimes depression does not appear as an overt behavioral syndrome but appears first in other symptomatic guises, hence the term "masked." There can be various kinds of surface manifestations behind which an actual clinical depression exists, depending on the person's age, ethnic background, socioeconomic status, and hereditary and constitutional background. Of particular relevance here are drug abuse syndromes and apparent physical disorders that have special frequency in adults. The fact that severe clinical depressions do not appear more among Blacks than Whites does not rule out the possibility that depressive response to social oppression may manifest in forms of behavior pathology other than frank clinical depression. It has long been known, for example, that alcohol is a widely used means of "self-treatment" for depression. The notion of masked depression, though not widely used, may have some value in understanding the effects of social oppression on Blacks.

Another area of behavior pathology—a special case of a longstanding social problem in the broader American society—is worth mentioning here. This is the issue of violence in the Black community. While the incidence of assault is a serious problem for the minority poor in general, inner-city African-American adolescents and youth are at greatest risk for death and injury (Bell, 1990; Gibbs, 1988; Hammond & Yung, 1993). As Bell (1990) notes in his review, in 1986 almost one-half the murder victims in the United States were African American, and 90% of them were killed by African-American offenders. Black men are about five times as likely as Black women to be homicide victims, and both men and women are likely to have known their assailants—as a friend or close family member. This is consistent with the Robins (1968) data we noted in Chapter 4. To phrase it in terms used earlier, violence is one of the pathological ways to seek self-affirmation in response to a sense of narcissistic injury (Miller, 1992). Bell (1990) and Hammond and Yung (1993) pose ways in which the Black community and the larger society must begin to deal with this problem to prevent the loss of a large portion of our youth.

Issues in Psychotherapy

Let's turn now to a discussion of the repair of distortions in self-functioning, issues having to do with psychotherapy among African Americans. There are many ways of conceptualizing the topic of psychotherapy. The term *therapy* is borrowed from the medical perspective, and it implies an intervention aimed at cure of an illness. Many researchers and practitioners in the field prefer to view psychological disorders and their amelioration from within the broad perspective of learning (White & Watt, 1981). In this view a disturbed individual has learned modes of behavior that get him or her through what s/he sees as dangerous situations but at considerable cost to adaptive functioning. Psychotherapy, a "talking therapy," is aimed at helping people to be able to relax their defenses, reappraise their anxieties, and consider new options for behavior. (Of course, some methods of intervening in emotional disorders are medical, that is, somatically oriented, such as electroconvulsive therapy for depression and drug therapy for various disorders. These are not psychotherapies, although drugs may at times be used as an aid to the psychotherapeutic process.)

Earlier in the chapter we noted that one aspect of emotional disorder is a diminution of the ability to bring one's intentions to bear on the world effectively. The aim of psychotherapy is to help an individual regain a sense of being "back in the saddle" of his or her own affairs again. The goal is to restore the individual's capacity to organize intentions more effectively in guiding behavior, restoring effectiveness and competence to self-activity and at the same time enhancing the sense of competence and self-esteem. Psychotherapy is not the only way of achieving these goals, but it is one way. The terms *therapy* and *mental health*, though borrowed from a medical context, are so much a part of everyday parlance that we shall continue to use them here. We shall also use the terms *client* and *patient* interchangeably here.[16]

We are continuing to emphasize the individual and his or her symbolizing processes. Throughout this book I have focused on the importance of such a perspective. In essence, what I am saying is that psychopathology represents a derailing of symbolizing processes so that an individual goes off into unproductive or outright bizarre paths, or perhaps spends energy "spinning his wheels," as it were, going nowhere. Psychotherapy is an opportunity to help people free their symbolizing processes from unproductive and destructive ways of conceptualizing their world, so that energy can be turned to more constructive modes of living. Szasz in his continuing critique of psychiatry, *The Myth of Psychotherapy* (1978/1979), made a similar point about the overall meaning of this enterprise when he cited (on the flyleaf of his book) Joseph Conrad's statement: "Strictly speaking, the question is not how to get cured, but how to live."

The focus on individual processes has come under fire in recent years from those who believe that the point of attack on mental disorder for minorities and the poor should be the community and social institutions rather than the individual. They argue that the pathology of oppressive social systems causes mental disorders and it is at the level of the social system that the major part of our resources should be directed. Some have even suggested that focusing on individual mental pathology and trying to ameliorate it without spending equal or greater energy on righting social conditions is a subtle form of blaming the victim (Billingsley, 1974). Further, it has been pointed out that there will not be in the near future—and may never be—enough trained human resources at the professional level to handle mental health problems on an individual or small-group level. (See cogent discussions of this "community mental health" point of view in Phares [1992] and Smith et al. [1978].)

The need for changes in mental health delivery is real. This is partly because the poor are more at risk for severe mental disorder, and services are not reaching them effectively. However, this doesn't mean that clinical attention to the individual participants in the struggle should be abandoned. Emotional disorder is the outcome of the individual's encounter with the tasks of living. People of all classes negotiate those tasks effectively, but a small segment of people of all social classes does not do so. Part of the critique calling for change in the kinds of mental health services delivered to the poor came from a view that communication abilities and capacity for insight into the personal styles of such persons were lacking. In response to this, Edelson's comment is appropriate:

> I am reminded of the criticism . . . [leveled at] many psychiatrists for their interest in psychotherapy as a treatment modality, not only on the grounds of difficulties in making psychotherapy widely available or of our own inadequacies as psychotherapists in symbolizing and communicating with those carrying on these activities in ways different from ourselves, but rather on the grounds that psychotherapy is culturally appropriate to the verbal middle-class but inapplicable to members of the so-called lower socioeconomic class who, so it is claimed, do not value words. For them, then, pills and advice.
>
> I wonder if it does not occur to such critics that a scarcity of language resources is not simply a preferred life style but rather a serious handicap in living, and that an inability to symbolize emotional, physiological, and sensory experience is not incidental to psychological illness but may in fact doom an individual to it. When we psychiatrists are exhorted to use other culturally more appropriate methods than psychotherapy in treating the lower socioeconomic class citizen—to accept, to adjust, so to speak, to his level of functioning—are we being asked to abandon him to a life of sleepwalking in a twilight zone of quasi-consciousness, in which he must depend for relief of his pain solely upon the efficient manipulation of his body and his environment? [1971, pp. 118–119]

Such questions about capacity are beginning to drop away as some of the parameters become clearer about what lubricates the flow of communication between people. It is generally recognized now that verbalness depends on the situation in which people find themselves (Labov, 1972; Lerner, 1972; Russell, 1988). When lower-class African Americans feel comfortable and understood, they are quite expressive and reflective (Evans, 1985; Geller, 1988).

Such expressiveness can be seen in the dreams of Blacks in therapy. One

Black man from an economically deprived childhood background, for example, dreamt of "Papa Doc," the President of Haiti at that time. His associations to the dream made it clear that he had condensed in this one symbol feelings about his father and similar ambivalent dependent feelings toward me, his therapist. I was in one sense a father figure (a "papa"), whom he usually greeted as "Doc." Another client's dream contained the image of her standing in the doorway of her childhood home looking at the strangely twisted hallway in her house. It corresponded perfectly to her often expressed feeling during that period of being "bent out of shape," that is, quite unhappy and frustrated. In work with Black clients of differing socioeconomic backgrounds and varying severity of psychopathology I have found them using beautifully expressive and apt metaphors to describe their psychological experience and using such material to make meaningful discoveries about themselves.

Psychotherapy with the Minority Poor

Is there evidence regarding the usefulness of psychotherapy for the minority poor? There are not many direct tests of this question, but some findings are worth looking at. In one intriguing study, Barbara Lerner (1972) investigated the effectiveness of short-term, psychodynamically oriented therapy in an inner-city community mental health center. Her client group was a diverse sample. It included "a Black Muslim incapacitated by an illness that had no physical basis, a suicidal prostitute, a welfare mother who abused her children . . . a child molester fearful of the police . . . a factory worker who felt that people on television were ridiculing him and broadcasting his deficiencies, and so on" (1972, p. 33). Not all of the group were poor or Black.

> The one thing all of these people had in common was a sense that something inside themselves prevented them from struggling effectively to realize their full psychosocial potential. None of them discounted real and often terrible external obstacles to such a realization, but all of them were dissatisfied with their ability to mobilize their own resources in the struggle against external obstacles. [p. 33]

In her study Lerner used a variety of measures of therapy outcome and assessed a large group of client characteristics such as diagnosis, previous therapy and/or previous hospitalizations for mental disturbance if any, race, social class, and other personality measures. She found that clients did improve with therapy and this improvement was not related to client characteristics. In other words, clients improved in spite of factors such as class and severity of diagnosis that should have hindered them from profiting from this kind of procedure according to the typical clinical wisdom. Karon and VandenBos (1972) found that psychotherapy as compared to medication alone was an effective treatment of clients who were "primarily poor, inner-city, and black" and who were diagnosed as being schizophrenic (p. 112). (This Michigan State Psychotherapy Project, as it was called, has been criticized by A. H. Tuma and P. R. A. May [1975], noted psychotherapy researchers in their own right; the critique has been rebutted by Karon and VandenBos [1975] and more recently by Karon [1989].)

The Therapeutic Relationship

Granted that psychotherapy with Blacks of varying classes can be effective, the question emerges as to what issues affect the therapy process favorably for the Black client. To some extent that is part of the broader and longstanding question as to how therapy works for anyone. The noted psychotherapy researcher Hans Strupp (1973) listed the establishment of a therapeutic relationship as the first of three "basic ingredients" of psychotherapy.

Most people coming to therapy in a state of demoralization, though wanting help, feel reluctant to expose to a stranger the sense of failure they feel at not being able to handle their problems independently. Part of the therapist's job is to create a relationship in which the client dares to relax defenses so that s/he can change nonproductive ways of conceptualizing and responding to life. This "helping relationship (patterned in significant respects after the parent-child relationship) [is] characterized by respect, interest, understanding, tact, maturity, and a firm belief in his ability to help" (Strupp, 1973, p. 1).

A key phrase to apply to this constellation of features would be "empathic understanding." *Empathy* refers to the ability to put oneself "in the other person's shoes" emotionally, while yet maintaining one's own identity and perspective. It involves trying to see another person's world, as much as one can, as that person sees it. This is an essential aspect of good parenting—being able to understand and respond to the child's sometimes inarticulately expressed needs not only for love and physical attention but also for discipline (lest the child's impulses run out of control). Thus, with respect to therapy, Kohut notes:

> Man can no more survive psychologically in a psychological milieu that does not respond empathically to him, than he can survive physically in an atmosphere that contains no oxygen. . . . The [therapist's] behavior vis-a-vis his patient should be the expected average one—i.e., the behavior of a psychologically perceptive person vis-a-vis someone who is suffering and has entrusted himself to him for help. [1977, p. 253]

From the perspective adopted here, the challenge to empathic understanding comes from the view that clients communicate about a number of different aspects of their strivings that reflect different aspects of self. For example, a client came into my office for her session on a brisk winter's day, and, spying the window open—the hospital's heating system was working overzealously—she stated emphatically: "I'm not getting undressed until you close that window!" At one level she meant she was not going to take off her coat in that (to her) cold office until the window was closed. At another level, less available to her awareness and reflective of her wariness about self-exploration, she was also saying: "I'm not going to reveal myself psychologically until I feel more comfortable with you." At a still "deeper," that is, more tightly defended, psychological level she was probably also making a comment that had overtones regarding sexual intimacy and nurturant physical contact consistent with hysterical character features in her personality make-up. (This does not exhaust the possible meanings in this comment, of course. Other ways of interpreting her statement are conceivable depending on one's theoretical orientation.) Thus, one sentence can be seen dialectically to have a variety of simultaneous, symbolic meanings. The tact and skill of the therapist involve understanding as many of the meanings as possible to get a sense of what the client's concerns are and also involves responding to the level the client is prepared to hear.

The ability to make these kinds of translations is essential to the dynamic therapies (Edelson, 1975), and one goal is to help the client do his or her own translations of thoughts and feelings so as to be able to awaken to more of what the self is about.[17] No therapist does this work of interpretation perfectly. Knowing what a client's words might refer to symbolically in his or her experience obviously makes this activity possible. When people already share a similarity of cultural background, they have a head start on the business of establishing a relationship.[18] This undoubtedly is a reason why private practitioners of psychotherapy tend to select as clients persons of their own religious-ethnic background (Catholic, Protestant, Jewish) more often than not (Henry, Sims, & Spray, 1973). If persons do not share such potentials for communication, establishing a relationship is far less likely to go well. (This is not just a matter of cognitive familiarity. Heiskell [1980/1981] found that the positive and negative reinforcement value (RV) ratings by subjects, who were responding as therapists might toward statements made by psychiatric patients, influenced the degree of empathy shown toward the patients.) When we add racial animosities and misunderstandings to cultural dissimilarities, the potential for a widened gap between client and therapist is greater. The interracial therapy situation—and we are interested in this discussion in the Black client/White therapist relationship, the most likely match-up for Black clients in most sections of the country—becomes something of a microcosm of the larger society.[19]

From the client's side, it is understandable that s/he might see the therapist as a representative of authority, the Establishment, the "Man"—more concerned about justifying society's positions than in empathic relating to the client and his or her actual troubles. The client, already reluctant to reveal himself or herself to anyone, might feel especially guarded about opening up in an interracial situation to provide another example of how Black folks "just can't make it." Such attitudes may not always be conscious, although for lower- and working-class persons they are likely to be. Nevertheless, they can be powerful determining factors in behavior.

From the therapist's side, A. Jones and Seagull (1977) suggest that White therapists may labor under a variety of pressures. They may act from unresolved unconscious racial guilt feelings, making them less able to respond accurately to the needs of specific Black clients. Or some therapists may unwittingly extend their wish to be helpful into needs for power and control and become paternalistic in their attitudes toward Black clients. These authors do not argue that all White therapists experience such problems, any more than all White people handle the pressures toward racist expression in this society in the same way. Similarly, particular kinds of questions exist for Black therapists. Racial pressures may foster unconscious attitudes in them that hinder their ability to be helpful to Black clients on one hand (Edwards, 1988) and White clients on the other (Gardner, 1971).[20]

Research on the Black Patient/White Therapist Interaction

Research on psychotherapy with Blacks confirms the notion that "the nature and quality of therapist-patient interaction is a critical determinant in whether a Black client continues psychotherapy" (Griffith & Jones, 1979, p. 229). Studies have shown that Blacks drop out of therapy at a high rate early in the contact (Sue, 1977; Sue et al., 1991). Some research has found that "depth of self-exploration" in Black clients was enhanced when those clients were seen by Black interviewers (W. M. Banks, 1972; Carkhuff & Pierce, 1967). A number of other writers (Atkinson, 1985; Atkinson & Schein, 1986; Griffith & Jones, 1979) report studies in which clients expressed preference for Black counselors or felt better understood by them. Griffith and Jones caution that many of these kinds of studies have been therapy "analogue" studies (see note 20) and may not reflect what the experience of therapy is like. They go on to point out, however, that since many Black clients leave after the initial session, these one-interview analogue studies may have some relevance to actual therapy situations in these kinds of instances.

When one looks at research relevant to these issues done in actual therapies, one finds that in a number of instances the White therapist–Black client setting was not a hindrance to creating an effective helping relationship. In Lerner's study (1972) the therapists were White and half of the patients were Black. In Atkinson's reviews there was little evidence that racial similarity in the counseling dyad improved counseling effectiveness. In the Karon and VandenBos study of severely disturbed schizophrenics (1972) the therapists were White and two-thirds of the patients were Black. Black patients from neurotic, middle-class populations have been shown to profit in cross-racial therapies also (Jones, 1978, 1982). In the Jones studies there was an opportunity to compare outcome and details of therapy process in the four kinds of Black-White/therapist-client matches. No differences were found in overall outcome—as a group, clients in all the different therapies got better to about the same degree, as far as could be told from the measures used. There were differences by racial match-up, however, in the process of the therapy relationships, that is, in the nature of the interpersonal dynamics that occurred between therapist and client.[21]

These results are consistent with Sue's (1988) recent analysis of data on cross-racial therapies. He notes that much of the thinking in this area confounds issues of ethnicity of client and therapist with those of culture. *Ethnicity* refers to the racial or national background of one's ancestors. *Culture* in this context refers to shared meanings among a particular group of people—values, behaviors, ways of experiencing. Sue notes:

> Ethnic matches can result in cultural mismatches if therapists and clients from the same ethnic group show markedly different values (e.g., a highly acculturated Chinese American therapist who works with a Chinese immigrant holding traditional Chinese values). Conversely, ethnic mismatches do not necessarily imply cultural mismatches, because therapists and clients from different ethnic groups may share similar values, life-styles and experiences. [p. 306]

Thus, as Juarez (1985) notes: "In effect, the issue is not whether patients are treated more effectively by same-race, same-class, or same-sex therapists, but whether the therapist's interpretation of the client's cultural experience creates the ambience that is necessary to establish rapport and an empathic bond which facilitate the therapeutic process" (p. 441).

An Ingredient for Success with Minority Clients
What characteristics of the participants are necessary to the establishment of a truly helping relationship with Blacks in such therapies? It has been typical, in the concept of "suitability" for psychodynamic therapy, to rest considerable responsibility on the client in principle if a helpful relationship can't be established. This criterion has by no means been leveled only at minority or lower-class clients. There is some merit in this notion. If a client persists in not seeing himself or herself as a significant contributor to personal difficulties or, while acknowledging this, does not feel sufficiently pained, or motivated, to change, such a person cannot be helped with psychotherapy—at least not while in that frame of mind.[22]

However, Lerner (1972) designed her study to test the possibility that success in psychotherapy had as much to do with characteristics of the *therapists* as it did with qualities in the clients. In addition to the considerable data that she had about clients, she also obtained information about the therapists—amount of therapeutic experience, capacity for being empathic, their own experience of having been in therapy, and other data. Of particular interest were therapist attitudes indicating the degree to which therapists held democratic as opposed to authoritarian values toward clients.[23] Recall that she found that none of the client variables were related to psychotherapeutic outcome. People improved in therapy without regard to race, social class, previous hospitalization, and so on. To her surprise, few of the therapist variables seemed to predict therapy outcome. One of those that did (as she hoped) had to do with degree of egalitarian values held toward the client. The more that therapists tended to believe in clients' right to autonomy and self-determination, that is, were free of authoritarian values, the more likely their particular clients were to improve in therapy. This effect was particularly strong for clients who were most disturbed. It makes particular sense that this latter group would be especially sensitive to such attitudes from their therapists since they are likely to be just the persons who do not get very tolerant or egalitarian treatment from society. (Lerner's general effect was further confirmed by Ross [1982/1983]. Using Lerner's construct, she found that Black patients seen by therapists who expressed egalitarianism remained in therapy longer than did those patients who found such an atmosphere missing in the early phases of the relationship.)

One of the things about an egalitarian attitude is that it is one way of communicating the dialectic implication in therapy that it is appropriate to have goals different from the therapist's. The therapist is there to help the client achieve the goals that s/he, the client, values. The effort with the Black Muslim man, for example, was to help him achieve his goal of living the life of a Muslim more effectively. An egalitarian attitude respects the many approaches to effective living that individuals choose. (It is of course not being implied that this only characterizes a humanistic point of view. Behavior therapists, being humanitarian, also work to help their clients achieve their own diverse goals.[24])

This result regarding egalitarian therapist attitudes was one of a very small number of significant trends from among a rather large number of other statistical tests that were not significant, so it requires replication. However, it calls attention to a possible factor involved in the creation of a helping relationship with minorities and the poor. Since it is likely that people will have egalitarian attitudes about groups they understand better, it is appropriate that therapists working with Black clients get to know more about Black people and the Black community, as has been suggested by many writers (Griffith & Jones, 1979; Jones & Seagull, 1977; Smith et al., 1978). Russell (1988) noted that even well-meaning therapists may diagnostically misconceptualize clients who speak with a pronounced dialect, such as Black English. He suggests that if one does not have much experience with a *nonclinical* sample of the group of which the minority client is a member, one should, among other things, be ready to enlist the aid of a knowledgeable consultant. (See also the recently published "Guidelines for Providers of Psychological Services to Ethnic, Linguistic, and Culturally Diverse Populations" [American Psychological Association, 1993].)

Relationship Issues: Managing the Early Sessions
We have noted Frank's idea that the prospective patient is struggling with a sense of demoralization. Basch (1980, 1988), from his particular pschodynamic perspective, suggests that in the quest to repair and further self-esteem the client is hoping to use the therapist as a "self object" (Kohut, 1977; Miller, 1992). From one view, a self object can be thought of as a special person whom the patient can use in a relationship to meet the specific personal needs of a developmentally weakened self. This would be true for the ethnic minority client as well. However, as I have suggested, the therapy situation is one naturally associated for many Blacks with the White Establishment. This may automatically conjure up the specter of an authoritarian institution operating on the potential client to his or her detriment. When a Black client acknowledges the need for psychological help, before s/he can make use of the therapist in the way Basch suggests, s/he must try to become certain about what kinds of attitudes the therapist brings from the larger society.

Speaking to the White therapist–Black client relationship, Griffith and Jones (1979) note:

> The race difference appears to have its greatest impact early in treatment, particularly at the first encounter. If the White therapist can establish effective rapport at initial contact and build a therapeutic alliance in relatively rapid fashion, successful outcomes can be achieved with lower-income Black clients, usually considered poor risks, and with middle-class Black clients despite their initial sense of wariness and consequently slower movement in therapy. [p. 230]

From this view the therapist's task is to establish his or her credibility as a sensitive and competent helper. Using this concept, Sue and Zane (1987) suggest that a therapist may have an "ascribed" credibility based on his or her age, gender, and/or ethnic background, if these match the client's expectations. These qualities may initially help build the relationship. But soon the therapist must move beyond this to develop an "achieved" credibility based on skill in dealing with the client. (This is consistent with the observation we have discussed that though Black clients may feel more at home with a Black therapist, other dynamics must be added in to determine a successful interaction.)

Gibbs (1985) has proposed a model for what is involved in achieving credibility with African-American clients. She notes that Black clients, mindful of racism, tend to take an interpersonal rather than an instrumental orientation in the therapy situation at first. That is, they are particularly sensitive to implicit atttitudes expressed by their potential therapists. They are less likely than typical middle-class patients to take for granted initially the therapist's readiness or ability to really be on their side. Thus, at first they are not yet ready to get to the task of looking at those feelings and behaviors that are more characterologically based and which are generating the problem that brought them to therapy.

Gibbs's experience has led her to view the interpersonal phase as one in which the relationship with the Black client evolves through several specific "micro-stages." These processes emerge in the first two or three sessions of the therapy. For example, the client tends first to be somewhat aloof but quite watchful in the effort to "size up" the therapist. Then the patient proceeds to "check out" the therapist by posing questions or statements in the course of conversation designed to elicit the therapist's values and qualifications. If the therapist fails to be sensitive to the patient's testing by responding skillfully, the relationship quickly begins to flounder and the patient is very likely to leave. To the extent that the therapist is attuned to this interpersonal sequence and responds appropriately the patient proceeds to the next stages and the relationship begins to deepen. In the final stage the patient moves on to the instrumental phase and begins to work on the personal problems in living that brought him or her into treatment.[25]

Affective Assessment and the Therapy Relationship

Another way of looking at the therapy relationship is in terms of the affective assessment process that we have been discussing throughout the book. That is, it is quite conceivable that Blacks (and probably other minorities as well) would approach therapy situations leading, so to speak, with their affective assessment capacities. Rychlak explained the propensity of minority groups to respond with RV modes in learning situations as a way of dealing with a cultural situation they did not feel at home with. Similarly, it may be that not only defensiveness about self-revelation and self-exploration is operating for many Blacks but a tendency to bring forward and be governed by their affective assessment processes as well. It may be that White clients, especially those of the middle class, are more comfortable with what they perceive initially and, even if not, are less likely to let the negative affective assessments immediately override their faith, albeit tentative, in the therapist. It is not just that Blacks, based on past experience, are expecting not to be treated well, although that is probably also a factor. This alone would only be an input from prior experience in the Lockean sense. But, in addition, the cultural unfamiliarity may heighten their tendency to rely more on affective assessments as a way of judging whether or not this is going to be a useful experience.

This may mean that the potential client will be more sensitive to initial difficulties in communicating that are bound to occur between strangers, especially when there are ethnic and class differences between them. And of course there will be times when the White therapist, being human, will not be sensitive to the Black client. While a reliance on the affective assessment process is natural, it may be detrimental in that it causes the potential client to shy away from a therapist who is well-meaning and, given more of an opportunity, really could be helpful. But let's be clear here. This doesn't mean that Black and other minority clients are to blame for this predicament. Falling back on the RV mode of assessing is due partly to the society's having excluded these clients from a fuller feeling of being a part of the dominant culture and its institutions and practices.

It is the therapist's responsibility, then, to work to overcome this tendency in the therapy situation. The research we have discussed indicates that the therapist's attitudes and efforts can achieve this. While the Black therapist presumably has some advantage over the White therapist in this initial period (holding constant other factors such as training and experience), s/he still has to work hard too in helping the patient discover that this process can work for him or her. This conception supports the observation of some writers (Griffith & Jones, 1979; Block, 1981) that it may be important for therapists treating lower/working-class Black clients to be more active than with White middle-class clients in communicating understanding of some of the client's psychological problems in initial sessions. Classical psychodynamic formulations on therapeutic technique emphasize the value of minimizing early interventions by the therapist. Such a technique may lead the minority client to regard the therapist as not being sufficiently caring, which would be consistent with the client's expectation regarding traditional authority. In addition, the neutral therapist may be seen as one who has little to offer the client (Block, 1981).[26]

Another way to increase the client's comfort is by educating him or her to the process of psychotherapy. To some extent this is a part of the technique of psychotherapy in general. Some have proposed the use of "role induction" procedures (Frank & Frank, 1991) to give clients without prior experience in therapy some sense of what to expect. In one kind of format such procedures involve an interview conducted by someone other than the therapist giving the rationale of treatment, expectations about how the patient is to respond (in terms of talking about what is on his or her mind, for example), and what to expect of the therapist.

Other methods have been used as well. Francois (1977/1978) reasoned that lower-class Black male adolescents referred to psychiatric outpatient facilities would be a particularly difficult group to keep in treatment. He devised a role induction procedure that involved showing subjects a brief film targeted, in the appearance and speech of the actors, at lower-class Black youth and depicting what therapy would be like. The design of this study was complicated, involving predictions about the effect of role induction, depression, and locus of control on his subject pool's response to psychotherapy. He found, as have others using some form of role induction process, that those experiencing the film continued longer in therapy than those who did not see the film. Paster (1985) in her work with such youngsters describes a process of negotiating a mutually developed contract regarding the nature and goals of treatment.

Psychotherapy and the Varieties of the Black Experience

Up to this point I have been talking about some of the general issues that can be posited about psychotherapy with African-American clients. However, I have also repeatedly emphasized the variability in experiences and problems engendered by social status, age, and gender in the African-American community. In the last chapter I noted that Blacks have developed a variety of psychological styles in reaction to their historical situation in America. It seems reasonable that, even within the broadly humanistic position taken here, such differences might make for differences in the ways that Black clients would approach mental health services. We shall look at just a few examples.

Recently a considerable amount of literature has emerged about work with specific demographic groups in the Black community. Noting the besieged position of young (especially lower-class) Black males in the United States, Franklin (1989), Paster (1985), and Roberts (1987) have discussed ways of understanding and intervening psychotherapeutically in the lives of Black adolescents. Boyd-Franklin (1989) and Coner-Edwards and Spurlock (1988) write of special issues for middle-class families. While many of the principles discussed in this chapter apply across gender, Comas-Diaz in her review (1988, chap. 13) notes that Black women bring their own set of issues to therapy as well.

As a general principle of working with Black clients we noted the literature that indicated that establishing the relationship calls for active attention by the therapist in the early phases. While this is an important caution, there is some indication that clients' reference group orientations, that is, their particular stage of nigrescence, might affect their attitudes toward therapy (Helms, 1984; Parham, 1989; Parham & Helms, 1981). One would expect that those stage 1 persons who are especially self-rejecting (and thus have fairly strong pro-White, anti-Black attitudes) would have an easier time entering what Gibbs would call the "instrumental" phase of therapy with a White therapist. On the other hand, stage 3 persons would be expected to rather quickly form a good working relationship with a Black counselor (Parham, 1989). The testing quality of Gibbs's "interpersonal" phase would be more prominent among this group if the counselor were White. (A similar kind of tension would exist with some stage 1 clients if the therapist were Black.) However, although there might be more suspicion of a White therapist by a stage 3 client, Parham does not argue that a cross-racial relationship with a stage 3 client is automatically doomed: "Indeed positive therapeutic work can occur if issues of the client's perception of the therapist are worked through in the *initial* stages of therapy" (Parham, 1989, p. 220). Thus, in general, while it may be necessary to move quickly to establish credibility with most Black clients, nigrescence theory suggests that it may be more of an issue with certain clients depending on their identity stage. The implication is that therapists should be sensitive to this or similar kinds of identity issues (Harrell, 1979) in their work with Black clients.

In an interesting recent paper Arthur Jones (1985) comes at within-group variability from a somewhat different direction. He delineates four classes of issues that describe different ways African Americans handle the task of adapting to society. These are: (1) their particular ways of reacting to racial oppression, (2) the influence that the values of the majority culture have on them, (3) the ties they feel to the traditional African-American culture, and (4) their particular individual or family experiences and endowments. These factors encompass socioeconomic, cultural, and individual issues, and they contribute in an interrelated way to a Black person's functioning. The individual's particular personal history might lead to one or another of these areas becoming more prominent in negotiating the task of adaptation to life:

> A person raised in a bigoted section of the South, for example, and whose parents were killed by members of the Ku Klux Klan, may well live a life so dominated by experiences of racial tension that the development of a way of coping with racism may overshadow other aspects of psychological functioning. In contrast, a person raised in an aristocratic black family in New England may be guided disproportionately by influences derived from the majority culture. [A. Jones, 1985, p. 367]

When a person experiences psychological disturbance, assessment of his or her condition should sort out which of these factors seems to be more prominent as an area where intervention should, at least initially, be focused. In one of his examples Jones described a man who had a paranoid psychotic break and became menacing to his neighbors. A psychologist who was consulted joined with a neighbor and relatives whom this man trusted to "talk him down" in someone's home. The support and caring shown him by friends and family helped him accept a referral for long-term individual and family treatment supplemented with antipsychotic medication. After several months he was able to function on his job again. In this instance the person's distress manifested itself in a sense of the disruption of important ties to his community. Jones argues that the relative weighting of the four classes of adaptational variables must be evaluated in each case to best understand how to approach Black clients.

It is true that minorities and the poor need to have the oppressive conditions that have been fostered by social institutions lifted from them. Real and profound social change is called for—the kind that actually allows for equality of opportunity. But when people are also saddled with their own personally generated problems, they are not in the best position to work for their own self-determination. The aim of therapy should not be to help people simply to get along and adjust to an unfair society, "playing more docilely and consistently with the loaded dice society hands them" (Lerner, 1974, p. 52).

> What poor people reduced to a state of psychological impotence usually need is a restoration of their sense of personal power, which will ultimately allow them to join with their fellows in an organized group struggle for social change—one in which they will be less vulnerable and more effective. Generic psychotherapy is fully compatible with social change because it is an attempt to restore personal power—self-understanding, self-control, self-direction, and self-esteem through the development of an honest, empathic, egalitarian relationship with another human being, the therapist. [ibid., p. 53]

Of course, individually tailored clinical approaches call not just for individual psychotherapy but for group, family, and/or vocational rehabilitation approaches as well. The technique and theory of therapy with Black and ethnic minority families have gained increasing prominence and sophistication (e.g., Boyd-Franklin, 1989; McGoldrick, Pearce, & Giordano, 1982). This is quite understandable considering our growing recognition of the sustaining value of family networks for minority people, as noted in Chapter 2. It is of additional interest to me that the guiding conceptions of the work of some family therapists are in line with Lerner's notion as stated above. For example, Boyd-Franklin (1989) notes that her treatment goal is "empowerment" of the families she works with:

> Empowerment . . . is defined as the process whereby the therapist restructures the family to facilitate the appropriate designation and use of power within the family system and to mobilize the family's ability to successfully interact with external systems. . . . Many of these families have a multigenerational history of victimization by poverty and racism. . . . Empowerment often involves helping parents to take back the control of their own families and feel that they can effect important changes for themselves. [p. 22]

This notion is very much in the spirit of the humanistic theme of this book. (Tharp [1991] suggests that the less the client is acculturated to the modern American society, the more likely it is that network therapy and family therapy interventions should be the first treatment considerations. Network treatment involves an organization of selected family and friends into a grouping that can be used by the therapist to support a client's psychological rehabilitation in a culturally syntonic way. A variant of such an approach was illustrated in the clinical example above from Arthur Jones.)

Conclusion

In this chapter I have focused on some of the ways of describing behavior when self-activity has become distorted, self-defeating, and unproductive. The mental health service delivery system has not been very successful in meeting the needs of those African Americans who could benefit from such help. Research has indicated that Black clients in clinical settings are considerably more prone than are White clients to drop out of therapy early. This has not been because Blacks are not potentially able to respond to the various treatment approaches available. It is partly because the mental health system has not effectively adapted itself to the minority client. The task for mental health workers is one of relating to African-American clients on their own terms, accepting their expressive styles and their special concerns, and recognizing their basic human effort to free themselves of the demoralizing sense of not being able to control major aspects of their psychological life.

In general, establishing credibility as a helper is easier for the therapist where cultural backgrounds and identity values are similar. In such cases the client more readily expects to be understood and is initially more at ease about self-disclosure. Usually, if the therapist is more familiar with the setting from which the client comes, establishing a therapeutic relationship is enhanced. However, it is also clear that Black clients can make good use of a therapy relationship with a White therapist when in addition to being well trained the latter is attentive to his or her own racial attitudes and makes the effort to learn about African-American culture and the Black community. In any event, psychotherapeutic procedures can help Black and other minority clients lift roadblocks to self-development by achieving a greater clarity in sense of self and enabling them to better carry out their competence strivings and intentions.

Notes

1. In Chapter 2 we noted that in the normal course of events, in order to come to terms with the world, we create our "reality" through the exercise of our symbolizing (conceptualizing) capacities. We are all busily at work construing

the import of the sensory events that confront us. As Harry Stack Sullivan noted, "From this viewpoint, it will be seen that any problem in psychopathology becomes a problem of symbol functioning, a matter of seeking to understand and interpret eccentric symbol performances" (1925–26/1962, p. 32). Thus, as the individual fashions a sense of self by taking one "road" or another of self-development, the choices made may arise out of eccentric or unusual ways of conceptualizing things. The bases for some of the person's choices may be shut out of awareness so that s/he comes to current situations with views influenced by unconscious conceptualizations of these events. I have suggested that racism poses special problems for African Americans. I have characterized Blacks as persons working hard to define themselves in ways that are dialectically different from the socially oppressive definitions applied to them. As such, African Americans run a greater risk than people not under such racist pressures of straining adaptive capacities and "going off the deep end," as it were, in trying to find dialectical solutions to their societal situation. Thus, from one perspective, Blacks have the special task of defining themselves in creative and productive ways against the odds stacked against them. But in doing so they must not allow the dialectic effort to become so intense that behavior becomes bizarre and ultimately self-defeating.

2. Although many of the persons typically identified with the modern humanistic approach to personality and psychotherapy, such as Rogers, Boss, and others (Rychlak, 1981), see themselves as being opposed to the psychoanalytic position, Rychlak has argued that the classic psychodynamic positions do have strong telic postulates central to their conceptions. Unconscious motivation, important to Freud, Jung, and Adler, represents one aspect of the individual proposing and often trying to pursue active intentions that are opposed (if the person deems it necessary) dialectically by other aspects of personality functioning (e.g., "defense" on the one hand vs. impulse on the other). When I use the term *humanistic* here, I am referring to those aspects of theories about personality that emphasize the goal-oriented, symbolizing activities operating simultaneously at conscious and subconscious levels. For me, while this can include the self-designated "humanistic" theorists, it also includes important portions of the psychoanalytic theories. (See also Holt [1972] and Jenkins [1992] on this point.) For a summary blending of some of the more useful aspects of traditional psychodynamic notions and the phenomenological-humanistic views, see Korchin (1976), chap. 3.

3. The study of abnormal psychology has yielded a kind of two-fold grouping of mental disorders in terms of the presumed origins of a particular disorder, namely, the psychogenic and the somatogenic. The psychogenic or functional disorders presumably have their origin in the disordered psychological processes of the individual—in a person's strivings and need patterns. Agoraphobia, a person's (learned) dread of crowded public places that re-

stricts his or her life severely, is an example. Somatogenic or organically based disorders have their origin in disorders of brain tissue, biochemistry, or other aspects of central nervous system physiology. Disorders of behavior stemming from poisoning the brain through alcohol abuse are an example of a somatogenic disorder. The hypothesis, backed up by some research evidence, that the two major psychoses, schizophrenia and affective disorder, are based in anomalies in genetic structure is an important modern somatogenic theory. (Some researchers are interested in demonstrating that even disorders such as agoraphobia have physiologic origins [Lipman, 1989].) The organic point of view stretched to cover all mental disorder is epitomized in the phrase attributed, I believe, to the Nobel laureate Linus Pauling, to the effect that "there is no twisted thought without a twisted molecule." The attempt to explain human behavior *solely* in terms of its biological bases (material and efficient causation) is a form of reductionism (Peele, 1983). The view in this book is that the understanding of physiological factors makes a necessary but not a sufficient contribution to comprehending experience and behavior. We must also understand the final-cause components (intentions, purposes) behind human action. In that sense, with respect to physical factors our humanistic view here is biologically *naturalistic* (Cameron & Rychlak, 1985).

In this chapter we shall be concerned primarily with a psychogenic approach to disorder in keeping with our overall concerns with self activity, which is a psychological process. However, more and more we are coming to see that there is considerable interaction between these two aspects of human existence and a sharp distinction is not productive. We should take note of the fact that modern behavioral research is greatly expanding our understanding of the biological (material-cause) contributions to behavior. This would be consistent with a biologically naturalist point of view. (See Gruen [1993] and Meltzer [1987] for further discussions of some of this literature.)

4. This is related to a fundamental point that Menninger, Mayman, and Pruyser (1963) made in their book. They suggested, contrary to the standard position on psychiatric nomenclature, that all psychological disorder can be placed on a single continuum ranging from effective functioning on one end to severe psychological dysfunction on the other. In this view, psychological disorders are similar in quality but differ from each other in the quantity of disturbance, ranging from relatively minor though perhaps continuing maladjustments to severely self-destructive behaviors. Each level of disorder, even a psychotic one, represents the effort to organize one's adaptive resources to maintain psychological survival and avoid the last level of disorder, that of giving up on life (examples that seem to fit this level are discussed by Seligman [1975]). Thus, one level of disintegration, let's say neurosis, while being less adapted than minor maladjustments (transient nervousness, irritability, or bodily symptoms during a life crisis, for example), is still a more integrated level of functioning than are explosive homicidal outbursts or psychosis. In Menninger's view, then, psychological adaptation is the active effort to maintain the best possible balance of functioning—the "vital balance"—under the given circumstances of personal intentions and environmental limitations. Such a position is in contrast to those who argue that severe mental disorder only represents the intrusion into functioning of less well-organized processes when the higher processes are disrupted. In other words, the higher-order processes are unable to do the usual job of active organizing of the lower processes.

5. People may manifest a variety of degrees of personality disruption in a state of demoralization, ranging from neurotic to psychotic. Historically the term *neurosis* has referred to a range of the less serious forms of disorder in which an individual's difficulty in balancing internal need pressures with environmental expectations is such that the person has to resort to defensive maneuvers that hamper efficiency but that allow the person to carry on daily living fairly well. For example, a woman who harbored since childhood a fear of her aggressive and hostile impulses developed the need to wash her hands and continually check to see that the stove was turned off so as to be sure that no one would be contaminated by germs or hurt in a gas explosion. She remained unaware of anger as the source of her compulsive behavior and generally did her clerical work on the job and her household duties adequately, although the psychological symptoms were becoming more and more of a nuisance because her ritual checking and washing behaviors were taking increasing amounts of time. All of us have areas of our lives that are less well adapted than others—so much so that in this age of super "sophistication" about psychological matters some are inclined to call the nonpsychiatrically disturbed person "normally neurotic."

There have been cogent criticisms of the term *neurotic* (see White & Watt, 1981). The latest edition of the American Psychiatric Association's diagnostic manual does not use the term *neurosis*. Those disorders formerly called neuroses are now put under headings that are more descriptive of the major symptom features, such as *anxiety disorder* (which would fit the woman struggling with her hostility), *somatoform disorders,* and *dissociative disorders.* The term *neurosis* is still being used out of habit to refer to this relatively milder though personally troubling range of mental disorders, and I will continue that fashion here.

The term *psychosis* refers to the more severe set of mental disorders marked by disruptions in the ability to appraise reality and to distinguish what is true about the world and what is a figment of one's imagination. Consider a man, generally depressed and reclusive, with longstanding deficiencies in his ability to relate to other people, who comes more and more to believe that people "have it in for him." He has always had a vivid imagination and an active fantasy life, and now he comes to the conclusion that the group of people he sees on the street corner beneath his window this morning are plotting to do away with him. That they are planning to kill him is possible, but improbable. He, however, for reasons of personal psychological history and perhaps factors in his constitution, believes that the thing he had imagined has in fact come to pass. Here we can see the human dialectical thinking process gone awry. In other words, one of the many possible alternative (and in this case unlikely) conceptualizations that one might consider about the street scene below has become an actuality for this poor man. In the most widely accepted psychological view of schizophrenia, it is greatly unrealistic and/or bizarre thinking that primarily characterizes the break with reality. In the other major set of psychotic disorders, the "affective" disorders—the manic and depressive disorders—the individual's mood or emotional state leads him or her to think or do highly irrational and unrealistic—and sometimes very dangerous—things.

6. Some argue that diagnosis is a dangerous activity and one that should not be conducted. They argue that trying to put a diagnostic label on people's behavior limits the understanding of people and creates expectations and stereotypes based on the diagnostic abstraction rather than on the actualities of the person's particular life and behavior. For example, in one frequently cited piece of research psychiatrically normal subjects who got themselves admitted to hospitals with diagnoses of schizophrenia were kept in hospitals although they were careful from then on to exhibit no behavior that was unusual (Rosenhan, 1973). The process of diagnosis was seen to cloud understanding rather than enhance it. Furthermore, recent criticism has suggested that diagnosticians have biases that make for inaccurate diagnoses of lower-class and minority clients, and even White females. Psychiatric and psychological diagnosis is usually done in a face-to-face interview situation often supplemented by the use of personality tests. These tests vary in their format, ranging from some that can be given in group formats to others that must be given in an individual situation. There is considerable literature on intellectual assessment of Blacks, as we saw in Chapter 3. In general there is much less written about the assessment of personality functioning and of psychopathology in Blacks and other minorities. (See, for example, G. Frank [1992].) This is partly because the clinical interpretation of some of the most widely used of these tests, such as the Rorschach test (see note 7) and the Thematic Apperception Test (telling stories based on a series of pictures), is grounded on rather complex theories of personality. The validity of these procedures has not been easy to measure by the usual methods of quantification for the general population or for minorities. On the other hand, a considerable amount has been written about the potential for racial bias in such tests as the widely used MMPI and the newer MCMI (Millon Clinical Multiaxial Inventory), but it would take us too far afield to deal with that or other issues of personality

testing with minorities here (see, for example, Davis, Greenblatt, & Pochyly, 1990; Greene, 1987; Gynther & Green, 1980; Hamberger & Hastings, 1992; Johnson & Brems, 1990; Powell & Johnson, 1976; Pritchard & Rosenblatt, 1980a, 1980b; W. D. Smith et al., 1978).

It is true that diagnostic categories are best seen as ideal types that are rarely seen in pure and unmixed form. From this perspective they should be seen as ways of developing hypotheses about a person's behavior for further, more specific investigation. It is also true that categorizing behavior has been used to put people into conceptual "pigeon holes" without due regard for their individual uniqueness, but I would argue that this is mostly a function of the way diagnostic activity is all too often carried out rather than a cogent criticism of the need for some kind of diagnosing activity (Schectman, 1977).

Actually, diagnosis represents a way of conceptualizing events, that is, putting an order or frame on them. In western society at least, some kinds of behaviors tend to occur more frequently together (e.g., emotional lability and an impulsive orientation to the world) than they do with other behaviors (e.g., emotional lability and a meticulous concern for facts and details). This tends to justify groupings of some sort. Such clusterings are broadly useful in that they might give a therapist a sense of whether under pressure a person might tend to do something ill-advised or, on the other hand, whether s/he might tend to be overly hesitant and indecisive. To a relatively young field of knowledge such as abnormal psychology, events—"reality"—present themselves much as they do to the newborn, as a "blooming, buzzing confusion." People must inevitably organize the data presented to them in some way or another in order to proceed. The activity of diagnosis is a particular case of what everyone has to do within a cultural context to come to know the world—we have to conceptualize it, in the humanistic sense. This does not mean as a field that we should rest too comfortably on any set of categories at which we have arrived. I am not suggesting that current diagnostic systems are satisfactory. There is much room for improvement in the way we carry on the activity of trying to understand the behavior of troubled individuals in general. Also, in the process of seeing a client, we should not be locked into the initial understanding (conceptualization) that we have of a particular person as we seek to help him or her. A diagnostic category, as the state of understanding of a given phenomenon, should be seen as a relatively temporary crystallization, a way station, to be abandoned as we develop better ones in the process of coming to understand behavior. This means mental health professionals trying to diagnose persons from quite different backgrounds from their own need to know as much as they can about the culture of the client and how that may affect the way that person might express himself or herself in an interview or on tests. Phillips (1968) and Tyler, Brome, and Williams (1991) have suggested frameworks that take into account an individual's social competence as well as his or her dysfunction. (See also Sugarman's

[1978] advocacy of diagnosis from a humanistic and humanitarian perspective.)

7. The Rorschach is the personality test that requests the subject's associations to a set of inkblots. Personality features are evaluated not only on the basis of what a person sees in the blots but also on how s/he expresses what is seen in the blots. "Thought disorder" is felt to be a hallmark of schizophrenic thinking, marked by unconventional, unrealistic, illogical ways of thinking about events and stimuli. It can usually be identified rather readily on psychological tests such as the WAIS (now published as the WAIS–R) and Rorschach (Exner, 1993; Johnston & Holzman, 1979; Weiner, 1966). Consider, for example, a subject who on the WAIS defines the word *winter* as "the ice house of the North wind," and does so without a "tongue-in-cheek" attitude or without the explicit intent to be metaphorical. If such kinds of productions amassed on this and other tests (psychologists usually do not draw such conclusions from a single response) we would have pretty good evidence for thinking disorder.

8. Block (1981) argues that while similar psychological principles apply to Blacks as to Whites, African-American clients tend because of their group history to accentuate different behavioral dimensions and may well respond differently to diagnostic and treatment situations. For example, she notes the reported tendency for Blacks to be diagnosed as paranoid schizophrenic more than Whites are. This may reflect the wariness and reluctance that Black clients feel about disclosing themselves in cross-racial situations. Such guardedness, although characteristic of persons experiencing forms of paranoid psychosis, may often reflect the kind of vigilance and self-containment that Blacks have had to develop historically as a means of survival (Grier & Cobbs, 1968; Ridley, 1984). G. Frank (1992) makes a similar point regarding the Rorschach. Failure on the part of the clinician to understand this may contribute to inaccurate conclusions about the presented behavior.

Raskin, Crook, and Herman (1975), while finding that Black and White inpatients were quite similar in depressive symptomatology, also found in their sample that Blacks tended to be diagnosed more as schizophrenic and Whites as depressed. They suggest, as did Brody, Derbyshire, and Schleifer (1967), that this may be because many Blacks do not arrive at psychiatric facilities unless their behavior has dangerous or strikingly bizarre features. This partly reflects the feeling in Black communities that you really have to be "crazy" before you go to a "shrink" or a mental hospital. On the other hand, as Baker (1988) notes, these differential diagnostic rates may represent the historic diagnostic biases toward African Americans I referred to earlier rather than true prevalence rates. To guard against such bias in the clinical situation, "the presence of psychotic symptoms in an Afro-American individual should stimulate a meticulous diagnostic effort" (Baker, 1988, p. 168). Particularly with the ready availability of drugs in present-day American society, "the importance of ascertaining prior substance abuse is key to preventing a misdiagnosis of schizophrenia or affective illness" (ibid.). Thus, careful use of interview and test procedures is particularly important in trying to learn more about the Black client's world. Baker gives examples (pp. 168–170) of how clients' responses and personal histories must be understood in the cultural context in which they emerge.

9. In recent years a considerable literature has developed on disorders in sense of self, which for some theorists include the narcissistic disorders and "borderline" conditions (e.g., Chessick, 1977; Masterson, 1981; Morrison, 1986). The term *narcissism* has been used not only to characterize features of individual personality functioning but also as a description of important aspects of western capitalist society (for example, Frosh, 1991, pp. 63–68). Obviously we are not able to consider these issues in depth from a clinical or sociological perspective. I have noted at various points in this book that attention to the quality of one's self-contributions to behavior, one's choices, is a necessary and desirable attitude in life. Thus, all people should be involved in what Miller (1992) calls "self-affirming activities." Such activities "increase one's feeling of self-esteem or feeling of self-cohesion or feeling that one is strong" (p. 218). The many kinds of self-affirming efforts a person might engage in (from using mood-altering substances to engaging in creative activities or involving oneself with people) could be done in a healthy or pathological way. I shall reserve the term *narcissism* for the dysfunctional ways of self-expression—modes of functioning worthy of clinical attention. As such the term refers to the defensive retreat from healthier self-affirming activities and mature interpersonal relationships in order to protect a vulnerable and frail sense of self. Although most Blacks are not clinically disturbed, I would suggest that such clinical language is useful in discussing some of the negative (often unconscious) pressures that the racial situation imposes on Blacks or on other minorities and the poor. No person is perfectly adjusted, and understanding more about the nature of the impacts on our lives can help us deal with the tensions we experience.

10. There are specific features of a person's behavior that as a cluster would merit a diagnosis of "narcissistic personality disorder." Some of these center around such tendencies as preoccupations with a sense of self-importance; fantasies of unlimited power, success, or ideal love; or interpersonal relationships marked by exploitativeness, lack of empathy, or sense of entitlement (A.P.A., 1987). Even when such focal symptoms are not prominent, the buffeting by racism increases the risk of defensive retreats taken in order to shield the self. Thus, problems in sense of self can also manifest in low self-esteem and chronic though not incapacitating depressive feelings. A person may have a disturbance in the sense of identity not just in the area of sexuality but as well in an inability to settle on a sense of personal direction. Difficulties in

sustaining gratifying, intimate interpersonal relationships may stem partly from a sense of secret shame over a feeling of unworthiness or from a fear that one's insignificance as a self makes one vulnerable to control by others (a feeling that might well fit the experience of the minority poor). Such symptoms per se are certainly not unique to Blacks, and they may well not be experienced by the Black client as being related to racial experiences. Further, severe psychological symptoms of any kind for anyone are often accompanied by an underlying sense of inadequacy. I am suggesting, however, that weakened defensive functioning as is present in emotional disorder may also expose other psychological difficulties that may have come as a result of racism. I am not suggesting here, either, that all Black clients manifest similar disorders or that they have developed similar personality responses to racism and other aspects of living. What I am suggesting is something that bears on psychotherapy with Blacks. As we shall see, in order for therapy to work, clients must be willing to disclose intimate and painful aspects of themselves. The special reluctance that a Black client may feel to do this with even a Black therapist may come partly from the need s/he has to defend the self against the hurts continually directed at him or her by the social scene.

11. The term *depression* is actually used in several ways. In common parlance it refers to the emotion of sadness that is common to us all. To be able to experience sadness after certain kinds of events is a sign that one's reactions are healthy. However, when the depressive response becomes unusually prolonged or intense or seems to emerge without an external provocation, we begin to speak of clinical depression. Such a symptom syndrome includes not only low self-esteem and deflated mood, sometimes accompanied by irrational guilt feelings, but in the more severe forms may include striking changes in eating habits, marked loss of interest in the environment, sleep disturbances, and suicidal ideation. Clinical depression can be the primary disorder in its own right, or depressive symptoms can occur secondarily to other emotional disorders such as schizophrenia or lesser problems such as the anxiety and personality disorders. Frank and Frank's (1991) concept of demoralization clearly implies that a feeling of dysphoria accompanies the sense of inability to cope effectively.

12. Depressive disorders can range from the relatively mild in which an individual is able to carry on his or her activities, though with something of an emotional albatross around the neck, to the severe reactions and syndromes just mentioned in which an individual is not able to function effectively and may even be psychotic. As pervasive a phenomenon as depression is among mental disorders, it has not been easy to classify. It used to be the fashion in diagnosing clinical depression to differentiate between "reactive" and "endogenous" depressions. Reactive depressions were seen to be more amenable to therapeutic intervention. Depressions of neurotic severity were labeled reac-

tive although transient psychotic reactions were also recognized. Most writers have been willing to see the reactive depressions as attributable to psychological conflict. The more severe syndromes that people show, however, sometimes seem to occur without reference to identifiable precipitating events. These were called the endogenous depressions, the implication being that these disorders spring from some aspects of the individual's physiological functioning that has gone askew (Akiskal & McKinney, 1975).

When psychological writers talk about the "cultural depression" presumably found among African Americans, they are not talking primarily about the endogenous disorders but, rather, the chronic mood responses that are reactive to the external crises of social oppression imposed on them. The Crain and Weisman data may well have referred to such relatively mild, though chronic, reactions. There is some evidence of different qualitative features in the clinical picture of depressed Blacks and Whites. In one study there were differences on the dimension of hostility, with Black men and women rating themselves higher than did Whites (Raskin, Crook, & Herman, 1975). Specifically, Blacks rated themselves higher on items tapping "negativism" (e.g., "When someone is bossy, I do the opposite of what he asks"; "Unless someone asks me in a nice way, I won't do what they want") and on items tapping "internalization." *Internalization* in this case refers to turning one's anger inward against oneself. Such a mechanism has the defensive purpose of preventing the escape of anger that would subject one to retaliatory punishment by a more powerful protagonist. (An example of an internalizing item would be "When I am mad or angry, I usually get a headache.") Black men reported themselves more ready to strike back verbally or physically when provoked. These tendencies to be more inhibiting (internalizing) or externalizing of hostility than Whites are quite consistent with the conclusions drawn by Crain and Weisman (1972) that racism has forced a different handling of aggression among African Americans.

The amount of severe clinical depression does not seem to show racial differences. However, as noted earlier with respect to the work of Gary and Weaver (1991), this is a rather complex matter when one considers the demographic variety that exists within the African-American community (Brown, 1990). For example, there is evidence that suicide, the lethal extreme of depressive mood, has remained higher among young Black men than in older Black men (J. J. Jackson, 1990). This pattern began to appear in the 1970s (Williams, 1986). In explanation, some writers (Gibbs, 1988; Parham & McDavis, 1987; Seiden, 1970) have emphasized the psychological impact of the blocking of opportunities for education and employment by the racist society. Of course, even using a system-blame approach, individual dynamics must be seen as playing a necessary part in the particular response to depressing external circumstances.

Seiden has suggested further that what looked like assaultive and potentially homicidal acts by young Blacks may in some instances have stemmed from suicidal impulses. He cites the example of one young Black man who started a commotion, seemingly with little cause, in a bar frequented by armed, off-duty policemen. He was shot to death as he pointed his loaded weapon at one of the officers. It is plausible to think that this man provoked his shooting. Seiden speculated that perhaps some "young Black revolutionaries are at least partially motivated by a wish to be martyred, to be ceremoniously executed, to be destroyed in violent confrontation in which they may momentarily respect themselves and from which they will gain posthumous status" (1970, p. 28). Such feelings presumably came from the intense sense of being confronted by hopeless odds in the society. Rather than passively submit, "better to go down in an explosion of masculine rage . . . and physical power" (p. 26). Again, although individual personality factors would contribute to choosing such an alternative, Seiden's primary emphasis is on the highly stressful load placed by American social structure on Black youth, especially those of lower and working-class status. Baker (1988) notes that a brief treatment intervention with the patient and his or her partner or family at the time of crisis can begin a process of changed adaptation. As a broader measure, public health education activities that teach family members of psychiatric patients how to be supportive and how to recognize signs of distress are in order.

13. The notion of self-hatred among minority group members has been a popular topic (Sarnoff, 1951; Poussaint, 1972). Bailey (1976) has suggested that what she has called "ethnic self-hatred" is an observable component of the complex of symptoms in Black psychotic patients. (Many of these persons were probably schizophrenic.) She devised a scale to rate the degree of ethnic self-hatred behavior displayed on a psychiatric ward and a scale for assessing ethnic self-hatred attitudes. She found that the patients evidenced significantly more ethnically self-rejecting attitudes than did a control group of nonpsychotic ward personnel. Further, those patients that showed more generally psychopathological ward behavior also scored higher on her measure of ethnic self-hatred behavior. She took her results as evidence that self-hatred plays "an important and central role in the emotional disturbance of Black psychotics" (1976, p. 1424B). Bailey seems to come very close to saying that ethnic self-hatred, fostered by a dehumanizing society, is a specific cause of psychotic behavior. While such social forces make a contribution, it seems safer to say that some Black persons with disturbed personalities and weakened defenses give more open expression to extreme feelings of what we might call "adaptive inferiority" (Pugh, 1972) with regard to racial self-concept. Psychotic persons often express in bold relief the experiences that others keep out of awareness or resolve effectively in their daily living. Put in terms that we used in Chapter 2, it is likely that these persons were unable to separate an extremely disturbed notion of racial self-concept from personal self-concept, as relatively normal African Americans have been able to do.

14. In this regard, Warheit, Holzer, and Arey (1975) found that while most of the racial difference in the mental health scales they administered disappeared when social class was controlled, on one scale, differences remained. These items tapped the degree to which people were bothered by phobias. Blacks, particularly Black women, scored higher than did Whites. A phobia is an intense and irrational fear of a situation, an object, or act and falls into the class of a neurotic level of disturbance. A phobia is irrational in that the thing feared actually represents only a small danger. Almost anything can become a phobic object or situation for an individual—fear of closed-in places, fear of crowds, and fear of flying are familiar examples. An analysis of the items used on this scale suggested that the greater presence of phobias among Blacks reflected something about the everyday realities to which they are exposed, especially in inner-city communities, in terms of bodily injury and threat from strangers. Warheit and his colleagues acknowledge that factors specific to Blacks' particular social situation may not account for all the difference between groups, but it is an important issue to take into account. The greater incidence of phobias in Warheit's sample (made up of Blacks from the southeastern part of the United States, incidentally) is in line with Halpern's observation about the prevalence of emotional reactivity in the symptom picture of the Black persons with whom she worked. Recent studies (Brown, Eaton, & Sussman, 1990; Neal & Turner, 1991) tend to confirm the higher prevalence of such disorders among Blacks.

15. Many Black Americans take pride in what appears to be a greater expressiveness with regard to their feelings as compared to some Euro-American groups. Some Blacks feel this stems from the African cultural heritage. Rychlak emphasizes in his discussion of reinforcement value (RV) preferences that the affective assessment capacity is not a learned style, that is, a product of sociocultural "input." All groups bring affective assessment potential to life at birth. How it is expressed later is a function of learning and circumstance, but the capacity is not. The implication of Black/White RV differences as personality characteristics might be that a philosophical heritage that emphasized oneness with nature, as in many African cultures, (see Chapter 1, note 2) may have supported a more direct response to the world along affective assessment lines than world views that make a sharp distinction between human beings and their rational mind on the one hand and the rest of nature on the other. Akbar (1991a) suggests that in "African Psychology," a framework which he sees as being basic to human psychology, the self is experienced most directly through emotion or affect. He cites a supportive reference from Vernon Dixon:

Homeland and overseas African persons know reality predominantly through the interaction of affect and symbolic imagery, i.e. the synthesis of these two factors produce knowledge. . . . Affect refers to the feeling self, the emotive self engaged in experiencing phenomena holistically. . . . Affect, however, is not intuition, for the latter term means direct or immediate knowledge (instinctive knowledge) without recourse to inference from or reasoning about evidence. Affect does interact with evidence, evidence in the form of symbolic imagery. [cited in Akbar, 1991a, p. 114]

Note that the emphasis on symbolizing functions is consistent with the humanistic perspective here (see note 1). It may be that people of African heritage have maintained as important the capacity to respond to the world with affective assessments more than have people from other cultural groups.

16. Among the differences in approach to psychotherapy the ones that concern us most here are those between psychodynamic and certain behavior therapy approaches to emotional disorder. A major distinction is that psychodynamic approaches depict much of behavior as stemming from unconscious motives and forces. (The terms *psychodynamic* and *psychoanalytic* are somewhat interchangeable. I prefer the term *psychodynamic* here because the term *psychoanalytic* is often associated primarily with Freudian theoretical notions—appropriately so since the many variants in modern psychoanalytic approaches issue from Freud's work. I want to be more inclusive of other related approaches than the term *psychoanalytic* might appear to be.) In this view, emotional disorder stems from unconsciously motivated distortions of reality (Silverman, 1974). Psychopathology, then, is remediated by recognizing and changing such distortions. The fact that distortion has occurred and still operates unconsciously to color the present situation is what makes distortions so powerful and so hard to change. From the humanistic perspective of this book we might describe a distortion as a conceptualization, a structuring of reality in a way that keeps a particular sense of self intact and free from anxiety but that nevertheless doesn't really square with socially constructed reality. So, without realizing it, a man responds to his wife's (in reality) reasonable demands as if they were those of his domineering mother, at least as he remembers her. The therapeutic interventions in psychodynamic psychotherapy are aimed at helping this client become clear on what the unconscious conceptualizations may be (e.g., wife = mother) that have been governing his actions, and he is then in a better position to strive to put other conceptualizations into effect in behavior. It is in this sense that Edelson says, "Psychotherapy is a process that increases the capacity of its participants . . . to attain voluntarily a state of becoming more fully awake" (1971, p. 117). This is akin to the notion of what the family can contribute to

the child's self-development in making it more aware (see Chapter 2, pp. 44–46).

Behavior therapies assume that an individual's current maladaptive behavior was learned as a way of reducing the anxiety aroused by a particular trauma or because the consequences in the environment produced by a particular behavior are rewarding. This is why the behavior persists, that is, becomes a habit. Traditionally in this approach no assumption is made that there is a set of unconscious conceptualizations held by the person that sustain the behavior. The therapeutic interventions in the behaviorist tradition are aimed at getting people to unlearn maladaptive habits by, for example, helping them to associate low anxiety (relaxed states) with feared situations or to associate negative and unrewarding connotations to the old habits. In recent years considerable emphasis in behavior therapy has been placed on cognition, that is, on helping people direct attention to the degree to which their thinking influences action. Such a focus is on thoughts and beliefs that are readily accessible rather then deeply subconscious (Phares, 1992).

There are varying opinions as to whether behavior therapy approaches are more appropriate for African Americans than are traditional psychodynamic approaches (Phares, 1992; Smith et al., 1978; Smith & Dejoie-Smith, 1984; Turner, 1982). My perspective would be that any theory that leaves out the role of the conceptualizing activity of the individual is inadequate to deal with the situation of African Americans—or any human beings for that matter. On the other hand, many of the techniques used by behavior therapists may well be quite useful to Blacks. In addition, there are recent trends to attempt to integrate behavioral and psychodynamic points of view, and African Americans can certainly benefit from these developments (Wachtel, 1977; Westerman, 1993).

It is customary to see psychoanalytic, behaviorist, and humanistic points of view as all differing from one another. But the humanistic position being advanced here is close in certain ways to the psychoanalytic view. The notion of a conceptualizing mind guided by conscious and unconscious intentions and using the dialectical meaning inherent in symbols for the purpose of adaptation and for defense—principles basic to psychodynamic thinking—are central to the kind of humanistic approach adopted here.

As an addendum to the discussion of behavior therapy, it is worth noting the special conceptualization of one of the principal techniques of behavior therapy called "assertiveness training" (Lanyon & Lanyon, 1978). This procedure has the aim of teaching people how to stand up for themselves and advance their legitimate interests without necessarily being hostile or destructive. It involves discussion with the counselor or therapist, "role playing" in the counseling sessions, directive encouragement from the therapist, and repeated efforts in the real-life situation.

Donald Cheek (1976) argued in his book *Assertive Black . . . Puzzled White,* which he labeled "a Black perspective on assertive behavior," that a different approach to assertiveness training is necessary for most Blacks. One of the key skills to be learned for Blacks in interracial situations is that of separating hostile from assertive impulses and knowing when to express one or the other of these feelings. Some people cannot be assertive *for fear of* being hostile; others seem often not to be able to be assertive *without* being hostile. As we have seen, various studies have suggested that historically Blacks have been kept from expressing their rage in productive ways.

Cheek notes that as Blacks have recently become more assertive in their expression of self, Whites have been puzzled that Blacks were impatient with the pace of change. "What do you want?" was the injured question addressed to Blacks in the sixties and early seventies. Cheek's approach to assertiveness training is to help Blacks learn to switch language codes and behavioral styles in shifting from a Black-Black to a Black-White interpersonal situation. He notes that what comes through as assertive in one setting, for instance, an all-Black setting, may be seen as hostile in an interracial setting by a White person.

> Because of the many pressures on a Black person . . . there is difficulty in finding the assertive manner of expressing oneself that is both comfortable (not giving up one's Black dignity and pride) and effective (manages to get the message across without harm). The usual Black response in a state of anxiety has either been passive or aggressive—either say nothing or become loud, threatening and abusive. For Whites, but particularly for Blacks, assertiveness is a social skill. It can open the door for many who occasionally need or want to "play the game." This doesn't mean that they must "sell out," act White or become a "handkerchief head." It means increasing choice and options in terms of ways of communicating honest feelings. It increases the repertoire of responses and makes one less subject to exploitation. [Cheek, 1976, p. 65]

His approach may have particular value for students on White campuses who come from lower- and working-class backgrounds and who are prone to "withdrawing" styles or to a sole use of separationist" or "assimilationist" styles (Gibbs, 1974).

17. The question of what happens when psychotherapy works is still unresolved. This is a particularly thorny issue in view of the large number of differing theoretical approaches, which all seem to have legitimate claim to at least some success. Chessick (1969) suggested a view that I have found persuasive and that is consistent with the ideas being developed in this book. In effect, he suggested that various approaches to psychotherapy can be viewed as different internally consistent ways of conceptualizing psychologi-

cal issues. A person gets "better" in therapy when s/he learns the therapist's way of conceptualizing events and applies them to life so as to live more competently. The test here is that the client is in fact able to achieve a more effective functioning of the self and has not simply slavishly adopted the therapist's style in order to please the latter. Therefore, different therapists may work well with different persons. Rychlak (1982a) puts that from within the teleological perspective:

> The logical learning theorist . . . begins from . . . the assumption that . . . what people need is a responsible, self-accepted premise or system of premises on the basis of which to behave. . . . [Each of the different approaches to psychotherapy] . . . Freudian, Adlerian, Rogerian, and so on . . . merely reflects a different set of premised meanings regarding the nature of human experience. Any one of them or some combination could serve to frame a given person's life adequately—or the person might concoct a suitable premise system entirely his or her own. [pp. 102–103]

Some persons are not as able to make sense of one kind of conceptualization, say a Freudian one, but may be able to make sense of a Jungian one. It may also be, of course, that a particular therapist because of his or her personal style and/or background is able to establish a relationship where other therapists have failed, and thus the client is willing to relax the "resistance" to accounting for his or her life in the new model that the therapist suggests.

This has implications also for the much debated question regarding the contribution to psychotherapeutic progress of gaining conscious "insight" into one's difficulties. Psychodynamic therapies have tended to imply that finding "the" origin of an individual's disturbance is necessary. What is being implied here is that gaining insight into one's difficulties involves learning a way to put one's self activities (intentions, some of which one becomes newly aware of in psychotherapy) into a framework that "makes sense." Therapists often recognize that a client in intensive psychotherapy may resolve a specific problem even when s/he is not clear on a specific insight into the self regarding that problem. This may be because even when a client is not able to fully acknowledge an issue as having been continually characteristic of himself or herself—and when there is good reason to believe that it is true about him or her—just the chance to discuss and experience hitherto suppressed or repressed material related to the conflict sometimes helps the individual to put it into perspective. In other words, the individual becomes better able to master these feelings—perhaps use a more mature set of defenses to handle them. (See Luborsky [1984, pp. 17–21] on this point.)

Related to these considerations is a recent trend in thinking that describes successful psychotherapy as involving the fashioning of a more coherent "narrative" or story (a conceptualization, in our terms) about one's past and present circumstances (e.g., Howard, 1991; Sarbin, 1990; Schafer, 1983, 1992; Spence, 1982). Such a reorganization of major themes in one's life (formal-cause factors) can be used to guide more effective living. As Howard (1991) notes, ". . .part of the work between client and therapist can be seen as life-story elaboration, adjustment, or repair" (p. 194).

18. Of course, creating a helping relationship is not the only aspect of the therapist's activity. Strupp (1973) suggests that as a second "basic ingredient" or condition of successful psychotherapy the therapist uses a well-established relationship as a kind of influence or power base, as it were, to encourage the client to reappraise defensive behavior, develop new conceptualizations, and try out new ways of acting. In the process of doing this the therapist may use "(a) suggestion (persuasion); (b) encouragement for openness of communication, self-scrutiny, and honesty . . .; (c) 'interpretations of unconscious material,' such as self-defeating and harmful strategies in interpersonal relations, fantasies, distorted beliefs about reality, etc.; (d) setting an example of 'maturity' and providing a model . . .; (e) manipulation of rewards" (p. 1).

19. The Ethnic Validity Model (Tyler, Brome, & Williams, 1991; Tyler, Sussewell, & Williams-McCoy, 1985) tries to conceptualize some of the complexities for psychotherapeutic practice in a multiethnic society such as ours. Briefly, the authors of this model note that heterogeneous societies "tend to be shaped or dominated by one of the ethnic groups within them. From a power position point of view that group functions as a culture-defining group (CDG). Its heritage and its members are preeminent in shaping the ethos of the culture" (Tyler, Sussewell, & Williams-McCoy, 1985, p. 312).

Individuals from other groups in the society, non–culture-defining-groups (NCDG), are likely to live with various limitations on their life options. Therapy dyads, of course, may represent differing CDG-NCDG combinations. The Ethnic Validity Model highlights three kinds of interactions that can emerge in psychotherapy: "convergence," "divergence," and "conflict." Convergent ethnic validity describes a situation in which world views of therapist and client are similar and compatible. Divergent ethnic validity refers to a pattern of interaction in which differences in certain important values exist but these are nevertheless tolerable and compatible. They do not impede communication and efforts at understanding. *Conflict* refers to an interaction situation in which differences in world view and ideas about competence are incompatible and intolerable so as to make fruitful dialogue between the dyad participants impossible.

Different CDG-NCDG combinations can have different implications for therapy process and outcome. One of the more relevant pairings from our perspective would be the CDG therapist—for example, one who is White, middle-class, and male—with an NCDG patient—Black, lower-class, and female. One would expect a diversity of experiences between these two persons as a function of their differing group memberships. In such a relationship each could learn about different cultural norms and ways of coping adaptively. While the patient would have the chance to evaluate dysfunctional aspects of her coping style, the therapist could get a direct view of the experience of being discriminated against and perhaps become more aware of some of his own cultural biases. For the therapy to work, the divergences in the dyad would have to be managed so that they do not become primarily conflictual. The authors note that one of the dangers of therapeutic failure might be that it would be harder for the participants to engage in other relationships with ethnically or socioeconomically different persons.

Even when client and therapist are Black—both from an NCDG group—there are pitfalls. While the client may feel particularly well understood, there may be a danger of client and therapist not seeing beyond their convergent points of view, about the racial situation for example. Unless the therapist is careful, s/he may not separate personal difficulties from racially imposed problems. Or, again, one or the other African-American participants in the dyad may strongly identify with CDG values (i.e., have a stage 1 orientation in Cross's terms), leading to problems in the process. As Tyler and his colleagues note, diversity of background does not necessarily block a constructive therapeutic exchange and similarity does not necessarily guarantee it.

Other writers come at the issue of cultural variability from a different perspective, although one we are familiar with. Helms (1984) proposes a model that expands on the nigrescence notion by suggesting that racial identity, as one aspect of the sense of self, goes through a process of evolution in Whites as well as Blacks. She suggests that there is first a "contact" stage in which Whites come to an awareness of Black people as being different. Whites may then evolve through four subsequent stages. These involve guilt about societal racism, retreat from interracial contact into a defensive prejudice, emergence into a curiosity about and intellectual acceptance of Blacks, and finally a genuine emotional acceptance of racial and cultural diversity. In this last stage there is a differentiated awareness of and valuing of their own White identity as well as a genuine appreciation for people from other backgrounds.

She suggests that the therapy process is influenced by the stage of racial identity development each member of the dyad is in. Even in same-race pairs, complications can emerge if the patient is at a more "advanced" stage than an otherwise quite competent therapist. Ponterotto (1988) described the responses of White counselor trainees to his classroom efforts to expand awareness of and appreciation for cultural differences. Drawing on Cross's and Helms's paradigms, he proposed a sequence of four stages from preexposure to integration that his students seemed to go through. The implication from all of these authors is that racial issues form an inevitable part of the background—the cultural ecology—of the therapeutic work.

20. Abramowitz (1978) in response to the Jones and Seagull article took sharp issue with the idea that "Black patients receive an appreciably less than fair shake from White therapists" (p. 957). His demurral stemmed from clinical analogue studies and from clinical judgment studies. The former are those in which subjects are not real patients and the interview is not an actual therapy session but rather a situation in which the participants are asked to role play a session for the purposes of the research. The clinical judgment study is one in which trained clinicians (usually) evaluate a bogus case profile on several dimensions posed by the researchers. The judges are then compared for their degree of bias, for example, in the kind of diagnosis made or their feeling about the hypothetical patient's suitability for therapy. Abramowitz concluded that such data do not support a picture of negative racial expectations on the part of White clinicians toward Blacks. However, he also noted that these kinds of studies do not provide compelling data. "The protocol [to be evaluated] is predetermined, the presumably evocative stimulus person is represented only skeletally, and the rater knows that his or her reactions are being monitored and do not have interpersonal consequences" (1978, p. 958). In other words, the therapist rater can give a socially acceptable response that does not necessarily reflect what his or her behavior would actually be in a real therapy situation. Jones and Seagull didn't say that Blacks must necessarily receive bad treatment from White professionals. However, they and other writers point out the pitfalls that therapists may run into on account of being products of their culture. We shall turn presently to studies of actual therapy situations.

21. In the opposite situation, when the therapist is Black, Holmes (1992) notes that sometimes the presence of racial feelings and fantasies can actually facilitate the work by providing a special entry into the patient's problem. This can be true for both Black and White patients. Among the examples from her clinical experience she cites patients who eventually acknowledged disappointment at having a Black female (hence "second-rate") therapist. Discussion of such feelings led to insight into the patients' intense feelings of personal inferiority.

22. As the third of his essential conditions for therapeutic change, Strupp postulates that what is called for is a client who is able to profit from this kind of help. This does not refer to those qualities that critics of psychotherapy often list about successful clients, that they are young, attractive, verbal, and only moderately disturbed. For Strupp, as suggested in his first condition, the therapy situation is one that has strong elements of a benign parent-child interaction—one in which a helpful, more knowledgeable authority attempts to guide a temporarily less expert and more dependent client. Thus, the kinds of clients who can best be helped are those who are open to letting themselves be influenced by such a figure. "Psychotherapy is potentially useful when the client has remained responsive to parental-type influences, and it is essentially

futile where such receptivity has either never existed or has been severely frustrated" (Strupp, 1973, p. 3). Sense of self grows out of family situations. The discussion in Chapter 2 pointed out that there have been strong sustaining influences in the Black family historically. This would certainly indicate that Blacks in general have the kind of background that is compatible with this condition that Strupp poses.

23. *Authoritarianism* (Adorno et al., 1950) refers to a much studied constellation of traits among which are attitudes of political and social conservatism associated with ethnic prejudice. This is an attitude cluster that researchers not infrequently attempt to assess in therapy clients, the typical prediction being that more authoritarian clients would do less well in psychotherapy. However, Lerner reasoned that, in addition, the presence of democratic-egalitarian as opposed to authoritarian values would be a particularly relevant dimension to assess in the therapist. "In the present study, it was hypothesized that the degree of authoritarianism initially manifested by clients would have no effect on outcome but that the degree of authoritarianism manifested by therapists would have a marked effect, with less authoritarian therapists achieving significantly better results" (1972, p. 88). She devised her own scale since the widespread familiarity among social science professionals with the "F Scale," as the authoritarianism measure is called, would have made it useless with this group. Examples of some of her items were: "If they had had a successful treatment experience, most political radicals of both the right and the left would change their views on society and its ills" and "Involvement of the poor in programs planned for their welfare is essential, but, because they are mainly oriented to immediate gratification, it is unrealistic to give them top level decision-making powers in planning such programs because long range goals would inevitably suffer" (p. 89). Responses of strong agreement with such statements would presumably be toward the authoritarian side.

24. A further word about authoritarianism and "authority" is in order. That the therapist should not be authoritarian does not mean s/he does not possess authority. Fromm, in his book *Man for himself* (1947), makes some conceptual distinctions that I have always found useful. He distinguishes between "irrational" and "rational" authority. Irrational authority is concerned with power over others. "This power can be physical or mental. . . . Power on the one side, fear on the other, are always the buttresses on which irrational authority is built" (p. 9). Its aim is to perpetuate itself and maintain others in subordination. In the political sphere the model is dictatorship. It is based on perpetuated inequality between authority and its object.

Rational authority, by contrast, stems from competence. The respect accruing to such a person stems from particular skill or knowledge that the authority possesses. This person's power lasts as long as s/he competently helps those who entrusted him or her with a particular task. The relationship between authority and object is one of equality as persons; the difference between them is with regard to expertise in a particular field. In some instances the aim of the rational authority is to balance out the differences, at least somewhat, by imparting the skills to those who do not have them. The model here is of a teacher or therapist. Indeed, the therapist begins with expertise about technique and soon develops knowledge about the client that the latter keeps out of consciousness and hence does not "know." Eventually, however, the client gains knowledge about the self and ideally uses the kinds of techniques the therapist has taught to continue to gain self-knowledge on his or her own. The client becomes the rational authority about himself or herself. Fromm proposes that one who holds power through irrational authority represents an authoritarian stance. One who has power on the basis of rational authority is "authoritative."

It is partly in this sense that therapy is like a parent-child interaction. Strupp (1973), as we have seen, suggests that clients in therapy are yearning for a benign and gratifying parent-child relationship. To greatly condense one view of the therapy process, the therapist with an egalitarian attitude offers a loving yet rationally authoritative relationship that substitutes for the less rational ones the client experienced in his or her life and thereby encourages trying out new and more mature behaviors in life.

25. This conception of the early stages of therapy process with African-American clients is similar in some respects to the "Control-Mastery" theoretical approach to psychoanalytic theory (Weiss & Sampson, 1986). According to this framework, the client harbors unconscious, unrealistic conceptualizations—"pathogenic beliefs"—that are hindrances to the individual's adaptation to reality. The client comes to therapy with the wish to master these maladaptive conceptualizations by gradually bringing them to consciousness where s/he can get better control over them. To do this the patient must ascertain that it is safe to bring this material into more frank expression. With this in mind the patient unconsciously "tests" the therapist by directing a portion of these expectations at the therapist to see whether s/he will, by attitude or behavior, support or disconfirm the pathogenic belief. If the therapist responds in ways that show that s/he is not threatened by the theme the patient is struggling with, the patient will feel it is safe to bring more of the issue into the open where greater understanding and mastery can be achieved. (Translating this notion into the cross-racial therapy situation, in Gibbs's interpersonal phase it might be said that the Black client comes into therapy hoping, before getting into the instrumental phase, to disconfirm the idea, perhaps held subconsciously, that the therapist is too biased racially to be of help.) This perspective clearly portrays the individual as being purposeful in trying to bring about his or her development and is fully consistent with the notions about agency that are central to this book (see Jenkins [1992] for a discussion of agency notions in psychoanalysis). A part of the therapist's growth-inducing, egalitarian attitude in Lerner's terms might well be the belief in such a mastery motivation in even severely disturbed, lower-class persons.

26. The emphasis put by Gibbs and Griffith and Jones on early relationship dynamics emphasizes therapy with African Americans in particular. However, concern with interpersonal processes is receiving wider attention in the general literature on psychotherapy (Gill, 1983; Luborsky, 1984; Strupp & Binder, 1984). For example, the psychoanalyst Merton Gill (1983) in the modern evolution of his thinking writes that "the interpersonal paradigm is the appropriate one for the therapeutic interaction" (p. 234). In his "supportive-expressive" approach to psychoanalytic therapy, Luborsky (1984) notes: "It is the relationship problems that are the most accessible and therapeutically usable expression of [the patient's] conflicts; they tend to be directly involved in the patient's suffering and therefore to require change" (p. 17). Accordingly, his approach is oriented toward concentrating the therapeutic work around a central focus, the "core conflictual relationship theme," that seems to characterize the patient's interpersonal functioning. Such a dynamic operates rigidly and to the detriment of the patient's better intentions and goals, and it tends to make life with other people recognizably difficult. This area serves as the point of attention for therapeutic intervention.

This broader emphasis on relationship issues in what Gibbs would call the instrumental phase of therapy also has application to African Americans. E. Jones (1985) notes that while work with minority clients must be based on sound knowledge of the culture from which they come, one always has the task of locating the particular (African-American) individual one is working with in his or her uniqueness. As I have been saying, there is much personal variability within ethnic identity groups. Granted that, Jones suggests that two fundamental interpersonal processes in therapeutic technique are relevant to work with African Americans as they are with all people. These are empathy, the capacity to share and understand affectively the experience of another, and "countertransference," the nature of the therapist's personal reactions to the patient.

We discussed empathy earlier as a central concept in psychodynamic therapy. It is typically seen as the capacity to involve oneself with another's experience emotionally by using one's own feelings as a reference point. Thus, I understand another's embarrassment or anger in a certain situation partly in terms of the experience of such feelings that I have had in the course of my life. But what of circumstances where cultural and social backgrounds are quite different? Jones suggests that in addition to focusing inward on one's own experience, an "outward movement of empathy" is called for. This would aim at focusing the imagination so as to "transpose oneself into another . . . [and thereby] achieve a more complete understanding of culturally varied predispositions . . . [and] personal constructs" (E. Jones, 1985, p. 178). In this regard the psychoanalyst Evelyne Schwaber calls empathy a *way* of perceiving—"experiencing from *within* the patient's experience" (1980, p. 216).

In addition, Jones notes that the therapist's failure to be able to take an empathic stance can lead to countertransference problems—inappropriate and personalized therapist reactions to the patient. In fact, as compared to White patients, "Black patients may evoke countertransference attitudes more frequently. The reason for this seems to lie in the fact that social images of Blacks still make them easier targets for therapists' projections, as well as the fact that the culturally different client provides more opportunities for empathic failures" (E. Jones, 1985, p. 178). He maintains that self-knowledge and the continuing effort to remain aware of one's ongoing psychological processes are the best ways of preventing dysfunctional intrusions of personal reactions into the therapy. Thus, "it is this therapist quality of *self-understanding* as much as *cultural understanding* that is important in treating the Black client" (p. 178). That is to say, one should know as much as one can about the culture of the person one is working with and recognize when the need arises for consultation with a knowledgeable colleague. But at the same time, there is no substitute for the therapist knowing his or her general personal biases and being sensitive to the reactions s/he is experiencing in *this* clinical interaction with *this* African-American client.

Epilogue

If a psychological conception of African Americans is to do justice to the reality of their current and historical struggles, it must not only focus on the psychosocial problems attendant on being a beleaguered minority in the United States but also account for how African Americans have continued to develop and sustain their humanity "despite and in rejection of the obstacles and meannesses imposed upon [them]" (Ellison, 1964, p. 39). This requirement poses a considerable challenge for psychology and the social sciences because these disciplines traditionally tend not to depict people as pro-active beings who attempt to make a difference in the circumstances that confront them. To redress the balance, the task for the social sciences becomes one of producing a credible image of the person as an active agent capable of taking charge of his or her life.

The Strengths of Black Americans

In this book I have argued that a teleological-humanistic view of psychological agency provides an excellent model for righting the human image. An agent is defined as a being who is capable of conforming to, adding to, opposing, or ignoring sociocultural and/or biological stimulations. That is to say, such a being may go along with the prevailing social norm, may capitulate to the pressing social forces, or not. I have argued that this capacity for agency, along with inherent strivings for psychological "competence," has enabled most African Americans to work to enhance personal growth in spite of the social obstacles they face.

We have discussed this capacity in various spheres of psychological functioning. For example, as we have seen, African Americans bring active intellectual abilities to life situations, though these skills have often been underappreciated and poorly developed by our educational system. In addition, we have noted that despite racist assaults on healthy self-affirming activities, African Americans struggle impressively against the anxiety and demoralization that tend to sabotage adaptive coping efforts. And in recent historical circumstances an increasingly greater number of Black people have linked personal self-esteem to positive group identity in the context of an increased appreciation of their cultural roots. Thus, in contrast to the traditional view, African Americans have been active agents in the circumstances that have confronted them. Though far from being without problems, Blacks have shown a remarkable ability to bring a sense of agency to bear in order to cope in the American social scene (J. Jones, 1991a; Ramseur, 1991) and, in fact, they have made positive contributions to this culture in the bargain.

In summing up, we can return to a point made in Chapter 6. There we noted that although many Blacks suffer the "double jeopardy" of oppressive race and social class pressures, as an ethnic group they do not seem to show greater mental disturbance than do Whites of similar socioeconomic status. The broad humanistic model that we have used is a powerful one in conceptualizing the strengths African Americans have shown as human beings. However, the data on comparative rates of mental disturbance in the Black and White communities suggest that the agency of Black Americans has been expressed in more culturally specific ways as well. Neighbors (1984) among others has indicated the need for research on cultural strengths that might help account for such findings. In this closing discussion I would like to highlight two features of cultural response of African Americans that may well be relevant to this issue. The first is that of biculturality and the second pertains to religiosity.

The "Twoness" of the African American

Bicultural functioning reflects a person's ability to participate in many aspects of mainstream American culture while at the same time having the interest and ability to take part in institutions and activities more distinctly characteristic of his or her ethnic background. Minority individuals often find such involvements to be psychologically nurturing. Consistent with this idea we have described the sense of self as having a dialectic quality—one that recognizes alternate, personally meaningful identity "anchor points" or reference group orientations. In reflecting on the ethnic minority experience in America, many writers ascribe a positive value to the idea of biculturalism/multiculturalism (Cross, 1991; Ramirez, 1983, 1991; Sue & Morishima, 1982).

With respect to African Americans specifically, the concept of biculturality brings us back to the quote from DuBois, written in 1903, to the effect that the African American ". . . ever feels his two-ness—an American, a Negro" (1961, p. 17). As we pursue the DuBois quote, we see that his perspective recognized the complexity inherent in this cultural duality. On the one hand he conceived this "twoness" as being represented by "two souls, two thoughts, two unreconciled strivings; two warring ideals in one dark body" (p. 17). On the other hand DuBois was not ultimately resigned to this quality of self experience as necessarily representing a "house divided against itself." In one sense we might say that he saw the American Negro in this dual consciousness as intent on achieving a particular kind of "integration." The goal was not that of assimilation on the part of the Negro but that of merging

> his double self into a better and truer self. In this merging he wishes neither of the older selves to be lost. He would not Africanize America, for America has too much to teach the world and Africa. He would not bleach his Negro soul in a flood of white Americanism, for he knows that Negro blood has a message for the world. He simply wishes to make it possible for a man to be both a Negro and an American. [p. 17]

Clearly, DuBois's words represent biculturality in a positive light.

Implied in DuBois's notion is the idea that "twoness" has the potential both for lending greater richness to personality and for imparting a greater strength in adaptive functioning. Such a perspective can be seen in the writing of a number of those interested in the issue of biculturalism. For example, Ramirez (1983) proposes that a bicultural/multicultural orientation is reflected, for one thing, in a person's openness to diversity. Accordingly, a person who embraces such a view "considers that all cultures and religions represent important sources of knowledge about life which can be helpful to his/her own development" (p. 9). This, of course, is consistent with DuBois's notion that "Negro blood has a message for the world." Ramirez goes on to note that the internalizing and use of these cultural alternatives as resources helps a person "to become more flexible and adaptable in meeting the diverse demands of life" (ibid.).

Along the same lines, James Jones (1991a) has recently noted that a bicultural adaptation, what he calls a "bifurcation" in the self, has historically allowed the African-American individual to combine "perspectives, preferences and styles as the situation demands" (p. 317). In some situations the individual might respond in ways that express the saliency of racial or group identity. But in other instances the person may choose to function on the basis of his or her individuality. Biculturality is not simply a (relatively static) trait that one *has*. It is more properly thought of as an ongoing *process* or style of activity that characterizes the way Blacks have tended to deal with the realities of America. In the terms of this book a bicultural stance has a dialectical quality—the capacity to imagine and use alternatives in conceptualizing a particular situation. Thus the term describes the fact that in their everyday efforts to enhance their competence many African Americans are intent on affirming their own cultural identity and are also open to making use of other cultural ways of adapting, depending on the situation.

Jones suggests several dialectically framed behavioral dimensions that illustrate ways a person might express acceptance of a mainstream cultural perspective or not, according to the situation. For example, opportunities present themselves to address an issue from "individual identity" as opposed to "group identity" vantage points. Both the history of racial oppression and the recent emergence of Black pride tend to support tendencies for African Americans to think about situations in terms of racial group identification. Jones (1991) argues, however, that Black people "vary in the degree to which and the circumstances under which group identity is espoused" (p. 316). Thus, many Blacks are also quite committed to the idea of a "colorblind" society in which they advocate that all persons be treated respectfully according to their *individual* merits. When they feel it is appropriate, they respond in ways that support this point of view.

Let's consider another example from Jones that highlights the issue of agency even more. The dimension of "personal accountability versus contextual blame" is one of considerable importance for Blacks. Jones's phrasing is something of a translation of the individual blame/system blame" dichotomy discussed in Chapter 5. As we saw, the emphasis of that frame of reference is on locating the source of responsibility for personal outcomes—either in the inadequacy of personal efforts or in the systematic blocking of opportunity by society. A modern, heightened Black consciousness tends to focus on the ways in which the sociohistorical context in America rather than personal failings of Black individuals has impeded the progress of African Americans. A too narrow focus on individual traits and behaviors tends to miss the larger field of negatively impacting social factors and can be somewhat demoralizing. However, Jones notes that an alternative perspective on this issue recognizes the possibility at times of assuming personal responsibility for outcomes no matter what the contextual circumstances.

> By choosing to be accountable, one is acknowledging the *determinacy of intention* [emphasis added]. Clearly we see this distinction when for example, an account of a black teenage mother shows her overcoming the difficulty of teenage poverty and motherhood to complete high school, care for her child, and build a career for herself. She accepted personal accountability, even though it might have been easy to blame her context for her misfortune. [p. 316]

In noting the "determinacy of intention," Jones highlights the power that final causes have when brought to bear on guiding choices, even in the face of painful alternatives. This capacity of Black individuals to vary the cultural and conceptual "anchor point" from which they approach a situation suggests an active stance in the situations that confront them. (Our discussion of Harrell's six coping styles [pp. 206–207] also implied this capacity to approach situations with an adaptive style attuned to the situation.) Such flexibility, that is, the capacity to conceive alternatives, is guided by the intention to maximize the competence of one's functioning. Jones argues that multidimensionality and biculturality represent "one of the major strengths of the reactions to racism" (p. 317). His emphasis highlights how biculturality is one vehicle for expressing the notion of agency advanced in this book.

Feeling the Spirit

Turning briefly to the area of religiosity, recent writing by a number of researchers points to the importance of religious experience for Black people in guiding their adaptation to America. Taylor and Chatters (1991), using data in the National Survey of Black Americans (Jackson, 1991, chaps. 1 and 2), document the high degree of religious involvement in the Black community. Such involvement includes not only official church membership and church attendance but also private religious behaviors, most notably daily prayer. Studies indicate that prayer is a coping device very frequently used by Blacks to handle stressful episodes (Neighbors et al., 1983). It is employed considerably more by African Americans than by Whites (Ramseur, 1991). As in the general population, level of religiosity varies across demographic groups in the Black community. For example, women, older persons, and married individuals have been found to show more of a religious commitment than their counterparts (Taylor & Chatters, 1991).

Participation in church life not only furnishes spiritual support but also provides other important social and economic services such as companionship, help in times of illness, goods and services, and financial assistance (Taylor & Chatters, 1991). Cross (1991) suggests that a religious orientation can be one of a set of coping strengths that can enrich the quality of functioning at the stage of internalization. He postulates that, for one thing, in dealing with the realities of prejudice in America a religious perspective can help keep the person focused on racism "as a form of human evil, rather than on [tending to demonize] white people, with its attendant hopelessness (one cannot negotiate with the devil)" (p. 216).

To an important degree, religiosity has traditionally provided Blacks an emotional and psychological haven from many of the meannesses of a discriminatory society. However, as Taylor and Chatters (1991) note, this does not mean that Black religious thought can be properly characterized as primarily "otherworldly" or "escapist."

> Historical and current evidence attests to the fact that black religious thought and organized religion has consistently functioned as a foundation for social action and reform. . . . Deeply held religious beliefs were incorporated into the ideological core and principles of the struggle for

civil and human rights and, further, provided the strategy and human resolution to participate in organized protest (i.e., civil disobedience, protest marches). . . . The weight of evidence attests to the fact that, while black religious traditions are dedicated to the spiritual lives and concerns of individuals, black religious thought and experience remain deeply committed to the political and social betterment and advancement of black Americans, individually and collectively. [p. 122]

From the viewpoint of this book, such an analysis is consistent with the idea that active involvement in religious activity has helped African Americans sustain their sense of competence and agency. Our humanistic focus has stressed the individual's capacity to have a personal causal impact through the exercise of intentions. The analysis throughout has had a nonreligious tone. However, this emphasis on the power of human action in the daily world need not be seen as necessarily at variance with a conception of a transcending spiritual power that seems to have been very important to countless African Americans. In Chapter 2 we noted Chein's view that the dignity of humanity rests in its capacity to be self-creating, a notion that can be found in the very genesis of the Judaeo-Christian religious conception. For the religious person the active stance that people take as agents to bring about social justice and the striving to become more and more capable and loving as individuals can certainly be carried out within their conception of God's intent and with an actively sustained consciousness of God's support and guidance. A telic-humanistic view is not antithetical to a spiritual perspective, though of course it does not require a religious orientation, either.

The "Afrocentric" View

This book has drawn on western philosophical traditions to ground a psychological perspective on people of African descent who have settled in the United States. Though my focus has been on Aristotelian thought, there is no claim being made here that this tradition was original with the ancient Greeks. In tracing these themes historically, Rychlak (1988) starts with Thales and Anaximander, who lived around 600 B.C. We know that intellectually sophisticated civilizations flourished in Africa, Asia, and the Middle East long before this. One tradition in current African-American scholarship argues that *all* human civilization began in Africa and fanned out across the globe, gradually changing into the ethnic variations we now know (Myers, 1988). It is this "Afrocentric" psychological perspective that I would like to briefly discuss now.

Following in a tradition of several African-American writers, White and Parham (1990) state that there is a longstanding "African world view" from which a basic African-American psychological perspective is derived. In this view the focus is "on emotional vitality, interdependence, collective survival, the oral tradition, perception of time, harmonious blending, and the role of the elderly" (White & Parham, 1990, p. 15). It begins with a holistic idea about the human condition that denies the validity of a dualism or split between mind and body or between affect and cognition. "The human organism is conceived as a totality made up of a series of interlocking systems" (ibid.).

In her recent book, Myers (1988) has developed what she calls an "optimal psychology" based on an Afrocentric point of view. Her perspective derives from an understanding of the world view and philosophy of the ancient Africans whose civilization began in the region around the Upper Nile. This Afrocentric conceptual system

> assumes that reality is at once spiritual and material. . . . [T]he notion is that there is an all pervasive "energy" which is the source, the sustainer, and the essence of all phenomena. In this regard everything becomes one thing, spirit manifesting. Spirit refers to that permeating essence known in an extra-sensory fashion (energy, consciousness, God). [p. 12]

With respect to the nature of the person, another Afrocentric theorist notes:

> African Psychology maintains that the essence of the human being is spiritual. This means that . . . [the human being] reduced to . . . lowest terms is invisible and of a universal substance. . . . [T]he African conception of personality is fundamentally built on the notion of a force which defines the . . . [person's] continuity with all things within the world. This implies that . . . [humans are] ultimately reducible to the universe itself which gives . . . [human beings] universal potential. This assumption of the ultimate spiritual nature of the human being hypothesizes the potential harmony of people with each other and the remainder of the universe. [Akbar, 1991a, p. 117]

In Myers' view, Afrocentric ideas are congruent with many notions that can be found in modern physics. For example, she points to the similarity between physicist G. F. Chew's "bootstrap" philosophy in physics with the African idea of identity. She cites Chew and his colleagues as saying "each particle helps to generate other particles which, in turn, generate it" (in Myers, 1988, p. 21). She goes on to note: "The African system of identity views human existence in the same way. 'I' do not exist alone, but out of the interaction and properties of the collective. I am created by the collective and in turn create it" (ibid.). This, of course, is consistent with the African notion of self that we noted in Chapter 2, in which the sense of "we," one's membership and commitment to the group, is a much stronger component of identity than is a sense of personal individuality, the "I" (Mbiti, 1970; Nobles, 1973). Perhaps the commitment to spirituality shown by many African Americans comes to an important degree from these presumed longstanding traditions in African culture. Further, to the extent that biculturalism is an important and positively adaptive aspect of the functioning of African Americans, perhaps at least some aspects of this Afrocentric perspective help define the African part of the sense of "twoness" felt by many Black Americans.

However, I think that it should be pointed out that some of the themes articulated here can be found in writing describing persons from other minority backgrounds. For example, we have noted that the criticism of the individualized self in Western social science and Western society is not confined to African-American scholars. Ramirez (1983) notes that Europeans pushing west on the American continent came in contact with native people who had a world view similar to what Myers and White and Parham describe and an orientation to the self that had a strong communal component. This has historically been true in Asian societies (Marsella, DeVos, & Hsu, 1985) and presumably remains important for Asian Americans as well (Sue & Morishima, 1982). Roland (1988) suggests that one must take this different nature of the self into consideration in doing psychoanalytic therapy with persons from India and Japan. Further, as we saw in Chapter 2, there is a line of theorizing growing out of western (European-American) social psychology (Sampson, 1985) and hermeneutic approaches to psychology (Sass, 1988) that is highly critical of the traditional notions of individualized self.

Myers acknowledges the similarity of the tenets of many world-view systems to the Afrocentric view. Further, one can see in her presentation of an "optimal psychology" some of the essential tenets of psychological agency as it has been defined in this book as well. For example, one can see the importance of the notion that people act according to intentions they set: "As individuals we can at any point in time choose to reason based upon whatever assumptions we decide" (Myers, 1988, p. 14). Again with reference to the bootstrap philosophy, her perspective is nonreductionistic: "The universe is a dynamic web of interrelated events or parts, all following from the properties of other parts; there are not fundamental entities like building blocks of matter" (p. 21). Or again, regarding what we would call a Kantian view of mental activity: "Perception is not a passive act in which the individual is simply an observer, but an active process where the perceiver can, to a degree, be said to 'construct' his/her perception" (p. 22) The Afrocentric perspective as articulated here is clearly a part of the nonmechanistic point of view emerging in psychology.

The question remains, "Is the Afrocentric view the historically original one that all other civilizations have adopted and later adapted to their particular geographical and cultural situation?" The Afrocentric theorists maintain that it is. However, it is quite possible that different groups having to face broadly similar social adaptive demands (e.g., dealing with gender differences, conceiving and rearing children, dealing with intragroup aggression) might come upon broadly similar social and moral tenets by which to govern their affairs and conceptualize their worlds. (The importance of allegiance to family and kinship group is certainly essential to many European peoples such as the Greeks and the Italians.)

The issue of whether the Afrocentric view was first to develop humanistic ideas is one for historians and anthropologists to solve. For the sake of the record and for the prideful consideration by African Americans of their past, the strong likelihood is that the earliest forebears of African Americans within their African cultures did develop what I am calling humanistic ideas, and it is quite possible these ideas were borrowed by later civilizations such as the Greeks. (The question of the influence on Far East Asian groups is another matter, however.) As African-American scholars develop the Afrocentric perspective more systematically, there will be the opportunity for making connections with recent developments in scholarship influenced by Euro-American thought. As I see it, however, the modern telic-humanistic framework that derives from western philosophical traditions, whatever its origins, is still very useful for considering the situation of African Americans today. Any conception of African Americans that fails to see them as engaged in exercising their human agency—sometimes successfully, sometimes not—cannot hope to grasp what they are about.

References

Abramowitz, S. I. (1978). Splitting data from theory on the black patient–white therapist relationship. *American Psychologist, 33,* 957–958 (Comment).

Adorno, T. W., Frenkel-Brunswik, E., Levinson, D. J., & Sanford, R. N. (1950). *The authoritarian personality.* New York: Harper.

Akbar, N. (1991a). The evolution of human psychology for African Americans. In R. Jones (Ed.), *Black psychology* (3d ed., pp. 99–123). Berkeley, CA: Cobb & Henry.

Akbar, N. (1991b). Mental disorder among African Americans. In R. L. Jones (Ed.), *Black psychology* (3d ed., pp. 339–352). Berkeley, CA: Cobb & Henry.

Akiskal, H. S., & McKinney, W. T., Jr. (1975). Overview of recent research in depression. *Archives of General Psychiatry, 32,* 285–305.

Alejandro-Wright, M. N. (1985). The child's conception of racial classification: A socio-cognitive developmental model. In M. B. Spencer, G. K. Brookins, & W. A. Allen (Eds.), *Beginnings: The social and affective development of black children* (pp. 185–200). Hillsdale, NJ: Erlbaum.

Allen, W. R., Epps, E. G., & Haniff, N. Z. (1991). *College in Black and White: African-American students in predominantly White and historically Black public universities.* Albany, NY: State University of New York Press.

American Psychiatric Association. (1987). *Diagnostic and statistical manual of mental disorders—DSM-III-R* (3d ed., rev.). Washington, DC.

American Psychological Association. (1993). Guidelines for providers of psychological services to ethnic, linguistic, and culturally diverse populations. *American Psychologist, 48,* 45–48.

Ames, R. A. (1950). Protest and irony in Negro folksong. *Science and Society, 14,* 193–213.

Anastasi, A. (1988). *Psychological testing* (6th ed.). New York: Macmillan.

Anderson, L. P. (1991). Acculturative stress: A theory of relevance to Black Americans. *Clinical Psychology Review, 11,* 685–702.

Arieti, S. (1974). *Interpretation of schizophrenia.* (2d ed.). New York: Basic Books.

Atkinson, D. R. (1985). A meta-review of research on cross-cultural counseling and psychotherapy. *Journal of Multicultural Counseling and Development, 1,* 138–153.

Atkinson, D. R., & Schein, S. (1986). Similarity in counseling. *The Counseling Psychologist, 14,* 319–354.

Bachman, J. G. (1970). *Youth in transition, vol. II: The impact of family background and intelligence on tenth-grade boys.* Ann Arbor, MI: Institute for Social Research, University of Michigan.

Bailey, S. T. (1976). Ethnic self-hatred in black psychotics (Doctoral dissertation, City University of New York, 1976). *Dissertation Abstracts International, 37,* 1423–1424B. (University Microfilms No. 76-21, 155.)

Baker, F. M. (1988). Afro Americans. In L. Comas-Diaz & E. E. H. Griffiths (Eds.), *Clinical guidelines in cross-cultural mental health* (pp. 151–181). New York: Wiley.

Baldwin, J. A. (1979). Theory and research concerning the notion of black self-hatred: A review and reinterpretation. *Journal of Black Psychology, 5,* 51–78.

Banks, W. C. (1976). White preference in blacks: A paradigm in search of a phenomenon. *Psychological Bulletin, 83,* 1179–1186.

Banks, W. C., McQuater, G. V., & Ross, J. A. (1979). On the importance of white preference and the comparative difference of blacks and others: Reply to Williams and Morland. *Psychological Bulletin, 86,* 33–36.

Banks, W. C., Ward, W. E., McQuater, G. V., & DeBritto, A. M. (1991). Are blacks external: On the status of locus of control in black populations. In R. L. Jones (Ed.), *Black psychology* (3d ed., pp. 181–192). Berkeley, CA: Cobb & Henry.

Banks, W. M. (1972). The differential effect of race and social class in helping. *Journal of Clinical Psychology, 28,* 90–92.

Baratz, J. C. (1970). Teaching reading in an urban Negro school system. In F. Williams (Ed.), *Language and poverty* (pp. 11–24). Chicago: Markham.

Barnes, E. J. (1991). The Black community as the source of positive self-concept for Black children: A theoretical perspective. In R. Jones (Ed.), *Black psychology* (3d ed., pp. 667–692). Berkeley, CA: Cobb & Henry.

Basch, M. F. (1980). *Doing psychotherapy.* New York: Basic Books.

Basch, M. F. (1988). *Understanding psychotherapy: The science behind the art.* New York: Basic Books.

Baughman, E. E. (1971). *Black Americans: A psychological analysis.* New York: Academic Press.

Bell, C. C. (1990). Black-on-Black homicide: The implications for Black community mental health. In D. S. Ruiz (Ed.), *Handbook of mental health and mental disorder among Black Americans* (pp. 191–207). Westport, CT: Greenwood.

Belle, D. (1990). Poverty and women's mental health. *American Psychologist, 45,* 385–389.

Belmont, J. M. (1989). Cognitive strategies and strategic learning: The socio-instructional approach. *American Psychologist, 44,* 142–148.

Bernhard, M. R. (1988). Activating variables and inhibitor deficits associated with violent male delinquents (Doctoral dissertation, New York University, 1987). *Dissertation Abstracts International, 48,* 3408B.

Bernstein, B. A. (1970). A sociolinguistic approach to socialization: With some reference to educability. In F. Williams (Ed.), *Language and poverty* (pp. 25–61). Chicago: Markham.

Berrueta-Clement, J. R., Schweinhart, L. J., Barnett, W. S., Epstein, A. S., & Weikart,

D. P. (1984). *Changed lives: The effects of the Perry Preschool Program on youths through age 19.* Ypsilanti, MI: The High/Scope Press.

Bibring, E. ([1953] 1968). The mechanism of depression. In W. Gaylin (Ed.), *The meaning of despair.* New York: Science House.

Billingsley, A. (1968). *Black families in white America.* Englewood Cliffs, NJ: Prentice-Hall.

Billingsley, A. (1974). The struggle for mental health. In D. A. Evans & W. L. Claiborn (Eds.), *Mental health issues and the urban poor* (pp. 27–35). Elmsford, NY: Pergamon Press.

Blatt, S. J. (1990). Interpersonal relatedness and self-definition: Two personality configurations and their implication for psychopathology and psychotherapy. In J. Singer (Ed.), *Repression and dissociation: Implications for personality theory, psychopathology and health* (pp. 299–335). Chicago: University of Chicago Press.

Blatt, S. J., Wild, C. M., & Ritzler, B. A. (1975). Disturbances of object representations in schizophrenia. *Psychoanalysis and Contemporary Science, 4,* 235–288.

Block, C. B. (1981). Black Americans and the cross-cultural counseling and psychotherapy experience. In A. J. Marsella & P. B. Pedersen (Eds.), *Cross-cultural counseling and psychotherapy* (pp. 177–194). Elmsford, NY: Pergamon Press.

Boggiano, A. K., & Katz, P. (1991). Maladaptive achievement patterns in students: The role of teachers' controlling strategies. *Journal of Social Issues, 47*(4), 35–51.

Bond, J. C. (1969). *Brown is a beautiful color.* New York: Franklin Watts.

Bortner, M., & Birch, H. G. (1971). Cognitive capacity and cognitive competence. In S. Chess & A. Thomas (Eds.), *Annual review and progress in child psychiatry and child development* (pp. 166–181). New York: Brunner/Mazel.

Bowman, P. J. (1989). Research perspectives on Black men: Role strain and adaptation across the Black adult male life cycle. In R. L. Jones (Ed.), *Black adult development and aging* (pp. 117–150). Berkeley, CA: Cobb & Henry.

Boyd-Franklin, N. (1989). *Black families in therapy: A multisystems approach.* New York: Guilford.

Boykin, A. W. (1977). Experimental psychology from a Black perspective: Issues and examples. *Journal of Black Psychology, 3,* 29–49.

Boykin, A. W. (1979). Psychological/behavioral verve: Some theoretical explanations and empirical manifestations. In A. W. Boykin, A. J. Franklin, & J. E. Yates (Eds.), *Research directions of black psychologists* (pp. 351–367). New York: Russell Sage Foundation.

Boykin, A. W. (1991). Black psychology and experimental psychology: A functional confluence. In R. L. Jones (Ed.), *Black psychology* (3d ed., pp 481–507). Berkeley, CA: Cobb & Henry.

Brand, E. S., Ruiz, R. A., & Padilla, A. (1974). Ethnic identification and preference: A review. *Psychological Bulletin, 81,* 860–890.

Brody, E. B., Derbyshire, R. L., & Schleifer, C. B. (1967). How the young adult Baltimore Negro male becomes a Maryland mental hospital statistic. In R. R. Monroe, G. D. Klee, & E. B. Brody (Eds.), *Psychiatric epidemiology and mental health planning* (Psychiatric research report No. 22, pp. 206–219). Washington, DC: American Psychiatric Association.

Bronfenbrenner, U. (1985). Summary, part I: Orienting issues for the study of black children. In M. B. Spencer, G. E. Brookins, & W. R. Allen (Eds.), *Beginnings: The social and affective development of black children* (pp. 67–73). NJ: Erlbaum.

Brown, A. L., Palincsar, A. S., & Purcell, L. (1986). Poor readers: Teach, don't label. In U. Neisser (Ed.), *The school achievement of minority children: New perspectives* (pp. 105–143). Hillsdale, NJ: Erlbaum.

Brown, D. R. (1990). Depression among Blacks: An epidemiological perspective. In D. S. Ruiz (Ed.), *Handbook of mental health and mental disorder among Black Americans* (pp. 71–93). Westport, CT: Greenwood.

Brown, D. R., Eaton, W. W., & Sussman, L. (1990). Racial differences in prevalence of phobic disorders. *Journal of Nervous and Mental Disease, 178*, 434–441.

Brown, L. M., & Steele, C. M. (1992, August). *The underperformance of African Americans and women in college*. Paper presented at the meeting of the American Psychological Association, Washington, DC.

Bryant-Tuckett, R. (1981). The effects of subliminal merging stimuli on the academic performance of emotionally handicapped students (Doctoral dissertation, New York University, 1980). *Dissertation Abstracts International, 41*, 4654B. (University Microfilms No. 8110724.)

Cameron, N., & Rychlak, J. F. (1985). *Personality development and psychopathology: A dynamic approach*. Boston: Houghton Mifflin.

Caplan, N. (1970). The new ghetto man: A review of recent empirical studies. *Journal of Social Issues, 26*(1), 59–73.

Caplan, N., & Nelson, S. D. (1974, November). Who's to blame? *Psychology Today*, 99–104.

Carey, P. M. (1979). Black women—a perspective. *Tenth-Year Anniversary Commemorative Monograph Series*, vol. 1, no. 3. New York: New York University, Institute for Afro-American Affairs.

Carkhuff, R. R., & Pierce, R. (1967). Differential effects of therapist race and social class upon patient depth of self-exploration in the initial clinical interview. *Journal of Consulting Psychology, 31*, 632–634.

Carter, K. E., & Steele, C. M. (1992, August). *Subverting stigma vulnerability: The effects of a "wise" environment*. Paper presented at the meeting of the American Psychological Association, Washington, DC.

Cauce, A. M., Comer, J. P., & Schwartz, D. (1987). Long term effects of a systems-oriented school prevention program. *American Journal of Orthopsychiatry, 57*, 127–131.

Cazden, C. B. (1970). The neglected situation in child language research and education. In F. Williams (Ed.), *Language and poverty*. Chicago: Markham.

Cheek, D. K. (1976). *Assertive black . . . puzzled white*. San Luis Obispo, CA: Impact.

Chein, I. (1972). *The science of behavior and the image of man*. New York: Basic Books.

Chessick, R. D. (1969). *How psychotherapy heals: The process of intensive psychotherapy*. New York: Science House.

Chessick, R. D. (1977). *Intensive psychotherapy of the borderline patient*. New York: Aronson.

Clark, K. B. (1965). *Dark ghetto*. New York: Harper.

Clark, K. B., & Clark, M. P. (1952). Racial identification and preference in Negro children. In G. E. Swanson, T. M. Newcomb, & E. L. Hartley (Eds.), *Readings in social psychology* (rev. ed., pp. 551–560). New York: Holt, Rinehart & Winston.

Cohen, R. A. (1969). Conceptual styles, culture conflict, and nonverbal tests of intelligence. *American Anthropologist, 71*, 828–856.
Cole, M., & Bruner, J. S. (1971). Cultural differences and inferences about psychological processes. *American Psychologist, 26*, 867–876.
Cole, M., & Scribner, S. (1974). *Culture and thought: A psychological introduction*. New York: Wiley.
Coleman, J. S., Campbell, E. Q., Hobson, C. J., McPartland, J., Mood, A. M., Weinfeld, F. D., & York, R. L. (1966). *Equality of educational opportunity*. Washington, DC: U.S. Department of Health, Education and Welfare. Government Printing Office.
Coles, R. (1967). *Children of crisis: A study of courage and fear*. New York: Dell.
Comas-Diaz, L. (1988). Cross-cultural mental health treatment. In L. Comas-Diaz & E. E. H. Griffiths (Eds.), *Clinical guidelines in cross-cultural mental health* (pp. 335–361). New York: Wiley.
Comer, J. P. (1972). *Beyond black and white*. New York: Quadrangle.
Comer, J. P. (1980). *School power: Implications of an intervention project*. New York: Free Press.
Comer, J. P. (1985). The Yale–New Haven Primary Prevention Project: A follow-up study. *Journal of the American Academy of Child Psychiatry, 24*, 154–160.
Coner-Edwards, A. F., & Spurlock, J. (Eds.). (1988). *Black families in crisis: The middle class*. New York: Brunner/Mazel.
Cook, S. W. (1988). The 1954 Social Science Statement and school desegregation: A reply to Gerard. In P. Katz & D. Taylor (Eds.), *Eliminating racism* (pp. 237–256). New York: Plenum.
Cook-Gumperz, J. (1973). *Social control and socialization: A study of class differences in the language of maternal control*. London: Routledge, Kegan & Paul.
Coughlin, E. K. (1992, Oct. 7). The renascence of Malcolm X. *The Chronicle of Higher Education*, A-8, A-14.
Crain, R. L., & Weisman, C. S. (1972). *Discrimination, personality, and achievement: A survey of northern blacks*. New York: Seminar Press.
Cross, W. E., Jr. (1978). The Thomas and Cross models of psychological nigrescence: A review. *Journal of Black Psychology, 5*, 13–31.
Cross, W. E., Jr. (1987). A two-factor theory of Black identity: Implications for the study of identity development in minority children. In J. S. Phinney & M. J. Rotheram (Eds.), *Children's ethnic socialization: Pluralism and development* (pp. 117–133). Newbury Park, CA: Sage.
Cross, W. E., Jr. (1991). *Shades of Black: Diversity in African-American identity*. Philadelphia: Temple University Press.
Cross, W. E., Jr., Parham, T. A., & Helms, J. E. (1991). The stages of Black identity development: Nigrescence models. In R. L. Jones (Ed.), *Black psychology* (3d ed., pp. 319–338). Berkeley, CA: Cobb & Henry.
Cushman, P. (1990). Why the self is empty: Toward a historically situated psychology. *American Psychologist, 45*, 599–611.
Cushman, P. (1991). Ideology obscured: Political uses of the self in Daniel Stern's infant. *American Psychologist, 46*, 206–219.
Davis, W. E., Greenblatt, R. L., & Pochyly, J. M. (1990). Test of MCMI Black norms for five scales. *Journal of Clinical Psychology, 46*, 175–178.

Deci, E., & Ryan, R. (1985). *Intrinsic motivation and self-determination in human behavior.* New York: Plenum.
Diggs, I. (1976). DuBois and children. *Phylon, 37*, 370–399.
Dressler, W. W. (1986). Unemployment and depressive symptoms in a southern Black community. *Journal of Nervous and Mental Disease, 174*, 639–645.
DuBois, W. E. B. (1961). *The souls of black folk.* New York: Fawcett.
Dweck, C. S. (1986). Motivational processes affecting learning. *American Psychologist, 41*, 1040–1048.
Edelson, M. (1971). *The idea of a mental illness.* New Haven, CT: Yale University Press.
Edelson, M. (1975). *Language and interpretation in psychoanalysis.* New Haven, CT: Yale University Press.
Edmonds, R. (1986). Characteristics of effective schools. In U. Neisser (Ed.), *The school achievement of minority children: New perspectives* (pp. 93–104). Hillsdale, NJ: Erlbaum.
Edwards, A., & Polite, C. K. (1992). *Children of the dream: The psychology of black success.* New York: Doubleday.
Edwards, H. E. (1988). Dynamic psychotherapy when both patient and therapist are Black. In A. F. Coner-Edwards & J. Spurlock (Eds.), *Black families in crisis: The middle class* (pp. 239–254). New York: Brunner/Mazel.
Ekstein, R., & Motto, R. L. (1969). *From learning for love to love of learning.* New York: Brunner/Mazel.
Ellison, R. (1952). *Invisible man.* New York: Signet Books.
Ellison, R. (1964). That same pain, that same pleasure: An interview. In R. Ellison, *Shadow and act* (pp. 23–41). New York: Signet Books.
Ellison, R., & McPherson, J. A. (1970, December). Indivisible man. *Atlantic*, 45–60.
Epps, E. G. (1975). The impact of school desegregation on aspirations, self-concepts and other aspects of personality. *Law and Contemporary Problems, 39*, 300–313.
Epstein, S. (1973). The self-concept revisited: Or a theory of a theory. *American Psychologist, 28*, 404–416.
Erikson, E. H. (1963). *Childhood and society* (2d ed.). New York: Norton.
Evans, D. A. (1985). Psychotherapy and Black patients: Problems of training, trainees, and trainers. *Psychotherapy, 22*, 457–460.
Evans, M. C., & Chein, I. (1948, September). *The Movie-Story Game: A projective test of interracial attitudes for use with Negro and white children.* Paper read at the annual meeting of the American Psychological Association, Boston.
Exner, J. E., Jr. (1993). *The Rorschach: A comprehensive system: vol. 1: Basic foundations* (3d ed.). New York: Wiley.
Fanon, F. (1967). *Black skin, white masks.* New York: Grove Press.
Faulconer, J. E., & Williams, R. N. (1985). Temporality in human action: An alternative to positivism and historicism. *American Psychologist, 40*, 1179–1188.
Feffer, M. (1988). *Radical constructionism: Rethinking the dynamics of development.* New York: New York University Press.
Feuerstein, R. (1979). *The dynamic assessment of retarded performers: The Learning Potential Assessment Device, theory, instruments, and techniques.* Baltimore, MD: University Park Press.
Feuerstein, R., Hoffman, M. B., Rand, Y., Jensen, M. R., Tzuriel, D., & Hoffman, D. B.

(1986). Learning to learn: Mediated learning experiences and instrumental enrichment. *Special Services in the Schools, 3*(1–2), 49–82.
Feuerstein, R., Rand, Y., Jensen, M., Kaniel, S., Tzuriel, D., Shachar, N. B., & Mintzker, Y. (1986). Learning potential assessment. *Special Services in the Schools, 2*(2–3), 85–106.
Figueroa, R. A., & Sassenrath, J. M. (1989). A longitudinal study of the predictive validity of the System of Multicultural Pluralistic Assessment (SOMPA). *Psychology in the Schools, 26*, 5–19.
Fischer, J. (1969). Negroes and Whites and rates of mental illness: Reconsideration of a myth. *Psychiatry, 32*, 428–446.
Fish, J. E., & Larr, C. J. (1972) A decade of change in drawings by black children. *American Journal of Psychiatry, 129*, 421–426.
Fleming, J. (1984). *Blacks in college: A comparative study of students' success in Black and in White institutions.* San Francisco: Jossey-Bass.
Flynn, J. T., & Anderson, B. E. (1976). The effect of test administration procedures on achievement test performance. *Journal of Negro Education, 45*, 37–45.
Forward, J. R., & Williams, J. R. (1970). Internal-external control and black militancy. *Journal of Social Issues, 26*(1), 75–92.
Frady, M. (1992, Oct. 12). The children of Malcolm. *The New Yorker*, 64–81.
Francois, T. V. (1978). The engagement of adolescent black males in psychotherapy: The relation of role induction, locus of control, and depression (Doctoral dissertation, New York University, 1977). *Dissertation Abstracts International, 38*, 6147B–6148B. (University Microfilms No. 7808524.)
Frank, G. H. (1992). The response of African Americans to the Rorschach: A review of the research. *Journal of Personality Assessment, 59*, 317–325.
Frank, J. D., & Frank, J. B. (1991). *Persuasion and healing* (3d ed.). Baltimore, MD: Johns Hopkins University Press.
Franklin, A. J. (1989). Therapeutic interventions with urban black adolescents. In R. L. Jones (Ed.), *Black adolescents* (pp. 309–337). Berkeley, CA: Cobb & Henry.
Franklin, A. J., & Fulani, L. (1979). Cultural content of materials and ethnic group performance in categorized recall. In A. W. Boykin, A. J. Franklin, & J. F. Yates (Eds.), *Research directions of black psychologists* (pp. 229–240). New York: Russell Sage Foundation.
Frazier, E. F. (1962). *Black bourgeoisie.* New York: Collier Books.
Freiberg, P. (1991, May). Separate classes for Black males? *APA Monitor*, pp. 1, 47.
Freud, S. ([1915, 1917] 1957). Mourning and melancholia. In J. Strachey (Ed.), *The standard edition of the complete psychological works of Sigmund Freud* (vol. 14, pp. 243–258). London: Hogarth Press and the Institute of Psychanalysis.
Frey, K. S., & Ruble, D. N. (1990). Strategies for comparative evaluation: Maintaining a sense of competence across the life span. In R. J. Sternberg & J. Kolligian, Jr. (Eds.), *Competence considered* (pp. 167–189). New Haven, CT: Yale University Press.
Fromm, E. (1947). *Man for himself.* New York: Rinehart.
Fromm, E. (1955). *The sane society.* New York: Rinehart.
Frosh, S. (1991). *Identity crisis: Modernity, psychoanalysis and the self.* New York: Routledge.

Frost, R. (1964). The road not taken. In *Complete poems of Robert Frost*. New York: Holt.
Garber, H. L., & Heber, R. (1981). The efficacy of early intervention with family rehabilitation. In M. J. Begab, H. C. Haywood, & H. L. Garber (Eds.), *Psychosocial influences in retarded performance: Vol. II. Strategies for improving competence* (pp. 71–87). Baltimore, MD: University Park Press.
Garcia, J. (1981). The logic and limits of mental aptitude testing. *American Psychologist, 36*, 1172–1180.
Gardner, H. (1985). *Frames of mind: The theory of multiple intelligences.* New York: Basic Books.
Gardner, LaM. H. (1971). The therapeutic relationship under varying conditions of race. *Psychotherapy, 8*, 78–87.
Gary, L. E., & Weaver, G. D. (1991). Mental health of African Americans: Research trends and directions. In R. L. Jones (Ed.), *Black psychology* (3d ed., pp. 727–745). Berkeley, CA: Cobb & Henry.
Gaylin, W. (Ed.). (1968). *The meaning of despair.* New York: Science House.
Geller, J. D. (1988). Racial bias in the evaluation of patients for psychotherapy. In L. Comas-Diaz & E. E. H. Griffiths (Eds.), *Clinical guidelines in cross-cultural mental health* (pp. 112–134). New York: Wiley.
Gerard, H. B. (1988). School desegregation: The social science role. In P. Katz & D. Taylor (Eds.), *Eliminating racism* (pp. 225–236). New York: Plenum.
Gergen, K. (1985). The social constructionist movement in modern psychology. *American Psychologist, 40*, 266–275.
Gerstein, A. I., Brodzinsky, D. M., & Reiskind, N. (1976). Perceptual integration on the Rorschach as an indicator of cognitive capacity: A developmental study of racial differences in a clinic population. *Journal of Consulting and Clinical Psychology, 44*, 760–765.
Gibbs, J. T. (1974). Patterns of adaptation among black students at a predominantly white university: Selected case studies. *American Journal of Orthopsychiatry, 44*, 728–740.
Gibbs, J. T. (1985). Establishing a treatment relationship with Black clients: Interpersonal vs. instrumental strategies. In C. Germain (Ed.), *Advances in clinical social work practice* (pp. 184–195). Silver Springs, MD: National Association of Social Work.
Gibbs, J. T. (Ed.). (1988). *Young, black and male in America: An endangered species.* Dover, MA: Auburn House.
Gill, M. M. (1983). The interpersonal paradigm and the degree of the therapist's involvement. *Contemporary Psychoanalysis, 19*, 200–237.
Golden, M., Birns, B., Bridger, W., & Moss, A. (1971). Social class differentiation in cognitive development among black preschool children. *Child Development, 42*, 37–45.
Golden, M., Bridger, W. H., & Montare, A. (1974). Social class differences in the ability of young children to use verbal information to facilitate learning. *American Journal of Orthopsychiatry, 44*, 86–91.
Goleman, D. (1991, July 16). New way to battle bias: Fight acts, not feelings. *New York Times*, pp. C1, C8.
Gopaul-McNicol, S. (1993). *Working with West Indian families.* New York: Guilford.

Gordon, V. V. (1977). *The self-concept of black Americans.* Washington, DC: University Press of America.
Gouldner, H., & Strong, M. S. (1978). *Teachers' pets, trouble-makers, and nobodies: Black children in elementary school.* Westport, CT: Greenwood.
Greene, R. L. (1987). Ethnicity and MMPI performance: A review. *Journal of Consulting and Clinical Psychology, 55,* 497–512.
Grier, W. H., & Cobbs, P. M. (1968). *Black rage.* New York: Basic Books.
Griffith, M. S., & Jones, E. E. (1979). Race and psychotherapy: Changing perspectives. In J. H. Masserman (Ed.), *Current psychiatric therapies* (vol. 18, pp. 225–235). New York: Grune & Stratton.
Gruen, R. J. (1993). Stress and depression: Toward the development of integrative models. In L. Goldberger & S. Breznitz (Eds.), *Handbook of stress: Theoretical and clinical aspects* (2d ed., pp. 550–569). New York: Free Press.
Gumperz, J. J. (1974). *The sociolinguistics of interpersonal communication.* (Working papers and prepublications, no. 33). Universita di Urbino, Italia: Centro Internazionale di Semiotica e di Linguistica.
Gumperz, J. J., & Herasimchuk, E. (1972). The conversational analysis of social meaning. In R. Shuy (Ed.), *Sociolinguistics: Current trends and prospects* (pp. 99–134). Georgetown University Monographs in Language and Linguistics. Washington, DC: Georgetown University Press.
Gumperz, J. J., & Hernandez-Chavez, E. (1972). Bilingualism, bidialectalism, and classroom interaction. In C. B. Cazden, V. P. John, & D. Hymes (Eds.), *Functions of language in the classroom* (pp. 84–108). New York: Teachers College Press.
Gurin, P., & Epps, E. G. (1975). *Black consciousness, identity, and achievement.* New York: Wiley.
Gurin, P., Gurin, G., Lao, R. C., & Beattie, M. (1969). Internal-external control in the motivational dynamics of Negro youth. *Journal of Social Issues, 25*(3), 29–53.
Gurin, P., Gurin, G., & Morrison, B. M. (1978). Personal and ideological aspects of Internal and External Control. *Social Psychology, 41,* 275–296.
Gurin, P., Hatchett, S., & Jackson, J. S. (1990). *Hope and independence: Blacks' response to electoral and party politics.* New York: Russell Sage.
Guthrie, R. V. (1976). *Even the rat was white: A historical view of psychology.* New York: Harper.
Gutman, H. G. (1976). *The black family in slavery and freedom, 1750–1925.* New York: Vintage.
Gynther, M. D., & Green, S. B. (1980). Accuracy may make a difference, but does a difference make for accuracy? A response to Pritchard and Greenblatt. *Journal of Consulting and Clinical Psychology, 48,* 268–272.
Haimo, S. E., & Holzman, P. S. (1979). Thought disorder in schizophrenics and normal controls: Social class and race differences. *Journal of Consulting and Clinical Psychology, 47,* 963–967.
Hale, J. E. (1982). *Black children: Their roots, culture and learning styles.* Provo, UT: Brigham Young University Press.
Haley, A. (1976). *Roots: The saga of an American family.* New York: Doubleday.
Hall, W. S., & Dore, J. (1980, March). *Lexical sharing in mother-child interaction.* (Tech. Report no. 161.) Urbana: University of Illinois, Center for the Study of Reading.
Hall, W. S., & Freedle, R. O. (1975). *Culture and language.* Washington, DC: Halsted.

Hall, W. S., & Guthrie, L. F. (1979a, May). *On the dialect question and reading*. (Tech. Report no. 121.) Urbana: University of Illinois, Center for the Study of Reading.

Hall, W. S., & Guthrie, L. F. (1979b, October). *Cultural and situational variation in language function and use: Methods and procedures for research.* (Tech. Report no. 148.) Urbana: University of Illinois, Center for the Study of Reading.

Hall, W. S., & Nagy, W. E. (1987). The semantic-pragmatic distinction in the investigation of mental state words: The role of the situation. [Special Issue: The language of thinking: Mental state words.] *Discourse Processes, 10,* 169–180.

Hall, W. S., Reder, S., & Cole, M. (1975). Story recall in young black and white children: Effects of racial group membership, race of experimenter, and dialect. *Developmental Psychology, 11,* 628–634.

Hall, W. S., & Tirre, W. C. (1979, May). *The communicative environment of young children: Social class, ethnic, and situational differences.* (Tech. Report no. 125.) Urbana: University of Illinois, Center for the Study of Reading.

Halpern, F. (1973). *Survival: Black/white.* Elmsford, NY: Pergamon Press.

Hamberger, L. K., & Hastings, J. E. (1992). Racial differences on the MCMI in an outpatient clinical sample. *Journal of Personality Assessment, 58,* 90–95.

Hammond, W. R., & Yung, B. (1993). Psychology's role in the public health response to assaultive violence among young African-American men. *American Psychologist, 48,* 142–154.

Harburg, E., Erfurt, J. C., Hauenstein, L. S., Chape, C., Schull, W. J., & Schork, M.A. (1973). Socio-ecological stress, suppressed hostility, skin color, and Black-White male blood pressure: Detroit. *Psychosomatic Medicine, 35,* 276–296.

Harburg, E., Gleiberman, L., Russell, M., & Cooper, M. L. (1991). Anger-coping styles and blood pressure in Black and White males: Buffalo, New York. *Psychosomatic Medicine, 53,* 153–164.

Hare, B. R., & Castenell, L. A. (1985). No place to run, no place to hide: Comparative status and future prospects of Black boys. In M. B. Spencer, G. K. Brookins, & W. R. Allen (Eds.), *Beginnings: The social and affective development of black children* (pp. 201–214). Hillsdale, NJ: Erlbaum.

Harre, R. (1986). *The social construction of emotions.* Oxford, England: Blackwell.

Harrell, J. P. (1979). Analyzing black coping styles: A supplemental diagnostic system. *Journal of Black Psychology, 5,* 99–108.

Harrison, A. O. (1989). Black working women: Introduction to a life span perspective. In R. L. Jones (Ed.), *Black adult development and aging* (pp. 91–115). Berkeley, CA: Cobb & Henry.

Harrison-Ross, P., & Wyden, B. (1973). *The black child: A parent's guide.* New York: Peter Wyden.

Hayes, W. A. (1991). Radical black behaviorism. In R. Jones (Ed.), *Black psychology* (3d ed., pp. 65–78). Berkeley, CA: Cobb & Henry.

Haynes, N. M., Comer, J. P., & Hamilton-Lee, M. (1988). The School Development Program: A model for school improvement. *Journal of Negro Education, 57,* 11–21.

Heath, S. B. (1982). Questioning at home and at school: A comparative study. In G. Spindler (Ed.), *Doing the ethnography of schooling: Educational anthropology in action* (pp. 103–127). New York: Holt, Rinehart & Winston.

Heath, S. B. (1986). Sociocultural contexts of language development. In *Beyond language: Social and cultural factors in schooling language minority students* (pp. 143–

186). Edited by Bilingual Education Office, California State Dept. of Education, Los Angeles: Evaluation, Dissemination and Assessment Center, California State University.

Heath, S. B. (1989). Oral and literate traditions among Black Americans living in poverty. *American Psychologist, 44,* 367–373.

Heber, R. F. (1978). Sociocultural mental retardation: A longitudinal study. In D. Forgays (Ed.), *Primary prevention of psychopathology, vol. 2. Environmental influences.* Hanover, NH: University Press of New England.

Heiskell, T. L. (1981). Empathy with liked and disliked patients (Doctoral dissertation, Purdue University, 1980). *Dissertation Abstracts International, 41,* 3180B. (University Microfilms No. 8102663.)

Helms, J. (1984). Toward a theoretical explanation of the effects of race on counseling: A Black and White model. *The Counseling Psychologist, 12,* 153–165.

Henry, W. E., Sims, J. H., & Spray, S. L. (1973). *Public and private lives of psychotherapists.* San Francisco: Jossey-Bass.

Hill, R. B. (1990). *Assessment of the status of African Americans: vol II. Research on the African-American family: A holistic perspective.* Boston: William Monroe Trotter Institute, University of Massachusetts–Boston.

Hollingshead, A. B., & Redlich, F. C. (1958). *Social class and mental illness.* New York: Wiley.

Holmes, D. E. (1992). Race and transference in psychoanalysis and psychotherapy. *International Journal of Psycho-analysis, 73,* 1–11.

Holt, R. R. (1972). Freud's mechanistic and humanistic images of man. *Psychoanalysis and contemporary science, 1,* 3–24.

Hoover, M. R. (1978). Community attitudes toward Black English. *Language in Society, 7,* 65–87.

Horowitz, M. J. (Ed.). (1977). *Hysterical personality.* New York: Aronson.

Houston, S. H. (1971). A reexamination of some assumptions about the language of the disadvantaged child. In S. Chess & A. Thomas (Eds.), *Annual progress in child psychiatry and child development* (pp. 233–250). New York: Brunner/Mazel.

Houston, S. H. (1973, March). Black English. *Psychology Today,* 45–48.

Howard, G. S. (1985). The role of values in the science of psychology. *American Psychologist, 40,* 255–265.

Howard, G. S. (1991). Culture tales: A narrative approach to thinking, cross-cultural psychology, and psychotherapy. *American Psychologist, 46,* 187–197.

Howard, G. S., & Conway, C. G. (1986). Can there be an empirical science of volitional action? *American Psychologist, 41,* 1241–1251.

Hraba, J., & Grant, G. (1970). Black is beautiful: A reexamination of racial preference and identification. *Journal of Personality and Social Psychology, 16,* 398–402.

Hughes, L. (1926). Mother to son. In *Selected poems of Langston Hughes.* New York: Knopf.

Jackson, J. J. (1990). Suicide trends of Blacks and Whites by sex and age. In D. S. Ruiz (Ed.), *Handbook of mental health and mental disorder among Black Americans* (pp. 95–109). Westport, CT: Greenwood.

Jackson, J. S. (Ed.). (1991). *Life in Black America.* Newbury Park, CA: Sage.

Jenkins, A. H. (1989). The liberating value of constructionism for minorities. *The Humanistic Psychologist, 17,* 161–168.

Jenkins, A. H. (1992). Hermeneutics versus science in psychoanalysis: A rigorous humanistic view. *Psychoanalytic Psychology, 9,* 509–527.

Jensen, A. R. (1969). How much can we boost I.Q. and scholastic achievement? *Harvard Educational Review, 39*, 1–123.

Johnson, F. (1985). The Western concept of self. In A. J. Marsella, G. DeVos, & F. L. K. Hsu (Eds.), *Culture and self: Asian and Western perspectives* (pp. 91–138). New York: Tavistock.

Johnson, M. E., & Brems, C. (1990). Psychiatric inpatient MMPI profiles: An exploration for potential racial bias. *Journal of Counseling Psychology, 37*, 213–215.

Johnston, M. H., & Holzman, P. S. (1979). *Assessing schizophrenic thinking.* San Francisco: Jossey-Bass.

Jones, A. C. (1985). Psychological functioning in Black Americans: A conceptual guide for use in psychotherapy. *Psychotherapy, 22*, 363–369.

Jones, A., & Seagull, A. A. (1977). Dimensions of the relationship between the black client and the white therapist: A theoretical overview. *American Psychologist, 32*, 850–855.

Jones, E. E. (1978). Effects of race on psychotherapy process and outcome: An exploratory investigation. *Psychotherapy, 15*, 226–236.

Jones, E. E. (1982). Psychotherapists' impressions of treatment outcome as a function of race. *Journal of Clinical Psychology, 38*, 722–731.

Jones, E. E. (1985). Psychotherapy and counseling with black clients. In P. Pedersen (Ed.), *Handbook of cross-cultural counseling and therapy* (pp. 173–179). Westport, CT: Greenwood.

Jones, E., & Thorne, A. (1987). Rediscovery of the subject: Intercultural approaches to clinical assessment. *Journal of Consulting and Clinical Psychology, 55*, 488–495.

Jones, F. (1989, October). Dancing to the music in our heads. *Brown Alumni Monthly,* 30–37.

Jones, F. (1992). *Jelly Roll-ing: Commentary on jazz in African-American culture.* Manuscript submitted for publication.

Jones, J. M. (1972). *Prejudice and racism.* Reading, MA: Addison-Wesley.

Jones, J. M. (1991a). The politics of personality: Being black in America. In R. L. Jones (Ed.), *Black psychology* (3d ed., pp. 305–318). Berkeley, CA: Cobb & Henry.

Jones, J. M. (1991b). Racism: A cultural analysis of the problem. In R. L. Jones (Ed.), *Black psychology* (3d ed., pp. 609–635). Berkeley, CA: Cobb & Henry.

Jonides, J., von Hippel, W., Lerner, J. S., & Nagda, B. A. (1992, August). *Evaluation of minority retention programs: The Undergraduate Research Opportunities Program at the University of Michigan.* Paper presented at the meeting of the American Psychological Association, Washington, DC.

Jordan, W. (1968). *White over black: American attitudes toward the Negro, 1550–1812.* Chapel Hill: University of North Carolina Press.

Juarez, R. (1985). Core issues in psychotherapy with the Hispanic child. *Psychotherapy, 22*, 441–448.

Kagan, J. (1976). Cognitive development. *JSAS Catalog of Selected Documents in Psychology, 6*, 96. (Ms. no. 1338, 36 pgs.)

Kagan, J. (1989). Commentary. *Human Development, 32*, 172–176.

Kagan, J., & Klein, R. E. (1973). Cross-cultural perspectives on early development. *American Psychologist, 28*, 947–961.

Kagan, S. (1986). Cooperative learning and sociocultural factors in schooling. In *Beyond language: Social and cultural factors in schooling language minority students* (pp. 231–298). Edited by Bilingual Education Office, California State Dept. of Education, Los Angeles: Evaluation, Dissemination and Assessment Center, California State University.

Kamin, L. J. (1974). *The science and politics of I.Q.* Potomac, MD: Erlbaum.

Kardiner, A., & Ovesey, L. ([1951] 1962). *The mark of oppression.* Cleveland, OH: Meridian Books. (Original edition, New York: Norton.)

Karon, B. P. (1989). Psychotherapy versus medication for schizophrenia: Empirical comparisons. In S. Fisher & R. P. Greenberg (Eds.), *The limits of biological treatments for psychological distress: Comparisons with psychotherapy and placebo* (pp. 105–150). Hillsdale, NJ: Erlbaum.

Karon, B. P., & VandenBos, G. R. (1972). The consequences of psychotherapy for schizophrenic patients. *Psychotherapy, 9,* 111–119.

Karon, B. P., & VandenBos, G. R. (1975). Issues in current research on psychotherapy vs. medication in treatment of schizophrenics. *Psychotherapy, 12,* 143–148.

Katz, P. A. (Ed.). (1976). *Towards the elimination of racism.* Elmsford, NY: Pergamon Press.

Katz, P. A., & Zalk, S. R. (1974). Doll preferences: An index of racial attitudes? *Journal of Educational Psychology, 66,* 663–668.

Keen, E. (1970). *Three faces of being: Toward an existential clinical psychology.* New York: Appleton-Century-Crofts.

Kennedy, T. R. (1980). *You gotta deal with it: Black family relations in a southern community.* New York: Oxford.

Kernan, C. M. (1971). Language behavior in a black urban community. *Monographs of the Language-Behavior Research Laboratory* (no. 2). University of California, Berkeley.

Kleinsmith, L. J., & Johnston, J. (1991). Tackling the fear of science: The impact of a computer-based study center on minority student achievement in biology. In W. R. Allen, E. G. Epps, & N. Z. Haniff (Eds.), *College in Black and White: African-American students in predominantly White and historically Black public universities* (pp. 239–246). Albany, NY: State University of New York Press.

Kohut, H. (1977). *The restoration of the self.* New York: International Universities Press.

Kohut, H., & Wolf, E. S. (1978). The disorders of the self and their treatment: An outline. *International Journal of Psycho-analysis, 59,* 413–425.

Korchin, S. J. (1976). *Modern clinical psychology.* New York: Basic Books.

Kovel, J. (1981). *The age of desire: Reflections of a radical psychoanalyst.* New York: Pantheon.

Kovel, J. (1984). *White racism: A psychohistory* (2d ed.). New York: Columbia University Press.

Kramer, M., Rosen, B. M., & Willis, E. M. (1973). Definitions and distributions of mental disorders in a racist society. In C. V. Willie, B. M. Kramer, & B. S. Brown (Eds.), *Racism and mental health* (pp. 353–459). Pittsburgh, PA: University of Pittsburgh Press.

Krebs, R. L. (1971). Some effects of a white institution on black psychiatric outpatients. *American Journal of Orthopsychiatry, 41,* 589–596.

Laboratory for Comparative Human Cognition. (1982). Culture and intelligence. In R. J. Sternberg (Ed.), *Handbook of human intelligence* (pp. 642–719). New York: Cambridge University Press.

Labov, W. (1972). *Language in the inner city: Studies in the Black English Vernacular.* Philadelphia: University of Pennsylvania Press.

Labov, W., & Harris, W. A. (1986). De facto segregation of black and white vernaculars. In D. Sankoff (Ed.), *Diversity and diachrony* (pp. 1–24). Philadelphia: John Benjamins.

Langer, E. J., & Park, K. (1990). Incompetence: A conceptual reconsideration. In R. J. Sternberg & J. Kolligian, Jr. (Eds.), *Competence considered* (pp. 149–166). New Haven, CT: Yale University Press.

Lanyon, R. I., & Lanyon, B. P. (1978). *Behavior therapy: A clinical introduction.* Reading, MA: Addison-Wesley.

Lerner, B. (1972). *Therapy in the ghetto: Political impotence and personal disintegration.* Baltimore, MD: Johns Hopkins University Press.

Lerner, B. (1974). Is psychotherapy relevant to the needs of the urban poor? In D. A. Evans & W. L. Claiborn (Eds.), *Mental health issues and the urban poor* (pp. 49–54). Elmsford, NY: Pergamon Press.

Lesse, S. (Ed.). (1974). *Masked depression.* New York: Aronson.

Lester, J. (1968). *Look out whitey! Black power's gon' get your mama!* New York: Grove.

Lester, J. (1991, Nov. 24). He said what no one dared to say. [Review of *Malcolm: The life of a man who changed Black America*]. *New York Times*, Sec. 7, Book Review Desk, p. 11.

Lewis, D. O., Balla, D. A., & Shanok, S. S. (1979). Some evidence of race bias in the diagnosis and treatment of the juvenile offender. *American Journal of Orthopsychiatry, 49,* 53–61.

Lewontin, R. C., Rose, S., & Kamin, L. J. (1984). *Not in our genes.* New York: Pantheon Books.

Lipman, R. S. (1989). Pharmacotherapy of the anxiety disorders. In S. Fisher & R. P. Greenberg (Eds.), *The limits of biological treatments for psychological distress: Comparisons with psychotherapy and placebo* (pp. 69–103). Hillsdale, NJ: Erlbaum.

Loehlin, J. C., Lindzey, G., & Spuhler, J. N. (1975) *Race differences in intelligence.* San Francisco: Freeman.

Luborsky, L. (1984). *Principles of psychoanalytic psychotherapy: A manual for supportive-expressive treatment.* New York: Basic Books.

Mackenzie, B. (1984). Explaining race differences in I.Q.: The logic, the methodology, and the evidence. *American Psychologist, 39,* 1214–1233.

MacMillan, M. (1988). The doll test studies—from cabbage patch to self-concept. *The Journal of Black Psychology, 14,* 69–72.

Mahl, G. F. (1969). Conflict and defense. In I. L. Janis (Ed.), *Personality: Dynamics, development, and assessment (part II).* New York: Harcourt Brace Jovanovich.

Mahler, M. S. (1974). Symbiosis and individuation: The psychological birth of the human infant. In R. S. Eissler, A. Freud, M. Kris, & A. J. Solnit (Eds.), *The psychoanalytic study of the child* (vol. 29, pp. 89–106). New Haven, CT: Yale University Press.

Majors, R. (1991). Nonverbal behaviors and communication styles among African Americans. In R. L. Jones (Ed.), *Black psychology* (3d ed., pp. 269–294). Berkeley, CA: Cobb & Henry.

Malcolm X. (1965). *The autobiography of Malcolm X.* New York: Grove.

Markus, H., Cross, S., & Wurf, E. (1990). The role of the self-system in competence. In R. J. Sternberg & J. Kolligian, Jr. (Eds.), *Competence considered* (pp. 205–225). New Haven, CT: Yale University Press.

Markus, H., & Nurius, P. (1986). Possible selves. *American Psychologist, 41,* 954–969.

Marsella, A. J., DeVos, G., & Hsu, F. S. K. (Eds.). (1985). *Culture and self.* New York: Tavistock.

Marshall, P. (1983, Jan. 9). The making of a writer: From the poets in the kitchen. *New York Times Book Review,* pp. 3, 34–35.

Marwit, S. J., Marwit, K. L., & Boswell, J. J. (1973). Negro children's use of nonstandard grammar. In S. Chess & A. Thomas (Eds.), *Annual progress in child psychiatry and child development* (pp. 285–296). New York: Brunner/Mazel.

Marwit, S. J., & Neumann, G. (1974). Black and white children's comprehension of standard and nonstandard English passages. *Journal of Educational Psychology, 66,* 329–332.

Maslow, A. H. (1968). *Toward a psychology of being* (2d ed.). New York: Van Nostrand Reinhold.

Masterson, J. (1981). *Narcissistic and borderline disorders: An integrated developmental approach.* New York: Brunner/Mazel.

Mbiti, J. S. (1970). *African religions and philosophy.* New York: Anchor Books.

McAdoo, H. P. (1977). The development of self-concept and race attitudes in black children: A longitudinal study. In W. E. Cross, Jr. (Ed.), *Proceedings: The third annual conference on empirical research in black psychology* (pp. 47–64). Washington, DC: U.S. Department of Health, Education, & Welfare, National Institute of Education.

McDonald, M. (1970). *Not by the color of their skin.* New York: International Universities Press.

McGoldrick, M., Pearce, J. K., & Giordano, J. (Eds.). (1982). *Ethnicity and family therapy.* NY: Guilford.

Mead, G. H. (1952). Language and the development of the self. In G. E. Swanson, T. M. Newcomb, & E. L. Hartley (Eds.), *Readings in social psychology* (rev. ed., pp. 44–54). New York: Holt.

Meltzer, H. Y. (Ed.). (1987). *Psychopharmacology: The third generation of progress.* New York: Raven.

Menninger, K. M., Mayman, M., & Pruyser, P. (1963). *The vital balance.* New York: Viking Press.

Mercer, J. R. (1973). *Labeling the mentally retarded.* Berkeley: University of California Press.

Mercer, J. R. (1979). *SOMPA: System of multicultural pluralistic assessment* (Technical Manual). New York: The Psychological Corporation.

Mercer, J. R. (1984). What is a racially and culturally nondiscriminatory test? A sociological and pluralistic perspective. In C. R. Reynolds & R. T. Brown (Eds.), *Perspectives on bias in mental testing* (pp. 293–356). New York: Plenum.

Mercer, J. R. (1992). The impact of changing patterns of disability on mental retardation in the year 2000. In L. Rowitz (Ed.), *Mental retardation in the year 2000* (pp. 15–38). New York: Springer-Verlag.

Messer, S., Sass, L., & Woolfolk, R. (Eds.). (1988). *Hermeneutics and psychological theory.* New Brunswick, NJ: Rutgers University Press.

Miller, I. J. (1992). Interpersonal vulnerability and narcissism: A conceptual continuum for understanding and treating narcissistic psychopathology. *Psychotherapy, 29,* 216–224.

Miller-Jones, D. (1989). Culture and testing. *American Psychologist, 44,* 360–366.
Milliones, J. (1980). Construction of a black consciousness measure: Psychotherapeutic implications. *Psychotherapy, 17,* 175–182.
Milner, D. (1983). *Children and race.* Beverly Hills, CA: Sage.
Modgil, S., & Modgil, C. (Eds.). (1987). *Arthur Jensen: Consensus and controversy.* Philadelphia: Falmer.
Moore, E. G. J. (1985). Ethnicity as a variable in child development. In M. B. Spencer, G. E. Brookins, & W. R. Allen (Eds.), *Beginnings: The social and affective development of black children* (pp. 101–115). Hillsdale, NJ: Erlbaum.
Morrison, A. P. (Ed.). (1986). *Essential papers on narcissism.* New York: New York University Press.
Myers, H. F., Anderson, N. B., & Strickland, T. L. (1989). A biobehavioral perspective on stress and hypertension in black adults. In R. L. Jones (Ed.), *Black adult development and aging* (pp. 311–349). Berkeley, CA: Cobb & Henry.
Myers, L. J. (1988). *Understanding an Afrocentric world view: Introduction to an optimal psychology.* Dubuque, IA: Kendall/Hunt.
Neal, A. M., & Turner, S. M. (1991). Anxiety disorders research with African Americans: Current status. *Psychological Bulletin, 109,* 400–410.
Neighbors, H. W. (1984). The distribution of psychiatric morbidity in Black Americans: A review and suggestions for research. *Community Mental Health Journal, 20,* 169–181.
Neighbors, H. W., Jackson, J. S., Bowman, P. J., & Gurin, G. (1983). Stress, coping, and Black mental health: Preliminary findings from a national study. *Prevention in Human Services, 2,* 5–29.
Nicholls, J. G., Cheung, P. C., Lauer, J., & Patashnick, M. (1989). Individual differences in academic motivation: Perceived ability, goals, beliefs, and values. *Learning and Individual Differences, 1,* 63–84.
Nobles, W. W. (1973). Psychological research and the black self-concept: A critical review. *Journal of Social Issues, 29(1),* 11–31.
Norem, J. K., & Cantor, N. (1990). Cognitive strategies, coping, and perceptions of competence. In R. J. Sternberg & J. Kolligian, Jr. (Eds.), *Competence considered* (pp. 190–204). New Haven, CT: Yale University Press.
Ogbu, J. U. (1985). A cultural ecology of competence among inner-city blacks. In M. B. Spencer, G. E. Brookins, & W. R. Allen (Eds.), *Beginnings: The social and affective development of black children* (pp. 45–66). Hillsdale, NJ: Erlbaum.
Ogbu, J. U. (1986). The consequences of the American caste system. In U. Neisser (Ed.), *The school achievement of minority children: New perspectives* (pp. 19–56). Hillsdale, NJ: Erlbaum.
Ogbu, J. U., & Matute-Bianchi, M. E. (1986). Understanding sociocultural factors: Knowledge, identity, and school adjustment. In *Beyond language: Social and cultural factors in schooling language minority students* (pp. 73–142). Edited by Bilingual Education Office, California State Dept. of Education, Los Angeles: Evaluation, Dissemination and Assessment Center, California State University.
Olim, E. G. (1970). Maternal language styles and cognitive development of children. In F. Williams (Ed.), *Language and poverty* (pp. 212–228). Chicago: Markham.
Orne, M. T. (1962). On the social psychology of the psychological experiment: With

particular reference to demand characteristics and their implications. *American Psychologist, 17,* 776–783.
Page, E. B. (1975). Miracle in Milwaukee: Raising the I.Q. In B. Z. Friedlander, G. M. Sterritt, & G. E. Kirk (Eds.), *Exceptional infant* (vol. 3, pp. 434–448). New York: Brunner/Mazel.
Parham, T. A. (1989). Cycles of psychological nigrescence. *The Counseling Psychologist, 17,* 187–226.
Parham, T. A., & Helms, J. E. (1981). The influence of Black students' racial identity attitudes on preferences for counselor's race. *Journal of Counseling Psychology, 28,* 250–257.
Parham, T. A., & McDavis, R. J. (1987). Black men, an endangered species: Who's really pulling the trigger? *Journal of Counseling and Development, 66,* 24–27.
Parker, K. (1978). The effects of subliminal merging stimuli on the academic performance of college students (Doctoral dissertation, New York University, 1977). *Dissertation Abstracts International, 38,* 6168B. (University Microfilms No. 7808550.)
Paster, V. S. (1985). Adapting psychotherapy for the depressed, unacculturated, acting-out, black male adolescent. *Psychotherapy, 22,* 408–417.
Peele, S. (1983). *The science of experience: A direction for psychology.* Lexington, MA: Lexington Books.
Pettigrew, T. F. (1964). *A profile of the Negro American.* Princeton, NJ: Van Nostrand.
Pettigrew, T. F. (1971). *Racially separate or together?* New York: McGraw-Hill.
Phares, E. J. (1992). *Clinical psychology: Concepts, methods, and profession* (4th ed.). Pacific Grove, CA: Brooks/Cole.
Phillips, L. (1968). *Human adaptation and its failures.* New York: Academic Press.
Piestrup, A. M. (1973). Black dialect interference and accommodation of reading instruction in first grade. *Monographs of the Language-Behavior Research Laboratory* (no. 4). University of California, Berkeley.
Pines, M. (1979, September). A head start in the nursery. *Psychology Today,* 56–68.
Polkinghorne, D. E. (1990). Language and qualitative research. *Theoretical and Philosophical Psychology, 10,* 3–24.
Ponterotto, J. G. (1988). Racial consciousness development among White counselor trainees: A stage model. *Journal of Multicultural Counseling and Development, 16,* 146–156.
Porter, J. R. (1971). *Black child, white child: The development of racial attitudes.* Cambridge, MA: Harvard University Press.
Porter, J. R., & Washington, R. E. (1979). Black identity and self-esteem: A review of studies of black self-concept. *Annual Review of Sociology, 5,* 53–74.
Poteat, G. M., Wuensch, K. L., & Gregg, N. B. (1988). An investigation of differential prediction with the WISC–R. *Journal of School Psychology, 26,* 59–68.
Poussaint, A. F. (1972). *Why blacks kill blacks.* New York: Emerson Hall.
Powdermaker, H. (1943). The channeling of Negro aggression by the cultural process. *American Journal of Sociology, 48,* 750–758.
Powell, G. J. (1973). Self-concept in white and black children. In C. V. Willie, B. M. Kramer, & B. S. Brown (Eds.), *Racism and mental health* (pp. 299–318). Pittsburgh, PA: University of Pittsburgh Press.

Powell, L., & Johnson, E. H. (1976). The black MMPI profile: Interpretive problems. *Journal of Negro Education, 45*, 27–36.

Powell-Hopson, D., & Hopson, D. S. (1988). Implications of doll color preferences among black preschool children and white preschool children. *Journal of Black Psychology, 14*, 57–63.

Pritchard, D. A., & Rosenblatt, A. (1980a). Racial bias in the MMPI: A methodological review. *Journal of Consulting and Clinical Psychology, 48*, 263–267.

Pritchard, D. A., & Rosenblatt, A. (1980b). Reply to Gynther and Green. *Journal of Consulting and Clinical Psychology, 48*, 273–274.

Pugh, R. W. (1972). *Psychology and the black experience.* Monterey, CA: Brooks/Cole.

Rainwater, L. (1966). Crucible of identity: The Negro lower-class family. In T. Parsons & K. B. Clark (Eds.), *The Negro-American* (pp. 160–204). Boston: Houghton Mifflin.

Ramirez, M. (1983). *Psychology of the Americas: Mestizo perspectives on personality and mental health.* Elmsford, NY: Pergamon Press.

Ramirez, M. (1991). *Psychotherapy and counseling with minorities: A cognitive approach to individual and cultural differences.* Elmsford, NY: Pergamon Press.

Ramseur, H. P. (1991). Psychologically healthy black adults. In R. L. Jones (Ed.), *Black psychology* (3d ed., pp. 353–378). Berkeley, CA: Cobb & Henry.

Ramsey, P. G. (1987). Young children's thinking about ethnic differences. In J. S. Phinney & M. J. Rotheram (Eds.), *Children's ethnic socialization: Pluralism and development* (pp. 56–72). Newbury Park, CA: Sage.

Raskin, A., Crook, T. H., & Herman, K. D. (1975). Psychiatric history and symptom differences in black and white depressed inpatients. *Journal of Consulting and Clinical Psychology, 43*, 73–80.

Redd, M. L. (1989). Alcoholism and drug addiction among Black adults. In R. L. Jones (Ed.), *Black adult development and aging* (pp. 351–374). Berkeley, CA: Cobb & Henry.

Reeves, C. (1976). An exploratory study: Modification of color concepts of low income black preschool youngsters (Doctoral dissertation, Stanford University). *Dissertation Abstracts International, 37*, 2751A–2752A. (University Microfilms No. 76-26, 064.)

Reschly, D. J. (1982). Assessing mild mental retardation: The influence of adaptive behavior, sociocultural status, and prospects for nonbiased assessment. In C. R. Reynolds & T. B. Gutkin (Eds.), *The handbook of school psychology* (pp. 209–242). New York: Wiley.

Reynolds, C. R., & Brown, R. T. (Eds.). (1984). *Perspectives on bias in mental testing.* New York: Plenum.

Rice, B. (1979, September). Brave new world of intelligence testing. *Psychology Today*, 27–41.

Ridley, C. R. (1984). Clinical treatment of the nondisclosing Black client: A therapeutic paradox. *American Psychologist, 39*, 1234–1244.

Roberts, H. B. (1987). *The inner world of the Black juvenile delinquent.* Hillsdale, NJ: Erlbaum.

Robins, L. N. (1968, June). Negro homicide victims—who will they be? *Trans-action*, 15–19.

Robins, L. N., Murphy, G. E., Woodruff, R. A., Jr., & King, L. J. (1971). Adult psychiatric status of black schoolboys. *Archives of General Psychiatry, 24*, 338–345.

Robinson, D. N. (1985). *Philosophy of psychology.* New York: Columbia University Press.
Robinson, D. N. (1991). Text, context and agency. *Theoretical and Philosophical Psychology, 11,* 1–10.
Rogoff, B., & Morelli, G. (1989). Perspectives on children's development from cultural psychology. *American Psychologist, 44,* 343–348.
Rohwer, W. D., Jr. (1980). How the smart get smarter. *Quarterly Newsletter of the Laboratory of Comparative Human Cognition, 2,* 35–39.
Roland, A. (1988). *In search of self in India and Japan: Toward a cross-cultural psychology.* Princeton, NJ: Princeton University Press.
Rorty, R. (1979). *Philosophy and the mirror of nature.* Princeton, NJ: Princeton University Press.
Rosen, H. (1974). Language and class: A critical look at the theories of Basil Bernstein. *Urban Review, 7,* 97–114.
Rosenberg, M., & Simmons, R. G. (1971). *Black and white self-esteem: The urban school child.* Washington, DC: American Sociological Association.
Rosenhan, D. L. (1973). On being sane in insane places. *Science, 179,* 250–258.
Rosenthal, J. (1984). If God ever listened: A portrait of Alice Walker. "Horizons" Series (#840307). Washington, DC: National Public Radio.
Rosenthal, R. (1973, September). The Pygmalion effect lives. *Psychology Today,* 56–63.
Rosenthal, R., & Jacobson, L. (1968). Self-fulfilling prophecies in the classroom: Teachers' expectations as unintended determinants of pupils' intellectual competence. In M. Deutsch, I. Katz, & A.R. Jensen (Eds.), *Social class, race, and psychological development* (pp. 219–253). New York: Holt.
Ross, S. A. (1983). Variables associated with dropping out of therapy (Doctoral Disseration, New York University, 1982). *Dissertation Abstracts International, 44,* 616B (University Microfilms No. DA830785.)
Rotter, J. B. (1966). Generalized expectancies for internal versus external control of reinforcement. *Psychological Monographs, 80* (1, entire issue no. 609).
Rumsey, J. M., & Rychlak, J. F. (1978). The role of affective assessment in intelligence testing. *Journal of Personality Assessment, 42,* 421–425.
Russell, D. M. (1988). Language and psychotherapy: The influence of nonstandard English in clinical practice. In L. Comas-Diaz & E. E. H. Griffiths (Eds.), *Clinical guidelines in cross-cultural mental health* (pp. 33–68). New York: Wiley.
Rychlak, J. F. (1976). Is a concept of "self" necessary in psychological theory, and if so why? A humanistic perspective. In A. Wandersman, P. J. Poppen, & D. F. Ricks (Eds.), *Humanism and behaviorism: Dialogue and growth* (pp. 121–145). Elmsford, NY: Pergamon Press.
Rychlak, J. F. (1979). *Discovering free will and personal responsibility.* New York: Oxford University Press.
Rychlak, J. F. (1981). *Introduction to personality and psychotherapy: A theory-construction approach* (2d ed.). Boston: Houghton Mifflin.
Rychlak, J. F. (1982a). Logical learning theory applications to psychotherapeutic practice. In L. E. Abt & I. R. Stuart (Eds.), *The newer therapies: A sourcebook* (pp. 96–116). New York: Van Nostrand Reinhold.
Rychlak, J. F. (1982b). *Personality and life-styles of young male managers: A logical learning theory analysis.* New York: Academic Press.

Rychlak, J. F. (1988). *The psychology of rigorous humanism* (2d ed.). New York: New York University Press.

Rychlak, J. F. (1990). Empirical evidence of Aristotle's concepts of predication and opposition. *Theoretical and Philosophical Psychology, 10,* 45–50.

Rychlak, J. F. (1991). *Artificial intelligence and human reason: A teleological critique.* New York: Columbia University Press.

Rychlak, J. F., & Barna, J. D. (1971). Causality and the proper image of man in scientific psychology. *Journal of Personality Assessment, 34,* 403–419.

Rychlak, J. F., & Ingwell, R. H. (1977). Causal orientation and personal adjustment of hospitalized veterans. *Journal of Personality Assessment, 41,* 299–303.

Sampson, E. E. (1985). The decentralization of identity: Toward a revised concept of personal and social order. *American Psychologist, 40,* 1203–1211.

Sampson, E. E. (1988). The debate on individualism: Indigenous psychologies of the individual and their role in personal and societal functioning. *American Psychologist, 43,* 15–22.

Sandoval, J. (1985). A review of the System of Multicultural Pluralistic Assessment. In J. V. Mitchell, Jr. (Ed.), *The ninth mental measurements yearbook* (vol. 2, pp. 1521–1526). Lincoln: The Buros Institute of Mental Measurements, The University of Nebraska.

Sarason, S. B. (1966). Mental subnormality. In F. C. Redlich & D. X. Freedman, *The theory and practice of psychiatry* (pp. 653–675). New York: Basic Books.

Sarbin, T. R. (1990). The narrative quality of action. *Theoretical and Philosophical Psychology, 10,* 49–65.

Sarnoff, I. (1951). Identification with the aggressor: Some personality correlates of antisemitism among Jews (Doctoral dissertation, University of Michigan). *Microfilm Abstracts, 11,* 753–754. (Publication no. 2647.)

Sass, L. (1988). Humanism, hermeneutics, and the concept of the human subject. In S. B. Messer, L. A. Sass, & R. L. Woolfolk (Eds.), *Hermeneutics and psychological theory* (pp. 222–271). New Brunswick, NJ: Rutgers University Press.

Savell, J. M., Twohig, P. T., & Rachford, D. L. (1986). Empirical status of Feuerstein's "Instrumental Enrichment" (FIE) technique as a method of teaching thinking skills. *Review of Educational Research, 56,* 381–409.

Scarr, S. (1977, September). *Genetic effects on human behavior: Recent family studies.* Paper presented in Master Lecture Series on Brain and Behavior Relationships at the annual meeting of the American Psychological Association, San Francisco.

Scarr, S. (1985). Constructing psychology: Making facts and fables for our times. *American Psychologist, 40,* 499–512.

Scarr, S., & Weinberg, R. A. (1976). I.Q. test performance of black children adopted by white families. *American Psychologist, 31,* 726–739.

Scarr, S., & Weinberg, R. A. (1978). The rights and responsibilities of the social scientist. (Comment.) *American Psychologist, 33,* 955–957.

Scarr-Salapatek, S. (1971). Race, social class and I.Q. *Science, 174,* 1285–1295.

Schacht, T., & Nathan, P. E. (1977). But is it good for the psychologists? Appraisal and status of DSM-III. *American Psychologist, 32,* 1017–1025.

Schafer, R. (1976). *A new language for psychoanalysis.* New Haven, CT: Yale University Press.

Schafer, R. (1977). Danger-situations. In P. W. Pruyser (Ed.), *Diagnosis and the difference it makes* (pp. 55–74). New York: Aronson.

Schafer, R. (1983). *The analytic attitude.* New York: Basic Books.

Schafer, R. (1992). *Retelling a life: Narration and dialogue in psychoanalysis.* New York: Basic Books.

Schectman, F. (1977). Provocative issues in psychiatric diagnosis: A dialogue. In P. W. Pruyser (Ed.), *Diagnosis and the difference it makes* (pp. 29–52). New York: Aronson.

Scheinfeld, D. R. (1983). Family relationships and school achievement among boys of lower-income urban black families. *American Journal of Orthopsychiatry, 53,* 127–143.

Schuman, H. (1974, September). Racial attitude change: Are whites really more liberal? Blacks aren't impressed. *Psychology Today,* 82–86.

Schwaber, E. (1980). Self psychology and the concept of psychopathology: A case presentation. In A. Goldberg (Ed.), *Advances in self psychology* (pp. 215–242). New York: International Universities Press.

Schweinhart, L. J., & Weikart, D. P. (1981). Perry Preschool effects nine years later: What do they mean? In M. J. Begab, H. C. Haywood, & H. L. Garber (Eds.), *Psychosocial influences in retarded performance: vol. II. Strategies for improving competence* (pp. 113–125). Baltimore, MD: University Park Press.

Scott, J. P., & Senay, E. C. (Eds.). (1973). *Separation and depression.* Washington, DC: American Association for the Advancement of Science.

Scrofani, P. J., Suziedelis, A., & Shore, M. F. (1973). Conceptual ability in black and white children of different social classes: An experimental test of Jensen's hypothesis. *American Journal of Orthopsychiatry, 43,* 541–553.

Secord, P. F. (1990). Explaining social behavior. *Theoretical and Philosophical Psychology, 11,* 25–38.

Sedlacek, W. E. (1986). [Review of *Blacks in college: A comparative study of students' success in Black and in White institutions*]. *Journal of Higher Education, 57,* 111–113.

Segall, M. H., Dasen, P. R., Berry, J. W., & Poortinga, Y. H. (1990). *Human behavior in global perspective: An introduction to cross-cultural psychology.* Elmsford, NY: Pergamon Press.

Seiden, R. H. (1970, August). We're driving young blacks to suicide. *Psychology Today,* 24–28.

Seligman, M. E. P. (1975). *Helplessness: On depression, development, and death.* San Francisco: Freeman.

Semaj, L. T. (1985). Afrikanity, cognition and extended self-identity. In M. B. Spencer, G. K. Brookins, & W. A. Allen (Eds.), *Beginnings: The social and affective development of black children* (pp. 173–183). Hillsdale, NJ: Erlbaum.

Shade, B. J. (1991). African-American patterns of cognition. In R. L. Jones (Ed.), *Black psychology* (3d ed., pp. 231–247). Berkeley, CA: Cobb & Henry.

Silverman, L. H. (1974). Some psychoanalytic considerations of non-psychoanalytic therapies: On the possibility of integrating treatment approaches and related issues. *Psychotherapy, 11,* 298–305.

Silverman, L. H. (1983). The subliminal psychodynamic activation method: Overview and comprehensive listing of studies. In J. Masling (Ed.), *Empirical studies of psychoanalytical theories* (vol. 1, pp. 69–100). Hillsdale, NJ: Erlbaum.

Simons, H. D. (1976). *Black dialect, reading interference and classroom interaction.* Unpublished manuscript, University of California, Berkeley.

Slaughter, D. T., & Epps, E. G. (1987). The home environment and academic achievement of Black American children and youth: An overview. *Journal of Negro Education, 56,* 3–20.

Slaughter, D. T., & McWorter, G. A. (1985). Social origins and early features of the scientific study of black American families and children. In M. B. Spencer, G. K. Brookins, & W. A. Allen (Eds.), *Beginnings: The social and affective development of black children* (pp. 5–18). Hillsdale, NJ: Erlbaum.

Smith, M., & Dejoie-Smith, M. (1984). Behavior therapy for non-White, non-YAVIS clients: Myth or panacea? *Psychotherapy, 21,* 524–529.

Smith, W. D., Burlew, A. K., Mosley, M. H., & Whitney, W. M. (1978). *Minority issues in mental health.* Reading, MA: Addison-Wesley.

Smitherman, G. (1991). Talkin and testifyin: Black English and the black experience. In R. L. Jones (Ed.), *Black psychology* (3d ed., pp. 249–267). Berkeley, CA: Cobb & Henry.

Snowden, L. R., & Cheung, F. K. (1990). Use of inpatient mental health services by members of ethnic minority groups. *American Psychologist, 45,* 347–355.

Spence, D. P. (1982). *Narrative and historical truth: Meaning and interpretation in psychoanalysis.* New York: Norton.

Spencer, M. B. (1985). Cultural cognition and social cognition as identity correlates of black children's personal-social development. In M. B. Spencer, G. K. Brookins, & W. A. Allen (Eds.), *Beginnings: The social and affective development of black children* (pp. 215–230). Hillsdale, NJ: Erlbaum.

Spindler, G. (Ed.). (1982). *Doing the ethnography of schooling: Educational anthropology in action.* New York: Holt, Rinehart & Winston.

Stack, C. B. (1974). *All our kin: Strategies for survival in a black urban community.* New York: Harper & Row.

Steele, C. M. (1992, April). Race and the schooling of Black Americans. *The Atlantic Monthly,* pp. 68, 70, 72, 74–78.

Sternberg, R. J. (1985). *Beyond IQ: A triarchic theory of human intelligence.* New York: Cambridge University Press.

Sternberg, R. J., & Kolligian, J., Jr. (Eds.). (1990). *Competence considered.* New Haven, CT: Yale University Press.

Stewart, W. A. (1970). Toward a history of American Negro dialect. In F. Williams (Ed.), *Language and poverty* (pp. 351–379). Chicago: Markham.

Strupp, H. H. (1973). On the basic ingredients of psychotherapy. *Journal of Consulting and Clinical Psychology, 41,* 1–8.

Strupp, H. H., & Binder, J. L. (1984). *Psychotherapy in a new key: A guide to time-limited dynamic psychotherapy.* New York: Basic Books.

Sudarkasa, N. (1981). Interpreting the African heritage in Afro-American family organization. In H. P. McAdoo (Ed.), *Black families* (pp. 37–53). Beverly Hills, CA: Sage.

Sue, S. (1977). Community mental health services to minority groups: Some optimism, some pessimism. *American Psychologist, 32,* 616–624.

Sue, S. (1988). Psychotherapeutic services for ethnic minorities: Two decades of research findings. *American Psychologist, 43,* 301–308.

Sue, S., Fujino, D. C., Li-tze, H., Takeuchi, D. T., & Zane, N. W. S. (1991). Community mental health services for ethnic minority groups: A test of the cultural responsiveness hypothesis. *Journal of Consulting and Clinical Psychology, 59,* 533–540.

Sue, S., & Morishima, J. (1982). *The mental health of Asian-Americans.* San Francisco: Jossey-Bass.

Sue, S., & Zane, N. (1987). The role of culture and cultural techniques in psychotherapy: A critique and reformulation. *American Psychologist, 42,* 37–45.

Sugarman, A. (1978). Is psychodiagnostic assessment humanistic? *Journal of Personality Assessment, 42,* 11–21.

Sullivan, H. S. ([1925–26] 1962). Peculiarity of thought in schizophrenia. In H. S. Sullivan, *Schizophrenia as a human process.* New York: Norton.

Szasz, T. S. (1974). *The myth of mental illness: Foundations of a theory of personal conduct* (rev. ed.). New York: Harper & Row.

Szasz, T. S. ([1978] 1979). *The myth of psychotherapy: Mental healing as religion, rhetoric, and repression.* Garden City, NY: Anchor Press/Doubleday.

Taylor, O. (1975). Black language and what to do about it: Some black community perspectives. In R. L. Williams (Ed.), *Ebonics: The true language of black folks* (pp. 28–39). St. Louis, MO: Institute of Black Studies.

Taylor, R. J., & Chatters, L. M. (1991). Religious life. In J. S. Jackson (Ed.), *Life in Black America* (pp. 105–123). Newbury Park, CA: Sage.

Taylor, R. L. (1976). Psychosocial development among black children and youth: A reexamination. *American Journal of Orthopsychiatry, 46,* 4–19.

Teale, W. H., & Sulzby, E. (1986). Introduction: Emergent literacy as a perspective for examining how young children become writers and readers. W. H. Teale & E. Sulzby (Eds.), *Emergent literacy: Writing and reading* (pp. vii–xxv). Norwood, NJ: Ablex.

Temoshok, L., & Attkisson, C. C. (1977). Epidemiology of hysterical phenomena: Evidence for a psychosocial theory. In M. J. Horowitz (Ed.), *Hysterical personality* (pp. 143–222). New York: Aronson.

Terrell, F., Taylor, J., & Terrell, S. L. (1978). Effects of type of social reinforcement on the intelligence test performance of lower-class black children. *Journal of Consulting and Clinical Psychology, 46,* 1538–1539.

Tharp, R. G. (1989). Psychocultural variables and constants: Effects on teaching and learning in schools. *American Psychologist, 44,* 349–359.

Tharp, R. G. (1991). Cultural diversity and treatment of children. *Journal of Consulting and Clinical Psychology, 59,* 799–812.

Thomas, A., Hertzig, M. E., Dryman, D., & Fernandez, P. (1971). Examiner effect in IQ testing of Puerto-Rican working-class children. *American Journal of Orthopsychiatry, 41,* 809–821.

Thomas, A., & Sillen, S. (1972). *Racism and psychiatry.* New York: Brunner/Mazel.

Thomas, C. W. (1970, September). Different strokes for different folks: Jo Ann E. Gardner (women's lib) and Charles W. Thomas (black psychology) in a conversation with T. George Harris. *Psychology Today,* 49–53; 78–80.

Thomas, C. W., & Thomas, S. W. (1971). Something borrowed, something black. In C. W. Thomas (Ed.), *Boys no more* (pp. 101–116). Beverly Hills, CA: Glencoe.

Tomes, H. (1976). The impact of cultural influences on psychotherapy. In J. L. Claghorn (Ed.), *Successful psychotherapy* (pp. 197–203). New York: Brunner/Mazel.

Trudgill, P. (1974). *Sociolinguistics: An introduction.* Harmondsworth, England: Penguin Books.

Trueba, H. T. (1986). [Review of *Beyond language: Social and cultural factors in schooling language minority students*]. *Anthropology and Education Quarterly, 17,* 255–259.

Tuma, A. H., & May, P. R. A. (1975). Psychotherapy, drugs and therapist experience in the treatment of schizophrenia: A critique of the Michigan State Project. *Psychotherapy, 12,* 138–142.

Turner, S. M. (1982). Behavior modification and black populations. In S. M. Turner & R. T. Jones (Eds.), *Behavior modification in black populations: Psychosocial issues and empirical findings* (pp. 1–19). New York: Plenum.

Tyler, F. B., Brome, D. R., & Williams, J. E. (1991). *Ethnic validity, ecology, and psychotherapy: A psychosocial competence model.* New York: Plenum.

Tyler, F. B., Sussewell, D. R., & Williams-McCoy, J. (1985). Ethnic validity in psychotherapy. *Psychotherapy, 22,* 311–320.

Vosk, J. S. (1966). Study of Negro children with learning difficulties at the outset of their careers. *American Journal of Orthopsychiatry, 36,* 32–40.

Vygotsky, L. S. (1978). *Mind in society: The development of higher psychological processes.* M. Cole, V. John-Steiner, S. Scribner, & E. Souberman, Eds., Cambridge, MA: Harvard University Press.

Wachtel, P. L. (1977). *Psychoanalysis and behavior therapy: Toward an integration.* New York: Basic Books.

Wakefield, J. C. (1992). The concept of mental disorder: On the boundary between biological facts and social values. *American Psychologist, 47,* 373–388.

Walker, A. (1982). *The color purple.* New York: Harcourt Brace Jovanovich.

Wallace, B. C. (1991). *Crack cocaine: A practical treatment approach for the chemically dependent.* New York: Brunner/Mazel.

Ward, M. C. (1971). *Them children: A study in language learning.* New York: Holt, Rinehart & Winston.

Ward, S. H., & Braun, J. (1972). Self-esteem and racial preference in black children. *American Journal of Orthopsychiatry, 42,* 644–647.

Warheit, G., Holzer, C. E., III, & Arey, S. A. (1975). Race and mental illness: An epidemiological update. *Journal of Health and Social Behavior, 16,* 243–256.

Watson, P. (1972, September). I.Q.: The racial gap. *Psychology Today,* 48–50; 97–99.

Webster's Ninth New Collegiate Dictionary. (1988). Springfield, MA: Merriam-Webster.

Weinberg, R. A. (1989). Intelligence and IQ: Landmark issues and great debates. *American Psychologist, 44,* 98–104.

Weinberger, J., & Hardaway, R. (1990). Separating science from myth in subliminal psychodynamic activation. *Clinical Psychology Review, 10,* 727–756.

Weiner, I. B. (1966). *Psychodiagnosis in schizophrenia.* New York: Wiley.

Weiss, B. L., & Kupfer, D. J. (1974). The black patient and research in a community mental health center: Where have all the patients gone? *American Journal of Psychiatry, 131,* 415–418.

Weiss, J., & Sampson, H. (1986). *The psychoanalytic process: Theory, clinical observation, and empirical research.* New York: Guilford.

Westerman, M. (1993). A hermeneutic approach to integration: Psychotherapy within the circle of practical activity. In G. Stricker & J. R. Gold (Eds.), *The comprehensive handbook of psychotherapy integration* (pp. 187–216). New York: Plenum.

White, J. L., & Parham, T. A. (1990). *The psychology of Blacks: An African-American perspective (2d ed.).* Englewood Cliffs, NJ: Prentice-Hall.

White, K. P. (1978). Toward a definition of the black self-concept: An analysis of meaning ascriptions (Doctoral dissertation, New York University, 1977). *Dissertation Abstracts International, 38,* 7249A. (University Microfilms No. 7808572.)

White, R. W. (1959). Motivation reconsidered: The concept of competence. *Psychological Review, 66,* 297–333.

White, R. W. (1963). Ego and reality in psychoanalytic theory. *Psychological Issues, 3* (Serial no. 11).

White, R. W., & Watt, N. F. (1981). *The abnormal personality* (5th ed.). New York: Wiley.

Williams, D. H. (1986). The epidemiology of mental illness in Afro-Americans. *Hospital and Community Psychiatry, 37,* 42–49.

Williams, F. (1970). Language, attitude, and social change. In F. Williams (Ed.), *Language and poverty* (pp. 380–399). Chicago: Markham.

Williams, J. E., & Morland, J. K. (1976). *Race, color, and the young child.* Chapel Hill: University of North Carolina Press.

Williams, J. E., & Morland, J. K. (1979). Comment on Bank's "White preference in blacks: A paradigm in search of a phenomenon." *Psychological Bulletin, 86,* 28–32.

Williams, R. L. (1975). Developing cultural specific assessment devices: An empirical rationale. In R. L. Williams (Ed.), *Ebonics: The true language of black folks* (pp. 110–132). St. Louis, MO: Institute of Black Studies.

Williams, R. L., & Mitchell, H. (1991). The testing game. In R. L. Jones (Ed.), *Black psychology* (3d ed., pp. 193–205). Berkeley, CA: Cobb & Henry.

Williamson, J. V. (1975). A look at Black English. In R. L. Williams (Ed.), *Ebonics: The true language of black folks* (pp. 11–21). St. Louis, MO: Institute of Black Studies.

Willie, C. V., Kramer, B. M., & Brown, B. S. (Eds.). (1973). *Racism and mental health.* Pittsburgh, PA: University of Pittsburgh Press.

Willis, M. G. (1989). Styles of African-American children: A review of the literature and interventions. *Journal of Black Psychology, 16,* 47–65.

Wilson, L., & Rogers, R. W. (1975). The fire this time: Effects of race of target, insult, and potential retaliation on black aggression. *Journal of Personality and Social Psychology, 32,* 857–864.

Wilson, M. N. (1989). Child development in the context of the Black extended family. *American Psychologist, 44,* 380–385.

Wilson, W. J. (1987). *The truly disadvantaged: The inner-city, the underclass, and public policy.* Chicago: University of Chicago Press.

Winslow, C. N., & Brainerd, J. E. (1950). A comparison of the reactions of whites and Negroes to frustration as measured by the Rosenzweig Picture-Frustration Test. *American Psychologist, 5,* 297.

Wright, R. (1975). Black English. *Language in Society, 4,* 185–198.

Wylie, R. (1974). *The self-concept: A review of methodological considerations and measuring instruments* (rev. ed.). Lincoln: University of Nebraska Press.

Yando, R., Seitz, V., & Zigler, E. F. (1979). *Intellectual and personality characteristics of children: Social-class and ethnic-group differences.* Hillsdale, NJ: Erlbaum.

Zigler, E. F. (1968). Familial mental retardation: A continuing dilemma. In S. Chess & A. Thomas (Eds.), *Annual progress in child psychiatry and child development* (pp. 281–299). New York: Brunner/Mazel.

Zigler, E. F. (1974). Project Head Start: Success or failure? In S. Chess & A. Thomas (Eds.), *Annual progress in child psychiatry and child development* (pp. 154–165). New York: Brunner/Mazel.

Zigler, E. F., Abelson, W. D., & Seitz, V. (1974). Motivational factors in the performance of economically disadvantaged children on the Peabody Picture Vocabulary Test. In S. Chess & A. Thomas (Eds.), *Annual progress in child psychiatry and child development* (pp. 199–215). New York: Brunner/Mazel.

Zigler, E. F., & Butterfield, E. C. (1968). Motivational aspects of changes in I.Q. test performance of culturally deprived nursery school children. *Child Development, 39*, 1–14.

Zigler, E. F., & Trickett, P. K. (1978). IQ, social competence, and evaluation of early childhood intervention programs. *American Psychologist, 33*, 789–798.

AUTHOR INDEX

A

Abelson, W. D., 109, 110, 135
Abramowitz, S. I., 265
Adorno, T. W., 266
Akbar, N., 15, 213, 258, 259, 277
Akiskal, H. S., 256
Alejandro-Wright, M. N., 50, 57, 58, 81
Allen, B., 85
Allen, W. R., 192, 210
American Psychiatric Association, 215, 250, 254
American Psychological Association, 241
Ames, R., 176
Anastasi, A., 73
Anderson, B. E., 109
Anderson, L. P., 225
Anderson, N. B., 231
Arey, S. A., 221, 258
Arieti, S., 38
Aristotle, 5, 6, 7
Atkinson, D. R., 238
Attkisson, C. C., 231

B

Bachman, J. G., 30, 41
Bailey, S. T., 257
Baker, F. M., 221, 253, 254, 257
Baldwin, J. A., 32
Balla, D. A., 222
Banks, W. C., 30, 203
Banks, W. M., 238
Baratz, J. C., 164
Barna, J. D., 203, 218
Barnes, E. J., 44
Basch, M. F., 241
Baughman, E. E., 30, 202
Bell, C. C., 232
Belle, D., 221
Belmont, J. M., 131
Bernhard, M. R., 223
Bernstein, B. A., 165, 166
Berrueta-Clement, J. P., 87, 89
Bibring, E., 227
Billingsley, A., 42, 43, 62, 233
Binder, J. L., 268
Birch, H. G., 109
Blatt, S. J., 129, 228
Block, C. B., 230, 243, 253
Boggiano, A. K., 116
Bond, J. C., 49
Bortner, M., 109
Boswell, J. J., 164
Bowman, P. J., 197, 228
Boyd-Franklin, N., 62, 63, 244, 246

307

Boykin, A. W., 13, 15, 85, 95, 97, 99, 111, 149, 167
Brainerd, J. E., 173, 177
Brand, E. S., 27
Braun, J., 30, 34
Brems, C., 252
Bridger, W. H., 82
Brody, E. B., 220, 253
Brodzinski, D. M., 135, 136
Brome, D. R., 252, 263. *See also* Sussewell, Deborah R.
Bronfenbrenner, U., 127
Brown, A. L., 157
Brown, B. S., x
Brown, D. R., 256, 258
Brown, L. M., 195
Brown, R. T., 101
Bruner, J. S., 112
Bryant-Tuckett, R., 130
Butterfield, E. C., 109

C

Cameron, N., xix, 13, 22, 249
Cantor, N., 117
Caplan, N., 175, 191, 202
Carey, P. M., 20
Carkhuff, R. R., 238
Carter, K. E., 194, 195, 196, 211
Castenell, L. A., 168
Cauce, A. M., 100
Cazden, C. B., 149
Chatters, L. M., 275, 276
Cheek, D. K., 171, 202, 260, 261
Chein, I., xix, xx, 3, 8, 18, 21, 28, 36, 45, 276
Chessick, R. D., 254, 261
Cheung, F. K., 220
Chew, G. F., 277
Clark, K. B., 27, 28, 34, 56, 65, 67, 77, 197
Clark, M. P., 27, 28, 34, 56, 65
Cobbs, P. M., 172, 175, 225, 226, 253
Cohen, R. A., 83, 84, 85, 128

Cole, M., 112, 164
Coleman, J. S., 46, 203
Coles, R., 25, 26, 43, 48, 49, 50
Comas-Diaz, L., 244
Comer, J. P., 99, 100, 119, 155, 225
Coner-Edwards, A. F., 244
Conway, C. G., xx, 3
Cook, S. W., 52
Cook-Gumperz, J., 166
Coughlin, E. K., 185
Crain, R. L., 1, 173, 174, 175, 176, 177, 178, 199, 202, 203, 205, 225, 256
Crook, T. H., 253, 256
Cross, S., 118
Cross, W. E., Jr., 31, 33, 34, 39, 55, 65, 177, 178, 179, 180, 181, 182, 184, 185, 186, 192, 199, 206, 207, 264, 272, 275
Cushman, P., 59

D

Davis, W. E., 252
Deci, E., xx, 116
Dejoie-Smith, M., 260
Derbyshire, R. L., 220, 253
DeVos, G., 278
Diggs, I., 43, 112
Dixon, V., 258, 259
Dore, J., 167
Dressler, W. W., 230
DuBois, W. E. B., 23, 43, 44, 46, 112, 272, 273
Dweck, C. S., 115, 116, 117, 119, 136

E

Eaton, W. W., 258
Edelson, M. 10, 19, 36, 59, 234, 237, 259
Edmonds, R., 97, 99
Edwards, A., 197, 198, 199

Edwards, H. E., 238
Ekstein, R. 129
Ellison, R., x, 9, 23, 271
Epps, E. G., 32, 33, 52, 112, 177, 186, 187, 189, 190, 191, 192, 194, 199, 209, 210
Epstein, S., 32, 54
Erikson, E. H., 50, 64, 181, 194
Evans, D. A., 234. *See also* Holmes, Dorothy Evans
Evans, M. C., 28
Exner, J. E., Jr., 253

F

Fanon, F., 142
Faulconer, J. E., xx
Feuerstein, R., 69, 72, 89, 90, 91, 92, 93, 94, 95, 101, 105, 110, 117, 118, 119, 122, 129, 130, 131, 132
Feffer, M., 14, 17
Figueroa, R. A., 132, 133, 134
Fischer, J., 220, 221
Fish, J. E., 30
Fleming, J., 193, 194, 195, 199, 210, 211
Flynn, J. T., 109
Forward, J. R., 175
Frady, M., 185
Francois, T. V., 243
Frank, G. H., 251, 253
Frank, J. B., 217, 218, 243, 255
Frank, J. D., 217, 218, 241, 243, 255
Franklin, A. J., 111, 244
Frazier, E. F., 162
Freedle, R. O., 140
Freiberg, P., 51
Freud, S., 216, 227
Frey, K. S., 117
Fromm, E., 213, 266, 267
Frosh, S., 254
Frost, R., 35, 36, 44
Fulani, L., 111

G

Garber, H., 87, 88
Garcia, J., 101, 123
Gardner, H., 75, 123, 124
Gardner, LaM. H., 238
Garza, R. T., 106
Gary, L. E., 220, 221, 256
Gaylin, W., 228
Geller, J. D., 221, 224, 234
Gerard, H. B., 52
Gergen, K., 22
Gerstein, A. I., 135, 136
Gibbs, J. T., xii, 51, 168, 204, 205, 232, 242, 244, 245, 256, 261, 267, 268
Gill, M. M., 268
Giordano, J., 246
Golden, M., 82, 152, 167
Goleman, D., 52
Gopaul-McNicol, S., xi
Gordon, V. V., 31, 33
Gouldner, H., 67, 150, 167, 229
Grant, G., 30, 34, 51
Green, S. B., 252
Greenblatt, R. L., 252
Greene, R. L., 252
Gregg, N. B., 133
Grier, W. H., 172, 175, 178, 225, 226, 253
Griffith, M. S., 238, 240, 241, 243, 268
Gruen, R. J., 249
Gumperz, J. J., 144, 150
Gurin, G., 209
Gurin, P., 177, 186, 187, 189, 190, 191, 192, 194, 199, 202, 206, 208, 209, 210
Guthrie, L. F., 147, 148, 167
Guthrie, R. V., 74
Gutman, H. G., 42
Gynther, M. D., 252

H

Haimo, S. F., 223
Hale, J., 84, 99

Haley, A., 20
Hall, W. S., 140, 147, 148, 149, 164, 167
Halpern, F., 102, 225, 230, 258
Hamberger, L. K., 252
Hamilton-Lee, M., 100
Hammond, W. R., 232
Haniff, N. Z., 192, 210
Harburg, E., 231
Hardaway, R., 129
Hare, B. R., 168
Harre, R., 22
Harrell, J. P., 199, 206, 207, 245, 274
Harris, W. A., 138, 140, 168, 169
Harrison, A. O., 197
Harrison-Ross, P., 48
Hastings, J. E., 252
Hatchett, S., 202, 206, 207
Hayes, W. A., 8, 10
Haynes, N. M., 100
Heath, S. B., 151, 152, 153, 154, 155, 159, 167, 196
Heber, R. F., 87, 88
Heiskell, T., 237
Helms, J. E., 206, 244, 264
Henry, W. E., 237
Herasimchuk, E., 150
Herman, K. D., 253, 256
Hernandez-Chavez, E., 144
Hill, R. B., 42, 62
Hilliard, A., 84
Hobbes, T., 14
Hoffman, M. B., 89, 90, 92, 94, 95
Hollingshead, A. B., 222
Holmes, D. E., 265. *See also* Evans, Dorothy A.
Holt, R. R., xviii, 248
Holzer, C. E., III, 221, 258
Holzman, P. S., 223, 253
Hoover, M. R., 140, 141, 160
Hopson, D. S., 57, 65
Horowitz, M. J., 230
Houston, S. H., 137, 149, 154, 155
Howard, G. S., xx, 3, 263

Hraba, J., 30, 34, 51
Hsu, F. S. K., 278
Hughes, L., ix, x
Hume, D., 14
Hunt, J. McV., 96

I

Ingwell, R. H., 135, 218

J

Jackson, J. J., 256
Jackson, J. S., 202, 206, 275
Jacobson, L., 110
James, W., 13
Jenkins, A. H., xx, 22, 248, 267
Jensen, A. R., 67, 68, 74, 77, 78, 121
Johnson, E. H., 252
Johnson, F., 60
Johnson, M. E., 252
Johnston, J., 196, 197
Johnston, M. H., 253
Jones, A., 238, 240, 265
Jones, A. C., 245, 247
Jones, E. E., 224, 238, 239, 240, 241, 243, 268, 269
Jones, F., 23
Jones, J., 162, 272, 273, 274, 275
Jonides, J., 192, 193, 210, 211
Juarez, R., 239

K

Kagan, J., 76, 80, 92, 97, 110, 123, 125, 126
Kagan, S., 97, 98, 99, 154, 196
Kamin, L. J., x, 74, 121
Kant, I., 12, 13, 14, 22
Kardiner, A., 1, 172, 204
Karon, B. P., 235, 236, 238
Katz, P. A., 53, 56, 116

Keen, E., 35, 55
Kennedy, T. R., 42
Kernan, C. M., 140, 141, 163
Klein, R. E., 80, 97
Kleinsmith, L. J., 196, 197
Kohut, H., 225, 229, 236, 241
Kolligian, J., xx, 114
Korchin, S. J., 215, 248
Kovel, J., 48, 162, 200, 201, 203, 213
Kramer, B. M., x
Kramer, M., 220
Krebs, R. L., 224
Kupfer, D. J., 222

L

Labov, W., 138, 140, 144, 145, 146, 148, 158, 168, 169, 234
Laboratory for Comparative Human Cognition (LCHC), 73, 74, 123, 131
Langer, E. J., 117
Lanyon, B. P., 260
Lanyon, R. I., 260
Larr, C. J., 30
Lerner, B., 234, 235, 238, 239, 240, 246, 266, 267
Lesse, S., 232
Lester, J., 11, 172, 183, 185
Lewis, D. O., 222, 223
Lewontin, R. C., 121
Lindzey, G., 88, 121
Lipman, R. S., 249
Locke, J., 12, 13, 14
Loehlin, J. C., 88, 121
Luborsky, L., 262, 268

M

Mackenzie, B., 121
MacMillan, M., 30
Mahl, G. F., 216

Mahler, M. S., 130
Majors, R., 142, 143
Malcolm X, 182, 183, 184, 185, 192, 206
Markus, H., 46, 63, 96, 118
Marsella, A. J., 278
Marshall, P., 160, 161
Marwit, K. L., 164
Marwit, S. J., 148, 164
Maslow, A. H., xix
Masterson, J., 254
Matute-Bianchi, M. E., 119, 126, 127, 209
May, P. R. A., 236
Mayman, M., 215, 249
Mbiti, J. S., 22, 278
McAdoo, H. P., 29, 30, 33, 34, 50
McDavis, R. J., 256
McDonald, M., 48, 56, 58
McGoldrick, M., 246
McKinney, W. T., Jr., 256
McPherson, J. A., 23
McQuater, G. V., 30
McWorter, G. A., 42
Mead, G. H., 37, 60
Meltzer, H. Y., 249
Menninger, K. M., 215, 249, 250
Mercer, J. R., 76, 81, 102, 103, 104, 105, 122, 132, 133, 134, 135
Messer, S., xx, 22
Miller, I. J., 232, 241, 254
Miller-Jones, D., 80, 95, 123
Milliones, J., 185
Milner, D., 30, 56
Mitchell, H., 102
Modgil, C., 101, 121
Modgil, S., 101, 121
Montare, A., 83
Moore, E. G. J., 81, 82-83, 125
Morelli, G., 80, 95, 131
Morishima, J., 272, 278
Morland, J. K., 29, 30, 50, 52, 53, 56, 63, 64
Morrison, A. P., 254
Morrison, B. M., 209

Motto, R. L., 129
Myers, H. F., 231
Myers, L. J., 22, 276, 277, 278

N

Nagy, W. E., 149
Nathan, P. E., 215
Neal, A. M., 220, 258
Neighbors, H. W., 221, 272, 275
Nelson, S. D., 202
Neumann, G., 148
Nicholls, J. G., 115
Nobles, W. W., 60, 61, 191, 278
Norem, J. K., 117
Nurius, P., 46, 63, 96

O

Ogbu, J. U., 114, 119, 121, 126, 127, 209
Olim, E. G., 166
Orne, M. T., 55
Ovesey, L., 1, 172, 204

P

Padilla, A., 27
Page, E. B., 88
Palincsar, A. S., 157
Parham, T. A., 181, 182, 206, 207, 244, 245, 256, 276, 277, 278
Park, K., 117
Parker, K., 130
Paster, V. S., 244
Pearce, J. K., 246
Peele, S., 22, 249
Pettigrew, T. F., 1, 43, 52, 99, 178, 204
Phares, E. J., 234, 260
Phillips, L., 252
Piaget, J., 57, 122, 126
Pierce, R., 238

Piestrup, A. M., 150, 156, 157, 158, 168
Pines, M., 96
Pochyly, J. M., 252
Polite, C. K., 197, 198, 199
Polkinghorne, D. E., xx
Ponterotto, J. G., 264
Porter, J. D. R., 28, 29, 30, 33, 34, 53, 54, 56, 57, 62, 64
Poteat, G. M., 133
Poussaint, A. F., 225, 257
Powdermaker, H., 8, 176
Powell, G. J., 30
Powell, L., 252
Powell-Hopson, D., 57, 65
Pritchard, D. A., 252
Pruyser, P., 215, 249
Pugh, R. W., 2, 3, 20, 22, 34, 172, 201, 257
Purcell, L., 157

R

Rachford, D. L., 95
Rainwater, L., 201, 202, 229
Ramirez, M., 61, 272, 273, 278
Ramseur, H. P., 272, 275
Ramsey, P. G., 58, 59
Rand, Y., 69, 89, 93
Raskin, A., 253, 256
Redd, M. L., 231
Reder, S., 164
Redlich, F. C., 222
Reeves, C., 52
Reiskind, N., 135, 136
Reschly, D. J., 133, 134
Reynolds, C. R., 101
Rice, B., 128
Ridley, C. R., 253
Ritzler, B. A., 129
Roberts, H. B., 244
Robins, L. N., 168, 221, 232
Robinson, D. N., xx, 3, 22

Rogers, R. W., 177
Rogoff, B., 80, 95, 131
Rohwer, W. D., 125
Roland, A., 60, 278
Rorty, R., 22
Rose, S., 121
Rosen, B. M., 220
Rosen, H., 166
Rosenberg, M., 30, 33, 41, 52
Rosenblatt, A., 252
Rosenhan, D. L., 251
Rosenthal, J., x, 168
Rosenthal, R., 110, 136
Ross, J. A., 30
Ross, S. A., 240
Rotter, J. B., 173, 203, 208
Ruble, D. N., 117
Ruiz, R. A., 27
Rumsey, J. M., 107, 108
Russell, D. M., 234, 240
Ryan, R., xx, 116
Rychlak, J. F., xix, xx, xxi, 3, 4, 5, 6, 7, 8, 10, 13, 14, 15, 17, 18, 22, 23, 24, 32, 35, 40, 44, 45, 55, 56, 61, 69, 70, 71, 72, 73, 83, 94, 95, 105, 106, 107, 108, 111, 120, 121, 124, 125, 135, 198, 203, 218, 242, 248, 249, 258, 262, 276

S

Sampson, E. E., 59, 60, 61, 191, 278
Sampson, H., 267
Sandoval, J., 133
Sarason, S. B., 122
Sarbin, T. R., xx, 263
Sarnoff, I., 257
Sass, L., xx, 22, 59, 278
Sassenrath, J. M., 132, 133, 134
Savell, J. M., 95
Scarr, S., 14, 81, 82, 125
Scarr-Salapatek, S., 81

Schact, T., 215
Schafer, R., xix, xx, 8, 19, 41, 45, 263
Schectman, F., 252
Schein, S., 238
Scheinfeld, D. R., 113, 136
Schleifer, C. B., 220, 253
Schuman, H., 177
Schwaber, E., 269
Schwartz, D., 100
Schweinhart, L. J., 88
Scott, J. P., 228
Scribner, S., 164
Scrofani, P. J., 77, 78, 79, 82, 89, 95, 107, 131
Seagull, A. A., 238, 240, 265
Secord, P. F., xx
Sedlacek, W. E., 210
Segall, M. H., 77, 112, 121
Seiden, R. H., 256, 257
Seitz, V., 109, 110, 112, 135
Seligman, M. E. P., 228, 249
Semaj, L. T., 57
Senay, E. C., 228
Shade, B. J., 84, 167
Shanok, S. S., 222
Sillen, S., x, 172, 219
Silverman, L. H., 129, 259
Simmons, R. G., 30, 33, 41, 52
Sims, J. H., 237
Simons, H. D., 147, 148, 150, 151, 154
Skinner, B. F., 24
Slaughter, D. T., 42, 112
Smith, M., 260
Smith, W. D., 214, 215, 234, 240, 252, 260
Smitherman, G., 147, 163, 164
Snowden, L. R., 220
Spence, D. P., 263
Spencer, M. B., 33, 34, 57, 58
Spindler, G., 167
Spray, S. L., 237
Spuhler, J. N., 88, 121
Spurlock, J., 244
Stack, C. B., 42

Steele, C. M., 120, 132, 194, 195, 196, 211
Sternberg, R. J., xx, 85, 114, 123, 125
Stewart, W. A., 139, 146
Strickland, T. L., 231
Strong, M. S., 67, 150, 167, 229
Strupp, H. H., 236, 263, 265, 266, 267, 268
Sudarkasa, N., 42
Sue, S., 238, 239, 241, 272, 278
Sugarman, A., 252, 253
Sullivan, H. S., 215, 221, 248
Sulzby, E., 158, 159
Sussman, L., 258
Sussewell, D. R., 263. *See also* Brome, Deborah R.
Szasz, T. S., 214, 231, 233

T

Taylor, J., 109
Taylor, O., 140, 142
Taylor, R. J., 275, 276
Taylor, R. L., 30, 39, 52
Teale, W. H., 158, 159
Temoshok, L., 231
Terrell, F., 109
Terrell, S. L., 109
Tharp, R. G., 167, 168, 247
Thomas, A., x, 109, 172, 219
Thomas, C. W., 178, 179
Thomas, S. W., 178
Thorne, A., 224
Tirre, W. C., 167
Tomes, H., 222
Trickett, P. K., 75, 109, 135
Trudgill, P., 138, 139, 140, 141, 164, 166
Trueba, H. T., 127
Tuck, K., 85
Tuma, A. H., 236
Turner, S. M., 220, 258, 260
Twohig, P. T., 95
Tyler, F. B., 252, 263, 264

V

VandenBos, G. R., 235, 236, 238
Vosk, J. S., 109
Vygotsky, L., 131, 132

W

Wachtel, P. L., 260
Wakefield, J. C., 214
Walker, A., x, 168
Wallace, B. C., 231
Ward, M. C., 166
Ward, S. H., 30, 34
Warheit, G. J., 221, 258
Washington, R. E., 30
Watson, P., 109
Watt, N. F., 31, 230, 232, 250
Weaver, G. D., 220, 221, 256
Weikart, D. P., 88
Weinberg, R. A., 81, 82, 121, 125
Weinberger, J., 129
Weiner, I. B., 253
Weisman, C. S., 1, 173, 174, 175, 176, 177, 178, 199, 202, 203, 205, 225, 256
Weiss, B. L., 222
Weiss, J., 267
Westerman, M., 260
White, J. L., 276, 277, 278
White, K. P., 204
White, R. W., xix, xx, 4, 8, 16, 17, 18, 19, 24, 31, 40, 64, 113, 201, 230, 232, 250
Wild, C. M., 129
Williams, D. H., 221, 256
Williams, F., 150
Williams, Janice E., 252, 263
Williams, John E., 29, 30, 50, 52, 53, 56, 63, 64
Williams, J. R., 175
Williams, R. L., 102, 132
Williams, R. N., xx
Williams-McCoy, J., 263

Williamson, J. V., 139
Willie, C. V., x
Willis, E. M., 220
Willis, M. G., 84, 85
Wilson, L., 177
Wilson, M. N., 42, 62
Wilson, W. J., xii, 129
Winslow, C. N., 173, 177
Wolf, E. S., 225, 229
Woolfolk, R., xx, 22
Wright, R., 140
Wuensch, K. L., 133
Wurf, E., 118
Wyden, B., 48
Wylie, R., 31

Y

Yando, R., 112
Yung, B., 232

Z

Zalk, S. R., 56
Zane, N. W. S., 241
Zigler, E. F., 75, 108, 109, 110, 112, 122, 135

SUBJECT INDEX

A

Abstract thinking, 67–70, 121, 125–126. 128. *See also* Level II (abstract abilities)
Achievement
  academic, 33, 46, 67, 80, 103, 127, 193, 194–197, 208, 210
  as content, 101–105
  "folk theory of success," 126–127
  individual and collective, 126, 186–191
  social background influence on, 126
Accepters, the, 174–175, 205
Achievers, the, 174–175, 205
Activity, 17, 19, 34–36, 68, 70–72, 84–85, 217, 230
Activists, the, 187–192
Adaptive inferiority, 2–3, 22, 172, 201–202, 257
Adoption, transracial, 81–82, 125
Adler, A., 248
Adulthood, 197–199
Affective assessment, 18, 23–24, 105–108
  and African heritage, 258–259
  and ethnic minority status, 106–108, 194–195, 242–243
  feeling of efficacy as, 24
  and IQ test performance, 107–108
  and learning, 71–72, 106–108, 121
  as reinforcement value (RV), 106–108, 135, 231, 237, 242
  in "self-schemas", 118
  and social class, 106–107, 108, 242–243
  of speech differences, 141–142, 150
  as transcendence, 24
Affirmation, 12, 17–18, 35, 39, 45, 59, 61, 105, 112, 121, 171
  in Gibbs's typology, 204–205
African American, the, 199–200
  bi-cultural status of, 23, 163, 181, 272–275
  as new cultural being, 23
  nonverbal communication styles of, 142–143
African heritage, 22, 178, 200. *See also* Affective assessment, and African heritage
  and African-American survival, 20
  and Black English, 139–140
  and popular culture, 23
  and sense of competence, 20
  and sense of self, 60–61, 178, 179–180
African world view, 22, 276–279
Afrocentrism, 180, 276–279

317

Agency, psychological, 3, 4, 60–62, 63, 268, 271, 274, 276
  and Afrocentric view, 278
Aggression, 171, 172–177, 200–201
  in Blacks, 1, 172–177, 200, 202, 215–216, 226, 256–257, 260–261
  by Blacks towards Blacks, 172, 176, 201–202, 221, 232
  by Blacks towards Whites, 176, 177, 178, 261
Anxiety, 2, 38, 62, 215–217, 255, 260
Aspirations, occupational, 187–192
Assertion, 171, 173–174, 183–185, 186–188, 199, 200, 260–261
  inhibition of, 172–174, 175
  training for, 260–261
Assertive Black . . . Puzzled White (Cheek), 260
Assimilation, 204–205. *See also* Accepters, the
Authoritarianism, 266–267
  and authority (Fromm), 266
  scale for therapists, 266
  in therapy, 240, 266–267
Awareness
  defined, 44–45,
  and personality functioning, 198, 206–207
  and school performance, 153, 212

B

Behaviorism
  behavior modification, 52, 65
  and Blacks, 8
  contingencies as used in, xviii, 20, 24, 124
  as mechanistic view, xviii, 124
Behavior therapy, 240, 260–261
BEV (Black English Vernacular). *See* Black English
Bias, cultural. *See* Intellectual tests, cultural bias in

Biculturalism, 180–181, 272–275
Bipolarity, 10, 18. *See also* Meaning, dialectical (bipolar)
Black bourgeoisie, 162
Black Consciousness, Identity and Achievement (Gurin & Epps), 186
Black English (BE)
  African origins of, 139–140
  and African-American culture, 159–163
  and cultural pluralism, 137–138, 146, 159, 162. *See also* Speech style, and pluralism
  deficiencies claimed for, 143–146, 150–151, 162
  as dialect, 138–140, 163–164
  and reading achievement, 147–148, 154–159
  social consequences of, 141–143, 159–160, 162, 168–169
  standard variety of, 140–142
  varieties of, 140–141
  vernacular features of, 138, 140, 163–164
Black English Vernacular (BEV). *See* Black English
Black Muslim, 184, 235, 240
Black nationalism, 180–181, 184–186, 206
Black pride, 2, 30, 33, 47, 48–50, 51, 162–163, 171, 199, 200, 274
Black Revolution. *See* Social protest
Boss, M., 248
Brown is a Beautiful Color (Bond), 49

C

Causal Construct Scale, 203, 218
Causation, 4–9. *See also* Efficient cause; Final cause; Formal cause; Material cause
  in Aristotle, 5–6
Children of the Dream (Edwards & Polite), 197

Choices, xxi, 17, 20, 32, 34–36, 38, 40, 41, 44, 198, 217, 254
   self-concept shaped by, 36, 38, 41, 198
   and self development, 35–36, 248
Civil Rights Movement. *See* Social protest
Clinical approach, the, 93, 214, 233, 246–247, 253–254
Cognitive processes, 70, 75–77, 93, 121, 124, 125–126
   deficiencies, 94–96
   as modifiable by intervention, 86–101
   and race, xxi, 76–77
   and social class, 76, 83, 128–129
Cognitive style, xxi, 83–86
   analytic vs. relational, 83–85, 128
   and behavioral verve, 85, 149
   in Black children, 84–85
   family influences on, 81–82
Colleges,
   Black, 186–190, 192, 193–194, 208, 210
   White, 193–197, 204–205, 210–212
color preferences, 2
   in children, 28–29, 57–59
   Color Meaning Test of, 28–29
Color Purple, The (Walker), 168
Committed Achievers, the, 187–190, 191
communication, non-verbal, 142
Community mental health, 214, 233–234
Competence
   and African-American survival, 19–21, 40–41, 271
   as critique of psychological theory, 16–17
   growth of, 16–19, 55
   as motivation, xix, 18, 40, 113, 114, 171, 201, 228, 229, 247
   sense of, 18–19, 30, 40–41, 51, 179, 208, 214, 233
   and Skinnerian model, 19
Conceptualizing, 12–13, 39, 59, 70, 71–72, 83, 120, 143, 214, 247–248, 252, 260, 261–262
   as creative activity, 59, 247–248
Creole, 139
Crisis, The, 43
Cultural differences
   between client and therapist, 239, 263–264
   in intellectual functioning, 75, 76–77, 80, 81–83, 84–86, 91, 104–105, 111
   and mental disorder. *See* Racial differences, in mental disorder; Social class differences, in mental disorder
Culture
   and affective assessment, 106–107
   and individual development, 20, 37–38, 47, 96
Culture conflict, 85, 263

D

Dark Ghetto (K.B. Clark), 67
Defense, psychological, 32, 38, 62, 172, 176–177, 202, 215–217, 237, 248, 254–255, 256, 263
   as dialectical activity, 216
   as displacement, 172–173, 176, 216
   as identification with aggressor, 2, 176
   as internalization, 256
   as projection, 202, 269
   as repression, 215, 216
   as suppression, 215
Dehumanization, 21, 213–214. *See also* Racism
Demand characteristics, 55
Depression, 225–226, 227–228, 255–257
   in African Americans, 225–228, 230, 231–232, 255–257
   "masked" form of, 231–232
Deprivation, cultural, 85–86, 91, 93
Desegregation, 25–26, 51–52, 198, 205, 219
   true integration, 52, 99
Diagnosis, 219–220, 251–253

in cross-racial settings, 221–224, 230, 253–254
Diagnostic and Statistical Manual of Mental Disorders, DSM-III-R, 215, 231, 250
Dialect, 138–139, 163–164
Dialectical thinking, 10, 11–12, 39–40, 43–44, 198, 216, 272
  as resistance by Blacks, 10–11, 21, 184, 216
Doll preference studies, 27–28, 29, 30, 33–34, 53–54, 55–56, 65
Drawings, children's
  aspects of self perception in, 25–27, 30, 49–50
Drifters, the, 174–175
Drive reduction, xviii, xix, 3, 16, 20–21, 38
Drives. *See also* Drive reduction
  in behaviorism, xviii
  critique of theory, xix
  in Freudian theory, xviii
  in infants, 16

E

Effectance, 17–18, 23, 39, 171
Efficacy, feeling of, 17, 18–19, 24, 50, 208
Efficient cause, 6, 8, 9, 249. *See also* Impetus construct
Ego strength, 216, 218, 219
Elijah Muhammad, 184
Emotional disorder. *See* Mental disorder
Emotionality
  and affective assessment, 231
  in African Americans, 230–231, 258–259
Emotions
  material-cause quality of, 23–24
Empathy, 222, 223, 229, 236–237, 254, 268–269
Environment
  as limiting Blacks, 8, 11, 47
Ethnic Validity Model, 263

Ethnocentrism, 30
Examiner effects, 55–56, 108–110, 238–239, 240, 265
External control, 173, 189–190, 203, 208, 209–210
Extraspective view, 11, 14, 21, 71

F

Family, Black
  cultural perspective of, 55
  as disorganized, 42
  extended kinship, 42, 62–63
  and self-awareness, 44–46
  and self-concept, 41–46, 229–230, 255–256
  as stable, 42–43, 202, 266
Final cause, 5, 7–9, 218, 249, 274. *See also* Intention construct
  and Black experience, 8–9
Formal cause, 5, 6, 8, 19, 22. *See also* Pattern construct

H

Head Start, 86–87
  evaluations of, 87–89
Horney, K., 204
Hostility. *See* Aggression
Human individual
  as active agent, 4, 21, 38, 217, 276
  as creator, 19, 21, 35–37, 216
  humanistic images of, xix, xx, 206–207, 276
  mechanistic image of, xviii, xix
  as research subject, 55–56
Humanistic view, xix, xx, xxi, 15–16, 19, 20, 167, 279
  and African-American survival, 11, 15–16, 19–20, 259
  as biologically "naturalistic", 249
  competence concept in, 16–19

of mental disorder, 215, 224, 240, 259
as a "psycho–logical" theory, 19, 121
in theories of personality, 206–207, 248, 260
and traditional psychology, 3, 15, 20–21, 68–69, 248
use of causal principles in, 5
Humanitarianism, xxi, 240
Hysterical personality, the, 230–231, 237

I

Identification with the aggressor. *See* Defense, psychological, identification with aggressor
Identity, 34–35, 40–41, 254–255
as continuity of self, 40–41, 179–180, 181–182
and language, 143
racial, 2–3, 21, 26, 27, 29–30, 33–34, 43, 48, 49, 51, 65, 171, 177–178, 179–181, 181–182, 272–275
Impetus construct, 4, 5, 6, 7, 218. *See also* Efficient cause
Individualistic Achievers, the, 187–190
Industry
as developmental stage (Erikson), 50, 64–65
Infant
psychological growth of, 16–19
Instrumental Enrichment (IE–Feuerstein), 93–95, 131
Intellectual ability. *See* Intellectual functioning
Intellectual functioning. *See also* Cultural differences, in intellectual functioning; Intellectual tests
and achievement, 101–105
affective/motivational factors in, 105–116, 121
and African Americans, 67–70, 74–75
as autonomous abilities, 124

cognitive aspects of, 75, 76–77, 122–123
and concrete operations (Piaget), 122–123
and conservation (Piaget), 123
content vs. process in, 76, 101
dynamic assessment of, 69, 89–96
and environmental background, 75, 76–77, 79–83, 124
and ethnically relevant materials, 85, 111, 128
genetic limitations on, 67–69, 79, 81, 90, 119–120, 121, 122
humanistic view of, 68–70, 79, 119–120, 121
Piaget's concepts of, 57, 122–123, 126
pluralistic views of, 84–86, 120
Rorschach Test assessment of, 135–136
and social class, 67–69, 72, 76–83, 86–89, 90, 96, 121, 128–129, 165–167
"triarchic" theory of (Sternberg), 123
and verbal skills, 82–83, 102
Intellectual performance. *See* Intellectual functioning
Intellectual tests, 72–75, 102–103, 124
and African-American children, 69, 77, 79, 104–105, 107–108, 109
Black Intelligence Test of Cultural Homogeneity (BITCH), 102, 132
components of, 75
cultural bias in, 101–105
as culture-free, 128
and developmental (Piagetian) approach, 122–123
Learning Performance Assessment Device (LPAD), 93–95, 130–131
and optimizing procedures, 109
Piagetian test, 78–79, 123
and social class, 69, 72–73, 74, 77, 79, 101–105, 107–108
System of Multicultural Pluralistic Assessment (SOMPA), 103–105, 133–134

Wechsler Intelligence Scale for Children (WISC, WISC-R, & WISC-III), 102, 103–105, 108, 109, 133–134
Intellectuals, black
 on social science, xxii–xviii, 13, 14
Intelligence, 72, 73, 90, 91, 93, 122, 123–124. *See also* Intellectual functioning
Intention construct, 7–8, 8–9, 203, 218. *See also* Final cause
Intentionality
 and Blacks, 8–9, 274–275
Intentions, 7–9, 71, 105, 248, 249, 250, 262, 274
 and language, 143
 and mental disorder, 214, 218, 248
 and self, 34–36
 and self-concept choices, 37–38
Internal Control, 173, 203
 and aggression, 173
 and Control Ideology, 189, 208–209
 and Personal Control, 208–209
 and self-esteem, 174–175
Internal–External Locus of Control Scale (Rotter), 173, 203
Intervention programs
 Cooperative learning, 97–99
 Head Start, 86–88
 "Instrumental Enrichment" (IE), 93–95, 131
 Kamehameha Early Education Project (KEEP), 167
 Learning Performance Assessment Device (LPAD), 93, 130
 Milwaukee Project, the, 87–88
 Perry Preschool Project, 88–89
 School Development Project, 99–101
Introspective view, 7–8, 11, 21
Invisible Man (Ellison), 9
I.Q., 64, 72–75, 124. *See also* Intellectual functioning; intellectual tests
I.Q. tests. *See* Intellectual tests

J

Jackson, Jesse, 205–206
Jazz, 23
Journal of Black Psychology, 22
Jung, C. G., 128, 205, 248

K

Kantian perspective, 12, 13–14, 15, 68, 129
 and African view of nature, 22, 278
 and the African American, 15
 on intellectual functioning, 68–69, 119
 transcendence in, 24
Knowledge
 Kantian perspective on, 12–13, 14, 22
 Lockean perspective on, 13–15
Kunta Kinte, 20

L

Labeling, 67
Labels, racial
 knowledge of, by children, 27, 53–54, 57–58
Language style. *See* Speech style
Larry P. v. Wilson Riles, 132
Learning
 associative, 67–69. *See also* Level I (rote) abilities
 and drive reduction, 17
 humanistic view of, 70–72, 121
 Lockean vs. Kantian view of, 12–14
 as mediated, 90–94, 94–95, 124, 129, 130
 motivation in, 115–117, 127
 and performance, 115, 120, 131. *See also* Intervention programs
Level I (rote) abilities, 67–69, 77–79, 121
Level II (abstract) abilities, 67–69, 70, 77–79, 82, 121, 125

Linguistic structure, 143–146
Literacy, 154, 158–159
Lockean perspective, 12, 13, 14, 15, 22, 97, 242
  on intellectual functioning, 67–68, 69, 91
  on self-development, 37
Locus of Control (LOC). See Internal–External Locus of Control Scale (Rotter)
Logical learning theory, 71, 143, 164, 231, 242–243, 262
  telosponse in, 124

M

Man for Himself (Fromm), 266
Mastery, 174, 201, 208, 267–268
Material cause, 5, 6, 8, 9, 38–39, 249. See also Substance construct
Meaning
  defined, 9
  demonstrative (unipolar), 9
  dialectical (bipolar), 10–12
  and infant's effectance behaviors, 16–18
  and learning, 70–71, 106–107, 121
  in mechanistic view, 9–10
Measurement of racial attitudes
  by doll preference techniques, 27–28, 29–30
  examiner race effects on, 56
  by Preschool Racial Attitude Measure (PRAM), 29
  racial classification in, 27, 53–54
  and racial similarity, 53–54
  and skin color salience, 53–54
  techniques in, 27–28, 29, 57–59, 62
  validity of techniques, 29, 30, 53–54, 56–57, 58–59
Mechanistic view, xviii
  in behaviorism, xviii, 8, 124
  and final cause explanation, 5
  in Freud, xviii, xix
  and material and efficient cause explanations, 6, 8
  in Pugh, 2
  and unipolar meaning, 11
Mediation
  in behaviorism, 124
  and intentionality, 92
  in parent-child relationship, 90–92, 129–130, 228–230
Medical model, 214, 232–233
Memory, 70, 107, 110–111
Mental activity. See Cognitive processes; Intellectual functioning; Mind
Mental disorder. See also Depression; Hysterical personality; Schizophrenic disorder
  and causal constructs, 218
  and conceptualizing, 217, 247–248
  as cry for help, 220
  and demoralization, 217, 218, 241, 250, 255
  and dialectical thinking, 247–248
  and drug abuse, 231
  and epidemiology, 219–221
  and intentions, 214, 218, 248
  as narcissistic damage, 225, 254–255
  neurotic vs. psychotic, 250–251
  as obsessive-compulsive behavior, 217, 231, 250
  as paranoia, 222–223, 245, 253
  as phobia, 217, 248–249, 258
  psychogenic vs. somatogenic, 248–249
  racial differences. See Racial differences, in mental disorder
  and self-activity, 217–218, 254, 262
  and sense of self. See Mental disorder, as narcissistic damage
  and symbolizing processes, 221–222, 233–234, 247–248
Mental health, 233
Michigan State Psychotherapy Project, 236
Militants, the, 174–176

Milwaukee Project, the, 87–88
Mind
　as blank slate (*tabula rasa*), 12
　as conceptualizing ability, 12–13, 13–14
　innate capacity of, 12–13
　models of, 12–15
　in Schafer, 19
Millon Clinical Multiaxial Inventory (MCMI), 251–252
Minnesota Multiphasic Personality Inventory (MMPI), 218, 251–252
Motivation, 20–21. *See also* Competence, as motivation; Drive reduction; Effectance
　unconscious, 44–45, 248, 259, 260
Multiculturalism. *See* Biculturalism
Myth of Psychotherapy, The (Szasz), 233

N

National Study of Black College Students (NSBCS), 210
New Ghetto Man, the, 175
Nigrescence, psychological, 177–178, 264
　Encounter stage (stage 2), 178, 182, 184, 185, 207
　Immersion-Emersion stage (stage 3), 178–179, 181, 182, 184, 199, 206, 244, 245
　Internalization stage (stage 4), 179, 180, 181, 182, 184, 186, 199, 207
　Internalization-Commitment stage (stage 5), 179, 184
　Pre–encounter stage (stage 1), 178, 179–180, 181, 183–184, 207, 244, 245
　recycling, 181–182

O

Oppression
　response to, 2, 199–200, 204

Outgroup Orientation, 33–34, 172, 180. *See also* Racial attitudes, and "Euro" figure preference

P

Parents, 16–17, 38–39, 41–42, 42–43, 44, 45, 46, 47, 49, 71–72, 76, 81, 87, 90–93, 100, 104, 112, 113–114, 116, 119, 125, 127, 129–130, 136, 152, 159, 167, 202, 226, 228–229, 236, 265–266, 267
Passive resistance, 21
Pattern construct, 6, 8, 38–39, 218. *See also* Formal cause
Persona, 205
Personality functioning, 172–173, 181–182, 202–203
　typologies of,
　Crain & Weisman, 173–175
　Cross, 178–179
　Gibbs, 204–205
　Gurin & Epps, 186–190
　Harrell, 206–207
　Pettigrew, 204
Pidgin, 139
Pluralism
　cultural, 84–86, 137–138, 159–163, 181
Polar reference, 9
Possible selves, 46–47, 63, 117–119
Postal clerk syndrome, 175
Preschool Racial Attitude Measure (PRAM), 29
Problem-solving abilities, 68–70, 75, 77–79, 84, 92, 101, 135
Psychoanalytic theory, xviii, xix, xx, 23, 129–130, 200, 227, 248, 259, 260, 267–268. *See also* Psychodynamic perspective
　action language (Schafer), xix–xx, 8, 19
　Freud, xviii, xix, xx, 64, 216, 248, 259
Psychodynamic perspective, 19, 62, 243, 254, 259–260. *See also* Psychoanalytic theory

dialectic conceptions in, 247–48
Psychological disorder. *See* Mental disorder
Psychology
   experimental, xix, 16
   pertinence to African Americans, xviii, 14–15
   portrayal of Blacks by, xvii, 1–3
   third force in, xix
Psychology and the Black Experience (Pugh), 2
Psychometric testing, 73–75. *See also* Standard intelligence tests
Psychopathology. *See* Mental disorder
Psychosomatic symptoms, 216–217, 231
Psychotherapy, 19, 232–233, 259–266. *See also* Therapeutic relationship, the
   Control-Mastery theory of, 267
   criticism of, 233–235, 260
   family, 246, 247
   goals of, 232–233, 246–247, 261–263
   "insight" in, 262
   interpersonal emphasis in, 268
   "microstages," 242
   and minority poor, 233–236
   "narrative" construction in, 262–263
   network, 247
   phases with Blacks, 242, 244–245, 268
   research in, 235–236, 238–241, 243–244
   role-induction procedures, 243–244
   and social change, 246
   teleological-humanistic view of, 259–260, 261–263
   and verbal skills, 234–235
Pygmalion effect, 110

R

Race consciousness, 177–179, 189
Racial attitudes
   and "Afro" figure preference, 50
   and "Euro" figure preference, 29
   origins of, 63–64
   and racial awareness, 53–54, 179, 181
   in therapy situation, 237–240, 241, 255, 265
Racial differences
   in mental disorder, 218–221, 221–224, 253–254, 256–257, 258
   in mental health services, 221–224, 243–244
   in response to treatment, 237–239, 239–242, 242–247
Racism, x, xvii, 1–2, 11, 21, 26, 41, 43, 44, 47, 48, 51, 127, 141–142, 160, 180, 194, 197, 198, 202, 215, 216, 217, 248, 256, 257, 272, 275
   as dehumanization, 213, 228
   and mental disorder, 213, 224–227, 228, 230–231, 245–246, 255
Reading instruction
   and teacher classroom style, 155–158, 167–168. *See also* Black English, and reading achievement
Reality, 19, 59, 70, 247, 251, 259, 263
Reality testing, 23
Reasoning, 70, 76, 128
Reductionism, 249
Religiosity, 275–276
Retardation, 67, 72–73, 77, 87–88, 89–91, 93, 102–105, 122, 133–134
"Road Not Taken, The" (Frost), 35
Rogers, C. R., 248
Rorschach Test, the, 135–136, 223, 251, 253

S

Sapir-Whorf hypothesis, 164
Schizophrenic disorder, 218, 223, 236, 249, 250, 251, 253, 255, 257
School performance
   and cognitive style, 83–86, 149

and culture conflict in classroom, 158, 168
and intervention. *See* Intervention programs
Science
  and final cause explanations, 7
  and Kantian-like thinking, 15
Scrofani study, the, 77–79, 82, 89, 95, 107, 131
Self, the, 31–33, 34–35, 39–41. *See also* Self-concept; Self–esteem
  as active agent, 34–38, 41
  as dialectic paradox, 31–33, 34
  as "ensembled individualism", 60–62
  and language, 143, 152, 159
  negative effects of, 41, 184–185
  as product of social environment, 37–38, 59–60, 63, 209–210
  as "self–contained individualism", 60
  as sense of identity, 34–35, 40, 41
Self-affirming activities, 232, 254
Self-awareness, 44–45, 49, 51, 199
Self-blaming, 174–175, 190, 209–210, 274
Self-concept, 25, 26–27, 31–34, 36, 39–41, 248
  Black family and, 41–46
  development of, in humanistic view, 36–38, 41–43
  doll preference studies of, 27–29
  and measurement problems, 27–29, 31, 40
  as multi-faceted, 31–34, 39–40, 43, 48–49, 50, 179. *See also* Self, the, as dialectic paradox; Possible selves
  "multiple reference point" view of, 33–34
  personal vs. racial, 2, 33–34, 42–43, 171, 173, 186–187
  racial, development of, 47–50, 179–180, 199
  as self-conceptualization, 32, 46–47, 54–55
  as self as object, 34–35

as theory about self, 34, 44, 54–55, 117–119
as "we", 60–62, 191–192, 277
Self-creation, 34–36, 37, 39, 44, 45, 179, 183, 184, 185, 186, 197, 199
Self-esteem, 1–2, 30–33, 171–172, 203–204, 214, 217, 233, 246, 254
  as affective assessment, 32
  change of, with age, 47–50
  change of, by direct intervention, 51–53, 210–212
  Crain & Weisman measure of, 173–175, 203–204
  defensive aspects of, 32, 62
  and family, 42–43, 45–46, 48–49, 51
  high, in Black children, 30–31
  in integrated vs. desegregated situations, 51–52
  low, in Black children, 27–30
  and measurement problems, 32–34. *See also* Self-concept, and measurement problems
  as sense of competence, 32–33
  as sustained by effectance behaviors, 31–33
Self-evaluation. *See* Self–esteem
Self-hatred, 2–3, 27, 54, 172, 176–177, 179, 257
Self-image, 25. *See also* Self–concept
Self-perception. *See* Self–concept
Self-realization, xix, 21, 183, 185
Self-rejection. *See* Self–hatred
Semantic evaluations, 29, 50, 204
Shades of Black (Cross), 179
Skinnerian framework, 19, 24
Slavery, 8, 11, 21, 42, 176, 213
Social class differences, 75, 77, 92–93, 182–183, 205, 261. *See also* Intellectual functioning, and social class; Intellectual tests, and social class; Speech style, social class differences in

in mental disorder, 220–221, 224, 230, 234–235
in mental health services, 222, 234, 243
in racial preference, 28
in response to treatment, 237–238, 242–244
Social competence, 135, 252
Social constructionism, 22
Social protest, xvii, 2, 30, 186, 188, 190, 199, 204, 205–206
Social science
  portrayal of Blacks in, xvii, 1
Sociolinguistic issues, 141–143
  in the classroom, 148–151, 156–159
Speech style
  and alienation from school, 158
  and code switching, 144, 157–158, 162–163, 261
  and colonialization, 142
  and elaborated and restricted codes, 165–167
  and family structure, 165
  and flair, 149
  fluency of, 148–149
  and mental disorder, 223
  and pluralism, 159–160, 161–163, 168–169
  and self-esteem, 142
  social class differences in, 144–146, 149–150, 165–167
  and social context, 148–150, 261
Standard Black English, 140–141
Standard English, 138, 141, 144, 162, 168
Standard intelligence tests, 72–75, 77–78, 81–83, 102–103, 121, 123. *See also* Intellectual tests
Stigma vulnerability, 194–195, 197, 211
Substance construct, 5, 8, 19, 203, 218.
  See also Material cause
Suicide
  and African Americans, 256–257
System–blaming, 174, 188–189, 209–210, 256

T

Teacher-pupil relationships. *See* Sociolinguistic issues, in the classroom
Teleological regression (Arieti), 38
Teleological (telic) view, 7, 248, 271, 276, 279
Tests. *See* Intellectual tests
Therapeutic relationship, the, 236–238, 263, 267
  affective assessment in, 242–243
  and egalitarianism, 239–241, 246, 267
  therapist/client race difference in, 238–241, 243–244, 263–264, 265, 267
  therapist "credibility" in, 241

U

Unconscious attitudes, 7, 32, 38, 45, 53–54, 62, 129–130, 176, 194, 214, 215, 218, 224, 237, 238, 248, 254
Unengaged, the, 187–188
Unipolarity. *See* Meaning, demonstrative (unipolar)
University Research Opportunities Program (UROP), 210–212

V

Verbal skills, 82–83, 152–154, 160–163
Verve, behavioral, 85, 111–112, 149
Victims
  African Americans as, xvii, 1, 20
  blaming the, xvii, 128, 202, 209–210, 212, 233–234
Violence, 232, 257

W

Waters, Maxine, 198
Wechsler Adult Intelligence Scale (WAIS), 223, 253
Wise Environment Program, 195–196, 199

Z

Zone of Proximal Development (ZPD – Vygotsky), 131–132